To my very special grandson

Sam   Allen

from Grandpa "Neddy" Neil Allen

who was fortunate enough to report:

14 Summer and Winter Olympic Games
1956 to 1996   for
The Times, London, Evening Standard, London
and, once, the New York Times and write as
a London correspondent, en français, for
the Paris daily newspaper L'Equipe.

Also reported more than 200 world boxing
championships around the world and two
Rugby Union World Cups

— while, their patience remarkable, also
managed somehow to bring up two sons, from 12 and
14, named Matthew ("Big M") and James
("Jimmy Jam Pot") of whom I am very proud.

SPORT IN BRITAIN

A SOCIAL HISTORY

SPORT IN BRITAIN

A SOCIAL HISTORY

EDITED BY

TONY MASON

CENTRE FOR THE STUDY OF SOCIAL
HISTORY, UNIVERSITY OF WARWICK

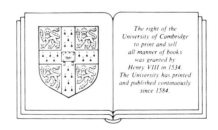

The right of the
University of Cambridge
to print and sell
all manner of books
was granted by
Henry VIII in 1534.
The University has printed
and published continuously
since 1584.

CAMBRIDGE UNIVERSITY PRESS

CAMBRIDGE
NEW YORK   PORT CHESTER
MELBOURNE   SYDNEY

Published by the Press Syndicate of the University of Cambridge
The Pitt Building, Trumpington Street, Cambridge CB2 1RP
40 West 20th Street, New York, NY 10011, USA
10 Stamford Road, Oakleigh, Melbourne 3166, Australia

First published 1989

Printed in Great Britain at The Bath Press, Avon

British Library cataloguing in publication data

Sport in Britain: a social history
1. Great Britain. Sports, history
I. Mason, Tony, *1938–*
796′.0941

Library of Congress cataloguing in publication data

Sport in Britain: a social history / edited by Tony Mason.
    p.   cm.
Includes index.
ISBN 0-521-35119-7
1. Sports – Great Britain – History. I. Mason, Tony.
GV605.S75 1989
796′.0941 – dc20 89-7048 CIP

ISBN 0 521 35119 7

BS

CONTENTS

The authors and publisher would like to thank the following for permission to reproduce illustrative material: *Angling Times* pp.13, 41; Artists and Mail Newspapers plc p.224; Associated Sports Photography pp.58, 60, 61; British Library Newspaper Library pp.70, 132, 142, 207b, 318; Colorsport p.154; Peter Dazeley p.213; Documentary Photography Archive pp.170a, 232a; Christopher Dodd pp.283, 292b, 295, 296, 297, 300, 301, 304; Greater London Photograph Library p.254; Frank Herman pp.232b, 233a, 233b; The Hulton Picture Company pp.18, 21, 25, 28, 33, 37a, 37b, 80, 106, 118, 122, 129, 136, 150, 153, 159, 170b, 171, 190, 197, 199, 207a, 218, 219, 225, 252, 253, 255, 261, 263, 264, 266, 279, 292a, 327, 330, 335a, 335b, 336; London Transport Museum p.181; Roger Mayne p.151; Manchester Public Libraries: Local History Library p.47; The University of Birmingham p.66; *The Oldham Chronicle* p.131; Oldham Local Studies Library pp.52, 133; Bill Shipley pp.82, 111; Sporting Pictures (UK) Ltd p.46.

Every effort has been made to reach copyright holders; the publishers would be pleased to hear from anyone whose rights they have unwittingly infringed.

NOTES ON CONTRIBUTORS

JEREMY CRUMP is a former student of history and now works in the civil service.

CHRISTOPHER DODD is features editor of *The Guardian*.

JOHN LOWERSON is reader in social history at the Centre for Continuing Education, University of Sussex.

TONY MASON is senior lecturer at the Centre for the Study of Social History, University of Warwick.

STAN SHIPLEY teaches history at Havering Technical College.

WRAY VAMPLEW is reader in economic history at Flinders University of South Australia.

HELEN WALKER is a part-time teacher of social history at the University of Sussex.

GARETH WILLIAMS is senior lecturer in history at Aberystwyth at the University College of Wales.

JACK WILLIAMS teaches history at Liverpool Polytechnic.

INTRODUCTION

In the summer of 1938, with no prospect of political preferment in view Mr Winston Churchill was earning good money by writing a series of articles, world copyright reserved, for the *News of the World*. The subject was contemporary Britain. On 4 September his theme was the effect of modern amusements on life and character. By its recreations and leisure the character and development of a civilisation could be judged. Sport was the 'first of all the British popular amusements'. A typically Churchillian exaggeration: a case for the premier place going to the cinema, the public house or the radio could certainly have been made. Nonetheless the future wartime Prime Minister was right to stress the important role played by sport in the life of Britain in this century.

Its place in the popular culture has been recognised by sportsmen and non-sportsmen, men and women, radicals and conservatives, intellectuals and hearties. In his *Notes Towards a Definition of Culture* of 1948, for example, T. S. Eliot wrote that it was 'all the characteristic activities and interests of a people: Derby Day, Henley Regatta, Cowes, the Twelfth of August, a cup final, the dog races, the pin table, the dart board, Wensleydale cheese, boiled cabbage cut into sections, beetroot in vinegar, nineteenth-century Gothic churches and the music of Elgar'.[1] Eight out of thirteen were sporting. In 1923 J. D. Bernal, eminent scientist and Communist Party member, modestly claimed ignorance of only two subjects, music and sport, but he told a friend that he was studying football and cricket on Party instructions because he had to be able to converse with working men about the things that interested them.[2]

When 400 old soldiers were asked in Burma in 1946 what they liked best about the army 108 put sport in first place. Comradeship and leave came a long way behind. Four hundred young soldiers newly conscripted were also asked the same questions: 104 said 'nothing' – but 70 said sport.[3] On the first day of the battle of the Somme, 1 July 1916, Captain W. P. Nevill of the 8th East Surreys provided his platoons with two footballs to kick towards the German trenches. On one was written 'The Great European Cup-Tie Finals, East Surreys v Bavarians. Kick-off at zero', and on the other 'no referee'. He offered a prize for the first platoon to dribble a ball as far as the German trenches. He did not live to present it.[4]

Keith Douglas in the western desert in 1942 recalled the delivery of new tanks to his unit. They 'needed every kind of elementary adjustment and repair, their insides were filthy and they lacked most of the detachable bits of equipment. The men of the other division who brought them up said they had not had time for maintenance because in their units sport took precedence over it. It is a horrible thought that this may have been true.'[5]

Well before 1900 sport was already an important part of the curriculum in grammar and public schools. In the state elementary schools it had been drill, with its connotations of obedience and discipline which had been provided for the children of the working classes. But enthusiastic teachers had been organising team games and setting up inter-school fixtures two decades before, in 1906, the Board of Education officially allowed sport as part of the curriculum. The state had also encouraged sport by a series of permissive acts which allowed local authorities to equip, maintain, and service facilities such as swimming baths, public parks and playing fields. The link between sport and recreation on the one hand and public health and public amenity on the other was clearly established by 1914. Even during the long inter-war depression local authorities continued to expand their provision of sporting facilities. The Physical Training and Recreation Act of 1937 channelled tax-payers' money both to local authorities and voluntary organisations to help build more swimming baths, gymnasia and playing fields. One of the more important clauses of the 1944 Education Act made mandatory the provision of facilities for physical training and recreation by local education authorities for all their schools.

The state also began to notice the cultural importance of sport in an international context. Although the British economy was greatly weakened by the First World War, British prestige was high and her culture widely admired. Sport was an important part both of the culture and the admiration. In the 1920s, for example, the Dutch, French, Germans, Greeks and Rumanians, together with Latin American and Middle Eastern countries, all asked the British Government for information about the structure and organisation of sport and physical recreation in Britain. Increasingly after 1918 the Foreign Office accepted the idea that sport had a role to play in the cultural competition between nations. It could be used to promote trade and cement alliances. The British legation in Athens in 1937, for example, noted that athletics was a promising field for the introduction of British sport and methods into Greece and might be a useful counterweight to German Olympic propaganda. The expansion of sport as an international phenomenon was at least in part a manifestation of the success of the British way and purpose. The number of competing countries in international sporting events doubled in the 1920s compared to the 1900s and doubled again by 1950. By then, another World War had further sapped Britain's economic sinews. The growth of sporting expertise elsewhere meant that victories in international sport became increasingly rare in the immediate post-war years. Several inquiries culminated in one set up by the Central Council of Physical Recreation, chaired by Sir John Wolfenden and entitled 'Sport and the Community'. In 1960 it claimed that 'decent living together in society' owed much to 'the traditional British love of sport'.[6] It recommended that the government should set up a Sports Development Council to increase participatory opportunity. Four years later the reforming Labour Government established the Sports Council. Since then sport has had its own propaganda agent inside the state's bureaucratic machine.

If any further illustration is needed of the important place of sport in twentieth-century Britain it can be provided by pointing to the extensive coverage given to it by the media. In newspapers, on radio and on the television screen the amount of space and time allotted to sport has both contributed to and reflected its social significance. A few examples must suffice. The *News of the World* was giving up 14 per cent of its total space to sporting news by 1900. In 1937 Henry Durant did a survey of the contents of 12 daily newspapers and 11 Sunday newspapers. The daily papers averaged 11.4 per cent of their total space to sport while the Sunday paper average was 17.7 per cent. He had deliberately excluded Monday. According to a Political and Economic Planning measurement in 1955, 46 per cent of the *Daily Mirror* and 35 per cent of the *Daily Mail* were filled by sport. Sport remains a predictable and considerable part of most national and local newspapers.[7]

Similarly it became and remains a significant portion of the output of radio and television. BBC radio was providing live commentaries as early as 1927 and Saturday afternoon sporting programmes by the middle of the 1930s. By the end of that decade radio reached into almost every home in Britain. Its coverage of certain key events in athletics, cricket, football, golf, rugby and tennis further underlined the existence of a national sporting calendar. Its treatment of events like the FA Cup Final helped to raise them to the level of an annual national ritual with royalty present and pre-match community singing culminating in 'Abide with me'.[8] Sport was bound to be popular with television especially in the 1950s and 1960s because it was already popular with the public. Nor was it very expensive to mount and transmit. ITV found it hard to break the BBC's historical relationship with the leading sports organisations. Even by the mid-1980s, when sport was charging television a much higher price for the privilege of showing it, and ITV had managed to prise athletics out of the BBC's grasp, the Corporation was responsible for two-thirds of British TV's sporting coverage. Out of an overall budget of £50 million in 1986, the BBC spent close on £20 million on sport.[9]

Of course playing and watching sport has always been a minority activity. Overall spectator rates appear to have been fairly steady through the last two decades. According to the General Household Survey between 10–11 per cent of the whole population watch live sport of some sort. A more recent study based on the analysis of time budgets has suggested that the proportion of men in full-time employment watching sport had not changed between 1961 and 1983–4. On the other hand the proportion of women in full-time employment watching sport had risen from 2 per cent to 6 per cent during the same period. The same study suggests more dramatic expansion in the numbers playing sport. Of men in full-time employment 9 per cent took part in some sport in 1961; 31 per cent did so in 1983–4. Of women in full-time employment 6 per cent took part in some sport in 1961; 17 per cent did so in 1983–4.[10]

We should also notice that such participation varies between social groups, age groups and indeed individuals within such wide categories. It is clear that life and family cycles are important influences on who plays and who watches sport. It is now well known not only that men still play and watch more than women, but that also the young play and watch more than the old, and non-manual workers play and watch more than manual workers. This is not the place to explore all the refinements of these general categorisations. For our purpose it is sufficient to point out sport's status as a minority activity while at the same time emphasising that its importance in the social life of the nation cannot be gauged by counting alone. Sport has always been gambled on, talked about, read about, listened to and casually played to a degree which constitutes an important additional dimension of its social role.

In the middle of the nineteenth century sport very often meant the so-called field sports of hunting, shooting and fishing. But it was also a word beginning to be applied to games played in the open air. Sports in the plural had been the name given to a series of athletic contests 'engaged in or held at one time and forming a spectacle or social event' since the sixteenth century.[11] A much greater number of activities are labelled sport in the Britain of the 1980s than at any previous time. For the purposes of this study sport has to be a more or less physically strenuous, competitive, recreational activity. It will usually, but not always, be in the open air and might involve team against team, athlete against athlete or athlete against nature, or the clock. The ten sports selected for detailed treatment cover the whole century and the whole country in terms of place and class. In terms of playing and watching they have been among the most popular sports. As late as 1960 the National Council for School Sports was only concerned with athletics, boxing, cricket, football, rugby and swimming and all are covered in this book save the latter. Swimming's absence is unfortunate. We would have liked to have found a place for it, in part because in excess of 6 per cent of the population were swimming by 1980 – more if you include the under-sixteens – and also because of its long-standing role in many communities as a competitive sport from the third quarter of the nineteenth century. Unfortunately not enough work has been done on the subject.

We have concentrated on competition, physical activity and spectacle. This has meant no place for the pub games of darts and snooker in which extended television coverage has both widened the economic opportunities for the few exceptional players and stimulated a new wave of participation. The popularity of both darts and snooker as a spectacle has been of very recent origin. The coming of colour television was crucial to both. The BBC began *Pot Black* in 1969 and 1976 was the start of the televised World Championships. The move to the Crucible Theatre, Sheffield took place the following year and 18.2 million viewers saw the 1985 final since when the audience for that event has fallen back.[12]

Badminton and squash are sports which have never been popular among spectators but whose expansion in the last two decades has been spectacular, owing a good deal to the perceived relationship between good health and physical exercise. In the case of badminton it grew 60 per cent in less than a decade in the 1970s with almost 5,000 clubs and over 115,000 players. There were only 260 squash courts in Great Britain in 1947 and they were mainly the property of about 150 private clubs. Squash became a craze in the 1970s, especially among young men in the professions, and squash courts proliferated in sports centres and were often provided by employers and added to clubs devoted to other sports. One estimate placed the number of players at almost 1,750,000 although it is not clear what level of commitment to the game all these players had. This growth from the bottom has also had the effect of revitalising the elite of professional players. In 1962 the professional championship of the British Isles was discontinued because of lack of entries. Jonah Barrington turned professional in 1969 and a new era for the professionals had begun. Both these sports have tended to be concentrated in London and the south but John Bale warns us against a simplistic middle-class categorisation of the bulk of the participants. He prefers to see them as part of a lifestyle which defines an 'outer metropolitan popular culture'. Both sports await their historian.[13]

Bowls is another omission we would like to have avoided. Its recent history epitomises many of the social and economic changes which have been altering the face of sport in Britain these last two decades. It was long popularly characterised as an old man's game, a stigma which may have inhibited younger recruits but which contained some truth. In 1955 a fifteen-year-old schoolboy reached a competition final and a schoolmaster refused to play against him. This led the English Bowling Association to wonder when a boy became a man and they decided that no one under the age of eighteen could enter their national championships. Today, most would agree with David Bryant, that 'bowls is a young man's game which old men can play'. This is most notably true at the highest levels where colour television and the accompanying sponsorship have transformed opportunities for a gradually growing number of professionals. The scoring has had to be changed to fit television's lust for the economical 'end' and 'set' and the number of indoor competitions has expanded to fit the medium's preference for viewing free from natural breaks. The Alexandra Palace indoor rink in the 1930s was quite a novelty. In the 1980s, England has over 200 indoor clubs, Scotland over 30 and Wales 10.[14]

Flat green bowls owes most of its early development to Scotland. All British bowlers played to the rules of the Scottish Bowling Association until after the 1914–18 war. Scotsmen were so dominant in the group of leading players before the First World War that when Scotland played England in an international match in 1909 both four-men-a-side teams were all Scots, the English team being made up of Scots who had migrated south for better jobs.

Bowls is also distinguished by another branch of the game with clear regional and social differences from the flat green variety. Crown green bowls is so-called because the green slopes away from the crown in the centre. The 'jack', as well as the 'woods', is biased and play goes on all over the green. Crown green bowls was centred in the north and midlands and supported a thriving professional sector throughout the whole of the years covered by this book. Men played for wagers, often on greens attached to public houses. They were often backed by small businessmen or even syndicates. The tournaments at the Talbot Hotel, Blackpool, became well known for their excitement and large crowds of spectators, the whole fuelled by a very vigorous betting culture. Crown green has not so far been able to take advantage of the opportunities presented to the flat green game by television and commercial sponsorship. But its parochialism makes it a fascinating sub-cultural survival of a way of life that was thought 'traditional' not so long ago.

The history of bowls is also interesting as one of the sites of the struggle of women to carve out for themselves a sporting life. If old men can play then so can old women but they had to meet a good deal of male opposition both before 1939 and after 1945. This was particularly true in the clubs, which were almost always controlled by men. This often led to male mono-poly of the greens in the evenings with women relegated to afternoon play. Such obstruction and more general ideological prejudice against women bowlers may have discouraged some. But there were estimated to be 100,000 women flat green players in 1948 and, by the middle of the 1980s, about one-third of the total of half a million bowlers were thought to be women. In 1985, 41,000 of them entered the English Women's Bowling Association Championship.

Bowling clubs were likely to be found almost anywhere in Britain between about 1905 and the present day. Rugby league clubs have never quite managed to construct for themselves a national place.[15] The image of rugby league remains essentially northern, with the bulk of its 34 professional clubs located in Yorkshire, Lancashire and Cumbria. But in those towns where the game has flourished it has played a similar role to soccer clubs elsewhere and has been a leading spectator sport for most of this century. The clubs have been run by the same middle-range businessmen who sat on the boards of so many professional football clubs. Shareholding was similarly thinly spread, such that in the 1960s one of the leading clubs, Wigan, had a share capital of £16,000 contributed by 1,700 largely local people few of whom had more than eight shares each. Like football clubs, dividends were rarely paid and the satisfaction was being part of an important and highly visible local institution. Where the professional rugby league club often differed from its soccer counterpart was that most of the rugby league players would probably be from the local district. Rugby league mattered in places like Wigan and Warrington, St Helens and Widnes, Featherstone and Castleford. During the boom in attendances at spectator sports immediately following the end of the 1939–45 war a quarter of Wigan's population would turn up for home matches.

The Northern Union was formed in August 1895 when 21 clubs broke away to form the NFU because they were frustrated at the refusal of the Rugby Football Union to allow broken-time payments for working men who had to lose time at their jobs in order to play. The middle-class business-men responsible for the new grouping did not want out and out profession-alism. By 1898 they had to agree to open payments but they insisted that playing rugby should not be a man's sole occupation. A series of 'work clauses' were laid down which stipulated that a man must have legitimate

employment. Unrespectable jobs such as billiard markers or bookies' runners were not allowed. In the early years of this century these regulations
were vigorously enforced. Some players were suspended for a whole season
for alleged infringements including a failure to work for the three days
immediately preceding a game. The work clauses did have a draconian
sound to them and they were abandoned in 1905. But the thrust behind
them remained. Full-time professionalism was discouraged. Most players
had other jobs, trained two nights a week and were paid a match fee plus
bonuses according to results. Before the Second World War backs often
received more than forwards.

The Rugby Union never forgave what became, in 1922, the name
adopted from Australia, the Rugby League. The RFU was outraged by
the open admission of payment and at the changes which the Northern
Union quickly introduced to the game in the hope of making it more attractive to the paying spectator: abolishing the line out, reducing the scoring
value of goals, limiting direct touch kicking and, in 1906, reducing the
number of players per side from 15 to 13 by eliminating two forwards.
A faster, more open game without the rucks, mauls and stoppages of rugby
union was claimed to be the result. The new game attracted some rugby
players in both Australia and New Zealand from which the first combined
touring team visited Britain in 1907–8. With the French Rugby League
being established in the 1930s the game did escape in part from its parochial
origins. But in spite of various missionary efforts, notably before 1914 in
Wales, the West Country and the midlands and after 1945 in part of the
south of England and Wales again, the League never managed to obtain
a firm foothold outside the English northwest.

This was partly due to the competition with other sports, particularly
soccer. It was partly due to the growing problem of finding grounds to
play on, especially in city centre areas in the south where land for building
was highly valued. It was partly due to the virulent opposition of the Rugby
Union which insisted that no amateur could play rugby league without
being infected by the professional virus. No amateur rugby league player
could be accepted into membership of a union club while still involved
in rugby league. Players who might have wished to sample the 13-a-side
game may often have been put off by the expulsion from the union code
that was almost certain to take place if discovered. It was a hypocritical
business which looks no better from the 1980s when a minority of rugby
union star players are little short of *de facto* professionals.

But rugby league seems to have been ambivalent about expanding the
game beyond its northern roots. It did move the cup final to Wembley
in 1929 but not everyone was satisfied that one of the climaxes to the

season should be played in London. 1932 saw it back at Wigan although it returned to Wembley the following year and has remained there ever since. This ambivalence was extended towards relations with the rugby union. It was strange that ex-union players received larger signing-on fees than former amateur league players. The reason given was compensation for loss of status. Expansion must also have been made difficult by the insensitive way northern clubs poached union players most notably from Wales. The only time the two codes came more or less amicably together was in the services during two World Wars. If you were good enough to fight with you had to be good enough to play with but when peace returned in 1918 and 1945, the armistice ended.

Professional rugby suffered a similar decline in support at the gate from the mid-1950s to that experienced by other sports. Over 4 million spectators had watched the matches in 1952–3: 20 years later the number had fallen to 1,365,700. In 1970 the receipts from the challenge cup final were twice as much as any club took in gate money over the whole season.

But rugby league also benefited from the expansion in playing sport which was a feature of the 1960s and beyond. Television coverage of top matches may have stimulated interest but another breakaway both reflected and promoted this new participatory growth. In 1973 the British Amateur Rugby League Association was formed in part as a result of discontent at the bottom with elite treatment of the grass roots. Three hundred amateur clubs in 1949 – for whom the broken-time principle had never applied – had grown to 500 clubs and 20,000 players in the middle of the 1980s. Moreover the amateurs had begun to form clubs well outside the traditional heartland of the game. Not only are teams found in many colleges, polytechnics and universities but since 1981 Oxford have played Cambridge in a sponsored annual fixture.[16] Perhaps the day when union and league might recognise each other's right to exist is not so far off.

Rugby league is a fascinating sub-culture which is only now beginning to be studied. Its contribution to images of the north and in particular to myths of northern hardness are well known. There is much to be said for a game in which, it has been alleged, some teams signalled rehearsed moves by calling the names of pubs. It is unfortunate that a detailed treatment proved impossible. Rugby league has a unique place in any history of twentieth-century British sport.

For each of the ten sports which we have covered we have tried to give some idea of its origins, the power structure within it, the relationship between the participatory mass and the spectacularly eminent. We have also paid attention to the role of women in what was for long thought of as a masculine world. The authors have all tried to take account of developments in Scotland, Wales and Ireland as well as England but the existing literature has rarely made this easy and it has occasionally proved impossible. British involvement in the spread of many of these sports to other countries has also been considered. Finally historians, almost as much as sociologists, recognise the danger of using sports to tell the reader about every societal phenomenon except sports. Each essay has tried not to leave out the particular sport itself, but the emphasis has inevitably been laid on showing that sport is part of the society in which it is experienced. Its changes and continuities cannot be understood without some awareness of the wider world. It would be especially rewarding if this book penetrated the world of the sports enthusiasts and added to their appreciation of the game. It is, after all, society that makes sport what it is.

NOTES

1 T. S. Eliot, *Notes Towards a Definition of Culture* (1948), p. 31.
2 Maurice Goldsmith, *Sage. A Life of J. D. Bernal* (1980), pp. 232–3.
3 E. W. Browne, W. B. Coates and A. F. Wells, *The Soldier and the Army. Opinions on Some Aspects of Army Life Expressed by Troops in SEAC* (RAMC–SEAC 1946), p. 38.
4 Peter Parker, *The Old Lie. The Great War and the Public School Ethos* (1987), pp. 213–14.
5 Keith Douglas, *Alamein to Zem Zem*, edited with an introduction by Desmond Graham (1979 edn), p. 109.
6 Sir John Wolfenden, *Sport and the Community* (1960), p. 6.
7 Henry Durant, *The Problem of Leisure* (1938), p. 188, *Planning*, 27 February 1956.
8 It is not clear how far this was a British ritual. The Scots, for example, had their own cup final and for many years now have held it on the same day as the English. 'Abide with me' was first sung at the Cup Final of 1928 apparently because it was the favourite hymn of Queen Mary. It is no longer sung at Wembley. P. C. McIntosh, *Sport and Society* (1963), p. 4.
9 According to figures compiled by the Henley Centre and published by the Sports Council sport-related economic activity had become the sixth largest employment sector by 1985 with only construction, transport, mechanical engineering, food and drink, tobacco and postal and telecommunications services ahead of it. 'Sport in the community. Which ways forward? A paper for consultation' (Sports Council 1987), p. 4.
10 Peter McIntosh and Valerie Charlton, *The Impact of Sport for All Policy 1966–1984 and a Way Forward* (Sports Council 1985), p. 117. Jonathan Gershuny and Sally Jones, 'The changing work–leisure balance in Britain, 1961–1984' in John Horne, David Jary, Alan Tomlinson (eds.), *Sport, Leisure and Social Relations* (1987), p. 40.
11 Oxford English Dictionary, vol. 2 (1973 edn), p. 2086.

12 Mike Bury, 'The social significance of snooker: sports-games in the age of television', *Theory, Culture and Society*, 3 2 (1986), pp. 49–62, *The Observer*, 8 May 1988.

13 J. R. Bale, *Sport and Place: A Geography of Sport in England and Wales* (1982), 100–9. J. Harry, *The History of Squash Rackets* (Brighton, 1979).

14 Most of this section is based on Phil Pilley (ed.), *The Story of Bowls* (1987).

15 For rugby league see Trevor R. Delaney, *The Roots of Rugby League* (Keighley, 1984) and Geoffrey Nicholson, *The Professionals* (1964), pp 64–81.

16 *The Guardian*, 8, 15 March 1988.

1 ANGLING

JOHN LOWERSON

If walking has now become the most popular outdoor participant sport in Britain then angling, with over 3 million regular followers, is certainly the second. There are major differences, not least in gender terms since comparatively few women fish, but both activities share strong roots in a popular arcadianism, the idea of a 'real England' and a time-limited escape from urban living. Both also have seen a significant shift in recent years from being largely an encounter with Nature requiring minimal financial outlay, towards a high level of consumption of 'high tec' access-ories with the inevitable accompanying tensions between design aes-thetics and function. The history of angling since the late nineteenth century shows significant shifts in the encounter of predominantly urban man with a 'natural' environment increasingly threatened by precisely the sort of activity which the urban escapee represents. It also demonstrates forcibly the main elements of class, economic and regional differences, par-ticularly in England, and their subtle shifts over the last hundred years or so.

I

Study to be quiet.
Izaak Walton and 1 Thessalonians 4, verse 16

Fishing is a 'sport' in the oldest British sense of the word; it involves a contest with Nature, albeit rarely one of great risk for the human partici-pant, and the attempt to hunt animal life. For much of its history that hunt has resulted in the death of the victim, either for food or trophy. In the modern sport the emphasis is now largely on releasing the catch, both to help conservation and because of the widely held but singularly unprovable belief that the released fish, having learned from experience, would be more challenging to catch in the future. Whilst that might well be true of the occasional solitary large carp or pike, it is less imaginable for most small fish. But it is the anthropomorphising of the quarry that is important; anglers have constructed a belief system which emphasises

1.1 Fishing's attraction lies in part in man's desire to return to nature. It's not always easy

the degree of skill the sport requires, and the wiliness of their minute opponents.

More than any other sport, angling is bolstered by a very widespread publishing enterprise. The roots of this are late medieval, but the key work is the mid-seventeenth-century classic, *The Compleat Angler* by Izaak Walton. Probably more referred to with reverence than actually read, these reflections of a High Church London Royalist during the interregnum embody much of what many practitioners would mouth less accurately about their sport. Walton became, by the late nineteenth century, a byword for genteel virtues, unofficially canonised when he was included in the reordering of Winchester Cathedral as a statue in the great reredos and with a stained glass window of his own. For many who probably never read him he seemed to represent what angling could do for mankind, refreshed physically and spiritually by being immersed in a pantheistic world of water and greenery. His gentle overshadowing of the sport's growth did a great deal to develop the common folk assumptions as to what were the fisherman's essential motives.[1] Inevitably there was a tension between these ascribed values and many actual practices in the sport; as with the Victorian ideals of athletic manliness, diffusion could only occur with some major modifications. The potential barbarism involved in killing wildlife had to be codified, brought within limits acceptable both to the majority of participants and to changing wider social mores. Any student of the Labour Party's fluctuating attitudes towards field sports will recognise only too easily the way in which their fiercer proponents have had to face the political realities of what might ensue if they pressed for the banning of the most popular working-class sporting activity.

Walton has produced many successors; Charles Kingsley, Edward Grey and Alec Douglas-Home have all added a distinct tone of literary elegance to the thousands of prosaic manuals of instruction which angling has generated.[2] An activity whose disciples have ranged in social dignity from the Queen Mother to Sheffield cutlers and Glasgow shipyard workers, all in pursuit of certain recognised common values, offers nevertheless most of the paradoxes and tensions of sport in an advanced industrial society. One major element is that of escape from oppressive townscapes, bolstered by the feeling that to do so is to express one's 'Englishness' in one of its deepest manifestations.[3] In many ways, this is the nationalist culture of the southern counties, expressed most clearly in the adulation of the finer chalk streams, and the cult of 'dry fly' purists, but angling offers both a national distribution of participants and a sense of regional variation and rivalry which has done much to maintain a 'north–south' divide within as well as between social classes. Both late Victorian factory owners and

1950s Labour politicians could laud it as both reducing the tendency to viciousness in manual workers' lives, and as offering to manufacturing a more contented and productive workforce.[4] Clergy, aware of the wholesale desertion of the churches by the working classes, could at least take comfort in its offering a 'sermon in stones' to the reflective angler contemplating God's handiwork.[5]

Angling provides both an individual challenge – sporting skill dependent on mature reflection – and the benefits of isolation in a hectically crowded society. Solitary contemplation beneath the spreading willow is still the landscaped dream, one reinforced in recent years by the televising and adaptation of some of Arthur Ransome's angling essays: the paradox lies in the extent to which the intrusive electronic medium can reinforce the sense of dedicated personal space.[6] But angling's history is that of a mass sport. In working-class terms in particular it is associated with a high degree of clubbability, underpinned very considerably by prize-bearing competition. To fish in some of the great Birmingham matches, with over 3,000 contestants, was to test the possibility of an isolated act of natural communion to virtual destruction. At this level, the sport's history is one of the growth of public transport, a wholesale acquisition of recreational space, the interplay between local self-determination and central 'bureaucratisation', and the opening up of relationships with local and national businesses in terms of providing equipment and sponsorship.

Angling may follow the essential pattern of all older field sports by being pan-class in its appeal but it has been quite sharply divided, at least in England and Wales. The Scots have tended to claim a 'democracy' of quarry and access which rarely stands the test of close scrutiny. Broadly speaking, the determinant of division in freshwater fishing has been between the 'game' fish of clear waters, salmon, seatrout, trout and grayling, and the 'coarse' or bottom-feeding fish of slow rivers and streams. In fact, the perverse inability of many fish themselves to recognise such clear-cut divisions has caused repeated human conflict; the mixed nature of the famous Royalty fishery on the Hampshire Avon has tended to push up the costs to all because of the presence of game fish, particularly salmon, in season. The best waters for game fish have tended to be annexed to the middle and upper classes by the simple expedient of high rents, whilst the other waters have been more readily available to the angling majority. In the south this has usually meant division of use within a comparatively short distance, as in the Thames Valley. In the north, the paradox has been that such unpolluted waters as could be found near large towns have tended to be taken over by the affluent bourgeois, whilst poorer anglers have had to travel up to 90 miles to find suitable sites. Sea fishing has demonstrated a different set of paradoxes. The late Victorian middle classes discovered it as a recreation, taking over for pleasure what many humbler men had had to do for work. Since the Second World War, in particular, it has grown considerably, reinforced less by a working-class hunt for food than by the availability of mass private transport and by the continued extension of the sponsored competitive fishing of riverbank to beach and boat. Cost and access are still major dividers in angling but, with the exception of Scottish salmon fishing, this has been blurred considerably by the spread of increased disposable incomes through the population since the late 1950s.

II

Anglers are, without doubt, pleasure-loving people.
Fishing Gazette, 25 February 1893

Angling for sport was certainly well established by the later middle ages. By the time of Walton's first publication in 1653, it was widely regarded both as a useful means of occupying the time of the landed classes when they found themselves in the countryside, and as a useful escape for urban merchants of Walton's own rank. But it also had a widespread popular following, as a means of augmenting limited working-class diets. The rapid spread of an urban industrial culture in the later eighteenth century confirmed and expanded this trend. Glasgow artisans organised themselves into fishing clubs, midlands weavers took to fishing such unpolluted parts of the Trent as they could find, selling their catch in Nottingham markets for 3d a pound. Before the wholesale availability of white sea fish after the development of the railways, the roach and dace may have been the only fresh fish many workers ever tasted. The tendency to catch and keep fish of any size remained a major problem until the First World War, for club officials increasingly worried about the impact on natural stocks as pressure from a growing number of participants developed. From the middle years of the nineteenth century fishing at this level developed away from the instrumentality of money or diet towards the recreational, the competitive and the honorific. Where market motives remained they were largely transferred from the possibility of sale to the recouping of prizes in kind or the fruits of bankside betting.[7]

   The greatest initial public (and, paradoxically, most private) growth was in the demand amongst the wealthier urban middle classes for game waters. From London this meant a spreading out into Hertfordshire and then westwards to the classic chalk streams of Berkshire, Hampshire and Wiltshire.

Disposable time and disposable income, a search for 'exclusiveness' and a growing concern with the health of highly stressed merchants, stock-brokers and professionals, all fuelled a remarkable growth. Even in the grim industrial midlands and north there were many trout and salmon waters within comparatively easy reach – the Severn for Birmingham, the Peak District for Sheffield, the Lakes for Lancashire, Northumberland for Durham and Newcastle. It was widely held that rod rents on the better streams doubled in the 1880s, as the wealth of a sport- and status-hungry middle class met the increasingly calculated needs of landowners severely affected by agricultural recession. The pressure on game stocks led to excise rod licensing in the 1870s (coarse fishing largely escaped this until new water boards were formed in the 1960s, and Scotland avoided it virtually altogether): 9,109 permits in 1879 developed into 55,069 by 1911. It could cost £50 a year to rent a rod in Hampshire by 1900 (the cost at the time of writing can be £120 per day). Healthy though the native stocks of brown trout were they were insufficient to meet demands at this level; one of the earliest of the sport's ancillary industries was pisciculture, with 25 trout farms scattered from Devonshire to Stirling by 1910. It was an industry that served the Empire as well: the hill streams of Kashmir were stocked by the turn of the century with exported trout ova – what began as a nostalgic reminder of home for exiled sahibs is now the basis of a tourist industry.[8] A reverse trend, the importing of Canadian rainbow trout to support depleted British fish stocks, was initially less successful but, as we shall see, has subsequently fostered a significant shift in the social balance of game angling and prompted a minor ecological crisis. At the peak of this world of privilege came Scottish salmon fishing, a product both of railway building and the pseudo-baronial mania produced by Sir Walter Scott and Prince Albert's Balmoral. It was effectively an English annexation of Scottish land, water following the deer forests into local legends of resent-ment, ameliorated only slightly by Punch cartoons about canny ghillies and the 'sporting' identification of poaching with patrician manliness in such works as John Buchan's *John MacNab*.[9] Deference was reinforced by the patterns of renting and tipping, so also was the dependence of a Scottish remnant upon a fickle English patronage.

It was among the lower-middle and working classes that angling gained its most significant popularity. Direct evidence of levels is very difficult to ascertain in coarse fishing; a quarter of a million regular addicts on the eve of the First World War would be a conservative estimate. Here regional differences were considerable, styles of angling being determined by the nature of available waters, methods reinforcing the fierce provincial allegiances which, local dialects apart, were often all that could be offered

1.2 Fishing also has its exclusive side. This was the Hon. Mrs MacDonald at
Lord Woolavington's house party in August 1922

for an urban life whose common elements of physical appeal were depressingly similar. Although all major centres eventually contributed to this there were two great poles of development before 1914; in London, inevitably, and Sheffield. In real terms, if not in actual numbers, it was the northern city which was the pacemaker. By the 1870s it had four-fifths of London's number of anglers, an effective ratio ten times better than the capital's: on the eve of the war there were over 21,000 members of Sheffield's affiliated clubs. It was the first major centre to move beyond local club organisation into the bureaucracy of modern sport when it formed an Angling Association in 1869, 15 years before London. The pattern was steadily copied by all the large towns by the 1890s.[10]

Instrumental requirements and extant patterns of working-class culture underpinned this growth. Angling's popularity grew in a world of male bonding, of workplace and street-life relationships focussed on small pubs. Weekday drinking, often moderate in tone and quantity, formed a central meeting point for building clublife. Few northern pubs were without an affiliated angling club by 1900 and London's 620 clubs were almost all pub-based. They often took their names from them although 'Brothers' was the single commonest element, such as the Great Northern Brothers of Clerkenwell. Some clubs eventually developed around the more adventurous churches and chapels or as offshoots of works-based clubs, particularly strong amongst railwaymen and civil servants, but most members preferred a focus which reinforced their sense of independence, comradeship and escape from domestic life. Upper rooms were let for nominal rents since anglers brought regular custom and fairly temperate behaviour – a pub festooned with stuffed fish, trophies and club signs was a virtual guarantee of its licensee's respectability. In addition, there was the mantle of an older form of organisation, the local benefit society. Most clubs maintained a fund for suffering members and their dependants, reinforced by regular charity matches. Paradoxically they were often most reluctant to hand this role over to a wider association, as the relatively low support for London's Anglers' Benevolent Society showed continually. Nor were they prepared to bother with official registration. In times of crisis, such as the late Victorian depressions, it was often the clubs which were first to offer help with bread, soup and clothing. Even in the worst years of the 1890s there was little decline in club membership and activities.

The basic purpose of organisation was to get access to waters. Walton's ideal of the solitary 'pleasure' angler had made sense in the relatively low demand levels of smallish forms of fishing in the seventeenth century. Urban growth, pollution and the sheer scale of sporting growth produced a very different reaction in the later Victorian industrialised society. London and

Nottingham had waters close at hand; the Lea in Essex, much of the Thames or the Trent free to all comers. But for the midland cities, for Lancashire and the West Riding there were considerable difficulties. In the Manchester area it meant finding access to, and stocking canals, for Birmingham, travelling out to those stretches of the Severn not preserved for salmon; for Sheffield it meant travelling 70 to 90 miles to fish the slow Lincolnshire rivers. In such towns, angling's popularity had one essential component; the growth of the nineteenth-century rail networks. Clubs and the wider associations became the agencies negotiating both bank access and low-cost travel. With powerful sanctions through their rules of exclusion, they could virtually guarantee good behaviour both on agricultural land and in crowded carriages, a major agency for self-directed reform of working-class manners. Sheffield anglers found it far easier to negotiate wholesale access to rural sites than did the town's walkers, but they represented virtually no threat to the preserved sports of the rich. What is surprising is that practically no landowners with coarse fishing rights sought to cash in on their properties' new potential, unlike their chalk stream counterparts. The great urban associations found fishing either free or so cheap that they were singularly ill-prepared for a much later period when landowners began the economic exploitation of their resources.

Leasing and stocking these waters was occasionally done with paternalistic upper-middle-class help but it was more usually the product of the clubs' and associations' careful financial management of funds made up from subscriptions and match entry fees. Peppercorn rents made little impact in their early years and probably allowed for a faster growth than might otherwise have been expected. Their other significant function was to negotiate cheap travel, with ticket privileges for their members often on chartered trains. In fact, the originator of this was a London publican, J. Clout, who founded fishing excursions to the picturesque Sussex village of Amberley in the 1870s: these turned into wholesale cockney family outings built around the husbands' sport. The urban associations soon came to dominate this market, negotiating near-monopoly rights with grateful railway companies. By the 1890s Sheffield ran 120 trains for 40,000 anglers in the main season. Since a concessionary ticket alone cost about a day's wage for a prosperous cutler the level of expenditure angling addicts were prepared to lay out appears to have been much higher, relatively speaking, than that faced by many of their middle-class counterparts. Club and association profits on operating the concessions paid for bailiffs and restocking. When extended fishing weekends in South Lincolnshire became possible by the early 1900s, the associations were effectively operating the first major working-class package holidays. But for most anglers the experience was

1.3 The railway stimulated competition angling as it did much else. A scene from 1950s South Yorkshire

packed into a hard-won day excursion. The regional pattern of this was very distinctive. In the south angling was usually fitted into a late Saturday afternoon or, increasingly, into Sunday. Whilst most middle-class clubs firmly eschewed fishing on the Lord's Day, the average London worker had little choice if the most was to be made of limited hours of daylight. Faced with much longer journeys, similar pressures operated in the north but there they clashed frequently with a popular, non-church attending, Sabbatarianism. The Sheffield response was pragmatic, a continuation of the cutlers' tradition of Saint Monday. Until 1914 the majority of Sheffield anglers fished on a Saturday and a Monday, working four days a week to pay for it. The national boom in working-class angling stopped abruptly with the outbreak of the First World War. Voluntary enrolment, long working hours and, ultimately, conscription called a virtual halt. The key implements of the sport, hooks and silk gut line, were very scarce as tackle manufacturers turned their skills to munitions work or assembling aircraft parts. A few local matches were fished to raise Red Cross and war relief funds and sporadic solitary pleasure angling attracted many a convalescent soldier trying to make sense of all the destruction, but the whole supportive infrastructure of concessionary fares and local hotels practically collapsed. Lead shot became available again in January 1919, and growth thereafter depended on varied local rates of demobilisation and reemployment.[11] Returning officers slotted as easily as before into their niche of rural escape, although some found that war profiteers had not only kept their waters open but were prepared to pay the increased rents that inflation and their newly acquired wealth could cover. Whilst many an infantryman stuck in the mud in Flanders must have dreamed of slow-flowing rivers, the officers of the Grand Fleet, incarcerated, with the exception of the Jutland episode, in Scotland for most of the war, had stocked a local loch and spent much of their time there.[12] Of the river Wye's 15 bailiffs, three had been killed and three were wounded in action. The conservators applied for the early demobilisation of the remaining nine to cope with post-war demand.[13] There were considerable divisions of opinions amongst anglers as to whether coarse fish should be widely netted to augment food shortages. A nation looking for explanations of its victory allowed angling a place among the manly sports whose fair play had ensured Germany's defeat, and rejoiced that the bulk of its returning participants would be too keen to get back to the riverbanks to allow for contamination by Bolshevism.[14]

Much of the club world of the pre-war era started off again, although the steady diminution of the role of the pub in working-class life meant that other agencies gradually came to represent a new focus for activity. Railway companies, moving into their long post-war decline, were less than ready to return to their wholesale concessions, and in many areas anything like parity with the 1914 position was not achieved until 1926. Angling's public profile increased, not least when F. H. Heald, the Clerk to the Trent Fishery Board, began a series of broadcasts on 2LO and then on BBC Nottingham during 1925.[15] The lake sunk at Beeston in front of the new Nottingham University College by Sir Jesse Boot was seen as a potential breeding pond for trout, which could widen the variety of species available to local working-class anglers. Old clubs were revived, new ones founded: 52 in the Birmingham area alone in 1925.[16] Despite continued recession in many of the heartlands of artisan angling, industrial growth in new sectors brought others into the sport. New collieries in South Yorkshire and Lancashire reflected a trend that had far greater importance than in the late nineteenth century, the firm-sponsored club provided with stocked and managed waters. Garswood Hall Collieries, outside Wigan, whose directors included Lord Colwyn MP, provided local waters for their workers to cut down travelling costs, offering copper kettles as match prizes:

for many such works, including the car firms of the midlands, the fishing club became as solid a symbol for worker pride as the brass band.[17] It was also seen as a valuable prophylactic to industrial unrest. Perhaps the most significant impact of the 'coal cloud' and the General Strike was to halt, briefly, the publication of the angling press, something even the First World War had been unable to achieve. The rail strike proved a hiccup, and little more, in the excursion calendar.

'Good fishing and good fellowship among artisan anglers' was something valued in Birmingham in the depths of the depression, despite the steady closure of licensed premises and slack employment.[18] Clubs based on small workshops in the city proved particularly vulnerable but the overall drop in the membership was slight – from 14,250 in 1930 to 13,510 in 1931. Although 22 clubs ceased to exist, 52 new ones were formed: angling could at least occupy the time of many unemployed, although this was easiest in those towns which had waters close by. In Worksop, where 90 per cent of the members were unemployed in 1932, it was walking or cycling to local rivers and ponds that kept the activity going.[19] In these conditions, the mass rail excursions of the past declined: in more fortunate areas the motor charabanc began its long ascendancy in the world of the travelling angler, not least because it was more open to direct bargaining with small operators and could be adapted to the timetables of the fishermen, rather than the other way around. The Wigan of Orwell's depressing survey could still boast 1,900 anglers on its local canals. With the economic revival of the mid-1930s angling recovered, particularly when fostered by large firms, 'who have found that angling conduces not only to the physical fitness and well-being of men engaged in the mass production but to their contentedness'.[20] Both the private sector, as in the Midland Road Passenger Transport Company, and municipal socialism, represented by Birmingham Corporation Tramways, fostered associations and offered competition prizes. Yet prosperity could have its disadvantages. Many coarse fishermen in the 1930s found the cost of their sport rising, particularly on smaller waters near to towns as middle-class car and working-class motorcycle owners pushed out the range of individual access to desirable fishing.

But it was the pan-class rather than the socially divisive aspects of the sport which attracted increasing comment in the later 1930s. The looming threat of war over the Czech crisis of 1938 made many clubs think about cancelling their arrangements, preparing to exchange rods for guns. In such circumstances, against the growing background of a national concern for physical fitness, the contented angler, refreshed by long periods in the open air, appeared as a valuable contribution to the nation's physical resources.

Much of the activity's sedentary nature was forgotten – reflectiveness could go hand in hand with a fitness augmented by the cunning manual dexterity and ingenuity the sport required. When 'Peace with Honour' was declared, Chamberlain received widespread adulation, not least among Birmingham anglers whose MP he was, because he was a fisherman:

Thank God our Prime Minister is a true angler! He possesses the patience, he strikes quickly at the right moment, he is willing to travel far for the fish he is after – whether the fish is salmon or Peace. His methods are always sporting and for the benefit of his brother anglers. He does not admit defeat.[21]

Only the war in Spain then provided an indication of the coming darkness, since it interfered with the supply of silk gut, the raw material of fishing lines, in which the country had a virtual monopoly. By 1939 the Prime Minister's angling virtues were quietly forgotten.

III

He had never known a good fisherman who was a bad fellow.
   Fishing Gazette, 10 September 1932

The emergence of angling as a mass participant sport involved singular tensions parallel to debates in many other more obviously athletic activities. If the emotional core which drove many towards joining was fashioned from a sense of the hunt and from popular romanticism, it soon became entangled in the competitive structure apparently inseparable from modern sports. Around this much ethical and class disagreement focussed. Although there was undoubtedly an element of informal competition among game anglers boasting of their catch at the end of the day in a fishing inn, the majority of middle-class participants in angling (at least above white-collar worker level) eschewed any notion of competition in their sport. 'Pleasure' angling was their predominant idea, the emphasis being primarily on the solitary encounter with nature bolstered, perhaps, by the occasional companionship of congenial individuals. The very nature of game fishing, covering quite large areas of water, fostered this but the very large number of middle-class coarse fishermen demonstrated similar ideals. For many men angling was an accompaniment of holidays away from home: it was this pattern that helped the late Victorian exploitation of the Norfolk Broads as a recreational centre. In them and in places like Yorkshire's Hornsea there could be found large pike or carp, to be hunted with singular skill, patience and, frequently, the help of professional boatmen, England's version of the cantankerous Scottish ghillie. Prowess here could be enshrined and shared through the benefits of photography or taxidermy. For these

1.4 Preparing to game fish from the Llanthony Abbey Hotel, Monmouthshire in the 1950s

men clubs were often little more than syndicates for acquiring favourable rents, the social model was often that of the London dining club, with the Flyfishers' at the top of the ladder; the more favoured, real fishing clubs such as the Piscatorial Society (founded in 1836), developed waiting lists similar to those of Pall Mall. Where the middle-class pleasure angler met working-class fishermen there could be social tension: few recreational spaces have been as socially zoned as riverbanks.

This is not to say that there were no working-class pleasure anglers. Wherever free waters could be found close to towns, as in Nottingham or London, then it was possible. But the very nature of organising access, of transport, and of the sociability of the pub-based club meant that competitive match fishing played a central role for the majority of coarse fishermen. It had a high profile, gave many clubs their *raison d'être*, and meant that anglers who wanted to fish solely for pleasure were largely obliged to do so as nominal participants in a match. Many contemporary observers of the first great fishing boom attributed it largely to the role that match prizes played in attracting poorer working-class participants. In many smaller local matches there was virtually a prize for every participant, usually donated by local businessmen and reflecting the symbiotic nature of the sport in urban culture. These prizes were usually utilitarian or mildly luxurious goods – blankets, kettles, pipes, food hampers and so on, at least until after the First World War.[22] Although a cash value often appeared in the prize lists, actual money was rarely given. It may be assumed that domestically appropriate goods might have done much to alleviate some of the repeated tensions resulting from male expenditure of significant amounts of spare time and household income upon their chosen sport.

Most club weekly outings seem to have involved matches, either internal ones or 'friendlies' with neighbouring bodies. There was a steady shift from the early 'roving' style, in which competitors wandered about until they formed a favoured spot of their own choosing, towards 'pegging'. This involved planning an entire match allocation and giving competitors a fixed spot, drawn through a bankside ballot, for a rigidly controlled period of fishing. The pressures making for this were partly ethical, to give an appearance of random fairness with its resultant demands on skill, thereby avoiding personal squabbles, and sharply practical, as a response to the growing numbers taking part. Voluntary officialdom and club leaderships were given full rein for the exercise of dignity and judgement in what became a highly ritualised pattern, usually taking longer than the actual fishing itself. Arrival, the draw, walking to the site, starting and finishing to the sound of the bugle or whistle, the ceremonial weighing of fish held in keepnets, and finally the awarding of prizes, this pattern was found at all levels, from matches with a dozen competitors to those with three thousand. To some, the scale of much of the activity was distinctly at variance with the pleasure angler's notion of allocating the maximum possible time to angling itself and being alone. One other major issue was that of catch weights. Most match scores depended on aggregated weights, with quantities of small fish at a premium, and holding those until the final weighing. Until various river authorities introduced minimum size regulations in the twentieth century, virtually anything caught could qualify, with a resulting wholesale slaughter of potential breeding stocks. Many clubs tried to limit this, with varying degrees of success since they were trapped by the prize expectations of their membership. Ethically, it raised the hoary middle-class complaint about workers' participation in pan-class sports; that they automatically brought with them the base activities of profit-seeking with its tendency both towards foul play and to over-regulation. Yet it was the clubs' and associations' response to such problems which did a great deal to develop the positive management and conservation of limited stocks in heavily exploited rivers. Indeed it helped them subsequently to become powerful forces in the late twentieth-century battle against pollution. The ethical division over competition has remained one of angling's most obvious features, particularly when it crept into game fishing.

Matches grew with the organisation of leases and travel. Originally fostered by publicans such as John Wreakes of Sheffield in the 1850s, they soon passed more firmly into club and association hands. Once again, Sheffield set the late Victorian pace. There the Association provided an annual series of 'All England' matches on their Lincolnshire waters. These were open to any individual but more essentially to locals – the title was as much an expression of regional pride as of national significance. With minimal entry fees of a shilling or so, organising costs could be considerable and by the early twentieth century the associations had often extended the small-scale sponsorship of small local businesses contributing simple prizes from stock, to significant financial support from larger firms, particularly breweries or local newspapers such as the *Hull Times*.

Imposing 'a strict and sportsmanlike spirit' in matches was not always easy: slipping in pre-caught fish, hidden in bait carriers, has remained a problem up to the present time, and there have been expulsions over the years. One other significant feature, but singularly difficult to trace systematically, has been the role of betting in match patterns: angling, together with pigeon- and dog-racing, has always had a strong underpinning of this, despite the anxiously coy denials of its existence by many embarrassed

1.5 For the matches the bookies come too. Fred Clark was at the national angling championships on the river Nene near Peterborough in September 1953

club officials. 'Loud voiced, brass-lunged bookies' were perhaps not as common as detractors claimed by 1900 but all matches (except among the few chapel and temperance clubs) attracted a betting network.[23] In many senses it was only a popular version of the private wagers between many members of game-fishing syndicates, but it was its scale and associated ethical problems that drew down some opprobrium. One side effect has been that it produced a limited (and not readily ascertainable) number of semi-professional match anglers who largely make up the sport's restricted pantheon of heroes. Few could live by angling, and few matchmen had the middle-class opportunity of paid angling journalism, but the highly skilled and very lucky could, and still can, considerably augment a manual workers' income. Walter Darwin of Sheffield in the 1890s was probably the first major figure of the type, fishing for £5 prizes in exhibition matches.[24] This has continued to the present day, typified now by the matchman sponsored by a tackle firm. Because of problems caused by the compatibility of this with many types of employment, these men often put their winnings into becoming minor local tackle dealers, effectively becoming angling freelance versions of the retired golf professional, or the retired footballer settling into his sports or tobacconist's shop. By the 1920s two men would often fish a one and a half-hour match for £10 to £20 a side, the winner taking 60 or 70 fish in that time, watched by a crowd of spectators anxiously shifting side bets. In the Wigan area this always took place on the Leeds and Liverpool canal; in cold weather, 'the two anglers are supplied with two hot bricks to sit on and roasted potatoes in their pockets to keep their fingers warm'.[25] In this world the non-betting match angler was a rarity, written up as such by the press. Such was George Bright, the captain of the Bristol and West of England team in the National Championship of 1938, who neither betted nor believed in Sunday fishing; his individual victory was widely regarded as a fluke.[26]

Pegged matches were introduced into the freer south from the north. Common though the mode became, organised match fishing enhanced both regional differences in actual fishing styles and their associated fierce loyalties. Methods were essentially a product of the requirements of locally different waters and their stocks. Sheffielders developed fine tackle with coloured maggot baits for small shoaling species in the slow-flowing Lincolnshire and Fenland rivers. The wide and quick-flowing Trent demanded heavier tackle, the Thames and its tributaries long poles. The technology of rods has changed considerably, from cane to steel, then to man-made glass or carbon fibres; reels have evolved from wood and brass to light alloys and carbon composites; and lines from woven silk gut to the ubiquitous nylon-derived monofilaments, but the essential styles have changed little and still produce an apparently endless refinement of debate. Regional variation was fostered initially by the essentially local nature of competition but pride was enhanced considerably by the significant early twentieth-century growth of 'national' matches. Those arranged by the Sheffield Association since the 1880s had been little more than national in name and it was a major step when the various regional associations began to develop a wider sense of cooperation. This had grown out of a fiercely negative reaction to various legislative proposals to introduce a 'rod tax', a national licence for coarse fishing. There was also some value in the constant monitoring of waterboard measures to cope with widespread industrial pollution and a growing perceived need to protect the general interests of anglers. The result was the formation of the National Federation of Anglers, at the behest of the Northern Anglers' Association at a meeting in Birmingham in May 1903. Without the minute regulatory role of many parallel organisations in sports bureaucracy and with a much larger and more independently-minded participatory affiliation than most of those ever enjoyed, the NFA found its main role in organising a national championship.

In so doing it avoided much of the controversy surrounding similar activities in other sports – both amateurs and 'shamateurs' appeared as contestants. The first match was mounted on the Thames at Pangbourne in October 1906. Significantly it was sponsored by the *Daily Mirror* which had realised the sport's role in the lives of many of its readers, and which gave it extensive coverage. This partnership lasted until the National Federation asserted its independence in 1938 and took sole responsibility for organisation and prizes. Unlike previous large matches this was not open to individuals but to club teams instead and the prizes were the cups and medals of organised sport, angling having been brought into line, at least at this level, with the general ethics of competition. The winners came from Boston, using Sheffield methods; northern hegemony was widely proclaimed. That predominance remained. It was 1959 before a 'southern association' (Bedford) won, despite the venue being moved to a different area each year. Paradoxically, all the records for individual coarse species caught before 1959 rested with southern pleasure anglers, with one rare exception, a 4lb 4oz gudgeon caught at Shipley in 1935.[27]

If the direct attraction of prizes in kind played a less important role in many matches after 1919, the level of competition increased as the war receded. As noted before, there had always been an altruistic element in those matches, organised primarily to raise charitable funds and this continued. If anything, matches developed an even greater role in bolstering regional pride and in scale of organisation. Here, at least, the preeminence passed from Sheffield to Birmingham; by 1926 the former city could only recruit 1,600 competitors for its largest match, whilst the 'Brummies' attracted 3,800 pegged at less than 10 yard intervals along 40 miles of bank, 18 on one side and 22 on the other.[28] With this size of match, peg allocations were done a fortnight before; there were 302 cash prizes (for once notional honour went largely by the board, although the winner received a shield) ranging from £12 to 10 shillings. Two fully equipped motor ambulances were provided for those overcome by strain and emotion. 1,770 anglers actually weighed in their results. The winner, W. Starmer of Aston, 'exclusively uses tackle made by Albert Smith and Company, Redditch'; if he was not paid a retainer, his tackle appears to have been provided free.[29] If Birmingham now dominated the match world in terms of organisation, it was a small cathedral city which offered the most valuable trophy, the 250 guinea City of Hereford Angling Challenge Trophy. The key difference was that it was fished for on different occasions, in four-hour matches, and the prize went to the club not with the greatest in aggregate weights but with a complex species / weighting points calculation which allowed 12 per pike pound and 128 per grayling pound.[30]

Regionalism rolled happily on, amidst occasional complaints that the successful and the gifted men of Lincolnshire should 'write articles showing the comparatively crude Londoners how to do it'.[31] But the 'unobtrusiveness of the angler's sport' continued, epitomised by a low-key London and affiliated associations' remembrance service at the Cenotaph in 1932.[32] As membership pressures continued, many clubs and associations withdrew even further from cash and kind prizes at matches, amid a general approbation for using surplus monies for restocking and improvement instead, although there was an undercurrent of feeling during the early 1930s Depression that prizes on the older model would do much to alleviate the misery of the old heartland of match fishing. In this world, the focus was inevitably the unemployed male angler. Rarely were women found on the banks. Even at the peak of the Birmingham matches only 30 women (less than 1 per cent of the entries) took part. Whilst game fishing had, at least since the 1870s, catered partly for women, even encouraging them in the interests of health and eugenics, gender separation remained very distinct further down the social scale. Some London bodies had a long tradition of refusing concessionary fares to hopeful women anglers, although they showed a common readiness to allow them on special trains as observant dependants of their husbands and fathers, largely on the ground that their presence might inhibit over-drinking and other forms of unsportsmanlike behaviour. The bigger matches often developed some of the aspects of a bank holiday carnival, but women were generally seen as a threat to the significant male bonding rituals of club and riverbank.[33]

There are many parallels to the experience, divisions and organisation of coarse fishing in a branch which the late Victorians could readily claim to have invented as a sport: sea fishing. The unlikely combination of the lure of the wilderness and the crowded imposition of social tone which produced the nineteenth-century seaside resort also fostered its sporting offspring. In close parallel to wildfowling there were some tensions in reactions from locals, when middle-class incomers took to doing for pleasure what they had had to do for a living, but the subservience of professional skills in the guise of boatmen (which we have already noted in the creation of the ghillie) marked the permanent ascendancy of the new pursuit. For the seasick or in stormy weather, beaches and piers provided suitable sites. Far more obviously tied in with urban holiday seasons than were other branches of fishing, sea fishing grew initially as a pursuit of the relatively affluent business and professional class. It was these men who sought to pool information and give recognition to suitably vetted local boatmen when they formed the British Sea Anglers' Society in 1893, with an initial membership drawn largely from Westminster politicians. It, and a volume in the *Badminton Library* gave the sport the publicity it needed: it is noticeable that, in the abundant history of angling literature, whilst much space has been given to the various forms of pursuit, only very few books actually deal with working-class organisations.[34] Sea angling's initial high profile was for a relatively limited clientele. It widened steadily, although with something of the esoteric appeal of wildfowling, because it came to attract not only the more affluent seaside visitor but also the resident middle classes who serviced the resorts themselves. Apart from being a useful, socially acceptable, way of adding to middle-class larders, it was eminently suited as a half-day sport for office and shopmen in the seaside towns. It was these who began to organise simple local matches, with some prizes similar to those of the coarse angling world, but with a far narrower social range of participant. The leading resorts in the Edwardian period, aiming largely at a middle-class clientele, soon saw the town competition, such as a Hastings Sea Fishing Festival, as a means of increasing their allure at relatively low cost. The British Sea Anglers' Society remained largely outside this development, more akin to the Alpine Club than to an urban angling association, and it was usually local businessmen and councils who took the initiative. Much more than with inland fishing, the First World War acted as a powerful inhibitor – who wanted to catch a mine? – and, even with the philathletic Lord Desborough offering active support, it remained the one branch of the sport which remained close to being a parody of an established industry. Its support in the inter-war years for a new Ministry of Fisheries actually reinforced this, but the sport grew slowly with the steady reemergence of resorts and a wider clientele.[35]

IV

Sport of which at one time you could only dream.
    Peter Stone, *Gravel Pit Angling*, (Newton Abbot 1978) p.15

Hitler's war made sea fishing very difficult indeed, and it led to the inevitable disruption of all other forms of angling. Once again such clubs as survived, largely for workers in the vital industries, managed to keep going by validating their activities with matches for service and medical charities, as when an Ely Sugar Beet Factory Fishing Club match raised £24 11s 8d for the Merchant Navy Comforts Service.[36] But with motoring and most rail travel out of the question wholesale activities were impossible. With members away at camps or fighting all over the world many of the bigger bodies, particularly in Birmingham, had considerable difficulties in raising enough funds to keep their waters rented, and there was widespread ambivalence as to how far associations should act as watchdogs against pollution arising from wartime production. The Second World War's more directive econ-

1.6 During the 1939–45 war coastal fishing was banned. This picture was taken somewhere on the south coast after the ban was lifted

omic management actually allowed a steady trickle of tackle to reach such anglers as could afford it – boots, waders, rods and bait could still be found, although many clubs felt that the traditional home mix for the latter of bread and cheese pastes was an undue pressure on the convoy system. But fishing represented part of the Arcadia for whose preservation the war was being fought. By comparison with the First World War far more British anglers found themselves incarcerated in prisoner of war camps, and the Red Cross ran an active campaign to provide them with artificial fly-tying gear to keep up morale and prepare them for the return of peace. The British Field Sport Society produced a series of booklets on hunting, shooting and fishing (presumably largely for officers) to remind them of what awaited them on release, and it was suggested that handicraft tackle-making classes in the camps might prepare the disabled for employment at the war's end.[37] The National Federation of Anglers overcame suggestions in 1943 that a journey was not really 'necessary' to attend its annual conference, the first to lunch in a British restaurant.[38] It did its own little bit for the war effort by encouraging its branches to let American troops stationed in Britain fish local waters free. It was the latter who introduced scarce nylon fishing lines and casts into their bartering arrangements. Other troops were rather less welcome when they took to poaching with explosives to augment the dubious quality of service food.[39] By the middle of the war the sense of a coming reconstruction found an echo in angling writers who came to suggest that municipalities should prepare to provide fishing on town reservoirs in much the way that some of them had fostered the spread of golf for the more fortunate.

The early years of peace and austerity saw a slow revival of the sport, conducted in many of its traditional ways until the later 1950s. The devastation of many cities had removed many of the street, pub or club props of the working-class coarse angler's life, giving firm-based clubs a new importance. The big urban associations found themselves operating less as amalgamations of clubs, although this still played a role, than as umbrella bodies for individual anglers often more interested in pleasure fishing. Matches still played a significant part as we shall see but, by the 1960s, the spread of individual motor transport and the steady erosion of rail facilities meant that the old symbiosis of membership and concessionary transport disappeared. Emphasis shifted to the individual or the small group of friends sharing a car. One major development of this was the emergence of one-species specialists, particularly concerned with catching large carp or pike. This became obsessional, a return to the skilled hunt away from the amassing of prize weights which this new breed despised. With its talisman, the 44lb carp caught by Dick Walker (an engineer turned fishing journalist who is widely held to be the greatest all-round exponent and practitioner of angling in the post-war decades) in Radmire Pool, Hertfordshire, and then placed live in London Zoo's aquarium, this movement represented a new technical elite with a much wider class base.

Its significance was far wider than the limited numbers of its leading practitioners, because it turned the attention of many working-class anglers away from distant rivers to local ponds and, significant as the delayed post-war building boom took off, to flooded gravel pits. These developed aquatic life remarkably rapidly, even when not stocked, and they represent the greatest impact of mass angling on the modern landscape. Although the larger ones could be match fished it was their role for the specialist and pleasure angler that really mattered. They were also generally less vulnerable than rivers to the growing threats from industrial and agricultural pollution. Some clubs even turned their funds to buying them. The specifically regional tackle and methods evolved over decades for river angling were rarely suited to these new venues, and the application of new ideas by men such as Walker, who put his Cambridge engineering training to superb use, did a great deal to move the focus of coarse angling pride from regional ascendancy to task-related problem solving. Far more time-consuming than the concentrated span of activity that older match fishing had required, this new growth fitted particularly well the needs and income of workers in what were becoming the car-rich English midlands.

They shared also in one of the greatest changes in angling that began just after the war but accelerated very rapidly in the 1960s, the availability of popular trout fishing. The classical trout stream had long since proved inadequate for growing middle-class demands on them and a limited stocking of streams near trout farms had begun before 1900. But it was to the great artificial lakes, the reservoirs produced to meet the drinking and sanitation needs of massive Victorian urbanisation, that some anglers' attention turned. It took a very long time to overcome the reluctance of some water authorities to let anglers near their 'pure' waters: the pressure came from bodies demanding more fresh air for the industrial working classes, but where access became possible, it was the urban upper middle classes who benefited initially. Bristol opened Blagdon reservoir in 1904, with a day-ticket price of 10 shillings, half a week's wages for some workers. By 1914 there were 150 rather smaller waters open, often much cheaper than Blagdon and largely in the north of England. But the great corporations, particularly Manchester, insisted that their *cordon sanitaire* around reservoirs in Wales and the Lake District remain unbreached. There were few additions in the inter-war period.[40]

The first significant shift took place in the late 1940s when Alex Behrendt created the Two Lakes fishery on land between the Test and Itchen in Hampshire by bulldozing and landscaping a small estate to create a relatively high cost 'exclusive' environment. In his words, 'Fishermen will be put off if the fishery is made to resemble a seaside resort.'[41] This method of building popularity was by careful stocking, the creation of a pleasant environment, and a low-key publicity grapevine that created a considerable waiting list for membership. Behrendt's model has been followed in a number of areas across Britain since, although by no means cheap to provide or maintain; in many places it worked best when associated with a fish farm for stocking. Here there has been a steady process in which angling has provided a spin-off from the growing popularity of trout for the table. Although the early anglers on these stillwaters wanted to hunt the prized fish of the chalk streams, the brown trout, the post-war boom has effectively been built upon farm breeding of a North American import, the rainbow trout. Edwardian experiments at introducing this had foundered, largely because the fish rarely spawned when released into the British wild. Now farming techniques and the growing acceptability of 'put and take' fishing offered, by the later 1960s, the possibility of a relatively cheap wholesale stocking of waters if such could be found.

In fact ample space became available with the creation of new 'super' reservoirs, particularly in the midlands to match the expansion of the car industry. Graffham Water (1,600 acres) in Huntingdonshire (now Cambridgeshire), and Rutland Water (3,100 acres), taking a large slice out of that small historic county, offered a model soon followed on Bewl Water in Kent, and then on most others in England and in Wales and Scotland as well. By the mid-1980s the 150 stillwaters of the inter-war period had become over 1,000 with a considerable difference in size, cost and social conduct for the trout angler. In a sense they represent a 'democratising' of fly-fishing, the essential element being the ability to pay the £10 or so currently required for a day-ticket on the larger waters. Loyalty to them is not that of club or often of setting: the key is the ability of each one to provide an adequate level of sporting demand throughout the season with a reasonable certainty of a sustained catching average. They rarely offer solitude, particularly on bank holidays, where 'hotspots' are as crowded as the banks at coarse fishing matches and they do vary considerably, ranging from flooded concrete bowls, such as Toft Newton in Lincolnshire, to Northumberland's Kielder Water, the largest man-made lake in Europe. The challenge has been to adapt the concealed stalking patterns of the chalk streams, where the quarry is usually visible, to acres of water where fish can often not be seen at all but lie deep. Some of the methods developed by Victorians for fishing the depths of Scottish lochs have been amalgamated with lake styles imported from North America to provide a singular hybrid. The basic work was done in the 1960s by the 'Northampton School' of fly-fisherman, led by Tom Ivens and Bob Church (now running a successful manufacturing and wholesale company specialising in reservoir tackle) and there is still something of the regionalism of both earlier trout and coarse fishing to attract loyalties. Essentially, the bulk of reservoir anglers use the 'wetfly' methods of older northern fishermen, although the 1980s have seen something of a reservoir dryfly and nymph cult develop in a latter-day purist reaction against the wholesale, and often very successful, trolling of the masses. And wholesale it became – by the mid-1980s there were about 700,000 regular reservoir anglers.

This growth was part of a much wider development, and one whose scale could be adequately measured for the first time when the River Boards generally introduced coarse fishing licences in the 1960s; all the old fears

Fishing has more in common with other sports than you might think. You have to learn and you have to practise

1.7 A joint LCC–CCPR project for instructing youngsters, Richmond, Surrey, August 1960

1.8 Members of the Camberley and District Sea Angling Club practising their casts in May 1967. Presumably their oilskins were for atmosphere

of a 'rod tax' on working-class anglers appears to have evaporated when it became clear that the Boards would undertake general maintenance and some stocking on their waters. In fact, the Scots continued to escape this as have sea anglers. By the late 1970s, there were 3,380,000 anglers in England and Wales and 354,000 in Scotland. Sixty per cent of these fished for coarse fish, 53 per cent for game and 20 per cent the sea – it became increasingly apparent that many moved between all three branches. A survey published in 1980 revealed that coarse fishing was most popular in the English midlands, game strongest in Scotland and the west midlands, and sea fishing in Wales, the southwest and the north of England. Forty-seven per cent of coarse anglers were skilled manual workers, about the same proportion of sea fishermen came from that social grouping, and 88 per cent of all anglers were male. Together, all anglers spent £633,000,000 in 1979 prices, with a coarse outing averaging £5.81 a trip as against £8.25 for a sea outing or £9.37 for game. Such averages conceal, on the one hand, the £3,000 a week that Scottish salmon fishing could now cost, or, at the other end of the scale, the small boy fishing a local canal with a bamboo pole and a simple line.[42]

What the figures did demonstrate was the economic role of the sport when viewed collectively; 15 per cent of men and boys aged over 12 were fishing regularly and the overall number had increased by 17.5 per cent during the 1970s, rather more than leisure planners had anticipated. Such an expansion had generated an accompanying business input, perhaps best exemplified by the (admittedly short-lived) appearance of fishing tackle stands in Woolworth's stores. Professionally made tackle had always had some part in modern angling, especially in hooks which had been developed in mass-production terms by large wire and needle firms such as Allcocks of Redditch, who came to dominate the market. Like guns, rods had usually been produced, particularly for game fishers, by small craft firms; the late Victorian boom had allowed one such, Hardy's of Alnwick, to transfer to factory production, which has since then dominated the quality end of the British market. These rods were built up from imported bamboo canes, the staple material until the 1960s, and still the preserve of absolute purists. Poorer anglers often built their own rods or bought cheap but serviceable imitations of the tackle used by match champions, adapted to regional needs.[43] The development of tubular steel technology between the wars had little effect on angling, although post-war austerity did see widespread adaptation of surplus radio aerials and similar gear. It was the introduction of the metal 'fixed spool' reel to all branches except fly-fishing in the mid-1960s that revolutionised casting and retrieval techniques using the increasingly popular and cheap nylon lines. Fibre glass followed quickly as the standard cheap rod material, to be replaced rapidly by carbon fibre in the 1980s. Much of this was produced abroad, in Sweden, Japan and Taiwan, but the 1980s saw the firm establishment of British production facilities for such foreign firms as Abu and Daiwa, widely regarded as the trend leaders in popular angling technology, the relative cheapness of whose products did a great deal to make growth possible.

The pressure of angling's growing post-war popularity saw another major role for the business world, as the provider of waters. Gravel pit angling, originally leased by a few individuals or clubs, was quickly exploited by large firms, particularly the extraction industry themselves. In the late 1970s the Redland Sand and Gravel Company developed its surplus pits in Buckinghamshire and Bedfordshire to offer 20 new venues.[44] Investment in angling space also became part of the 1970s property investment boom; the Leisure Sport Angling Club, a subsidiary of RMC (Feltham) became the largest of the commercial coarse syndicates, with 43 gravel pits and 11 river stretches, as far apart as the London area, Nottinghamshire and Norfolk. From their Leisure Sport Tackle shop and office in Staines, Middlesex, they serviced 15,000 permit holders by the late 1970s.[45] In this new pattern the older clubs and big urban associations found themselves under considerable pressure. With the spread of car ownership and specialist angling, individual fishermen appeared less dependent on their local bodies and more selective in the waters they sought. As angling became much more recognisably a revenue-producing investment, landowners who had traditionally let out waters at nominal rates began to renegotiate leases at much higher prices, which the weakened associations, having lost their privileged access position, could no longer afford. Sheffield began a sustained withdrawal from Lincolnshire; the number of anglers did not diminish, it was their mode of organisation and access which did.[46]

Older forms of voluntarist organisations continued but often with a different emphasis, particularly since rod licensing focussed many anglers' attentions on the water boards. The clubs and associations continued to manage matches, but developed very significantly as watchdogs as angling faced singular post-war pressures. The effective collapse of inland water transport in the 1950s pushed the bodies into battle to keep canals open as recreation facilities and this produced further problems as angling was joined by other activities in a general water activities boom.[47] With the growth of recreational boating, canal cruising, river canoeing and sailing on reservoirs, fishermen found themselves sharply at odds with other water users, negotiation often being less common than mutual abuse. But there were other, greater problems. Anglers became one of the greatest pressure groups against the growing risk of pollution from new chemical industries, from an agriculture increasingly dependent on artificial nitrates and, ironically, from the slurry from fish farms. In 1948 a small group founded the Anglers' Cooperative Association which undertook the frequent and successful prosecution of the worst offenders. Although vociferous in its defence of freshwater interests, it has never enjoyed more than a very limited support from the bulk of the sport's followers.[48] The water boards which are now responsible for the oversight of all freshwater angling are themselves often faced by the difficulties which increased water extraction can cause and they have recently begun to 'privatise' their fishing facilities under government pressure. But there have been major successes; by the mid-1980s salmon had once again appeared in the Thames, a rare sign of returning purity. Angling has developed a much higher and wider profile since the late 1960s, not only because of the growing number of participants. Not least has been the role of commercial sponsorship, particularly from tackle firms, for competitive fishing. One tackle firm, Gladding, arranged a Masters Tournament, on the lines of golf's model, on the Trent in 1977, with all the implications for angling as a spectator sport; 4,000 came to watch. When it was revived in 1987, it was with the aim of recapturing 'all the glamour, prestige and entertainment of the original series'.[49] Many other firms with no links with tackle production were similarly involved, such as Ladbroke's, the betting conglomerate, and Embassy, the cigarette producers. The semiprofessional, often fishing for a tackle firm such as Daiwa, became a sports hero in angling, hyped through a widespread tabloid fishing press such as no previous generation had been able to supply. A Coventry tackle dealer, Billy Lane, was the key figure of the 1960s but a new, younger group appeared by the later 1970s. Mark Downes, the 'Birmingham Star', hoped to see match fishing organised like football with 'a more professional approach.'[50] Kenny Collings gave up window cleaning in 1977 to be the 'first truly professional angler' in the south of England, contracted to a London tackle manufacturer, Henry W. Aiken Ltd.[51] A semi-professional, Harry Settle of Bolton, reckoned to spend twenty hours a week on preparing his tackle and bait; with first prizes of £1,000 or more for the sponsored matches it could be well worthwhile.[52] Similar men could be found in sea fishing, particularly when the television companies, both BBC and Independent, started to produce programmes of match highlights or, as in the case of TVS, sponsor their own competitions.

In this sense, coarse angling went the way of most sports in the leisure boom that emerged in the 1960s. It reflects the recreational potential and the inbuilt tensions of all sport in an industrial society in which leisure is now a major economic sector. But, for all the media hype, the cash prizes and the adulation of the new technology which supports the activity,

1.9 But this is the big one, a modern division one national championship. The
year is 1985 and the place, the Leeds–Liverpool canal

there is still a major core of Waltonian arcadianism. The anarchic hero
of Alan Sillitoe's 1960s novel, *Saturday Night and Sunday Morning*, Arthur
Seaton, found his hope of real peace in fishing the local canal just as the
hero of Orwell's *Coming Up For Air*, George Bowling, had sought solace
in the 1930s. And men (with a few women) of all social classes still take
cheerfully to a sport which could be described in a 1970s conference on
freshwater recreation as 'an intensely personal activity which may at times
place the individual in a sort of mesmeric trance'.[53]

NOTES

1 See J. Lowerson, 'Izaak Walton: father of a dream', *History Today* (December
   1983).
2 E.g. Charles Kingsley, *Chalk Stream Studies; Miscellanies I* (1859), Edward
   Grey, *Flyfishing* (1899), Alec Douglas-Home, *Border Reflections* (1979).

3 See R. Colls and P. Dodd, *Englishness* (1986).

4 For instance, *Fishing Gazette*, 12 February 1955.

5 J. Lowerson, 'Sport and the Victorian Sunday', *British Journal of Sports History*, vol. 1, no. 2 (September 1984).

6 Arthur Ransome, *Rod and Line* (Various edns).

7 The rise of coarse fishing is discussed more fully in J. Lowerson, 'Brothers of the angle; coarse fishing and working-class culture' in J. A. Mangan (ed.), *Pleasure, Profit, Proselytism* (1988).

8 Ibid.

9 John Buchan, *John MacNab* (1925).

10 Lowerson, 'Brothers of the Angle'.

11 *Fishing Gazette*, 4 January 1919.

12 *Fishing Gazette*, 15 February 1919.

13 *Fishing Gazette*, 8 March 1919.

14 *Fishing Gazette*, 16 August 1919.

15 *Fishing Gazette*, 6 February 1926.

16 *Fishing Gazette*, 13 March 1926.

17 *Fishing Gazette*, 24 April 1926.

18 *Fishing Gazette*, 22 March 1930.

19 *Fishing Gazette*, 21 May 1932.

20 *Fishing Gazette*, 10 September 1938.

21 *Fishing Gazette*, 8 October 1938.

22 See J. Lowerson, 'Brothers of the angle', *passim*.

23 Ibid.

24 *Fishing Gazette*, 19 November 1892.

25 *Fishing Gazette*, 15 March 1919.

26 *Fishing Gazette*, 10 October 1938.

27 For records see 'Angling' in C. Harvey (ed.), *Encyclopedia of Sport* (1959).

28 *Fishing Gazette*, 16 October 1926.

29 *Fishing Gazette*, 13 November 1926.

30 *Fishing Gazette*, 29 May 1926.

31 *Fishing Gazette*, 11 January 1930.

32 *Fishing Gazette*, 18 January 1932.

33 J. Lowerson, 'Brothers of the angle', *passim*.

34 J. Bickerdyke, *Sea Fishing* (1902).

35 *Fishing Gazette*, 29 March 1919.

36 *Fishing Gazette*, 18 September 1943.

37 *Fishing Gazette*, 21 January 1943.

38 *Fishing Gazette*, 1 May 1943.

39 *Fishing Gazette*, 17 April 1943.

40 See J. Lowerson, 'Green wellies and still waters', *New Society*, 28 April 1983.

41 Alex Behrendt, *The Management of Angling Waters* (1978), p. 200.

42 *National Angling Survey 1980*.

43 *Fishing Gazette*, 24 May 1930.

44 Bill Howes, *Fishing for Londoners* (1978), p. 9ff.

45 Ibid.

46 *Angling Times*, 4 February 1987.

47 *Fishing Gazette*, 2 April 1955.

48 Bernard Venables, *Fishing* (1953), p. 263ff.
49 *Angling Times*, 4 February 1987.
50 *Coarse Angler*, June 1977.
51 Ibid.
52 Ibid.
53 J. S. Alabaster (ed.), *Recreational Freshwater Fisheries* (1978), p. 133.

2 ATHLETICS

JEREMY CRUMP

I

> The athletic movement which commenced with the 'classes' and first drew its
> strength from the Universities and public schools, has finally, like most other
> movements and fashions, good or bad, spread downwards, to the masses.
>
> Montague Shearman, *Athletics and Football*, (1889) pp.226–7

Athletics in its modern form came into being in the 1860s and the modern
programme of events is based on that of the first championship of the
Amateur Athletic Club held in 1865. The sport was given institutional form
by the clubs which grew up at that time. Their origins were various,
although they were often made up of army officers, civil servants, university
men, professionals and businessmen many of whom had taken part in running races at Oxford, Cambridge or the major public schools. The Amateur
Athletic Club (f. 1866) itself was the most exclusive. The Mincing Lane
Athletic Club (f. 1863), which became the London Athletic Club in 1866,
drew its membership largely from the City. The Civil Service Athletic Club
was founded in 1866. Many clubs were set up by enthusiasts for other
sports who saw them as a means of keeping fit. This was the case with
the West London Racing Club's Athletics Section (f. 1861) and the Peckham
Hounds (later the Blackheath Harriers) (f. 1869). Elsewhere, clubs were
set up in conjunction with the volunteer movement, as was the Liverpool
Athletic Club (f. 1862). At first, the driving force behind many clubs was
social as much as athletic *per se*, but the assimilation of athletics to the
respectable club model was important in distancing the sport from pedestrianism. In the latter, runners were very much on their own, competing
for prize money on tracks owned by sports ground companies. Athletics
stressed individual achievement to an extent which could undermine the
team spirit fostered by other games favoured by the Victorian middle class.
The club provided an element of collective endeavour. Moreover, the club
was a microcosm of the way in which the sport's more influential patrons
wanted athletics as a whole to be run, somewhat akin to the MCC's role
in cricket.

During the 1870s, the membership of many clubs grew as the sport became officially less exclusive (see pp. 50–1 below). By 1874, for example, the London AC had 900 members and the Blackheath Harriers had reached 200 by 1883. The number of clubs grew as well. There were 45 affiliated to the AAA (f. 1879) in 1880, rising to 185 by 1887, 200 by 1897 and 502 by 1914. The geographical spread of the clubs took in most areas of the country, as is shown by strong regional associations in the north and midlands.

The 1920s saw a rapid growth in the number of athletic clubs, so that the AAA had about 1,000 affiliates by 1930. The AAA was hard pressed to provide support for the new clubs, and it has been suggested that the development of coaching was necessarily neglected in the inter-war years.[1] At the same time, the establishment of new organisations such as the Inter-University Athletics Board of Great Britain and Ireland (1919), and the Women's Amateur Athletic Association (1925) point to the broadening social base of the sport. The number of clubs declined in the late 1930s, but there was a resurgence of interest after the war, stimulated in part by the encouragement given to athletics by the armed forces. The AAA was able to launch a national scheme to train coaches in 1946 and from 1947 the scheme was 80 per cent funded by the Ministry of Education. By 1965, it had provided over 2,000 trained coaches. The AAA's 5-Star Award Scheme was launched in 1968 as a means of encouraging young athletes to improve, and over 1 million awards have been made per year.

At another level, participation in athletics has reached unprecedented levels since the mid-1970s with the popularity of marathon running, fun runs and jogging. Some long-distance events date from the early years of the century, such as the Poly Marathon, established by the Polytechnic Harriers in 1909, or even from the nineteenth century, such as the London to Brighton run. Social running was an important aspect of the early clubs, but had declined as cross-country running replaced paper chasing. But in the 1960s, clubs again experienced an upsurge of interest from runners whose principal interest was not competition. By the early 1980s, running, whether in clubs or, more often, informally, had become highly popular and track-suited joggers ubiquitous, in part a response to worries about health. Joggers have been organised into truly massive sporting events on occasions. Notable events such as the London Marathon and the Great North Run (both f. 1981) have attracted tens of thousands of applicants. In 1985, for example, 70,000 applied for 22,000 places in the London Marathon. Such events cater for novices alongside the country's leading marathon runners. In May 1986, hundreds of thousands of people ran six miles over courses throughout the country for the Sport Aid charity in aid of famine in Africa, and there have been innumerable lesser fund-raising events.

2.1 The importance of taking part can rarely have been better exemplified than by the massed ranks of the London Marathon. This one was in 1985

2.2 This was a posed picture but it also illustrates the popularity of track and field over 80 years ago in the Salford of 1907

Major athletic events have attracted large crowds from the early years of the AAA Championship (f. 1880) onwards. Indeed, even before then grounds such as the Lillie Bridge Ground in West Brompton (f. 1869) and its successor at Stamford Bridge (f. 1877) could draw crowds of 10,000 or more, comparable with the larger football crowds of the day. The prevalence of betting led on occasions to disorder, particularly if a disqualification frustrated hopes of winnings. In 1881, the AAA provided policemen at 30 yard intervals around the track as a precaution against disorder. It was also often necessary to take steps to prevent the crowd overflowing onto the track to follow the leader to the line, overwhelming those further down the field. In 1887, the Lillie Bridge Ground was burned down by a gang who were involved in betting at a professional sprinting match. The AAA's campaign against professionalism and illegal payments in the 1890s led to a decline in crowds in 1896–7, but the subsequent growth of international athletics was to stimulate renewed interest. The 1908 Olympic Games produced very large crowds, including one of 90,000 which remains the largest recorded for an athletics event in Britain.

In parallel with the growth of club athletics, the 1920s saw the transformation of athletics into a major spectator sport. Crowds of over 20,000 were usual for the largest events. In 1928, there were 41,000 at Stamford Bridge to watch the British Empire compete against the USA. The AAA Championships were drawing 30,000 by the early 1930s, but there was a decline in the popularity of the sport after the mid-1930s, reflecting the poorer performances of British athletes in international competition when compared with those of the 1920s. In 1932, the AAA had transferred its headquarters to the White City Stadium as Stamford Bridge was increasingly used for the more profitable speedway. The White City was also a major greyhound racing stadium. In the late 1940s and early 1950s it hosted crowds of 40–50,000 as athletics shared in the post-war boom experienced by football and cricket, and indeed by other forms of entertainment such as the cinema. The first international after the war drew a crowd of 52,000 to witness Sidney Wooderson compete against the leading Swedish miler Arne Andersson. The athletics crowd at the White City seems to have had a character of its own in these years. Roger Bannister recalls the encouragement he received from 'the deep-throated White City roar' at the British Games in 1951.[2] At that time, even a club event such as the Blackheath Harriers annual championship in 1946 at Motspur Park in South London could draw 7,000 spectators, although Wooderson's presence made this something of a special occasion.

By the later 1950s, athletics had entered a long decline as a spectator sport. Only the presence of leading international athletes could produce a large crowd. The attendance at the AAA championships fell year by year, to 17,000 in 1959, 8,000 on the Saturday of the two-day meeting in 1969 and to 4,271 in 1970. The move to the Crystal Palace stadium in Norwood the following year improved the crowd, but it has only been sponsorship which has kept athletics solvent since the late 1950s. In the years since 1970, athletics has been a popular television spectacle, and the biggest meetings have continued to attract crowds, but it is an important aspect of the transformation of athletics that the sport is no longer supported by gate money.

II

The ruling class of British athletics have drawn up a constitution which has created and perpetuated an aristocracy.
    Geoff Capes, *Big Shot*, (1981) p.66

The Amateur Athletic Association was formed in 1880 at a meeting instigated by three Oxford University men, each a former athlete, who had recognised the need for a single authoritative body in English athletics. During the 1870s, the Amateur Athletic Club's authority had declined to the extent that its championships were no longer universally accepted as the national championships. In 1879, there were rival English national championships. The AAA was to be governed by a committee including representatives of the major clubs and associations.[3] It succeeded in its immediate aim of unifying amateur athletics in England, and at once undertook the defence of its relatively liberal interpretation of amateurism. In 1889 it promulgated its first set of Rules for Competition which, with subsequent revisions, won general acceptance in Britain and formed the basis for later international sets of rules. Only with the establishment of the International Amateur Athletics Federation in 1912, to which the AAA affiliated two years later, was it finally apparent that the AAA was not to have the same dominant relationship to athletics as the MCC had to cricket.

Although the AAA succeeded in bringing together the various bodies with an interest in the administration of amateur athletics in late nineteenth-century Britain, it failed to maintain single-handed control of athletics in the twentieth century. The AAA's patrician leadership, its metropolitan base and above all its unwillingness to extend its responsibilities meant that the administration of athletics grew by the creation of further governing bodies with specific interests. Thus the British Olympic Association was set up to organise the 1908 Games and served as a fund-raising body for future Games, as well as coordinating the contribution of the various sports. The AAA did not take up the opportunity to control women's athletics, so an autonomous Women's Association was set up in 1922. The AAA was forced in 1932 to pass on its function of selecting and supporting the national team to the British Amateur Athletics Board (BAAB) which was set up at the instigation of the IAAF when the Scottish AAA objected to the AAA's continuing domination. When Neil MacFarlane took over the office of Minister of Sport in 1981, he was astonished to learn that there were no less than 19 organisations with a controlling interest in athletics in the UK.

The financial crisis of athletics, particularly of the AAA, in the mid-1960s, arising in part from the decline of attendances at major meetings, led to calls for the unification of the various administrative bodies. The Byers report, published in 1968, found that unification, along with the appointment of professional directors, was essential for the financial health of the sport. Similar conclusions were reached in 1983 by a committee set up by the Sports Council at the instigation of Mr MacFarlane. There was increasing concern that the complex administrative structure would be incapable of handling the large and growing sponsorship income which athletics have enjoyed since the late 1970s, and that money would not be directed where it was most needed. But there was strong opposition to reform from the many vested interests among the 19 governing bodies. Jack Crump, secretary of the BAAB from 1937 to 1964, and very much from the tradition of amateur administrators, had defended the status quo in terms of safeguarding the domestic customs of the governing bodies.[4] Circumstances were to dictate the rationalisation of the administration, although not for 20 years after the Byers report. By the mid-1980s, the AAA's financial position was by far the most favourable since it received the largest part of the income from television contracts. On the other hand, the BAAB, which had to fund international teams and the UK coaching scheme, was running a deficit which by 1987 had reached £300,000. The AAA's price for rescuing the BAAB was nothing short of the creation of a single unified governing body and, despite the resistance of the regional associations and the WAAA, it was agreed that such a body should come into being as the British Athletics Federation by 1 January 1989.

The emergence of a single governing body may signal the achievement of an administrative structure capable of dealing with the demands placed upon it. Several of the governing bodies have had full-time staff since 1945, but the division of authority, overlapping responsibilities and the frequent intervention of amateur administrators have led to numerous disputes and failures. Relations between the administration and coaches, athletes and the media have often been touchy, and reached low levels in the late 1950s when the BAAB alienated the chief coach, Dyson, and many of the athletes (see pp. 53–4 below). More recently, the failure has been to exploit fully the opportunities for raising revenue which a sport on the verge of professionalism has needed to exploit. The nadir of amateur administration was reached at the Edinburgh Commonwealth Games in 1986 when the organisers found their old-fashioned system, based on committees staffed by unpaid part-timers, quite unequal to the task of running the games.

III

An amateur is a person who has never competed in an open competition, or for public money, or for admission money, and who has never at any period of his life taught or assisted in the pursuit of athletic exercise as a means of livelihood, or is a mechanic, artisan or labourer.

Amateur Athletic Club Rules, 1867

The university men who sought to make athletics a respectable pursuit in the 1860s were acutely aware of the need to disassociate themselves from professional pedestrians and the inheritance of eighteenth-century traditions of races for wages between the servants of gentlemen. Pedestrianism was associated with betting and roping (the fixing of races), and by the

1850s had lost its aristocratic patronage and become entirely plebeian. For the founders of the Amateur Athletic Club it was essential that their sport be seen to contribute to the all-round development of the gentleman and that it was not open to those who, as a result of their trade, had developed athletic prowess which would give them what was seen as an unfair advantage. The definition in the club's first code of rules of 1866 of those eligible to compete was among the most openly exclusive of all the codes of the newly regulated sports. The 1867 code made it more so by adding the explicit exclusion of any mechanic, artisan or labourer. In 1868 this clause was excluded and instead the definition was amended to begin 'An amateur is any gentleman who has never competed'.

It is unlikely that the rule was strictly enforced, and the AAC's championship was certainly less exclusive than the club itself. Even so the formal exclusion of all but gentlemen from the sport was not revoked until the formation of the Amateur Athletic Association in 1880. Part of the pressure for the formation of the association came from the growth of athletic competition in the midlands and north where the enforcement of the rule was impossible. But although social status was no longer an issue, professionalism was. Whereas association football accommodated professionalism and rugby split into distinct codes, one amateur the other not, the athletics authorities fought to uphold amateurism in as pure a form as possible. From the 1890s, they received further support from Olympianism, inspired by a mythic classical past refracted through de Coubertin's Anglophilia.

Professional athletics persisted, especially in the Highland Games and in the north of England. The AAA sought throughout the later nineteenth century to strengthen its grip on the sport and to exclude professionals from other sports, notably cricketers (1883) and footballers (1899). In 1882 a fund was established for prosecuting those found guilty of contravening the ban on professionals and several were sentenced to six months hard labour for fraud. In 1892, a further rule banned the paying of expenses. In 1896, six leading athletes were banned for receiving appearance money and by the end of 1897, several leading runners in all events from 100 yards to 20 miles had been banned for life. F. A. M. Webster expressed a view consistent with AAA orthodoxy in 1929 when he suggested that in the 1870s and 1880s there was extensive roping and betting in events in the midlands where all the athletes were artisans or labourers.[5] Perhaps it is a measure of the success of the AAA's campaign against professionalism that in 1899 they felt able to authorise the payment of athletes' travelling expenses. No further major change in the rules for payments to British athletes was to take place until pocket money was allowed in 1956.

By the first decade of the twentieth century, the amateur ethos was

2.3 Winners were usually rewarded. It seems fitting that the prize for the first athlete home in the Royston Hall Plate should be cutlery. Note the mill manager on the left

dominant in British athletics. Writing in *The Granta* in 1912, Philip Noel Baker, then a Cambridge University athlete, complained about the methods used by American athletes to achieve their early dominance in the sport. He observed that

The American athlete specializes in one or two events; before any race of great importance he devotes most of his energies and time to his training; he has a coach – often a professional – who likewise devotes his whole time and energies to his coaching; he has an organization behind him which is managed by paid organizers – which system depends on organizing ability and intelligence, supported by a reasonable amount of money.[6]

Noel Baker admitted that cricket and racing were similarly organised in Britain, but felt that it lowered sport to the status of a commercial enterprise. It was of course contrary to the amateur ethos. The article was typical of many down the years, and similar arguments continued to be made about unfair contravention of the amateur ethos by more successful competitors until the transformation of the status of British athletes in the 1970s.

The 1920s represented the high point of the cult of the gentleman amateur.

They were the second of what Lovesey has identified as the three flowerings of Oxbridge athletics. The first was that of the founders of the sport and of the AAA, the third, much briefer, that of Bannister, Brasher and Chataway in the mid-1950s.[7] The 1920s was the period of domination of the national team by members of the Achilles Club, formed for Oxbridge graduates to continue practising their sport after leaving the university. Its most prominent members, including Abrahams, Lowe and Burghley, were the first athletes to achieve national fame and respectability at the same time. Athletes (or pedestrians) may have attracted a large following and press attention before 1914, but the Achilles men, and others of comparably unimpeachable amateur credentials such as the Scot, Liddell, were acceptable to all classes of society.

The respectability of athletics, and the implications of Olympic and other international performance for national prestige, were such that, by the 1930s, the sport began to become subject to forces which were to undermine the ethos of the gentleman amateur. The spread of county associations and the growth of the number of clubs provided opportunities to compete to far more people. The AAA contributed to the view that the sport had a scientific basis by launching its first summer school at Loughborough in 1934. Two years later, the School of Athletics, Games and Physical Education was opened at Loughborough College under the direction of F. A. M. Webster. Britain's poor showing at the 1936 Olympic Games demonstrated to many, even to correspondents to *The Daily Telegraph*, that the amateur ethos was not compatible with success against highly organised teams trained at the State's expense.[8] But for all that, the British athlete who attracted most public attention in the years between 1936 and the end of the war was the middle distance runner Sidney Wooderson. Wooderson was a London clerk, and a member of the Blackheath Harriers. He was certainly not in the Achilles mould, but his relatively light training and his attitude to competition hardly suggest that the old spirit was under threat.

The status of athletes was to change only slowly during the 25 years after the Second World War. In part, this reflected the domination of the administration until the 1960s by people such as Abrahams, Burghley and Crump who were imbued with the spirit of pre-war athletics. It is also the case that university athletics was particularly strong in the early 1950s. The changing status of athletes was a consequence of a lengthy and at times bitter struggle between a tradition-minded administration and new generations of athletes and their coaches who regarded the former as out of touch. At times, there were unequivocal signs that questions of social status were involved. In 1950, for example, Jack Crump found the choice

of team captain for the 1950 British and Empire Games less than straightforward. He recalled that

Donald Finlay was the outstanding choice, but he occupied a very high rank,
that of group captain in the Royal Air Force, and we felt that position made him
somewhat remote from some members of the team who had served 'in the ranks'
of the RAF. Members of the team had made it abundantly clear that they would
feel uncomfortable and ill at ease with Donald Finlay as captain.[9]

The 1956 Olympics brought matters to a head. The conditions under
which the team travelled, with Crump insisting that men sat at one end
of the plane to Australia and women at the other, must have served as
an irritant to athletes who resented the administration's paternalistic management. Once in Melbourne, there was conflict between the university
athletes and the rest. The latter complained to Crump about the Oxford
contingent's cliquishness. Crump's recollection leaves little doubt as to
where his sympathies lay. He commented that 'In general, the less fortunately educated tended to display a slight inferiority complex and were less
ready to feel on equal terms with the university athletes, as the latter were
fully prepared to accept.'[10] There was further trouble over the payment
of pocket money, which other nations' athletes were already receiving,
but which had yet to be given to the British. The dispute set in train the
events which led to the formation of the International Athletes Club in
1958. This represented a major change, in effect the formation of a collective
body representing the athletes' view against that of the administration.
It was an outsider group, by contrast to groups such as the Achilles Club
which were wholly acceptable to the authorities.

The formation of the IAC did not of itself bring the athletes the improved
status which they sought. The 1964 Olympics, Crump's last as secretary
to the BAAB, was the occasion for bitter confrontation between the BAAB
and the IAC, and particularly with the team captain, Robbie Brightwell.
Crump sought to maintain the custom that the composition of the team
should remain secret until athletes received their official invitations, signed
by Prince Philip in his role as President of the BOA. Brightwell sought,
unsuccessfully, prior disclosure before that so that he could discuss the
selection. There followed an acrimonious row between athletes and administrators over fees for interviews on the BBC *Sportsview* programme before
the departure for Tokyo. Brightwell and others refused to appear if the
fees were not paid to the IAC. The BAAB found this unacceptable, and
a number of athletes refused to be interviewed. Athletes were quoted in
the press accusing Crump in person for souring relations between athletes
and officials. Brightwell contributed an article to the *Sun* on his return
from Tokyo denying that officials had contributed to British success at

the Games. A number of legal actions followed, although Crump dropped them on his retirement in 1965.[11]

Alongside the growing assertiveness of leading athletes, there were signs in the early post-war years that the athletics authorities realised that some means needed to be found to support them financially. Such support continued to be on an *ad hoc* basis, and at times was little publicised for obvious reasons. In 1958, for example, Sir James Bowman of the National Coal Board wrote to Noel Baker to say that arrangements had been made for the shot-putter Arthur Rowe to be paid his wages and shift allowances, even when absent to compete in athletic events. The previous year he had lost 10 weeks' money.[12] Such indirect support was still rare at that time, but the authorities were implicated in a breach of the amateur code as originally intended. Similarly, the sponsorship of individual athletes, although strictly controlled, was beginning to appear. The donation of gifts to the British team for the 1948 Olympic Games was restricted and donors were forbidden to advertise goods as supplied to individual athletes.[13] By 1964, however, the *News of the World* was able to benefit from the publicity arising from its sponsorship of Brightwell to attend the US Championships as part of his pre-Olympic schedule.[14]

During the 1960s and 1970s, the status of athletes was transformed. To the athletes' demands for more open management by officials were added commercial pressures which were to prove irresistible. The growth of commercial sponsorship meant that leading athletes at least had access to training resources far in excess of those enjoyed by Abrahams or Bannister. The contribution of trust funds has meant that they remain amateurs in name only.

As early as 1974, the pole vaulter Mike Bull remarked that 'There are so many pressures now in international athletics that even in Britain the good loser is no longer accepted as a good sportsman.'[15] The poor performance of the British team in the 1976 Olympics further drove home the point that, if Britain was to win medals, there was a need to develop an elite squad. Steve Ovett was the sole British gold medallist in the European championships in 1978. In response, the BAAB allocated £160,000 for preparation for the 1980 Olympics, with support from the Sport Aid Foundation. In effect, this meant that each of the probable squad received about £4,000 towards training expenses. At the same time, the problem of payments to athletes remained unresolved. The IOC had left it to the IAAF to decide what was permissible within amateur status throughout the 1970s. Only in 1982 was the trust fund accepted as the solution. It is a system whereby appearance money and income from sponsorship and advertising contracts is paid into a fund which can be used for subsistence and training, but the bulk of which is likely to be enjoyed by the athletes on retirement. The system, a half-way house to professionalism, leaves the officials with a residual paternalistic grip since only the BAAB can authorise trust fund arrangements. The experience of trust funds has not been a happy one and it seems to have given new form to the long-running conflict between officials and athletes. At the same time, the associations are hardly in a position to take the rigorous approach to thinly veiled professionalism which their predecessors had done in the 1880s and 1890s. As the ex-Minister of Sport, Neil MacFarlane remarked about charges of illegal payments to athletes (not just British ones) at the 1984 Olympics, it seemed that officials had no intention of digging too deep into charges of illegal payments 'and who can blame them as they watched the way the sport is sprinting towards pure professionalism?'[16]

The scale of payments to top athletes has been remarkable by any standards. The highest payment to a British athlete was made in 1985 when Zola Budd was paid £90,000 to run against Mary Slaney. The latter received £54,000 for participating in a rematch of their ill-fated Olympic 3,000 metres final of the year before. The meeting at Crystal Palace received £200,000 sponsorship from a TV company. Such payments are of course exceptionally high, but since 1985 various systems of subvention have been used to support leading athletes, most of the money coming from ITV's contract with the AAA. The money has been very unevenly distributed. In 1986, 15 athletes took 77 per cent of the subvention provided by the Joint Standing Committee, and the rest was shared among 135 others. In 1987, a system of appearance payments operated, whereby the BAAB decided how much each of the top athletes should receive for appearing at certain events. There was much dispute over the relative status of individual athletes which this implied. Steve Ovett in particular was affronted to be on only £1,000 per appearance as against the £10,000 paid to Steve Cram, Sebastian Coe and Fatima Whitbread. He told John Rodda that

I don't have to run for money, I don't need to. But I had to speak out, because the whole thing damaged the creditability of the sport. It was insulting and embarrassing.[17]

The value of success on the track is great. In 1986, the sprinter Linford Christie received £400 per appearance from his sponsor. After running the fastest time in Europe in 1986, it rose to £5,000.

Subventions make up only a part of the modern athlete's income. Sponsorship deals provide far more. Daley Thompson has received as much as £300,000 a year from the sports goods firm Adidas and £50,000 for a national TV advertisement for Lucozade. In 1987, Cram was sponsored by Kelloggs,

Coe by C and A, and Budd by Brooks, all for over £100,000 a year. Meanwhile disputes with the authorities have shown no sign of abating. Indeed, there is now much more at stake. The President of the IOC expressed the official view in 1983 when he commented that 'the only thing we don't want in the Olympic movement is athletes living only for sport and belonging to a sport federation but working only for promoters.'[18] Leading athletes seem to think otherwise. Of course they cannot afford to alienate the association which selects them for the international competitions on which their fame (and hence their earning power) depends. Nevertheless, disputes over the officials' right to determine when athletes can compete overseas are endemic. Notable cases have involved Steve Ovett, threatened with suspension in 1979 for racing at a 1500 metres at Nijmegen rather than for the British team in West Germany. In 1980, Daley Thompson's refusal to let the BAAB determine which decathlon he should enter led to him losing support from the Sport Aid Foundation. Seven years later, athletes (including Steve Cram) were in dispute over participation at a Grand Prix meeting at Koblenz. The Scottish AAA even went as far as to refuse licences to two athletes who wanted to run there rather than at the Scottish national championships.[19]

Looking back on his career in the 1960s and 1970s, the shot-putter Geoff Capes, recalled the authoritarianism and lack of professionalism of the athletics authorities with ill-concealed resentment.

Basically, the difference between athletes and officials was one of age. The officials thought all athletes were students on summer vacation with a family stipend. They still thought in terms of Lord Burghley and Harold Abrahams. It did not occur to them that there were athletes who had no money, who do not get paid if they did not work.[20]

By the 1980s, Capes thought, team management had improved as ex-international athletes, such as Mary Peters and Lynn Davies took over responsibility. Certainly there was a lot more money in athletics, but it was unevenly distributed. As Chris Brasher has commented, the effect of the injection of millions of pounds for TV sponsorship has been to make megastars out of a few while the rest, from lesser internationals to club athletes, count as little more than a chorus line.[21] Yet if team management, coaching and the events themselves have all been transformed by commerce, the administration has changed more slowly, relinquishing its paternalistic control and the remnants of the amateur ethos with the greatest reluctance. In this respect too, as in the matter of payments, athletes had yet to achieve the status of professionals, free to make their own contractual arrangements by the mid-1980s.

Meanwhile, what of athletes' motivation and the nature of their

2.4 Not a good picture but an historic one. Roger Bannister has just become the
first athlete to run a mile in under four minutes, at Oxford 6 May 1954

commitment to the sport? It is of course difficult to generalise on the basis
of statements published in autobiographies or made in interviews. Nevertheless, there is an illuminating contrast between the image projected by Bannister, for example, and several athletes whose careers span the later 1970s
and 1980s. In the autobiographical account of his career as an athlete,
Bannister recalled his motivation on the occasion of the Benjamin Franklin
mile in Philadelphia in 1951.

Though I had barely dared to admit it, I knew that in England the publicity about
the race had been enormous, and the result had great significance for the British
public. On this occasion, rightly or wrongly, I had become a symbol in athletics
of British spirit against American, and for the sake of national prestige I felt I
had to win.[22]

More recently, a number of athletes have described a less straightforward view of their motivation when competing for the national team. Geoff Capes, for example, wrote that 'of course it is an honour to be the person representing all the other athletes and people in your country. But athletes are individuals. We are not training three hours a day only for Britain. It's for ourselves as well.'[23] Capes was of course very much an outsider to the charmed circle of university educated athletes and administrators such as Bannister or Sir Arthur Gold, but he was a popular team captain and a serving international athlete. His statement encapsulates a view of the world in which the athlete's effort and dedication are directed at least as much to self-realisation and to the peer group of athletes as to the national team and the wider public. It is open to speculation how far such an ethic has been fostered by or has increased the apparent alienation of athletes from officials in the last 30 years. It is certainly a view prevalent in many sports which are already fully professionalised, notably tennis and to a lesser extent football, and one which the growing professionalisation of athletics may well encourage.

IV

I am fed up to the ears with women as track and field competitors.
> Attributed to Avery Brundage in 1936. Quoted in Tom McNab, *The Complete Book of Athletics*, (1980) p.25

The development of women's athletics in Britain began some 50 years after the establishment of athletics for men, and also after other sports such as croquet and tennis had become acceptable for middle-class women. The dress, exertion and freedom of movement which athletics entailed were hardly compatible with Victorian notions of respectable womanhood. By the turn of the century, such restrictive views received the support of eugenicists and some medical opinion. In 1911, for example, Doctor Mary Scherlieb claimed that 'Doctors and schoolmistresses observe that excessive devotion to athletics and gymnastics tends to produce what may perhaps be called the neuter type of girl'. Athletics was claimed to be detrimental to grace, figure and child-bearing alike. Indeed, the proponents of Swedish gymnastics as suitable physical education for girls, including its founder Mme Osterberg, were willing to stress the superiority of their discipline because it lacked such unwelcome side effects. Sheila Fletcher certainly gives little indication that track and field athletics played a part in women's physical education before 1914.[24]

There were still those hostile to women's athletics on the grounds of its defeminising effect in the 1920s, and there were fears that the sport might contribute to the decline of the birth rate, still regarded as of crucial

2.5 You cannot begin too early. This was a boys' international in 1956

military importance. But such views were increasingly challenged from
influential quarters. In 1921, for example, the conference of the Medical
Officers of Schools Association rejected the view that athletics and gymnastics were bad for the health of girls. The increased participation of women
in the sport from the war years onwards, the formation of clubs and international events along with challenges to established notions of what women
should wear and how they should behave provided an environment in which
the sport could win acceptance. Even so, this was on the basis of the institutional separation of men's and women's athletics to a remarkable degree
well into the 1930s.

   Despite the social acceptability of women's athletics from the 1920s on,
there has been an influential current of opinion which has felt it necessary
to assert the compatibility of the sport with conventional notions of femininity. In 1955, for example, George Pallett, who coached many of the leading
British women athletes of the time wrote that

2.6 Nor do you have to let the downs interrupt your stride. This steeplechase took place at Wolverhampton in 1962

one can run through a list of the world's outstanding women athletes and pick out any number who are feminine to a degree, healthy in mind and body, and pictures of grace in movement . . . The girl athletes of today can adorn a ballroom as well as they do an athletics meeting.[25]

For a long time, women were excluded from a wide range of events on the grounds that they were unfeminine, either too strenuous or too lacking in grace. That was certainly the view of Avery Brundage, chairman of the IOC from 1964 to 1975. Women were first allowed to compete over 800 metres at the Olympics in 1964 and the longer distances have only become open to them in the last ten years or so. They remain barred from the hammer, triple jump or pole vault. From the late 1950s, the British press at least began to question the femininity of many successful Eastern Europe athletes, and it became a widely held belief that Britain's relative lack of success was because the Eastern Europeans, their musculature highly developed by training (and perhaps on some occasions also by steroids), were not real women at all. In many ways this argument was analogous to that which condemned the American athletes before 1914 for cheating because they trained seriously.

Riordan has suggested that the success of East German women, particularly in the swimming events at the 1976 Olympics, was the occasion of a major shift in dominant western views about femininity and athleticism.[26] The popularity of aerobics and other forms of fitness training and the sympathetic publicity given to women marathon runners such as Greta Weiss and Ingrid Kristiansen in the later 1970s and 1980s may be indicative of such change. Even so, as Riordan points out, media coverage in Britain still tends to trivialise women's athletics. A comparison of the attention given to the American Mary Slaney and the Czech Ludmilla Kratochvilova shows the obsession of commentators with the physical appearance of women athletes.

The first recorded women's athletics meeting may have been held in the USA in 1895, but there is little evidence of the sport in anything like its modern form in Britain until the First World War. Women's work in the armed forces and in occupations hitherto barred to them provided a context in which their participation in athletics became possible. In 1918, the WRAF entered a team for a relay (presumably against men) at Stamford Bridge and the following year the Inter-Services Championships included a women's 440 yards relay. Women students began their own meetings at the same time, and the first Northern Counties Ladies Championships was also held in 1919. Eighteen British women competed at the first multinational women's games, at Monte Carlo, in 1921 and the following year the Women's Amateur Athletic Association was formed. Its first championships followed in 1923. There was clearly much popular interest in women's athletics. The *News of the World* sponsored a women's meeting in 1924 which drew 25,000 spectators to Stamford Bridge.

The initial reception of women's athletics by men's organisations was hostile, both at home and abroad. The IOC refused in 1919 to accept women's athletics for the first post-war games and did not reverse its decision until 1926. The first women's athletic events were not held until the Amsterdam Games of 1928, although other women's sports (tennis and swimming) had been included in the Paris games in 1924. All-women's games had been organised by the Fédération Sportive Féminine Internationale (f. 1921) from 1922. The British men, along with Australia, New Zealand, Finland, Hungary and Ireland, had voted at the IOC meeting in 1926 against the inclusion of women's events, and had spoken out at the IAAF congress the same year against the AAA taking control of women's athletics. Opposition to the organisational integration of men's and women's athletics seems to have gone to greater lengths in Britain than elsewhere. By the 1950s, Great Britain was the only nation which retained separate organisations, and although the BAAB was obliged by the IAAF's insistence on a single representative body for international purposes to select the teams, the WAAA kept control of the rules for women's athletics. Only the merger of all the British associations, planned for 1989, will end this anomaly.

The persistence of separate women's organisations was by no means due wholly to male exclusiveness. Jennifer Hargreaves has argued that the separation was a precondition for the rapid growth of the sport in the early days.[27] There was a strong separatist element within women's athletics, as within the women's physical education colleges, which sought to protect the women's sport from male domination. Mrs V. Searle, formerly the WAAA 440 yards champion, said in 1928 that

We strongly object to the mixing up of men and women in the Olympic Games or at any other meeting. If this actually happened it would kill our movement, and we should be absorbed by the men as in other countries. In England, we have nothing to do with the AAA; we are entirely a separate body.

British women first competed at the Olympic Games in 1932, although they opposed (unsuccessfully) the merging of the FSFI and the IAAF in 1936. The women's world games continued to be held in the 1930s, though, and in 1934 took place in London.

The first women's clubs had links with colleges. The Kensington Athletics Club (f. 1921) was made up mainly of members of the Borough Polytechnic. The team for Monte Carlo in 1921 was drawn largely from the departments of physical education at Regent Street Polytechnic and Woolwich Polytechnic. Although the Inter-University Athletics Board was opposed to women's athletics in 1919, Manchester University women established a team in 1921 and in 1923 the Women's Inter-Varsity Athletics Board was set up. Girls were able to compete in the first schools athletics championships in 1925. Encouragement for the sport seems to have come from the press. As well as the *News of the World* sponsorship of meetings, the *Sporting Life* sponsored the Monte Carlo team and in 1925 the *Daily Mirror* gave a trophy for club contests. The growth of the county associations seems also to have boosted women's athletics, and by the mid-1920s the WAAA had 23,000 members.

Yet for all the suddenness with which women's athletics was able to establish itself in the 1920s, questions have been asked about the strength of the sport in Britain. With notable exceptions such as Mary Rand, Ann Packer and Mary Peters, there were relatively few successes internationally until the 1980s. Even then, Fatima Whitbread, the most successful British woman athlete to date, was able to argue that women's athletics was failing to contribute as much as it should to international performance because at all levels it lacked a professional outlook. Certainly it could still be argued that women's athletics is not given the priority in Britain and other western societies that it is in eastern Europe. Overt hostility to sportswomen may have diminished, but perhaps deeper cultural patterns persist.

V

> Exactly where in the table athletics are placed depends on how sponsorship spending is defined, but by any standards . . . the sport is one of the major beneficiaries of sponsorship.
>
> *Economic Intelligence Unit Special Report No. 86*, 1980, p.13

Public support for athletics was available in the form of funding for school and university athletics and the provision of courses at training colleges, notably Loughborough, from at least the 1930s. There has been little doubt in this century that the sport was considered worthy of encouragement from both local and central government, but the bulk of the finance has come from local authorities, most significantly in the provision of track and sports centres. Direct aid to the sport's governing bodies for training, preparation for major events and the development of national facilities has since 1972 been directed by the Sports Council. During the 1970s, emphasis has been on initiatives such as the Sports Aid Foundation, established in 1976, to raise mixed funding from industry, voluntary bodies and the public with pump-priming grants from the Sports Council. The success of athletics in obtaining sponsorship from business and television has meant that the sport has become largely independent of central government funding in the 1980s. Indeed, the report of a Sports Council Committee chaired by Sebastian Coe, entitled 'Preparing for '88', reported in 1985 that athletics didn't need any of the proposed £5.2m extra funding which would be required to prepare for the Seoul Olympics.[28] Similarly, when the Department of the Environment was criticised in 1986 for what was seen as a failure to increase the Sports Council's budget for 1987–8, the chairman of the AAA, Arthur MacAllister, observed that 'As one of the relatively better off sports we would not be unduly affected.'[29] Local authorities, however, continue to provide considerable resources. Here too, though, change is possible. In September 1987 the Department of the Environment issued a consultation paper entitled 'Competition in the Management of Local Authority Sport and Leisure Facilities' which outlined the government's proposals to introduce compulsory competitive tendering to the management of facilities. In commenting, the AAA argued that 'athletics is a multifarious sport, requiring complicated facilities at unsocial hours. This would not present an attractive return to a company bent on profit.' The Department replied that it certainly had not hoped to bring about increased charges to young athletes in inner city areas.[30]

It is beyond question though that the most dynamic source of funds for athletics comes from the private sector in the form of sponsorship. The AAA had long been willing to accept support for events, tours and facilities, although always with close attention to the implications for the amateur identity of the sport. Sponsorship in the early post-war years was discreet and limited in scope. Strict rules were imposed on the advertising advantages which companies could seek. The *News of the World*, for example, was willing to underwrite Oxford and Cambridge matches against leading American universities in the 1950s, although this rarely involved a loss once receipts had been taken into account.[31] In some ways, the 1950s were a transitional period to the fully developed sponsorship of subsequent decades. Fund-raising for the 1956 Olympics, for example, was largely aimed at wealthy individuals and the public rather than at business. Crump noted how

Few people realise the strain imposed on sporting executives by the appeal for funds inseparable from an Olympic Games year... Going around the country, speaking at lunches, dinners, dances, sports brain-trusts and similar functions designed to produce financial support from the public is time consuming, physically fatiguing...

Crump met at least two such engagements per week for a year before the Melbourne Games.[32]

In the 1960s, the search for sponsorship became a vital matter as other sources of income dried up and demands for professional coaching and administration grew. The AAA won sponsorship from the Carborundum Company, the *Daily Herald* and Pepsi Cola in the early 1960s before becoming heavily reliant for support on the *News of the World*. The paper's withdrawal in 1968 caused difficulties which remain a warning of the need to find a diversity of sponsors. By 1980, athletics enjoyed a total sponsorship income estimated at about £1m per annum,[33] comparable to golf but rather less than horse-racing (£2m) and far less than motor sport (£8m). The position was transformed in 1984 when ITV offered a deal for exclusive coverage of athletics in Britain which was worth £10m over four years. It was widely felt that the sport was awash with money, although there was doubt over whether it was likely to be used in its long-term interest. The governing bodies' response to the question of how to handle their new-

2.7 Tobacco manufacturers have consistently used sport to market their product.
This mile race was actually run at Penrhiwceiber in 1964

found attractiveness to would-be sponsors was to contract with the firm
of the ex-international athlete Alan Pascoe to market the sport. In return
for a cut of 25 per cent, Pascoe agreed to raise £3m from selling advertising
over five years. Pascoe was soon able to increase the advertising revenue
for an international meeting from £12,000 to £100,000.[34] However effectively income is maximised, though, the effectiveness of the use of the money
is likely to depend on the administrative structure set up to distribute it.

Sponsorship in athletics has largely gone to fund events or to support
individual athletes. It has proved much more difficult to get sponsors for
coaching schemes. The largest sums have inevitably gone to the most prestigious athlete or to international events such as the Peugeot-Talbot Games,
but sponsorship has also been forthcoming for lesser events. In its *Report
on the allocation of monies by companies towards sponsorship of sport
in the UK* (1981), the Sports Council listed sponsorship ranging from the
£80,000 paid by the Guardian Legal Exchange Company to the UK Closed

Championships to £250 paid by the Woolwich Equitable Building Society to the Cambridge Harriers.

VI

I believe that [athletics] may prove a medium for the wiping out of so many of those misunderstandings which made the Great War popular.
F. A. M. Webster, *Athletics of Today* (1929) p.vii

Athletics has undoubtedly contributed to developments in twentieth-century Britain which are in the widest sense political. Women's sport has provided a forum in which significant issues about emancipation and equality have been, and continue to be raised. The importance for ethnic relations of the strong and growing representation of black athletes at club and international level is as yet difficult to gauge. Christopher Brasher has noted that 33 per cent of the English team for the 1986 Commonwealth Games were from the 2 per cent of the national population who are of Afro-Caribbean origin.[35] In common with other sports, athletics has been taken up in policies for the regeneration of the inner city, largely by means of the provision of facilities by local authorities. At the same time, recent initiatives in improving the nation's health have given impetus to marathons, fun runs and jogging. But athletics has also become involved in more sharply focussed political controversy, and with greater frequency in the last decade. Athletics has not been plagued by crowd disorder in the twentieth century, and the athletics authorities needed little persuasion to join in the campaign to stamp out street betting in the years before the First World War. Its most salient political involvement has been in international relations, in so far as it has been thought to contribute to national prestige, and in the role which athletic contacts have played in fostering relations with other countries.

Early in the present century, international athletics became closely identified with the nation state. British athletes competing at the first modern Olympic Games in 1896 did not do so as part of a national team. In 1900 and 1908 they did, and from 1912, participation at the Games was open only to members of national teams. The IOC came to insist that teams represented sovereign states, hence the need for a British team drawn from all four home countries, and for the formation of the BAAB in 1932 to affiliate to the IAAF. At the same time, the constitutional autonomy of governing bodies of sports in Britain has meant that quasi-diplomatic functions have fallen to organisations that are outside direct government control. It has been claimed that such a degree of autonomy on the part of the British Olympic Association is unique.[36] The worldwide prominence given to the Olympic Games, where track and field athletics remain the most prestigious events, and especially since 1960 with television and the participation of more and more national teams, has made the role of the athletics authorities a very sensitive one indeed. Moreover, track and field athletics is the only major sport in which Britain has been prominent which regularly provides opportunities for meetings between all the major political powers and the Third World nations. Athletics has also been central to the British Empire Games (f. 1930) subsequently recast as the British Empire and Commonwealth Games (1952) and the Commonwealth Games (1970).

In the earlier part of the century, athletics was among those sports which benefited from concern about national efficiency and the ability of the nation to field effective fighting forces. The Board of Education's Syllabus of Physical Training (1909), although more concerned with gymnastic exercises than athletics as such, was the first such practical sign of the government's concern. Fear of German and Italian superiority in physical fitness, a reflection in part of the poor showing of the British team at the 1936 Olympics, and also a response to the Nazi Strength through Joy movement, led to the Physical Training and Recreation Act of 1937 and the National Fitness Campaign of the same year. More recently, initiatives following the report of the Wolfenden Committee in 1960 and the works of the Sports Council and local authorities have been directed at the need to provide creative opportunities for urban youth and at improving the health of an increasingly affluent nation as well as at producing a strong national team. Even so, it has been questions of international diplomacy which have drawn British governments into involvement with athletics most directly.

The early development of amateur athletics in Britain meant that, at the beginning of the twentieth century, there was still a widespread assumption that Britain rightfully occupied a leading position both on the track and in the administration of the sport. Despite a highly successful Games in Paris in 1924, at which British athletes won medals at every distance from 100m to 1500m, there could be no pretence after 1912 that Britain was a dominant power as far as performance was concerned. American and Scandinavian athletes from the first decade of the century, Germans in the 1930s and eastern Europeans from the 1950s outperformed British athletes in most events. British prestige has been maintained to a greater or lesser extent in certain events, in particular in middle distance running. The 1972 and 1976 games produced such poor results that the Sports Council was persuaded to provide more funds in preparation for the 1980 Games and an 'Action Plan for Moscow' was drawn up. Certainly the 1980s produced British success in terms of medals and records on a scale unknown since the 1920s.

As for organisation, Britain's reputation for effective organisation probably benefited from hosting the Olympic Games in London in 1908 and 1948, and the Commonwealth Games in Edinburgh in 1970. The 1908 Olympics did rather less for the reputation of British officials. The Americans accused the judges of persistent bias against them, and destroyed the myth of British impartiality. Moreover, contacts with the USAAA ceased for a time.[37] More recently, the calamitous Edinburgh Commonwealth Games of 1986, which were boycotted by a majority of Commonwealth countries and which lost over £4m, did little for national prestige.[38] The escalating cost of staging the Olympic Games, culminating in the massive losses borne by the City of Montreal in 1976, have effectively deterred recent British governments from giving extensive financial backing to proposals to host the Games. The government welcomed Birmingham's approach in bidding for the 1992 Games in which it was made clear that the Games would be entirely privately financed. It is interesting to note, however, that Neil Macfarlane claimed that the Prime Minister was little pleased by bids from Birmingham and Manchester for the 1992 Games, not least because of Treasury estimates that security alone would cost the exchequer £25m.[39]

If central government has had serious doubts about whether any prestige accruing from hosting major events is worth the considerable financial and political commitment required, there are signs that local authorities still believe that there are benefits to be had. In particular, Birmingham's bid for the 1992 Games, to be renewed in respect of the 1996 Games, reflects the importance attached to such an event by the local business community and by local politicians. The Birmingham bid, led by the City Council but fronted by a local MP and ex-Minister of Sport, Denis Howell, raised £2.3m from midland businesses, the local authorities for Birmingham, Wolverhampton and Coventry and national firms including British Rail and British Airways. The Sports Council provided £250,000 towards the fund. Denis Howell has since claimed that, although the bid failed, it succeeded in putting Birmingham on the map and has helped to attract £50m worth of investment to the west midlands. He commented that 'Our first objective was to get Birmingham acknowledged worldwide as an international city of significance and so attract investment and help us to solve our great problem of industrial decline and unemployment.'[40]

But it has not been the staging of major events in Britain which has presented the greatest challenge to the constitutional position of the athletic and Olympic authorities or which has most clearly undermined the authorities' wish to steer clear of political involvement. Rather, it has been the question of whether British teams should be involved in sporting contests

2.8 Women's athletics has had a long struggle for recognition. In this picture some
members of the England team in a match against Germany in July 1930 found
a novel way of presenting themselves to the public

with regimes of which a significant body of opinion in the country, at
times even the government itself, disapproves. The issue has come to a
head in relation to participation in the Olympic Games in Berlin in 1936
and Moscow in 1980, and in a less decisive manner over the question of
sporting contacts with South Africa.

The pattern of sporting contacts with Germany in the inter-war years
followed that of diplomatic relations in general. German athletes were
banned from AAA events until 1926 and did not compete in the Olympic
Games until 1932. At the same time, an increasing number of voices asserted
the Olympic view that sporting contact would encourage international
understanding, a view which had triumphed by the time of Hitler's rise
to power. During the year or so before the Berlin Olympics in 1936, there
were an increasing number of protests against sporting contacts with Germany, focussing at first on football matches and then on the Games themselves. The National Workers' Sports Association (f. 1931) asked to set up
an alternative games in Barcelona (it was cancelled due to the outbreak
of the Spanish Civil War),[41] having first failed to persuade the AAA to
withdraw from Berlin. At the same time Archbishop William Temple tried
to win the BOC's support for his call for an Olympic amnesty for religious
prisoners but without success. It was feared that the Games would be

exploited to propagate Nazi ideology and German superiority, and that Jewish athletes were excluded from the German team. There was also concern on the part of the athletics authorities that the German athletes were being allowed a month's leave with pay in order to train, in contravention of the British interpretation of the amateur code. Yet even the occupation of the Rhineland in March 1936 did not deflect the BOC from their view that there should be no boycott. Shortly afterwards, the BOC wrote to *The Times* to state that

The British Olympic Council are convinced that in sending a team to Berlin they are acting in the best interests of sport. The Olympic Games have always stood for the ideal of harmony and reconciliation between nations, and it would have been nothing short of a calamity if, at this very critical stage in world affairs, the country to whom the world so often looks for a lead, were not fully represented at a gathering which will include athletes from almost every other nation.[42]

Such commitment to a belief in the value of the Games as a force for peace received further expression when Lord Desborough, who had founded the BOA in 1905, spoke for a faction in the BOC who favoured continuing with the Games planned for Tokyo in 1940. The opposite view prevailed. Nor were the Berlin Olympics the last athletics meeting between Britain and Germany before the war. In the last week of August 1939, Jack Crump was in Cologne with a British team.[43]

There was little satisfaction in British athletic circles with the Berlin Games. Athletes and officials commented on the contrast with the open atmosphere and sporting spirit which they considered to have prevailed in Los Angeles four years earlier.[44] The government had made it clear throughout that participation was wholly a matter for the BOC, and there are indications that they were satisfied with their hands-off approach. A Foreign Office minute on a letter from the ambassador in Berlin of 10 May 1936 about pressure which the French Left was putting on its government, observes that

This sort of thing leads one to believe that HMG are right to have no official contact connection whatever with the Olympic Games. They lend themselves to every possible kind of propaganda.[45]

During the 1950s, however, the Foreign Office were more willing to risk involvement with international athletics. Athletics provided a vehicle for improving relations with both the USA and the USSR. In 1954, 30,000 spectators turned out to see a Moscow team (in effect the Russian national squad) compete against London at the White City. Crump thought that a British tour of the USSR, Czechoslovakia and Hungary was good for peace, and noted later that 'Our Foreign Office ... entirely subscribed to this view and I was told that our ambassadors in these countries referred to the good work which these visits constituted.'[46] The Soviet team's visit to Britain in 1956 was less fortunate though. The international match was cancelled when the British authorities insisted that they were unable to get the courts to drop charges against a member of the Soviet team who was prosecuted for shoplifting three hats from a London store. By the following year (and apparently without reference to the Hungarian crisis which had intervened), relations between the athletic associations were back to normal. A crowd of 40,000 watched the match against the USSR at the White City on the first day of the football season. Meanwhile, following the 4-minute mile in 1954, the Foreign Office had suggested to Bannister that he should travel to New York to make broadcasts of a goodwill nature. Selwyn Lloyd commented in the Commons in May 1954, in response to questions about Bannister's amateur status, that he was sure that the visit had been 'a very good thing for Anglo-American relations'.[47]

In the decades after these early experiments in the use of athletics for diplomatic ends, there were increasingly powerful forces which, perhaps inevitably, led to further government involvement. Major athletics events became popular television spectacles, and it was widely perceived that Olympic sports were valued in Eastern Europe as a major test of national prestige and the success of the political system. Successive Olympic Games became embroiled in political campaigns which had little to do with athletics – black power demonstrations in 1968, the massacre of Israeli athletes in 1972, the African boycott in 1976. Against such a background, the 1980 Olympics in Moscow were always likely to be the occasion for some kind of political demonstration. In the event, the Soviet occupation of Afghanistan precipitated an American boycott of the Games and a diplomatic initiative in Europe to win support for the boycott. The response in Britain serves principally to illustrate the autonomy of the sporting authorities, and perhaps also the good fortune of the Foreign Office in being able to avoid involvement in controversy over the 1936 Games. The political response of the government was to give full support to the American boycott and to call on the British Olympic Association to join in. A full day's debate in both Houses of Parliament produced resolutions calling for withdrawal, the first time that a sporting matter had been debated at such length. It was notable, though, that the Minister for Sport, Hector Munro, did not speak in the debate and considered resigning over the issue. The Prime Minister wrote on three occasions to the BOA calling for their withdrawal, and further pressure was exerted by the Foreign Office, the Department of the Environment and the Home Office. All this was without success. The

BOA left the matter to individual sporting authorities and, with a very few exceptions, they chose to attend.

Neil MacFarlane, Hector Munro's successor as Minister of Sport recalled that

The clear feeling in British sport during the build-up to Moscow and for some time afterwards was that the British Olympic Association, and Sir Denis Follows in particular, had been subjected to intense and unreasonable pressure by the Government, that the debate was kept in people's minds by carefully planted questions in the House and that Mrs. Thatcher and her senior ministers were guilty of interference of the worst kind.[48]

There was also resentment that the Olympic boycott seemed to be the only measure taken against the Soviet government. Trade links remained largely unaffected, it was thought. The government continued to try to use such means as it had at its disposal to hinder the team. No help was to be forthcoming from the Moscow embassy. Those competitors who were civil servants or members of the armed forces were not to be granted preferential treatment for leave to attend the Games. The Sports Council, which is grant aided by the Department of Environment, would not support the boycott though and elsewhere responses were mixed. The boycott hindered fund-raising and the British Olympic Appeal Committee, chaired by Sir Anthony Tuke of Barclays, cut off its support. The BBC and IBA agreed on greatly reduced broadcast coverage, 40 hours replacing the 180 hours which had been planned. The television coverage played down the nationalistic and ceremonial aspects by ignoring the medal ceremonies, and was often accompanied by commentary which was critical of the hosts' motives and political system.[49] The British team had already agreed to use the Olympic flag and anthem, not the national ones. The attempt to enforce a boycott of the Moscow Olympics was not successful in unifying the nation in a common cause, and the controversy suggested that the government could not directly control the British Olympic Association, and still less the governing bodies of individual sports.

For a long time, British athletics had escaped relatively lightly from disruption on account of the politics of sporting contacts with South Africa. Prior to the expulsion of South Africa from the IOC in 1961, the British view had largely been that South African team selection was an internal matter. Once banned, there was little incentive for contact with South African athletics. In an amateur sport, money was unlikely to lure rebel tourists and the South Africans were hardly the power in athletics that they were in rugby. Athletics suffered first in 1976 when African nations refused to compete alongside New Zealand in the Montreal Olympics as a protest against a rugby tour earlier in the year. One consequence was the drafting of the 1977 Commonwealth Statement on Apartheid in Sport ('The Gleneagles Agreement') which bound Commonwealth nations to do all in their power to dissuade sporting bodies from maintaining contacts with South Africa.

Controversy arose in Britain in 1984 when the South African middle and long distance runner, Zola Budd was granted UK citizenship only two weeks after being flown to Britain by the *Daily Mail*. That compared with an average of 21 months for naturalisation and 14 months for registration in other cases. The immigration minister, David Waddington, admitted that this was a special case and it has been suggested that a personal appeal had been made by the *Mail*'s editor, David English, to the then Home Secretary.[50] Zola Budd qualified for selection for the British team for the Los Angeles Olympics, although it later became apparent that she had by no means abandoned her Afrikaans roots and for a time lived largely in South Africa. A number of Labour-dominated local authorities tried to protest about the appearance of Zola Budd in events at their tracks, notably Edinburgh City Council and Tarfaen DC (who own Cwmbran stadium). Their efforts to display anti-apartheid slogans by the track led to difficulty with TV coverage, threats of withdrawal of sponsorship and the derision of the popular press.

It was not Zola Budd who precipitated the boycott by 32 of the 58 Commonwealth teams of the 1986 Edinburgh Games. Indeed, it was not a sports matter at all but rather the British government's resolute refusal to implement the programme of economic sanctions against South Africa favoured by the other Commonwealth countries. Protests were also made against the participation of Zola Budd and the South African-born swimmer Annett Cowley in the English team, and both were subsequently dropped. The boycott, led by Ghana and Nigeria, represented a further example of international athletics, and indeed sport in general, serving as a battleground for conflict over an issue which was not directly related to the event which was consequently disrupted. The burden on this occasion fell particularly heavily on the same Edinburgh City Council which had previously been to the fore in demonstrations against Zola Budd.

VII

Sport internationally is at the point where it has to think hard about its marketing, at a time when television is paying less and says it will be paying nothing. You have to think about your host broadcaster – whether he is competent to operate, can he take in outside help. It means thinking hard before taking events behind the Iron Curtain and it means thinking hard about placing events in the right time zones and where they can be marketed properly.

Alan Pascoe to John Rodda, *The Guardian*, 28 November 1987

The events of the 1980s have suggested that athletics, at least at the level of its governing bodies and leading competitors, is undergoing a fundamental transformation in terms of both its economic base and its social function. The decade has seen the establishment of trust funds (1983), a massive increase in the overall level of sponsorship (1984) and a resolution to implement a coherent administrative structure capable of more effective management (1987). It has also withstood the political débâcles of Moscow (1980) and Edinburgh (1986). There is seemingly little left of the amateur ethos of the sport's pioneers. Amateur athletics was developed initially as a means of recreation for professional men from university and public school backgrounds. It soon achieved a wider social constituency but its leadership remained committed to traditions of participation for its own sake, of competing rather than winning, well into the 1960s. Amateur athletics was one of the last major sports whose governing bodies sought to isolate the sport from the commercial pressures which surrounded it. In part this was a function of the generational effect whereby the officials who dominated the sport throughout the 1950s had competed as athletes in the very different circumstances of the 1920s. It was also the case that the growth of the sport by multiplication of governing bodies created vested interests in the maintenance of existing relations between officials, athletes, the media and commerce.

In the early nineteenth century, pedestrianism had been a sport based on patronage and betting, as was horse-racing. The century or so from the 1860s may well come to be seen as a period when the economic base of the sport was more or less effectively hidden. The emergent phase is one of explicit commercialism, an era of logos and sponsorship deals, of international athletes appearing in TV commercials and amassing large balances in trust funds. The prospect may be an alarming one for the athletics authorities and governments alike since neither can continue to depend on existing means of controlling athletes. As Moscow showed, the British government's influence over the sport is weak anyway, yet the sport will remain important for national prestige unless, as in tennis and golf, professionalism weakens the identification of athletes with their national teams.

But the continued advance of commercialism also offers the possibility that more funds will be available for the humbler levels of the sport. Whatever the mix of local authority and private enterprise involvement, provision of athletics facilities is likely to play a part in the development of inner cities. Moreover, there is little evidence that the popularity of mass participation in running is about to diminish. While greater commercial investment and incipient professionalism will continue to stimulate the most intense competition at the upper reaches of the sport, it is likely that at the least formal end, large numbers will run for fitness or sociability. To that extent at least something akin to the spirit of the Victorian founders of amateur athletics persists.

NOTES

1   Peter Lovesey, *The Official Centenary History of the AAA* (1979), p. 120.
2   Roger Bannister, *Four-minute Mile* (1955), p. xx.
3   They were the AAC, Oxford University AC, Cambridge University AC, the London AC, the Civil Service AC and the German Gymnastic Club.
4   Jack Crump, *Running Round the World* (1966), p. 51.
5   F. A. M. Webster, *Athletics of Today* (1929), p. 170.
6   Philip Noel Baker papers in Churchill College, Cambridge, NBKR 6 / 22–1.
7   Lovesey, *The Official Centenary History*, p. 113.
8   Duff Hart-Davis, *Hitler's Games* (1986), pp. 230ff.
9   Crump, *Running Round the World*, p. 109.
10 Ibid., pp. 42–3.
11 Ibid., pp. 237ff.
12 NBKR 6 / 10–19.
13 NBKR 6 / 15–1.
14 Crump, *Running Round the World*, p. 236.
15 Quoted in Tom Donohoe and Neil Johnson, *Foul Play: Drug Abuse in Sport* (Oxford, 1986) pp. 128–9.
16 Neil MacFarlane, *Sport and Politics* (1986).
17 *The Guardian*, 30 May 1987.
18 Juan Samaranch quoted in the *International Herald Tribune*, 30 March 1983.
19 Harry Wilson, *Running Dialogue. A Coach's Story* (1982), p. 147; Skip Rozin, *Daley Thompson* (1983), pp. 162–6; *Independent*, 2 July 1987.
20 Geoff Capes with Neil Wilson, *Big Shot* (1981), pp. 68–9.
21 *The Observer*, 10 November 1985.
22 Bannister, *Four-minute Mile*, p. 126.
23 Capes, *Big Shot*, p. 75.
24 Sheila Fletcher, *Women First: The Female Tradition in English Physical Education 1880–1980* (1984), p. 25.
25 George Pallett, *Women's Athletics* (1955), p. 15.
26 Jim Riordan, 'The social emancipation of women through sport' in *British Journal of Sports History*, vol. 2, no. 1, May 1985.
27 Jennifer A. Hargreaves, 'Playing like gentlemen while behaving like ladies: contradictory features of the formative years of women's sport' in *British Journal of Sports History*, vol. 2, no. 1, May 1985.
28 *The Guardian*, 6 December 1985.
29 Ibid., 26 November 1986.
30 Ibid., 21 December 1987.
31 NBKR 6 / 10–24.

32 Crump, *Running Round the World*, p. 165.

33 Jean Simpkins, *Sponsorship* 1980/81, Economist Intelligence Unit Special Report No. 86, 1980.

34 *The Guardian*, 20 December 1986; 28 November 1987.

35 *The Observer*, 27 July 1986.

36 Denis Howell in *Hansard*, 24 March 1987, Col. 229.

37 Lord Killanin and John Rodda (eds.), *The Olympic Games* 1984 (1983).

38 Derek Bateman and Derek Douglas, *Unfriendly Games. Boycotted and Broke. The Inside Story of the 1986 Commonwealth Games* (Glasgow, 1986).

39 MacFarlane, *Sport and Politics*, p. 242.

40 *The Guardian*, 13 October 1986; *The Independent*, 3 December 1987. In the event Manchester defeated Birmingham to secure the United Kingdom nomination to host the 1996 Games.

41 James Riordan, 'The workers' olympics' in Alan Tomlinson and Gary Whannel (eds.), *Five Ring Circus. Money, Power and Politics at the Olympic Games* (1984).

42 *The Times*, 17 March 1936.

43 NBKR 6/15–3; Crump, *Running Round the World*, p. 71.

44 NBKR 6/14–3.

45 Quoted in Hart-Davis, *Hitler's Games*, ch. 8.

46 Crump, *Running Round the World*, p. 155.

47 Bannister, *Four-minute Mile*, p. 194.

48 MacFarlane, *Sport and Politics*, pp. 229–30.

49 Tomlinson and Whannel, *Five Ring Circus*, pp. 35ff.; John Hargreaves, *Sport, Power and Culture* (Cambridge, 1986) pp. 156–7. See also Christopher Brooker, *The Games War* (1981).

50 See MacFarlane, *Sport and Politics*, ch. 7.

3 BOXING

STAN SHIPLEY

> Now Sam was ever readier for a fight than Billy was; but the sum of Billy's
> half-pints was large: wherefore the fight began.
> Arthur Morrison on 'Lizerunt' in *Tales of Mean Streets* (Leipzig 1895) p.32

From the first Wednesday in March 1987 until the following Saturday, Britain had three world professional boxing champions. The British Boxing Board of Control recognises twelve weights for their championships, and with three different international organisations offering versions of world titles, professional boxing is in a tangle. The proliferation of world titles from the simple six of 1900 can be largely explained by the huge fees which can be obtained from televising live boxing, and this commenced in the USA in the 1950s.[1] Yet boxing as an organised professional and amateur sport began in England.

Bare-knuckle contests between two men fighting for money prizes took place in the seventeenth century. Boxing was already an old English word when pugilism entered the language from Latin. Prizefighting, which this fisticuffs can be conveniently called, gained written rules in the 1740s (Broughton's Rules), and these allowed wrestling holds and falls, though not hitting a man who was down, or punching below the belt. Prizefighting technique borrowed movement of the feet from sword fighting, and when giving ground became acceptable to spectators and contestants, a bloodier, though much slower, variety of the modern sport would have been recognisable. Professors of boxing also taught gentlemen how to spar using padded gloves, though there was no organisation of contests for amateurs until 1867. The professional sport exploded into popularity in the 1790s with the interaction of manufacturing, deep coal-mining, busy ports, the city as premier marketplace, and a Jewish lad from Whitechapel, named Daniel Mendoza.

Mendoza (1764–1836) was described in 1789 as 'the most Scientific Boxer ever known'. He was the build of a modern middleweight in an age when prizefighters were classed simply heavy or light, thus he would have been obliged to use ringcraft when his opponents outweighed him by two or three stones. Mendoza's schooling was good (he wrote two books)[2] and he summarily resigned his glass-cutting apprenticeship after a fight with his master's son. At 19 Mendoza was a professional pugilist. He fought mostly around London, usually on grass, though to win the heavyweight championship of England he went to Doncaster where he won easily in 15 minutes, and, unusually, this contest was fought on a raised stage. Five hundred tickets at half a guinea were sold, Mendoza tells us, but there were gatecrashers; and prizefighting, an open-air sport, never was able to control and charge spectators like indoor boxing which arose rapidly and flourished from the 1880s. By 1900 the bare-knuckle variety of boxing, with national and regional champions, had ceased to exist. Prizefights still took place all over the country, but their prestige had vanished, and newspaper coverage dwelt on a new breed of heroes who fought three-minute rounds wearing six-ounce gloves. The rounds in prizefighting went on until at least one man was on the ground, and a round could last 40 minutes. The interest of the public in this style of combat is evidenced by Mendoza pottery (mugs and jugs) and paintings and prints of him shaping up. His name was introduced into dialogue at the theatre, and a song commemorating his first victory over Richard 'Gentleman' Humphreys went like this:

> My Dickie was all the delight of half the genteels in the town;
> Their tables were scarcely compleat, unless my Dickie sat down;
> So very polite, so genteel, such a soft complaisant face,
> What a damnable shame to be spoil'd by a curst little Jew from Duke's Place!

Humphreys mixed with the 'upper crust', and the hint of working-class consciousness in 1789 is unmistakable. A hundred years later boxing was to become the most proletarian of all sports, as boys from poor families tanned university graduates and army officers in the amateur ring. Public schoolboys retreated into their own private championships, held at Aldershot, and well reported by P. G. Wodehouse.[3] Medals and trophies in open competitions fled from gentlemen's boxing clubs like the Belsize, in St John's Wood, to a wholly different type of club organised in the rougher quarters of Birmingham and London. Prizefighters had always been workers because by definition gentlemen could not box for money.

During a prizefight either or both contestants could be knocked unconscious more than once because their attendants were allowed 30 or 40 seconds in which to bring them round. Thus William Hazlitt's description of Tom Hickman's face:

I never saw anything more terrific than his aspect just before he fell. All traces of life, of natural expression, were gone from him. His face was like a human skull, a death's head spouting blood.[4]

refers to the eighth, not the eighteenth round when this prizefight finished

3.1 The London County Council encouraged entertainment in the parks like open-air ballroom dancing after the Second World War had ended. This photograph was taken in 1947 at Victoria Park in Hackney, and the concentration of the audience is strikingly captured. Whether amateur or professional, outdoor boxing is exceptional in this country

with Bill Neate of Bristol the winner. At the end of the first round the betting had been seven to four on 'Gasman' (Hickman), and it was calculated that £150,000 had been gambled on this inter-city match (London v. Bristol) held in Berkshire in 1821.[5] Nineteenth-century prizefights, however, seldom became the subjects of essays by figures with a place in the pantheon of English literature. Prizefighting was ubiquitous, and it took place at many levels. In 1889, for instance, bantamweights from London and Nottingham fought for £200, a highly organised affair which took place at Gravesend, in Kent.[6] Of considerably lower order, was the prizefight reported in 1897 between two market porters (Spitalfields v. Covent Garden).[7] Yet again, the argument started in a pub would be settled outside by prizefighting convention, and boys in schoolyards from Newcastle upon Tyne to Plymouth observed the same canonicals. It is more than a sport with which this chapter deals.

AMATEUR BOXING

Give the average Briton the choice between a warm turn-up with the gloves and the best of gymnastic displays, and he will generally choose the former.

P. G. Wodehouse, 'The schools at Aldershot' in *Sandow's Magazine of Physical Culture*, vol. 6, January to June 1901

John Graham Chambers, who was born in Llanelli, Carmarthenshire, in 1843, was the original organiser of competitive amateur boxing. Educated at Eton and Trinity College, Cambridge, he founded the Amateur Athletic Club at Walham Green in 1866. The club held an annual sports meeting in the spring, and from 1867 this included outdoor boxing at three weights. Chambers wrote the rules for these gloved competitions, which required umpires to score points over three timed rounds and then decide upon a winner giving heed to style. Chambers persuaded a friend from Cambridge, John Sholto Douglas, the 8th Marquis of Queensberry, to give challenge cups to the winners of the boxing competitions, and these Queensberry Cup championships ran from 1867 until 1885. At the same time Douglas allowed Chambers' rules to be captioned with the Marquis's prestigious title. In 1869 a turnstiled sports ground was opened at Lillie Bridge in West Brompton, and the Amateur Athletic Club's annual meeting was shifted to here. It was ideal; because it was enclosed, the riff-raff could be kept out, and gentlemen could relax unless they were competing at walking, running, hurdling, high and broad jumping, putting the weight, throwing the hammer, pole jumping, wrestling, bicycling or boxing.

Lillie Bridge boxing championship contestants came from a narrow social spectrum. They were invariably middle-class. References could be demanded upon entry, there was also a fee, but the chief reason was the exclusiveness of amateur boxing clubs. At Cestus BC, for example, which met at the Oval cricket ground, membership was by ballot at a general meeting, 'one black ball in five to exclude'.[8] These gentlemen's boxing clubs employed 'a Professor of Boxing', who was always a former prize-fighter, to teach members to spar. The Professor, who was no fool to be there in the first place, did not punch too hard. Few clubs like this survived much beyond the First World War. Queensberry Cup competitions died in 1885 because an alternative championship had arisen which allowed working boys and men to enter. The Amateur Boxing Association (hereafter the ABA) was founded in 1880, and this most interesting decade (of economic trough then boom; of socialist agitation; of trade union organisation) saw a change in the nature of amateur boxing clubs.

New model clubs arose specifically for amateur boxing. Their gym was frequently at a pub, or a volunteers' drill hall, and the new polytechnics, with their wood-block floors and wall-bars, had produced an ABA cham-

3.2   The contest: an early match in the Northwest London ABA championships
held at Tottenham in February 1988. Photographer Bill Shipley

pion by 1890. In London particularly, working men's clubs formed boxing sections. The federal body, the Club and Institute Union, was cool about the new recreation (it never offered prizes as it did for angling, billiards and chess) yet members packed the hall for a boxing show. At the United Radical Club in Hackney, for example, a thousand men watched a feather-weight competition in 1891, and by 1898 three CIU clubs were affiliated to the ABA. At this time boys took to boxing in huge numbers at university settlement clubs, at church clubs, and at works' clubs. This should not be seen as street fighting moving indoors and using gloves. This was a new interest for boys because the clubs had only just been established, and street fighting, which the young can usually avoid if they choose to, carried on. The youth clubs bought boxing equipment, and paid an instructor, because this was what boys who joined wanted to do in the evenings after work. Street-fighting youth tended not to join clubs. They were anarchistic, and clubs had rules.

The enthusiasm for amateur boxing was inspired by professional boxers. Small halls running weekly shows began in London, Birmingham and Newcastle in the economic boom of 1887–97, and local heroes inspired others to try the gloves on. Newspaper coverage[9] of professional champions who were ring artists encouraged a compulsorily-educated readership to share their victories in newsprint, and some to try to emulate their prowess. Boxing needed to be learned. First there was footwork, then blocking a punch, ducking and weaving, feinting, drawing a lead, timing a rally, using the ropes, inside work to the body. This curriculum was best commenced at an amateur boxing club, and hundreds of these were formed from around 1890, several of which still exist like the Repton BC in East London. A minority of this stream of amateur boxers gave up winning trophies in order to 'turn pro'. The records show, however, that before the First World War they were rarely successful at the highest level of paid boxing. Though the amateur championships began in 1881, it was not until 1911 that a former ABA champion won a British professional boxing title. This was when Matt Wells, who won the unpaid lightweight championship four times in a row (1904–7), outpointed Freddie Welsh over 20 rounds at the National Sporting Club in Covent Garden. Between the Wars ex-amateurs were much more likely to become professional champions and this trend has developed until in 1988, Tony Sibson, then British and Commonwealth professional champion at middleweight, was regarded as slightly unusual because he did not have an illustrious record as an amateur. A secular change has taken place in amateur boxing which is confirmed by language. The hallmark of style which was once the 'straight left' has gone; the term is never used because it would be laughed at as old fashioned. The cry now is 'left jab', and this expresses a world of difference in boxing.

Orthodox boxers shape up to opponents with their left side forward. The important minority who reverse this posture, 'southpaws', have to be overlooked in the next two paragraphs except to say that they are rarely elegant to watch. The straight left was delivered standing sideways with the arm fully extended and the weight of the body behind it. This was the text-book punch in British boxing for the first half of the twentieth century. It opened exchanges, stopped the spoiler rushing in, was enthusiastically applauded by spectators, and won contests almost without the use of right arm swings. Boxers would be described with some admiration as 'left hand merchants' because of their timing and accuracy with this one punch. The ABA lightweight champion of 1937, Arthur Danahar, of Bethnal Green, had an exquisite straight left. It leapt out magically, and this was perfect style. He turned professional and in 1939 was matched for the British title with an equally young man Eric Boon, of Chatteris, who had recently become the champion. This contest at Harringay Arena between the artist and the fighter was outstanding, and the latter won.

The classical straight left punch was possessed by boxers who balanced themselves on the balls of their feet. It was accompanied invariably by neat footwork and smart use of the ring. Boxers who lacked a points-amassing straight left lead tended to rely on punches that were swung, left hooks and right crosses, to equalise their disability. But such punches were likely to miss and exhausting to throw, so each one needed to count more heavily than rapidly repeatable straight lefts. The boxer who swung needed purchase on the floor so he stood more flat-footed. Standing sideways on, the right swing had a long way to travel, so this type of puncher used an 'on guard' position which made him squarer to his opponent. Artist and fighter, as described, are ideal types: boxers lean towards one or the other. Danahar outclassed Boon for seven rounds, then Boon's right got through. In the eighth round the boxing classicist was down twice, but he struggled back, regaining his stride to win the tenth round with superior boxing. Towards the close of the next round Boon knocked Danahar down with a left hook, and though he fought on and resisted a knockout, the Londoner lost in round 14 when the referee intervened. Twelve thousand people saw this boxing contest whilst many without tickets stood outside listening to the sounds from a packed arena.[10] Artist versus punching specialist was the key to successful matchmaking.

The most significant change in amateur boxing since the Second World War has been the decline of the straight left style, and the rise of the squarer-stanced, swinger of punches, whose style is described (for reasons which will be explained later) as American.

THE ORGANISATION OF AMATEURS

The past month has been rendered remarkable by the fact that we have attained
our first success in a Federation Competition. It was in the *Boxing Competition*
... We entered S. Higgins in Class Four, and to our great gratification he secured
the medal. Our heartiest congratulations to him, for except for a tendency to
use a little more force than was necessary, he undoubtedly boxed very well.

St Anthony's Boys' Club report in *Oxford House Chronicle*, May 1905

From its foundation in 1880 the Amateur Boxing Association organised
championship competitions, held indoors every spring. The only years in
which these did not take place were 1940–3. These competitions were open,
keenly contested, and popular with spectators. For example, at Alexandra
Palace in April 1924, there were 72 competitors at eight weights, and the
show made a profit of £582.[11] Competitions are the foundation stone of
amateur boxing and they take place at every level from novices upwards.
If the entries at any one weight exceed four the eventual victor must probably
win three bouts over three rounds, each round lasting three minutes. Thus
amateur boxing competitions, which are most frequently held during one
day, are a tough test of skill, pluck and endurance, and the boxing goes
on, with a short break, from mid-afternoon until late evening. The spectators are usually vociferous; the numerous officials act in an honorary capacity; the shows rarely make a profit, and crowd disorder is unknown. By
the 1920s there were school boys' boxing championships (held at Birkbeck
College in 1923); a Business Houses' and a Boy Scouts' championships;
and the Federation of Social Clubs, centred on Oxford House, had held
their championships since the previous century. The ABA took all these
competitions under its wing, and itself spawned three regions in an attempt
to ease the dominance of London. They were Midland Counties, Northern
Counties and the Welsh Association. Scotland had its own United Scottish
ABA; and the Irish ABA, first formed in 1911, was heavily indebted to
police (the Garda) participation and organisational support.[12] Team
matches between the four countries, arranged 'on the same terms as the
Calcutta Cup meetings of the Rugby Union',[13] were discussed in 1939,
but dropped because of the war. Ireland by this time had built a National
Stadium in Dublin, the only one in the world owned by an amateur boxing
association. When the European Championships were held here in April
1939 these prestigious titles were won by two Irish boxers (Jimmy Ingle
and Paddy Dowdall), two Italians, and one each by boxers from Germany,
Poland, Estonia, and Sweden. The ABA played a major part in starting
international amateur boxing, and it is to this that we must now turn.

At the instigation of France and England the International Amateur Boxing Federation was formed in 1920 by five countries. At the Olympic Games,

held in Paris four years later, there were 181 boxing contests over six days, involving boxers from 29 nations. The Great Britain team provided winners at middle- and light-heavy weights. Harry Mallin, a Metropolitan police-man who boxed at 11st. 6lb, causes us to pause, because he was one of the best amateur boxers ever produced in these islands. He won the ABA championships five times in succession (1919–23), and Olympic gold medals twice, the first time at Antwerp in 1920. He and H. J. Mitchell, the light-heavyweight, were the last British or Irish boxers to win Olympic titles until the Scot, Dick McTaggart, and the Londoner, Terry Spinks, won in Melbourne in 1956. For the Paris Games in 1924 the British Olympic Association made a grant of £577 to the ABA towards 'training and prepara-tion of the Olympic Team'. Amateur boxing has rarely had so much money.

The British Empire Games in August 1934 included two days of boxing (Wednesday and Friday) at Wembley Stadium. The winners came from Australia, South Africa, and six from England; Wales had three runners-up, and a winner of a contest for third place. The Northern Ireland team gained two third places, and in other international competitions Ireland would have boxed as an all-Ireland side. Scotland had a runner-up and two third places, and their heavyweight boxer, almost unbelievably, was a member of the aristocracy, Lord D. D. Hamilton. He came third. The outstanding boxer at these second Empire Games to include the sport (it was first staged at Hamilton, Canada, in 1930) was probably Dave McCleave, and he went on to become the British professional welterweight champion in 1936.

Amateur boxing clubs were the bricks, the ABA the mortar, from which British boxing, not for cash but for fun and tokens, was built up. The clubs ranged from the enormously successful, like Lynn in the early 1900s, through to a group of lads sparring in an inhospitable basement with few thoughts of winning national championships. Nevertheless all clubs boxed to the same rules, and these rules spread to other countries. The gentlemen of the ABA were much more likely to be stockbrokers than clock punchers at a factory, yet they administered a sport at which the working class won almost all the prizes. The ABA obtained royal patronage through the Prince of Wales in the early 1920s, and the social class of the administrators changed only slightly during the first half of this body's history. The sport was never organised to make profits, and clubs often had, and have, local businessmen as benefactors. Club officials labour hard mainly for the love of the sport, for there is no money to be made out of amateur boxing. In 1987 the ABA received £50,000 from sponsorship by business (George Wimpey plc), and £29,000 for television fees, and this is spent on training schemes for coaches, rent, salaries and taking senior and junior teams abroad. Nevertheless by comparison with some other countries our amateur boxing is run on a shoestring, and this is reflected in results at international level. Since 1956 only one British boxer (Chris Finnigan) has won an Olympic gold medal, and performances at the quadrennial World Amateur Boxing Championship have been disappointing for Ireland and this country.

THE DOMESTIC SCENE

Suddenly, I was aware of young Alf by my side, in his chair at his own corner. But young Alf translated. Young Alf in pink breeches, white stockings and shoes. Young Alf holding out his hands superciliously for his second ... to put his gloves on.

Clarence Rook on 'All for her' in *The Hooligan Nights* (1899) p.244

England started amateur boxing championships, and from 1881 these were open to anyone who was not a professional boxer. The first seven competitions were held at the St James's Hall, in Piccadilly, and they were dominated by boxers from Birmingham and London. A Dublin Boxing Club affiliated to the ABA in 1884, and the first Welsh club, Cardiff BC, became a member three years later. Not until 1898 did an entrant from outside England become a champion, and this was the lightweight, H. Marks, from Cardiff Harlequin Harriers. These finals were also noteworthy because two clubs from polytechnics (Goldsmiths' Institute and Finsbury Poly) supplied five of the ten finalists. To summarise amateur boxing before the First World War it is fair to say London clubs made up the vast majority of affiliates to the ABA; the April championships were staged in the capital, and they drew large audiences; and London boxers won the bulk of the titles.

In the seasons 1910–11, Scotland, Wales and Ireland started holding their own national championships. These had the then standard five weights (bantam, feather, light, middle and heavy) though Ireland added welterweight (not exceeding 10st. 7lb), which the others included in 1920. Little fellows, not exceeding 8st., were also given a better chance around this time by the institution of the further category, flyweight. In this respect amateur boxing trailed some ten years behind the professionals. Team matches between the four countries naturally followed, with England usually much too strong for the other teams. The English team's record was remarkable. Boxing in England they never lost a match until 1951 when a team from the USA won by six bouts to four. The best-remembered performance by an England team came ten years later, and a huge audience watched television to see England 'whitewash' a United States team, ten bouts to nil.

Wales lagged behind the other countries in amateur boxing. Organisationally it remained a division of the English ruling body until 1954, an extraordinary subservience, which may help to explain, or may have resulted in, a sad lack of brilliant Welsh amateur boxers. More likely, this lack of exceptional talent wearing vests, stems from a tradition of 'mountain' fighters who always boxed for cash. One of the best Welsh boxers, Howard Winstone, MBE, from Merthyr Tydfil, illustrates how this tendency works to the disadvantage of the amateur sport. Winstone was the British ABA champion at bantamweight in 1958. From 1961 until he retired in 1968, this outstandingly skilful boxer was the professional champion, a talent lost to the amateur ranks.

Scotland won two of the five titles at the ABA championships of 1903 held at the Northampton Institute, in London. Harold Feargus and Edward Dickson came from the same club, Edinburgh Harriers.[14] Leith Victoria provided a winner and a losing finalist (R. and J. Watson) at the Albert Hall in 1939, when eight weights were being contested. Thus Scotland made successful forays into the British base of amateur boxing, the deep south. Scotland was keen on amateur boxing, and in 1909 there was a furious row between rival ruling bodies.[15] The surviving one remained affiliated to the English ABA until 1947. Scottish amateur boxing achieved great heights in the 1960s. Dick McTaggart started it off by winning the Olympics, and he also won one European, and five British ABA championships. Tom Imrie dominated Scottish light-middleweight boxing; won the ABA's in London twice, and a European bronze medal at Bucharest. Walter McGowan, Ken Buchanan, John McCluskey and Jim Watt were among other top Scottish amateur boxers of the 1960s.

Irish amateur boxing was different. There was almost no professional boxing outside Belfast, so an easy opportunity to turn professional was lacking. Public attention was deflected to Irish-born boxers who were successful abroad, such as Jimmy McLarnin, a world welterweight champion in the 1930s, whose family had emigrated to Canada whilst he was still a baby.[16] The opening of the National Stadium in Dublin in 1939 altered the situation. Here was a fine new stadium purpose-built for amateur boxing. It held amateur boxing shows almost weekly throughout the season and crowd-pleasing amateurs at the Dublin Stadium gained a following of supporters because they boxed there regularly. In British cities the fans would watch their boxing weekly at a professional show. So the atmosphere at the Dublin Stadium contained the excitement generated at professional boxing shows at Belle Vue, Manchester, or the Liverpool Stadium. Thus in Dublin amateur boxing had the glamour attached to professional boxing in other cities. A lad could become a hero at the National Stadium without turning professional or even becoming a national amateur champion. As a corollary, the best boxer at any weight in Ireland was as likely to be an amateur as a professional, an impossibility in England, Scotland and Wales.

PARTICIPATION AND CULTURE

I was a zealous youngster with a belief that the blue uniform was so impressive that I need fear no odds. One evening I met a group of hilarious spirits emerging from a local boxing-saloon and spreading themselves arm-in-arm across the pavement. A more experienced man would have turned a blind eye. I, however, reproved them for obstruction . . . I was laid up for about four months.

Frederick Porter Wensley, OBE, *Detective Days* (1931) p.2

Women have neither boxed nor occupied a great deal of the seating at amateur boxing shows. In 1900 women in small numbers went with men to see gymnastics and sparring at what were called 'assaults-at-arms'. At the music hall, in far greater numbers, women must have seen professional boxers going through their training routine because, particularly in the 1890s, they sometimes topped the bill.[17] Otherwise the sport excluded females. This gender exclusiveness has not been expressed in boxing advertising since 1914, yet in marked contrast to professional wrestling, women have never formed a significant component of the live audience for boxing. As popular culture boxing was masculine.

The number of men taking part in amateur boxing has never been identified. Only the clubs, not the individual boxers, are registered with the governing bodies. In England presently (February 1988) there are 850 clubs affiliated to the ABA. Since a club could scarcely function with less than 30 boxers, it is safe to guess that there are upwards of 25,000 active amateur boxers in England, including juniors, who are under 18 years of age, and schoolboys, who must have reached the age of eleven. Yet boxing as a part of the national culture should not be measured by those taking part in it at any particular time. Whenever a male squares up to an opponent he automatically draws upon the culture of boxing. In spite of the British Medical Association's report on *Boxing*, which was published and well publicised in 1984, young men and boys have not yet stopped taking up the sport. Clearly punches to the head damage the brain cumulatively. Headguards were required to be worn at the Los Angeles Olympic Games, yet this practice has not been adopted in the UK. Social pressure against wearing headguards is enormous, and it comes from boxers and spectators.

Amateur boxing is not saintly but it always has been remarkably free from undercover cash payments to boxers, and any other forms of professionalism. Amateur clubs are faced with expulsion if they allow professionals to train with their members.[18] There are no bookmakers laying the odds in this sport, and advertising agencies do not ask amateur champions to endorse products. In many ways boxing is a paradigm of virtue compared to athletics and football. Of course, discreet clubs have occasionally given a few notes to entice boxers to appear on their show,[19] but this practice

has never been widespread. Much more commonly, boxers, having honourably won a canteen of cutlery, might sell it on the following day, and
do so regularly with all their prizes. This was ethically tolerable when
one considers that boxers have usually worked at low-paid jobs.

The great transformation of amateur boxing took place in the 1890s
when a middle-class recreation was transformed into a popular activity
of the masses. This participatory sport was not imposed on workers in
industrial centres by employers, landlords, ministers of any church, or
school teachers. The working class, which had enjoyed prizefighting and
gloved contests for a century, observed the organisation of briefer contests
which were less painful, and wanted to take part. They already had a
boxing culture of contests for cash on the heath or in the skittle alley,
which was reinforced by their customary manner of settling a dispute at
work or outside the pub. The class exclusiveness of Queensberry Cups
boxing was fractured in 1880 by the formation of the ABA by stockbrokers
like Jack Angle, who encouraged the sport to become truly competitive.
The outlay for kit was modest, some gloves and skipping ropes, punch
bag and ball, eventually a proper ring, and a club was well equipped.
Amateur boxing clubs began in their hundreds at pubs and polytechnics,
working men's clubs and church halls, not because gentlemen wanted to
encourage it, though some leaders of boys' clubs did, but because the proletariat itself adopted boxing for sport, and promptly won all the prizes.
Amateur boxing was democratised at this time by a complex of factors.
First, more money was circulating in working-class quarters; secondly,
workers had experience of organising prizefights, and the taste for this
sport declined as rapidly as the demand for boxing rose. Yet prizefighting
at the highest level had been elitist within the working class, a sub-culture
within a culture, whilst boxing was open to all. Thirdly, increased literacy
and wider newspaper coverage spread the popularity of sporting heroes,
and boxing lifted off as *the* sport in inner cities. Fourthly, there was a
commingling of substrata within the working class with the unskilled
workers becoming more organised and emulating the stability and continuity of journeymen's life-styles. Finally, the locality around home sprouted
cultural property beyond the public house. Music halls and boxing saloons
offered places to watch, but clubs, evening institutes, church and drill halls
were spaces in which to take part in this new stimulating recreation which
kept you physically fit. The swift rise of amateur boxing was, however,
only possible because contests between two men in a ring of any construction
had already been part of working-class culture since Daniel Mendoza.

PROFESSIONAL BOXING

The right cross-counter is distinctly one of those things which it is more blessed
to give than to receive.

    P. G. Wodehouse, *The Pothunters* (1902) p.30

Boxing became a popular spectator sport when unskilled and casual workers
became able to afford sixpence regularly each week for extra entertainment.
Between 1887 and 1900 when living standards amongst working people
rose, boxing deserted public houses in favour of small halls with greater
audience capacity. At the same time prizefighting was displaced in the columns of newspapers, and new papers were published which gave space
to boxing. By 1909 two weekly papers were started which were entirely
devoted to boxing. Small hall boxing immediately flourished in cities like
London, Birmingham and Newcastle upon Tyne. The feature of this new
entertainment was that it was frequent and regular. Usually held twice
weekly, on Saturday evenings the boxing had its own crowd of supporters
who came week after week. They overlapped with the mid-week crowd
who could often afford a shilling, but that night too had its own ambience,
determined in both cases by the regular supporters. Boxing attracted working-class customers who came regularly, and they set the tone of the entertainment. This clientele did not have to adapt in order to watch this sport,
as they would have had to attending cricket with its large establishment
of middle-class 'County' followers. Boxing, from Plymouth through Mountain Ash to Liverpool and South Shields, was not only a new spectator
sport, it was the first popular, country-wide, working-class sport until football penetrated the inner cities.

    Boxing as an entertainment was always available. Saturday evening shows
were the most popular, but in London one could find a show on every
night of the week, including Sundays. Holidays were used by promoters,
though ironically shows held on Boxing Day were rarely crowded. At the
Ring, in Blackfriars, matinees were well attended from 1912, presumably
by market porters and others who finished work early. Besides top-line
contests, an added attraction were professional competitions which were
completed over several weeks, thus boxing had serials running long before
cinema came along with the same idea. Boxing audiences were noisy, and
since they attended regularly, they were knowledgeable; many of them
would have fought in a ring themselves, and the level of understanding
of the sport was high.[20] They loved to watch a local boy winning his early
contests, or putting up a good fight (they had probably worked or drunk
with his father or brother) and his boxing career would be followed with
some fervour at the same hall for several years. Boxers before the 1950s
would box frequently. For example, Len Harvey, a smart eight-stone boxer

3.3 The front page of the weekly paper *Boxing* in its third year of publication.
Its 24 pages included 'Scottish News', 'Irish Ring Notes', 'News from South Wales',
'Midland Gossip' and 'Round the London Ring'. In this issue there were nine still
photographs of boxers, and an excellent half-page cartoon

from Plymouth, engaged in 27 contests at the Ring, Blackfriars, in two years (1924–5) after his arrival in London, and he had four contests elsewhere. He was 16 years old when boxing 15-round contests, but Harvey was so clever defensively that his career lasted over 20 years and he won British championships from middle to heavyweight. The Ring crowd adopted the boy from the West Country.[21] It would be quite misleading, however, to see small hall boxing audiences as benign, for part of this same crowd could be anti-semitic,[22] and in Belfast in the 1940s boxing audiences made it uncomfortable for Catholic boxers. Yet crowd disorder at professional boxing throughout this century has been rare. Ethnic, religious and racial tension could make the atmosphere ugly, but boxing crowds were mostly fair-minded. The underdog especially aroused a well of sympathy from a boxing crowd, and the toppling of a cocky performer delighted it.

Boxers at the turn of the century were often young and tiny. They sparred at pubs and clubs and music halls, billed as somebody's 'midgets', and, aged 12, would progress to six- or eight-round contests. Competitions were held at the Lambeth School of Arms, for boxers not exceeding 6st. 6lb.[23] They had little or no amateur experience, and often came from boxing families. This helps to explain the proliferation of boxers whose names were prefixed by 'Kid', 'Young', 'Nipper' or 'Tich' before 1930. In this period most boxers trained by taking contests almost fortnightly; for instance, Jackie Berg had 21 contests in 1925, involving 262 rounds of boxing. In such cases, one must ask, how on earth did they avoid brain damage? Unlike Kid Berg, many didn't, yet there is a second explanation. Small hall crowds appreciated defensive skills, and would applaud artistry in avoiding punches; delicate footwork was admired, and style was important to the audience. Their level of understanding of the art in boxing encouraged skill and discouraged sloggers. With the advent of vastly ignorant television audiences a current has flowed in the opposite direction. Boxers have not regressed, on the contrary, the watchers have, and aggression, for its own sake, has become more important because of this. The influence on the sport of the devotees has declined, and one part of working-class culture has been diminished. Consumers sample sports through television and their choice is enormous. Financially, professional boxing has been hugely rewarded by fees from television companies. The loser, standing almost forgotten in society's corner, has been community. Tommy Farr made all feel proud, yet ineffaceably he was Tonypandy's delegate, just as Teddy Baldock represented Poplar's fighting spirit, and Benny Lynch epitomised neighbourhood networks in Glaswegian slum tenements. Local heroes were lost to professional boxing in the 1950s with the start of universalised consumerism.

Early boxing promoters were local businessmen like Jonas (Jack) Woolf of Wonderland, who kept the East London Tavern in the Whitechapel Road. The £3,000 nominal capital of 'Wonderland' Limited, when the company was set up in 1895, came from five other shareholders besides the licensed victualler. They were described as a dramatic author, a music publisher, a publisher's manager, a printer and a solicitor, but Woolf ran the highly successful boxing shows until Wonderland was burnt down in 1911. The hall, which had been built in 1834 and rebuilt twice, had been used as a theatre. It could hold 2,000 spectators, and though the company was wound up in 1906, the boxing carried on, making, one suspects, large profits. By this time the telephone had been installed, and Wonderland favourites, like Young Joseph from Aldgate, were in contention for national championships. Woolf seems to have been popular, and he was famous for taking round his collection box for charities.[24]

The promoter at the Ring, Blackfriars, offers interesting comparisons with Woolf. Dick Burge had been an outstanding boxer of the 1890s. Born in Cheltenham in 1865, he had been adopted as a prizefighter and boxer by the *cognoscenti* of Newcastle upon Tyne. At about ten stone he was difficult to beat; he won the English title in 1891 (from Birmingham's Jem Carney) and was only just outpunched (by Kid Lavigne) for the world championship. Burge was used to having money and a heavy gambler when he was imprisoned for seven years over the Liverpool bank frauds. After his release he turned to completely honest boxing promotion at the old chapel in Blackfriars Road. The new small hall, opened in 1910, was soon a success. Burge, like Woolf, exploited the boxers by paying them very little money, yet those who shone could still earn more than a skilled artisan. Burge, however, did not live where his wealth was created, his house was situated in the leafy suburb of Golders Green. Here, during the war, Burge staged a different order of boxing show when he paid over £700 in purse money to four top-of-the-bill boxers. Two champions, Billy Wells and Pat O'Keefe, succeeded in beating their challengers at the new and palatial Hippodrome. The point is not that boxing promotion was unaffected by the war (though most boxers joined the army) but that Burge bridged the gap between small hall twice-weekly promotion, and the irregular spectacular show aimed at a larger audience which was not entirely working-class.[25] It is to promoters of large hall / high purse boxing that we must now turn, because boxing developed with a twin thrust.

London has always been the capital of boxing. Throughout the century most major contests have taken place there. The big purse money, however, arrived late, not until 1910, when Hugh D. McIntosh came over from Australia. At Sydney in December 1908 he had raised the cash to tempt Tommy Burns to defend his world heavyweight championship against Jack Johnson.

McIntosh himself refereed the contest which the black man won decisively. For the next five years promoters and managers sought a white boxer who could win the title back from Johnson, and one such was found in India. Bombardier Billy Wells, who had learned to box at an East End youth club, became heavyweight champion of (the British forces in) 'All-India' by winning a competition at Simla, and in 1909 this was an important British boxing title. Wells's release from the 6th Mountain Battery was purchased, and he returned to London, aged 22, and a heavyweight prospect. For a contest at Wonderland, Jack Woolf paid him £8; then McIntosh paid Wells £100 for his next three matches,[26] the third of which was billed as 'The Search for a White Champion'. Ticket prices were high as the advertisement in *Mirror of Life* shows. Soon afterwards McIntosh and Wells took boxing promotion beyond the local arena. In the *Referee* 'Sporting Notions' wrote:

I had not been to Olympia before – that is to say, to the Annexe to watch boxing. There is no doubt that the place has caught on. Every seat was occupied. I heard that all sorts of prices were offered for admission by late-comers, but there was no room . . . Boxing at Olympia is going to be a great success.[27]

The cinematograph cameras were there in January 1911, and at the end of the first round the betting was 20–1 on Billy Wells. The attraction of boxing lies in its unpredictability, however, and Gunner Moir knocked him out in round three. Professional boxing in the form of a spectacular sporting entertainment was established in Britain at this time by the coincidence of several connecting factors. National income per head of population was rising after a period of slow growth. Jack Johnson's skill as a boxer, and the colour of his skin, had drawn the attention of a wider public to the sport, and he was popular in this country though he had boxed here only once, at Plymouth. Wells, despite his vulnerability to heavy punchers, was an exciting boxer to watch, and he became much loved by the boxing fraternity. Through newspaper coverage and music hall appearances boxers became personalities rather than athletes. Finally, the purses offered by promoters rose astronomically. When the Johnson–Wells match was set for the Empress Hall, Earls Court, on 2 October 1911, they were to receive £6,000 and £2,000 respectively. Johnson, in light training in North London, appeared at the Walthamstow Palace, and a local paper reported:

The star . . . is Jack Johnson, the boxing champion of the world. It is almost inadequate to say that every seat is occupied at every performance, for large numbers have been quite content if they only can have standing room. The huge black's exhibition bouts . . . have been rapturously applauded and his genial way of either making a speech or singing a song . . . considerably enhances the popularity of the smiling giant.[28]

A tidal wave of opposition to the match was started by the Free Church Council on the grounds that the contest would be repulsive, and the film of it even more so. Lord Lonsdale objected on the grounds that Wells stood no chance against Johnson. The London County Council threatened to refuse to renew the entertainment licence, and the Metropolitan Railway Company, who were the freeholders of the premises, obtained a court injunction forbidding the contest to take place. The promoter, a Lancashire capitalist, called Jimmy White, was forced to cancel the show a week before the scheduled date.[29] There is no evidence whatsoever to suggest that the general public, without access to the press and the law, wanted the match to be suppressed. Boxing had become a big business that attracted business-men with no background in boxing. Woolf, Burge and McIntosh had in common some roots in the sport which made them rich. From this time showmen, like C. B. Cochrane, the theatrical impresario, would make box-ing an extension of their other financial activities.[30] The local entrepreneur continued, and continues, with small hall boxing, but public attention was drawn more and more towards the 'spectaculars' at Albert Hall, Harringay Arena, and Wembley. The two forms are closely linked, yet music hall, cinema, radio, television, and the press enhanced the latter. When increased affluence multiplied people's choice of spectator and participatory sports in the 1960s, small hall boxing almost died. Unemployment has helped to revive this side of the sport in the 1980s, by increasing the numbers of professional boxers. There are presently over 600 professional boxers in the United Kingdom, compared to less than half that number in 1974.[31] Whilst boxing flagged, a caucus (Mike Barrett, Mickey Duff, Jarvis Astaire, Terry Lawless) gained a monopoly of large boxing promotions. Their power was broken largely by the efforts of a newcomer to boxing, Frank Warren. Warren combines promotion of shows (which are usually televised, some-times worldwide) with the management of boxers. When Warren promoted the Colin Jones–Don Curry world welterweight championship contest at the National Exhibition Centre at Birmingham in January 1985, he was prising open an economic cartel. Three years of vertical integration has resulted in his presently managing upwards of 50 boxers. Promoters have always used individual boxers in order to maximise profits. Jack Solomons and Bruce Woodcock are a typical example of this relationship in the 1940s, but the Doncaster heavyweight had a manager to look after his interests, fellow Yorkshireman, Tom Hurst. The promoter who manages boxers must at times face a conflict of interest and the recent bitter proceedings between Belfast's Barney Eastwood and Barry McGuigan[32] suggest that the functions of promoter and manager are best kept separate, though McGuigan is currently managed by Warren.

GOVERNING BODIES

Wilson tells a good yarn about his contest with Moir. Hawker was something akin to the stranger in a strange land when he made his début at the Club, and totally unused to some of the London ringcraft methods. His surprise when Moir led off by asking him what he thought of the Insurance Bill as they sparred up can therefore be imagined.

'North of England Notes' on Newcastle in the weekly paper *Boxing*, 4 January 1913

The British Boxing Board of Control grew out of the National Sporting Club. The embryo Board kept minutes of its meetings from 1914,[33] but it was a self-appointed body of interested gentlemen without power or recognition, except through the Club which produced Lonsdale Belts as the symbols of British professional boxing championships.[34] The Club had been founded in Covent Garden in 1891 for members only, and it soon decreed that only on its premises could contests for titles take place.[35] Surprisingly the sporting press supported this assumption until the end of the First World War. This monopoly was finally made to look absurd in 1919 when the 'authorised' heavyweight champion, Bombardier Billy Wells, was knocked out in six rounds by Joe Beckett at the Holborn Stadium. With the exception of the hierarchy of the National Sporting Club, no one, especially Billy, could any longer believe that Wells was the British heavyweight champion.

The 'wee free' Liberal MP for Hull Central, Lieutenant Commander J. M. Kenworthy, who had boxed in the navy, suggested legislation could be used to institute a governing body for professional boxing. His model was taken from the USA. The subject was soon dropped, however, and the statute book has never been used to regulate boxing in this country.[36] Voluntary means of control were preferred, and they developed gradually from 1930.

The Board licensed promoters, managers, ring officials, and boxers, and gained sufficient support to apply sanctions. For example, in 1933 they fined heavyweight Jack Doyle over £2,000 for his infraction of the rules at the White City Stadium. In his challenge for the British title the ex-Irish Guardsman had struck Jack Peterson of Wales, several times below the belt for which he was disqualified in the second round. Doyle sued the Board and won his case, but the Board appealed and the court upheld Doyle's punishment. The withdrawal of a licence holder's registration became a powerful sanction as the Board gained more and more control of the sport. Referee Joe Palmer was unconcerned in 1926 when (probably unjustly) this happened to him as a result of the John Sullivan–Len Harvey contest. Ten years later, such was its growth in authority that any referee's progress would have been wrecked or blighted by the same disciplinary action taken by the Board. Within the ruling body promoters had, and have, the largest say. Boxers' unions have been started but they have always failed in this individualistic occupation. Unlicensed boxing shows are now few and far between. Some local authorities will not allow their halls to be used for them, and the public are wary because of much greater general knowledge about medical aspects of boxing. The British Boxing Board of Control probably has greater control presently than at any time in its history, which is good, because professional boxing needs firm government.[37] A statutory body might still be the best way forward. Professional boxing was banned in Sweden in 1969, and in Norway in 1982. For it to continue in this country legislation should include a minimum wage for boxers; separation of managers and promoters without any fraudulent overlap; and a levy on the professional sport to fund the amateur game. The former has lived far too long, rent-free, off the back of the latter.

In 1902 A. F. (Peggy) Bettinson devoted a chapter of his book *The National Sporting Club* to 'The decline of English champions ...' By English he meant British, and the decline was relative to the rise of American boxers. He had taken Pedlar Palmer to New York in 1899 only for the so-called 'Box of Tricks' to be knocked out in the first round by a Pennsylvanian, aptly named 'Terrible' Terry McGovern. What Bettinson wrote is of limited interest yet the premise was sound, for from about 1880 the United States had displaced Britain as the top boxing nation and their relative positions have remained unchanged ever since. Boxing is the sport of the big city and industrialisation. A few boxers may have been born in rural places, but they learnt their trade in small halls situated beside factories, docks and railway arches. Boxing thrives where the proletariat is working overtime. Comparative studies in economic history would be informed by a glance at the rise of boxing in cities like Cardiff, Detroit, Mexico City and Seoul. The American style of boxing can be summarised as two-fisted infighting, going forward territorially, always aiming for the knock-out and the quickest possible finish to a contest. The difference between the two styles has greatly diminished since Danahar in 1938, yet the emphasis on upright posture, straight left and backing off, is recognisably British.

World championship titles won by boxers from these Isles are collated in Table 1. There will be arguments about why some names have been left out (Howard Winstone, of Wales, for example) yet, these 30 boxers represent my judgement of *not* who were the best, but who unequivocally won world professional boxing championships. The 30 champions can be broken down as follows, there are:

2 Welshmen	5 Scotsmen	2 Nigerians
2 Irishmen	18 Englishmen	1 Ugandan

Comparisons with census figures show that Scotland has produced the most world champions per head of population in these Isles, closely followed by Wales. Ten of the 18 Englishmen have come from London, and the capital could fairly claim Ugandan-born Boza-Edwards, who boxed as an amateur with the Fitzroy Lodge club. Furthermore, Salford's Joe Bowker made his name in London, and had few matches up north. The lack of a genuine representative of the north of England in this table before the 1930s is surprising, and the absence of boxers from the north-east is difficult to explain because Tynemouth in the 1890s had the strongest boxing culture along with Birmingham and London. The midlands, famous as a nursery of boxers at the turn of the century, had to wait patiently before Randolph Turpin surprised everyone by beating Sugar Ray Robinson in 1951. Liverpool's Boxing Stadium was flourishing in 1912 and the tradition created, played its part in the making of two African-born world champion boxers, Hogan Bassey and Dick Tiger.

World championship titles numbered six in 1900. There were seven weight divisions when light-heavy gained approval three years later. Flyweight was added in 1910, at which time professional boxing was confined to the United States, Britain and its white colonies, and France. In 1983 the weight divisions had risen to 14 or 15, and with three bodies offering their versions of titles, 62 world championship contests took place in 11 different countries.[38] Of these contests 15 were held in Asia (Japan, South Korea and Thailand) where small men win world championships as readily as they did in Britain before the welfare state raised body weights generally. Contenders come from all five continents to compete just as they do in amateur boxing. Professional world championships are not necessarily easier to win now than they were in 1900 because the boxing world has massively expanded.

The question of race can be illustrated by Table 1. Boxing promoters, from Jack Woolf onwards, have often been Jewish, and so were the boxers until around 1950. A Jewish boxer won the ABA heavyweight championship as early as 1889, but the orthodox community frowned upon their boys taking up professional boxing.[39] As religion weakened, and the numbers of Jews increased (particularly in London and Leeds) through immigration from Central Europe, Jewish boys took to boxing in droves. The large number can partly be explained because the Jewish sabbath ruled out the alternative sport, football, for it was chiefly played on Saturday before sundown. Thus halls like Premierland in East London almost specialised in Jewish boxers. A large proportion of Britain's top professional boxers between the wars were Jewish,[40] and Ted 'Kid' Lewis and Jack 'Kid' Berg went even further, and their names appear in Table 1. Jewish youth in

Table 1. *Domestically based boxers who won World Professional titles*
1900–88

Index number	Years of professional boxing	Ring name, and place usually billed from	When title won, from whom, and where; when title lost, to whom and where
Flyweight			
1	1910–23	Jimmy Wilde of Tylorstown, South Wales	December 1916, Young Zulu Kid, London
			June 1923, Pancho Villa, New York
2	1926–39	Jackie Brown of Manchester	October 1932, Young Perez, Manchester
			September 1935, Benny Lynch, Manchester
3	1931–38	Benny Lynch of Glasgow	September 1935, Jackie Brown, Manchester
			June 1938, unable to make the weight
4	1934–48	Peter Kane of Golborne, Lancashire	September 1938, Jackie Jurich, Liverpool
			June 1943, Jackie Paterson, Glasgow
5	1938–50	Jackie Paterson of Scotland	June 1943, Peter Kane, Glasgow
			March 1948, Rinty Monaghan, Belfast
6	1934–49	Rinty Monaghan of Belfast	March 1948, Jackie Paterson, Belfast
			April 1950, retired
7	1942–54	Terry Allen of Islington, London	April 1950, Honore Pratesi, London
			August 1950, Dado Marino, Honolulu
8	1961–69	Walter McGowan of Hamilton, Scotland	June 1966, Salvatore Burruni, London
			December 1966, Chartchai Chionoi, Bangkok
9	1977–86	Charlie Magri of Stepney, East London	March 1983, Eleoncio Mercedes, London
			September 1983, Frank Cedeno, London
10	1982–	Duke McKenzie of Croydon	October 1988, Rolando Bohol, London

Table 1. *Cont.*

Index number	Years of professional boxing	Ring name, and place usually billed from	When title won, from whom, and where; when title lost, to whom and where
Bantamweight			
11	1900–19	Joe Bowker of Salford, Lancashire	October 1904, Frank Neil, London March 1905, outgrew the weight limit
Featherweight			
12	1949–59	Hogan Bassey of Nigeria then, from 1951, Liverpool	June 1957, Cherif Hamia, Paris March 1959, Davey Moore, Los Angeles
13	1981–	Barry McGuigan of Clones, Monaghan	June 1985, Eusebio Pedroza, London June 1986, Steve Cruz, Las Vegas
Junior-lightweight			
14	1976–	Cornelius Boza-Edwards of Uganda, then London	March 1981, Rafael Limón, Stockton August 1981, Rolando Navarette, Via Reggio
Lightweight			
15	1905–22	Freddie Welsh of Pontypridd, South Wales	July 1914, Willie Ritchie, London May 1917, Benny Leonard, New York
16	1965–82	Ken Buchanan of Edinburgh	September 1970, Ismael Laguna, San Juan, Rico June 1972, Roberto Durán, New York
17	1968–81	Jim Watt of Glasgow	April 1979, Alfredo Pitalua, Glasgow June 1981, Alexis Argüello, London
Light-welterweight			
18	1924–45	Jack 'Kid' Berg of Whitechapel, East London	February 1930, Mushy Callahan, London March 1931, Tony Canzoneri, Chicago
19	1981–87	Terry Marsh of Stepney then Basildon, Essex	March 1987, Joe Manley, Basildon September 1987, retired due to ill health

Table 1. *Cont.*

Index number	Years of professional boxing	Ring name, and place usually billed from	When title won, from whom, and where; when title lost, to whom and where
Welterweight			
20	1909–29	Ted 'Kid' Lewis of St George's-in-the-East, London	August 1915, Jack Britton, Boston April 1916, Jack Britton, New Orleans regained title June 1917, Jack Britton, Dayton, Ohio March 1919, Jack Britton, Canton, Ohio
21	1969–78	John H. Stracey of Bethnal Green, East London	December 1975, José Napoles, Mexico City June 1976, Carlos Palomino, London
22	1980–	Lloyd Honeygan of Bermondsey, South London	September 1986, Don Curry, Atlantic City November 1987, Jorge Vaca, London Regained title March 1988, Jorge Vaca, London
Light-middleweight			
23	1973–82	Maurice Hope of Hackney, East London	March 1979, Rocky Mattioli, San Remo May 1981, Wilfred Benítez, Las Vegas
Middleweight			
24	1946–58	Randolph Turpin of Leamington, Warwickshire	July 1951, Sugar Ray Robinson, London September 1951, Sugar Ray Robinson, New York
25	1957–64	Terry Downes of London	July 1961, Paul Pender, London April 1962, Paul Pender, Boston
26	1952–68	Dick Tiger of Nigeria, and, from 1955, Liverpool	October 1962, Gene Fullmer, San Francisco December 1963, Joey Giardello, Atlantic City regained title October 1965, Joey Giardello, New York April 1966, Emile Griffith, New York

Table 1. *Cont.*

Index number	Years of professional boxing	Ring name, and place usually billed from	When title won, from whom, and where; when title lost, to whom and where
27	1972–81	Alan Minter of Crawley, Sussex	March 1980, Vito Antuofermo, Las Vegas September 1980, Marvin Hagler, London
Light-Heavyweight			
28	1936–50	Freddie Mills of Bournemouth, Hampshire	July 1948, Gus Lesnevich, London January 1950, Joey Maxim, London
See also 26	1952–68	Dick Tiger of Nigeria; then from 1955 boxed in Britain	see middleweight December 1966, José Torres, New York May 1968, Bob Foster, New York
29	1971–80	John Conteh of Liverpool	October 1974, Jorge Ahumada, London June 1978, Mate Parlov, Belgrade
30	1978–	Dennis Andries of Hackney, East London	April 1986, J. B. Williamson, London March 1987, Thomas Hearns, Detroit

Sources: Nat Fleischer (ed.), *The 1968 Ring Boxing Encyclopedia and Record Book*, and Herbert G. Goldman (ed.), *1984 Ring Record Book and Boxing Encyclopedia*, both published in New York City. Barry J. Hugman (ed.), *British Boxing Yearbook 1988*; Harry Mullan (ed.), *Boxing News Annual and Record Book 1985*; Maurice Golesworthy (ed.), *Encyclopedia of Boxing*, 1970; *'Boxing's' Book of Records up to 30th June, 1914*; Ernest A. Bland (ed.), *52 Years of Sport*, n.d. (1949).

Britain largely gave up boxing at the same time as their counterparts in the USA. Full employment and rising standards of living played a part in this, as did the increase in Britain of newer ethnic groups, fresh 'outsiders', and we must now look at black boxers.

A colour bar did not allow a black man to box for a British title until 1948, even if he had been born in the British Isles. One example of the effect this had must suffice. Len Johnson was born in Manchester in 1902, the son of Bill Johnson, a West African seaman, who had married a local white girl, and Len boxed from 1921 until 1933. Black boxers' careers are difficult to trace because only champions find a place in the record books. Fortunately, the late Denis Fleming did the necessary research for his splendid book *The Manchester Fighters* published in 1986. Len had 116 professional contests, and won 86 of them. In his prime, around the age of 25, Johnson was probably the best welterweight in Europe when he outpointed Len Harvey over 20 rounds at the Ring, Blackfriars; yet the rematch at the Albert Hall five years later was denied the status of a British championship contest, though Harvey, by this time the champion, wanted this. The sporting press acquiesced, whilst boxing supporters' attitude towards the colour bar imposed by the British Boxing Board of Control is difficult to assess. The late Larry Gains, the black Canadian heavyweight, who chose to box out of Leicester during the 1930s, simply did not mention racial discrimination in this period in his thoughtful autobiography, *The Impossible Dream*, though the title of his book is significant. The British public had respected the quality of black boxers since Nova Scotia's George Dixon knocked out Birmingham's Nunc Wallace in 1890, and as they sat round their wireless sets in 1937 listening to Tommy Farr's gallant attempt to beat Joe Louis, one suspects national pride not racial prejudice got them out of their beds at 3 a.m.

Boxing has been the most popular sport with black people in the British Isles, though this hypothesis may be exaggerated by their singular ability to rise to the top at this sport rather than other national pastimes like cricket and football. Of the ten British title holders in December 1987 (two titles were vacant) four of them were black. At the same time there was not a single licensed black referee in British professional boxing. Since there are over 2,400,000 people in Britain of all ethnic minorities both facts are worth pondering. British boxers who are black usually have families from the West Indies, hence the success rate of this ethnic group at boxing, compared to the number in Britain's population which is perhaps 750,000, is remarkable.[41] Asian families in Britain have produced very few boxers in total, and no champions. West Indian-born boxers lacked a home-based professional boxing industry, and if as adults they chose this trade the obvious country to move to was the USA. Britain's successful black boxers, however, are usually sons of families who came from Guyana, St Lucia, Curaçao, Barbados and Jamaica during the 1950s to settle in places like Nottingham, Sheffield, Leicester, Leeds, Birmingham, and East London north and south of the river.[42] Arrival as immigrants and success a generation later at boxing represents a remarkable parallel between Jews from Central Europe and, seventy years later, West Indians. Both waves of newcomers came from countries without a strong boxing culture, settled where there was one, and adopted it. If the production of outstanding sportspeople gives any guide to levels of participation amongst the general citizenry, then West Indians may well have been effectively screened from English cricket and from following their national game. Central European Jewry had no national sport and they moved, unlike West Indians, into all the spaces in professional boxing (promoting, managing, training); there never has been the equivalent of Premierland for black boxers. In Table 1 Honeygan, Hope, Andries and McKenzie are the black boxers from West Indian families who should be analysed alongside Berg and Lewis, the Jewish sportsmen. All six, it should be noted, lived in London, the chief marketplace of British professional boxing.

In the twentieth century the boxing industry has had periods of high activity, heightened public interest, and success in producing splendid champions and contenders, between troughs when the native sport seemed languid. General interest going beyond regular spectators was most stirred by heavy and middleweight boxers, thus Table 1 gives almost no guide to boxing's trade cycle. Boxing activity rose with promoters' profits, yet the correlation with gross national product is not close, and the nexus between rising living standards in the late 1880s and the making of the industry was not observable later. Professional boxing peaked in the years 1910–19, 1929–39, 1947–51, and 1980–7. The first period was most closely associated with Welsh boxers, such as Johnny Basham, Jim Driscoll and Jimmy Wilde,[43] and the heavyweights Billy Wells and Joe Beckett from Southampton. The second period belonged to Glasgow, through flyweight Benny Lynch, and to Manchester through manager Harry Fleming's stable, which included Jackie Brown and the Rochdale middleweight, Jock McAvoy.[44] The third period revolved around promoter Jack Solomons and three English boxers, Bruce Woodcock, of Doncaster, Freddy Mills and Randolph Turpin. The last named was the brother of the first coloured man to hold a British boxing title, and when Randy outpointed Sugar Ray Robinson at Earls Court, he beat an awesome opponent in the black middleweight from Detroit. Woodcock, Mills and Turpin illustrate three routes which were then common in British boxing. The Yorkshireman started off by winning the amateur light-heavyweight championship in 1939; Mills polished his skills between 1937 and 1939 working for two West Country boxing booths; and Turpin underlines the importance of family tradition in boxing.[45] The latest boxing boom might almost be claimed for Belfast through Eastwood, McGuigan, and the Larne waiter, flyweight Dave McAuley, who was literally one punch away from the world's championship in April 1987.[46] This would be unfair to Terry Lawless (the most remarkable manager since Fleming) whose boxers have included Magri, Watt, Stracey and Hope from Table 1, and heavyweight Frank

3.4 Alf Weston's boxing academy at Newbury fairground in 1954. The boxing booth produced innumerable champions including Joe Bowker and Jimmy Wilde. So popular was this mixture of sport and one-sided pushovers in the 1930s, that at some fairs there were two boxing booths. The non-serious state of the proceedings, which can be detected in the spectators' faces, suggests that theatre outweighed sporting considerations. For an insider's analysis of this contradiction see Harry Legge, *A Penny a Punch* (Christchurch, Dorset, 1981)

Bruno. Boxing perhaps more than any other sport tends to produce national heroes, mostly heavyweights who have fought international opponents. British and Irish heavyweights invariably lose, yet they gain enormous attention, and in some cases great public affection.

Bombardier Billy Wells' career coincided with the commercialising of British boxing. He twice lost to the gifted and popular French boxer Georges Carpentier, yet the press continually wrote about him, using still then action photographs. He made a comedy one-reel film, and when he was matched against an American, in 1915, the London Opera House was packed to capacity. 'Look out Billy'[47] yelled a voice from the gallery, for Frank Moran telegraphed his punches, yet Wells succumbed in the tenth round. Whether Wells won or lost made no difference to his personal following between 1910 and 1922. The popular weekly magazine *Answers* ran his 'My life and fights' continuously from May 1914 until March 1915; and in 1920 *Thomson's Weekly News* carried a freshly written autobiography in 41 instalments. His hardback book, *Modern Boxing* (1913?), reached seven editions, and when the boys' magazine *The Rocket* issued a set of eleven photographs in 1923 called 'Famous Knock-Outs', at least four were of Billy Wells, though, rather unkindly, in three he was on the floor. Wells's ups and downs made news as boxing became a national entertainment.

The world of boxing had become dull when Cassius Clay woke it up. The Rome Olympics' winner had turned professional and won 18 contests (in the USA) when he was matched, in 1963, with the British champion at Wembley. In the picturesque language of the sport, Henry Cooper was 'a bleeder', and his face was badly cut when the contest was stopped by the referee. In the round previously, however, Henry had scored with a strong left hook which knocked his opponent off his feet. Through television this punch has become the best known in British boxing history. The likeable 29-year-old champion, who had won ABA titles ten years earlier, happened to have floored the man who, as Muhammad Ali, became one of the best-known men in the world. Cooper gradually became the most popular UK boxer since Bombardier Billy Wells, and Cooper's popularity has lasted longer.

CONCLUSION

Brian London took on Patterson and then came out, unaccountably, for more of the same medicine from Ali – and then got the train back to Blackpool uttering the immortal line 'I'm only a prawn in this game.' Not many boxers have been so realistic when the hype gets going ... Richard Dunn also took on Ali. It did not last long. The Yorkshireman wore his pink Parachute Regiment trunks, and soon fluttered down to terra firma. After the fight I went up to commiserate; Richard was tucked up in bed, looking none the worse for wear, and reading *A Bridge Too Far*.

Frank Keating on 'Bruno flat out to defy tradition' in the *Guardian*, 19 July 1986

The significant changes in domestic boxing over three generations can be summarised briefly. Boxing technique has altered. Before the First World War the American style was rare and disliked, yet it has gradually become standard practice. Professional top-of-the-bill contests have become shorter. Matches of 20 rounds ceased to be made from the late 1920s, and the classical distance became five rounds shorter for over half a century; now the maximum is 12 rounds, and this has recently been endorsed by the High Court. Boxing has certainly speeded up, and boxers are probably fitter than they used to be. Whilst this judgement cannot be measured, video recordings of Tommy Milligan in 1927 and Alan Minter in 1981 provide sufficient evidence for this writer. Medical inspections, seriously

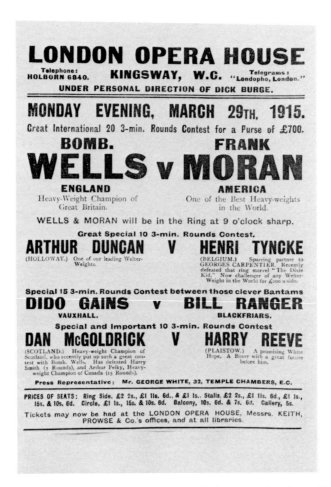

3.5 The London Opera House was built in 1911 for Oscar Hammerstein with seating for 2,660 people. It was only occasionally used for boxing, and became the Stoll Picture Theatre in 1919. Moran beat Wells. *Boxing* reported 'The Opera House was crowded to its utmost capacity, and there were more ladies present than we ever remember . . . In fact, the fair sex were (*sic*) almost as well represented as the Khaki-coloured element . . .' In the previous month Wells had boxed at Plymouth and Belfast and he was subject to some criticism for not having rejoined the army

undertaken since the introduction of brain scans and the death of Welshman Johnny Owen (in Los Angeles in 1980), have probably ensured that boxers with detached retinas and similar boxing injuries are not allowed to compete as they regularly used to be. Boxers box much less frequently since the twice-weekly hall closed its doors, or was bombed out, during the Second World War. The equalisation of food intake between social classes; school milk which was free, orange juice for expectant mothers, a buoyant labour market, brought an end to malnutrition in the 1940s, and this began to decimate the ranks of flyweight boxers. Senior amateur competitions for men weighing up to eight stones usually became walkovers, and active professional flyweight boxers in the UK now add up to eight, a number probably exceeded in 1938 from the Gorbals district of Glasgow on its own.

The earnings of boxers are surrounded in mystery. The vast majority (preliminary boxers) would work at another job, and, for example, in the 1920s, pick up £1.50 for a win (£1 if they lost) for a six-rounds, small hall contest.[48] In 1927 a skilled engineer's wages for a week's work plain time was £3 in London, and slightly less elsewhere.[49] In this year promoter Cochran paid Scotland's Tommy Milligan £3,000 to box the American Micky Walker at Olympia.[50] This tremendous disparity in earnings has always been a feature of the sport. The lowest price for a ticket to a boxing show has been remarkably consistent. From sixpence (2½p) to £7.50 has usually represented approximately 4 per cent of a male industrial worker's average weekly wage, and a night's boxing presently costs slightly more than standing on the terraces at a first division football match.

Boxing spectators have changed more than the boxers since 1900. My argument is that young, unskilled male workers made boxing part of the entertainment industry by regularly attending small halls around the country in the years after 1890.[51] The broadcasting of radio commentaries on boxing from 1927 widened public interest and W. Barrington Dalby became a national name ('come in Barry') simply through his expert between-rounds' summaries of how the contest was going.[52] In 1951 the Turpin–Robinson match was shown on television on the following evening,[53] and this practice grew without noticeably affecting the numbers of actual spectators. These declined substantially in the 1960s and 1970s, closing small hall boxing almost throughout the country, because of consumerism. Teenage boys bought guitars and enjoyed playing recordings of popular music as well as, or more than, the rigours of training for amateur boxing; and pop music concerts drew larger audiences than top professional boxing shows. Boxing in both forms returned to favour in the 1980s when the real spending power of young labour was reduced and unemployment, particularly in inner cities, rose rapidly. The revival of boxing has been paralleled by the televising of boxing matches live, and this has had the effect of diminishing the importance of the spectators gathered in the arena. Fees for worldwide television broadcasts have the potential to dwarf ticket sales, and did so as early as 1974 when Muhammad Ali regained the heavyweight championship of the world from George Foreman in a contest staged at Kinshasa in Zaire. In Britain the effect of millions watching boxing in their homes has been to widen the social class of the audience.[54] Its presentation by this means, however, contains two serious faults. First, as Roland Barthes wrote, a 'boxing match is a story which is constructed before the eyes of the spectator', it has a flow of action which shapes the whole,[55] and the perpetual editing of contests, both amateur and professional which are not shown live, has trivialised the sport. Such commercial packaging ruins the story and almost eliminates pure endeavour, an important element in the history of boxing. Secondly, the producers of boxing on television love a winner and abhor a loser, a feeling which has never been natural within the boxing arena. Television has done away with the traditional cheer for the loser, and it promises to remove eventually all the subtleties in the ancient sport in favour of the aggressive strong man. Boxing has always had its 'Cast Iron' Jack Caseys,[56] but found greater admiration for ring artists. Television sells boxing with power as the magic ingredient, and it sells the sport short on skill and tactics. To use a metaphor, the televised boxer seldom picks the lock, he charges down the door. Television encourages boxers to drop craft because producers assume that viewers prefer knockdowns, and the machine in the living room has had a recent tendency to reduce the artistry in boxing.[57]

Amateur boxing in Britain has changed very little. When the first Olympic Games including boxing were held in London in 1908 we supplied most of the entrants and won all the titles. Since then the rest of the world has joined in with this popular activity which organisationally dates from 1880, when the ABA was founded and allowed working-class boxers to compete. Throughout the twentieth century Britain and Ireland have contained a strong amateur boxing culture which produces sound boxers for ever more challenging international competitions. One doubts whether domestic amateur boxing has ever been fitter, though such speculation is best left to the reader.

The development of professional boxing in Britain has been considerably more complicated, and the changes wrought come largely from outside agencies. Boxing as a job has always appealed to manual workers. As miners, market porters, tailors' pressers and the like have become a smaller proportion of the labour force the number of professional boxers has shrunk. Boxing has remained a working-class sport. The growth of alternative forms of entertainment (greyhound racing, cinema, television) reduced boxing shows at local halls because they became unprofitable. The profitability of dance halls in the 1930s and 1940s suggests that masculine recreations were perhaps losing their hold. Suburbanisation and private motor cars have extended the boxing supporters' range, yet the sport has tenaciously claimed a sense of place. Boxers have always been seen as coming from

3.6 Welterweight M. Lloyd of Northolt Boxing Club during the Northwest London division of the ABA championships at the Municipal Hall, Tottenham, on 11 February 1988. He had just beaten P. Quarrie, of Islington, but lost the final to F. Finn of the All-Stars. Photographer: Bill Shipley

a working-class community. The boxers are still so billed; whether the community remains is another matter.

NOTES

1 *Professional Boxing: Hearings before the Subcommittee on Administrative Practice and Procedure of the Committee on the Judiciary, United States Senate, Eighty-Sixth Congress, Second Session, Pursuant to S. Res. 234*, Washington, 1960; and *ibid., Part 2, Pursuant to S. Res. 238, Frank Carbo*, Washington, 1961. The two parts of this report, which followed two-and-a-half years of investigation into monopoly in professional boxing, ran to 1,247 pages.
2 Daniel Mendoza, *The Art of Boxing*, n.d. (1789), 95 pp.; Daniel Mendoza, *Memoirs of the Life of Daniel Mendoza* (1816), 320 pp. An edited version of

the second book was published in 1951 by Batsford. It has several excellent illustrations, some coloured, and a scholarly introduction by Paul Magriel.

3 P. G. Wodehouse, 'The schools at Aldershot', *Sandow's Magazine of Physical Culture*, vol. 6, January–June 1901, pp. 438–42. For a perceptive fictional account see the first few chapters of P. G. Wodehouse, *The Pothunters* (1924).

4 Hazlitt's essay 'The fight' appeared in *The New Monthly Magazine*, February 1822.

5 Henry Downes Miles, *Pugilistica: The History of British Boxing*, vol. 2 (Edinburgh 1906) pp. 104–37. Miles left the final 'e' off the Bristol man's surname. Miles's splendid three-volume history of prizefighting appeared first in numbers in the 1860s.

6 *Southwark Recorder*, 10 August 1889; Harry Preston, *Memories* (1928), p. 92; Sir Harry Preston, *Leaves from My Unwritten Diary*, n.d. (1936), pp. 150–1; R. P. Watson, *Memoirs of Robert Patrick Watson: A Journalist's Experience of Mixed Society*, n.d. (1899), p. 84.

7 *Sporting Mirror*, 11 October 1897.

8 The newspaper which catered for the Lillie Bridge sporting set was *The Sportsman*. It was a four-page, sporting newspaper, published in Fleet Street, price one penny. It was started in 1865 and discontinued in 1924. For the rules of the Cestus Boxing Club see Charles Dickens Jnr, *Dickens Dictionary of London*, n.d., pp. 40–1.

9 Newspaper reports of boxing matches were numerous. They were to be found in 1900 in two daily sporting newspapers, *Sporting Life* and *Sporting Chronicle* (Manchester); and the weeklies included *Referee* and *Mirror of Life*. In 1909 two weekly papers solely devoted to boxing were started, *Boxing* and *Boxing World*. *The Times* covered boxing from 1906, and the two newspapers associated with the beer trade, *Morning Advertiser* and *Licensed Victuallers' Gazette*, gave much space to boxing from the early 1890s.

10 O. F. Snelling, *A Bedside Book of Boxing* (1972), pp. 109–19; Charlie Rose, *Life's a Knock-out* (1953), p. 143; Gilbert E. Odd, *Ring Battles of the Century* (1949), pp. 35–45; Jack Solomons, *Jack Solomons Tells All* (1956), pp. 27–43, the author was Boon's manager.

11 ABA, *Report of the Council to be presented at the 44th AGM*, 1924. With many more entries the championships now occupy months of the season, and the semi-finals and finals are staged on separate evenings.

12 Jimmy Ingle, *The Jimmy Ingle Story* (Dingle, Co. Kerry 1984), pp. 45–6; Noel Carroll, *Sport in Ireland* (Dublin 1979).

13 ABA, *Report* (1939). I am indebted to Clive Howe, the Executive Director of the English ABA, for his warm welcome and for allowing me to inspect these *Annual Reports and Accounts*, which run from 1924 to date.

14 *Sporting Chronicle*, 8, 11 April 1903; *Sporting Life*, 8 April 1903; *Sandow's Magazine*, vol. 10, January–June 1903, pp. 314–18.

15 *Boxing*, 6 November, 4 December 1909.

16 For Jimmy McLarnin see Patrick Myler, *The Fighting Irish: Ireland's Role in World Boxing History* (Dingle, Co. Kerry 1987), pp. 91–5.

17 Ladies were 'specially invited' to an Assault-at-Arms in an advertisement in *The Sportsman*, 8 April 1893. There was a report of ladies attending 'in goodly numbers' the Public Schools' boxing championships in *The Sportsman*, 6 April

1895. For professional boxers as music hall attractions see, for example, *Mirror of Life*, 2 February 1895.

18 For the Colvestone Club's expulsion from the ABA in 1985 see *Hackney Gazette*, 30 April 1985; *Boxing News*, 10 May 1985.

19 Jimmy Ingle, *The Jimmy Ingle Story*, pp. 54–5.

20 'I realised that I was fighting before a much more expert audience than any in France at that time. These knowledgeable men . . . were not impressed easily.' *Carpentier by Himself* (1955), p. 44. Georges was recalling his first contest in England in October 1911 when at Earls Court, as a welterweight, he out-pointed Sid Burns.

21 Gilbert Odd, *Len Harvey: Prince of Boxers*, 1978, pp. 35–46; Charlie Rose, *Life's a Knock-out*, pp. 125–33; L. A. G. Strong, *Shake Hands and Come Out Fighting* (1953), pp. 232–4.

22 *Boxing*, 16 July 1919.

23 *Sporting Life*, 29 May, 9 October 1897.

24 Public Record Office, BT31 / 6470 / 45578; Diana Howard, *London Theatres and Music Halls 1850-1950*, 1979, pp. 75–6; *Vim Magazine*, no. 1, vol. 4, January 1905, pp. 9–13; *Sporting Chronicle*, 9 January 1901; *Sporting Life*, 9 April 1906; *Boxing*, 18 September 1909.

25 Leslie Bell, *Bella of Blackfriars*, 1961; *Boxing*, 19 January, 23 February 1916; *Thomson's Weekly News*, 21 August 1920.

26 *Ibid.*, 8 May 1920; *Mirror of Life*, 30 July, 13 August 1910; Eugene Corri, *Refereeing 1,000 Fights: Reminiscences of Boxing* (1919), p. 57; Denzil Batchelor, *Jack Johnson and His Times* (1957), pp. 61–2.

27 *Referee*, 15 January 1911.

28 *District Times*, 28 July 1911.

29 *Mirror of Life*, 30 July, 13 August 1910; *The Times*, 12, 16, 19, 21, 23, 27, 28 September 1911; Randy Roberts, *Papa Jack: Jack Johnson and the Era of White Hopes* (New York, 1983) pp. 126–9; Jack Johnson, *In the Ring and Out* (1977), p. 57; James Barr, 'Is the prize ring doomed?', *Red Magazine*, vol. 11, no. 66, pp. 725–32.

30 Charles B. Cochran, *Secrets of a Showman* (1925), pp. 189–93, 285–337; Cochran, *I had almost Forgotten . . .* (1932), pp. 151–82; Cochran, *Cock-a-doodle-do* (1941), pp. 215–26; Cochran, *Showman Looks On* (1945), pp. 263–78; Charles Graves, *The Cochran Story*, n.d., pp. 48–51, 74–82, 142–3. Promoters of major boxing shows between the Wars included Major Arnold Wilson, Jeff Dickson and Arthur Elvin.

31 *Boxing News Annual and Record Book, 1975*, pp. 6–77; *Boxing News*, 4 December 1987.

32 McGuigan lost his world title to Steve Cruz in June 1986, and his subsequent dispute with his manager / promoter Eastwood can be followed in *Irish Post*, 15 August 1987, 12 March 1988, *The Guardian*, 28 January, 3 March 1988, *The Observer*, 6 March 1988.

33 British Boxing Board of Control No. 1 Minutes Book covers the period 5 February 1914-13 September 1923. The Board has a wonderfully full archive from 1929 which I was kindly allowed to inspect.

34 The first Lord Lonsdale Challenge Belt was put round the waist of Freddie Welsh by the 5th Earl of Lonsdale (1857-1944) in 1909. The Pontypridd-born

boxer (1886–1927) became a professional in the USA, and learnt the trade in Philadelphia. The occasion was when he outpointed Middlesbrough-born Johnny Summers, who boxed out of Canning Town, over 20 rounds at the National Sporting Club for the British lightweight title.

35 Guy Deghy, *Noble and Manly* (1956); A. F. Bettinson and W. Outram Tristram, *The National Sporting Club* (1902); A. F. Bettinson and Ben Bennison, *Home of Boxing* (1922); Bernard John Angle, *My Sporting Memories* (1925), pp. 87–120; Norman Clark, *All in the Game* (1935), pp. 192–241; Douglas Sutherland, *The Yellow Earl* (1965), pp. 170–7.

36 Harry Preston, *Memories* (1928), pp. 122–6; Sir Harry Preston, *Leaves*, pp. 240–4. Kenworthy joined the Labour Party in 1926, the year after the abortive plan to legislate for boxing.

37 Patrick Myler, *Fighting Irish*, pp. 97–103; Joe Palmer, *Recollections of a Boxing Referee* (1927), pp. 231–5. *Waltham Forest Extra*, 12 January, 2 February 1988; *The Guardian*, 13 February 1988, for unlicensed Bobby Frankham's shows being cancelled.

38 Herbert G. Goldman (ed.), *1984 Ring Record Book and Boxing Encyclopedia* (New York City, 1984), p. 46.

39 Alf Bowman belonged to the Jewish Working Men's Club and Institute, and the Royal Victor Athletic Club which specialised in boxing. Both clubs were in the East End of London. Bowman turned professional and boxed locally as well as at the National Sporting Club. ABA Minute Book No. 2, 10 February 1899, 25 February 1901; *Referee*, 7 April, 1 December 1889; *Sporting Life*, 5 April 1892; Harold Pollins, *A History of the Jewish Working Men's Club and Institute* (Oxford, 1981), p. 23.

40 *Boxing*, 7 June 1922; Fred Dartnell, *Seconds Out*, n.d. (1924), pp. 204–6; Louis Behr, 'Boxing memories', *East London Record*, no. 5, 1982, pp. 34–6; Norman Clark, *All in the Game*, pp. 216, 304–6; James Butler, *Kings of the Ring*, n.d. (1936), pp. 219–25; Joe Jacobs, *Out of the Ghetto* (1978), p. 39; Jack Goodwin, *Myself and My Boxers* (1924), pp. 239–41; Hedley Trembath (ed.), *British Sport*, n.d. (1947), p. 89; Robert Barltrop, *Bright Summer – Dark Autumn* (1986), p. 31–2; Nat Fleischer (ed.), *1968 Ring Boxing Encyclopedia and Record Book* (New York City, 1968), pp. 258–9; John Harding, *Jack Kid Berg: The Whitechapel Windmill* (1987), 256 pp.

41 Central Statistical Office, *Social Trends 18* (1988), p. 26; *Boxing News*, 4 December 1987.

42 Black men and women are now achieving similar success in track and field athletics.

43 Dai Smith, 'Champions of a fighting cause', *The Listener*, 15 October 1987; Joe Palmer, *Recollections* (1927), pp. 56–63, 91–102; Jim Driscoll, *The Straight Left*, 6th edn, n.d.; 'Boxing', Handbooks no. 3, *Favourite Ring Tricks of Champions*, n.d. (1913?); Jimmy Wilde, *The Art of Boxing*, n.d. (1923?); O. F. Snelling, *Bedside Book of Boxing* (1972), pp. 197–9; Charles Platt, *Famous Fights and Fighters*, n.d. (1920?), pp. 183–8; Alexander Cordell, *Peerless Jim* (1984). Freddie Welsh wrote articles for the weekly paper *Boxing* (see issues dated 5 October 1912, 20 September 1913), yet the boxing scenario is best enjoyed by reading Chas. A. Barnett's regular column in the same paper 'News from South Wales'.

44 Denis Fleming, *The Manchester Fighters* (Manchester, 1986). The tragic story of Benny Lynch who beat the best, then died of drink and self-neglect in his early thirties, is well described in John Macadam, *The Macadam Road* (1957), pp. 148–51. Other sources for the second period are: Gilbert E. Odd, *Ring Battles of the Century* (1949), pp. 24–34, 234–43; R. A. Haldane, *Champions and Challengers* (1967), pp. 138–9, 149–51; 216–22; Hedley Trembath, *British Sport*, pp. 99, 172. Other cities, of course, also produced great boxers, for example, Liverpool had Nel Tarleton, and Belfast, Tommy Armour.

45 Bruce Woodcock, *Two Fists – and a Fortune* (1951); Freddie Mills, *Twenty Years: An Autobiography* (1950); Ted Broadribb, *Fighting is My Life*, n.d., pp. 102–23, Broadribb was Mills's manager; Freddie Mills, *Battling for a Title* (1954); *Jack Solomons Tells All*, pp. 52–191; Denzil Batchelor, *Big Fight* (1955), pp. 214–24; Charlie Rose, *Life's a Knock-out*, pp. 190–200; Maurice Smith (ed.), *'The People' Boxing Guide* (1950), pp. 2–13, 30–3.

46 *Boxing News*, 15 May 1987.

47 *Boxing*, 31 March 1915; *The Bioscope*, 26 December 1912, p. 1003.

48 Interview with Teddy Reeder at Woodford Green on 29 October 1983. Tape in possession of the author who conducted the interview. Teddy Reeder boxed professionally from 1928 at places like Premierland and Ipswich Baths. He once earned £10 at Aston in Birmingham, when he topped the bill against Tom Cartwright.

49 Wal Hannington, *The Rights of Engineers* (1944), pp. 24–5.

50 Charles B. Cochran, *I had almost Forgotten . . .* (1932), p. 166.

51 Stan Shipley, *The Boxer as Hero: Social Class, Community and Sport in Late-Victorian London* (forthcoming).

52 O. F. Snelling, *A Bedside Book of Boxing*, pp. 24–5.

53 Leslie Bell, *Inside the Fight Game* (1952), p. 166.

54 Steve Grant, 'Ring Swing', *Time Out*, 10–17 June 1987.

55 Roland Barthes, *Mythologies* (1976), pp. 15–25.

56 Edith Summerskill, *The Ignoble Art* (1956), p. 42.

57 I am not suggesting that contemporary boxing is less skilled than it used to be, only that the greater emphasis given by television to power allows boxers less room for artistry. For example, a defensively inclined boxer like Sheffield's Herol Graham changed his style to suit the cameras (*The Guardian*, 27 May 1987; *Daily Mail* and *Daily News*, *ibid.*) because this enhanced his world title ambitions. Graham lost to Italian-based, Zaire-born Sumbu Kalambay as it happened.

4 CRICKET

JACK WILLIAMS

I

> I think that the deficiency of good amateur players is the crucial defect of our cricket.
>
> Lord Hawke speaking in 1921

Throughout the twentieth century cricket has been inseparably intertwined with the class system and its history does much to make clear the changing nuances of social relationships within Britain. Until 1968 control of first-class cricket[1] in the United Kingdom was shared between the Marylebone Cricket Club and those county clubs that contested the County Championship, though the MCC was the more powerful member of this partnership. Founded in 1787 and owner of Lord's cricket ground, the MCC remains an all-male private club with the privilege of framing the game's laws. It selected players and officials for overseas tours on which England played test matches and represented England on the Imperial Cricket Conference (after 1965, the International Cricket Conference) which arranged test matches and other matters between cricket-playing nations. The County Championship, the sole major domestic first-class cricket competition before 1963, was regulated by the Advisory County Cricket Committee, which first met in 1904 and on which all first-class counties had representatives but the chair at its meetings was usually taken by the MCC president and the MCC could veto its recommendations, though this hardly ever happened. The first-class counties had more representatives than the MCC upon the Board of Control, established in 1898, the body responsible for test matches played in England.

Descriptive evidence shows a close association between the MCC and the elite of British society. MCC membership has been an eagerly sought mark of social distinction. A requirement that only existing members may propose the addition of names to the waiting list of candidates for membership can be interpreted as a device for maintaining the club's social exclusiveness. Members numbered around 4,000 in 1900, over 7,000 in 1945 and above 18,000 by the 1980s but unfortunately there has been little empirical research into whether the social background of members has broadened. In 1925 16,000 names were on the waiting list and 9,000 in 1987, but membership can be granted more quickly to those with cricketing ability. Since 1945 the MCC committee has tended to become chosen from a wider social spectrum, though these changes have not been dramatic and the committee is still one of economic and social privilege. During the first half of this century committee members were usually aristocrats and senior military officers with a fair sprinkling of wealthy professional men and businessmen. In the 1950s Lord Monckton, a Conservative minister, said that beside the MCC committee Macmillan's cabinet was 'a band of pinkos'.[2] In 1980 the committee contained only one aristocrat but also a former professional cricketer. Most of the 1980 committee had attended private schools and played first-class cricket as amateurs. The individuals who appear to have exercised most influence with the MCC all belonged to the social elite. The six secretaries between 1898 and 1986 were all products of public schools as were the seven treasurers between 1916 and 1980, who included such dominant figures as Lord Harris (Eton), Lord Hawke (Eton), H. S. Altham (Repton) and G. O. Allen (Eton).

Like the MCC first-class counties have remained members' clubs, controlled in theory by executive committees elected by members at annual meetings, though only a small proportion usually attend these. Samples of Yorkshire members in 1919, 1926 and 1940 from around Sheffield, perhaps too few to be representative of members in general, included owners and managers of businesses, professional men and financiers but by 1940 the numbers of teachers and shop-keepers had increased. No blue-collar workers were found in the samples. At most counties, subscriptions of a guinea before 1914 and up to two guineas between the Wars were probably prohibitively expensive for working men whilst appeals for new members were usually addressed to 'gentlemen'. Indeed, it was often stressed that membership of a county club was obligatory for 'gentlemen'. Throughout the twentieth century wide variations existed between the numbers of members at different counties. In 1982 Lancashire and Yorkshire each had more than 11,000 but Derbyshire, Gloucestershire, Northamptonshire and Worcestershire all had below 3,000. At most counties the number of members remained more or less constant between 1900 and 1914, doubled between the Wars and doubled again between 1945 and the early 1960s but then declined. By 1963 members totalled 135,000, just under 100,000 in 1974 and 95,000 in 1980. The real value of subscriptions was lower in the 1960s and 1970s, yet whether the social profile of members changed is unclear.

Annual reports of county clubs indicate that county committees in the first half of this century included landed aristocrats, country gentlemen,

4.1 Lord's and privilege. The Eton and Harrow match remained an important part of the Season well into this century as this interval promenade in 1934 clearly shows

professional and businessmen. During the 1960s and 1970s successful businessmen emerged as the dominant personalities at some clubs and though it is uncertain whether significant shifts were occurring in the social composition of county committees, Keith Sandiford has demonstrated that since the early 1960s management of county clubs became more businesslike in the commercial presentation of cricket.[3] For much of the twentieth century it would appear that those controlling county clubs had backgrounds similar to those who dominated the MCC and shared their opinions about how cricket should be played and administered. Most leading personalities within the MCC were also influential figures at county clubs. No doubt it appeared natural that those exercising political and social leadership in other spheres should control cricket.[4]

Since 1968 the MCC's influence over first-class cricket has diminished whilst that of the county clubs has grown. In 1968 the creation of the Cricket Council, established partly to facilitate financial assistance from the Sports Council, transformed cricket's structure of authority. Initially power within the Cricket Council was shared equally between the MCC, the National Cricket Association, set up in 1963 to further non-first-class and recreational cricket, and a new body, the Test and County Cricket Board which absorbed the Board of Control and the ACCC and was dominated by the first-class counties. In 1983 the TCCB was given eight votes on the Cricket Council, the NCA five and the MCC three. This rise of the TCCB coincided with control of cricket becoming less socially exclusive. Though all chairmen of the MCC and the Cricket Council after 1968 had been educated at public schools, a significant minority of those serving on TCCB sub-committees had been professional cricketers,[5] but possibly this reflected growing recognition within society of professional expertise. Unlike in Australia, the Packer affair during the late 1970s did not result in the promotion of a rival form of first-class cricket but moves by the TCCB to ban from county cricket those who played for Packer were defeated in the courts.

Biographies of cricketers and Michael Marshall's conversations[6] with retired cricketers indicate that for much of this century first-class cricket was riddled with social distinctions. Until 1963 first-class cricketers were divided into Gentlemen, or amateurs who were not supposed to receive money for playing, and Players or professionals who played for cash. Some professionals had middle-class backgrounds, but the overwhelming majority were working-class though it is not certain what sections within this class produced the greatest proportion and whether this varied over time or between regions. Most amateurs had relatively privileged backgrounds. Obituaries for those killed in the World Wars show that almost all were officers and had attended private schools. In 1900 and 1920 nearly 40 per cent of all appearances in County Championship matches were by amateurs, 30 per cent in 1910 and around 20 per cent in 1930 and 1939 but by the 1950s the proportion had fallen to between 10 and 15 per cent. Until the 1930s the numbers of amateurs varied enormously between counties. Nottinghamshire and Yorkshire rarely played more than one amateur but in 1920 Middlesex, who won the County Championship, played only four professionals, Somerset two and Worcestershire six over the whole season.

The status of professionals was inferior to that of Gentlemen. Except at Leicestershire in 1935, captains of county sides before 1939 were amateurs though in emergencies senior professionals could lead sides and amateur captains whose playing skills scarcely merited a regular place in a county side were not uncommon. By 1963 only three counties had not appointed professional captains. In 1952 Hutton became England's first professional captain since the 1880s. Until 1939 most grounds had separate dressing rooms for amateurs and professionals, though in 1926 England's amateurs and professionals began sharing entrances to the field of play and the same dressing room. Before the Second World War professionals were usually expected to address amateurs as Sir or Mr. How far these social distinctions were resented is unclear. In the 1920s Fred Root, the Worcestershire fast bowler, complained of them but Surrey's senior professionals wished to retain separate dressing rooms and until 1939 class distinctions within cricket were probably typical of those found in other walks of life.

Marshall's *Gentlemen and Players* reveals rising bitterness among professionals about shamateurism in the late 1950s. Precise measurements of shamateurism are impossible but in the 1930s Arthur Carr, an amateur captain of Nottinghamshire and England, claimed that some amateurs received up to £500 in expenses[7] when the recommended maximum annual wage for county professionals was £440[8] and leading amateurs have admitted that in the 1950s appointments as assistant county secretaries or assistant treasurers were lucrative fiddles which allowed them to play as amateurs. Scrapping the amateur/professional distinction seems to have resulted from growing unease over shamateurism, a sense that such distinctions had become anachronistic and perhaps more importantly the hope that allowing those with privileged backgrounds to receive payment would encourage them to pursue cricket as a career. This hope was partially realised. In 1983 15 per cent of those who played at least ten county matches had attended a public school or Oxbridge but this could reflect the continuing high quality of facilities and coaching at private schools which had long equipped so many amateurs to play first-class cricket, and the decline of cricket as a school sport in public sector education.

The survival of an amateur/professional divide until 1963 was related to cricket's structure of authority. It seems likely that the domination of so many aspects of British life by the elite who controlled cricket led to an assumption that amateurs should exercise authority in cricket sides. Having amateur captains was often justified on the grounds that professionals would be reluctant to discipline fellow professionals, or that the Gentlemen versus Players matches had shown professional captains to be tactically unadventurous, but the achievements of professional captains in the 1950s undermined the plausibility of such arguments. It was also contended that amateur batsmen could afford to play in a less inhibited style with greater spectator appeal than professionals, whose livelihoods depended upon developing defensive techniques on which reliable performances could be built, but in the 1950s leading amateurs such as Bailey and Cowdrey could be just as determined and defensive as professionals.

II

Cricketers do not expect anyone to watch three-day games. They do not really *want* anyone to watch. To a cricketer, the longer game is the only serious test of his skill . . . In one-day games, batsmen are as homogeneous as tins of baked beans.

       Peter Roebuck, of Somerset, *Sunday Times*, 22 September 1985

Assessments of cricket's role within popular culture have to consider its appeal as a spectator sport. After 1952 the MCC collated statistics of attendances at first-class matches but although archives of county clubs contain materials about gate receipts, no study has drawn these together though Wray Vamplew and Keith Sandiford have demonstrated that in the Edwardian period, often called cricket's 'Golden Age', county cricket was not attracting sufficient spectators to be financially self-supporting.[9] Fragmentary data suggest that attendances were higher in the early and mid-1920s than just before the First World War, but a decline in the 1930s caused several counties financial embarrassment. In the late 1940s seasonal attendances of around two million for county matches were probably the twentieth-century peak but fell to 580,000 by 1963. However, these figures for both dates ignore members whose subscriptions granted free admission to matches. By 1980 just over 600,000 paid to watch all forms of county cricket but only 160,000 attended County Championship games although the programme of these matches was a quarter less than in 1963. Until the 1960s the numbers of paying spectators attending home matches of different counties differed enormously though attendances moved in more or less the same direction at all counties throughout the twentieth century. In 1925, 326,000 paid to watch Yorkshire's home matches, the county's highest inter-war attendances, and nearly 183,000 in 1935, whilst those for Essex in the same seasons almost certainly did not exceed 40,000 and 22,000.[10]

Not even crude estimates of the number watching non-first-class cricket are available but possibly spectators at club matches exceeded those for county cricket in the 1920s. Attendances in the Lancashire League, whose clubs were situated within 20 miles of Blackburn but which was only one of several leagues in the county, surpassed 35,000 in 1921 and 300,000 in 1922. In Yorkshire, Bradford League matches attracted 225,000 in 1921 and crowds of between 2,000 and 4,000 were common in the First Division, and occasionally the Second Division, of the South Wales and Monmouthshire Cricket Association during the late 1920s and 1930s.[11] Numbers of spectators at league matches around Bolton fluctuated more or less in step with those of county clubs, reaching peaks in the early 1920s and late 1940s. In 1921 probably at least 100,000 watched league matches in the

4.2 Photographers and spectators watching England v. Australia in 1938 from outside the Oval. In 1926 one householder who charged for viewing cricket from her balcony was prosecuted for failing to pay entertainment tax on her takings

Bolton area but by the 1970s spectators were so few that often no admission charges were made, a trend also found in the Birmingham League.

In 1965–6 a social survey found that 14 per cent of males over sixteen and 4 per cent of females in England and Wales watched a match at some level at least once a month but another in 1977 produced figures of 2.8 per cent and 1.3 per cent. Both showed that among most social groups cricket was the second or third most popular spectator sport although in 1977 only just above 6 per cent of all sports spectators watched cricket. In 1977 over half of all cricket spectators were aged over 45 and two-thirds belonged to social classes I, II and III.[12]

Michael Down has argued convincingly that more widely dispersed affluence led to smaller attendances at county cricket after the early 1950s by adding to the range of counter-attractions, but economic change alone does not provide a totally satisfactory explanation for fluctuations in the numbers of spectators during other periods of this century. At most counties, attendances fell during the depression of the early 1930s but declined even more sharply during the economic recovery of the late 1930s. Peak attendances following the World Wars are often attributed to reactions against wartime cessation of sport and after 1945 to a desire for excitement in a period of austerity but full employment. Higher attendances for one-day matches in the 1960s and 1970s showed that a faster tempo of play and the obtaining of a definite result were more attractive than traditional three-day matches. Multiple regression analysis of gate receipts for Sunday League matches in 1976 and 1977 emphasised that playing success, the point in a season when a match was played, weather and population base could attract spectators whilst admission costs within limits, television coverage and the appearance of international players except 'superstars' had little impact.[13] In all periods it would appear that playing success, fine weather and location within densely populated conurbations stimulated attendances. The buoyancy of test match attendances may be associated with greater media coverage and the presence of so many well-known players.

Apologists for cricket stress that interest in the game has always been greater than attendances at matches indicate. An opinion poll in 1966 showed that 39 per cent of males over sixteen were interested in cricket, a proportion exceeded only by soccer and boxing but the nature of this 'interest' was not defined.[14] More books on cricket have been published than for any other sport. The 1984 edition of Padwick's *A Bibliography of Cricket* listed more than 5,000 titles dealing with cricket in Britain and this excluded articles in periodicals. Such a reading public for cricket may reflect the game's 'middle-class' connections though all levels of the press report cricket extensively. In the 1970s more cricket was televised live than any other team sport but the small amount of cricket broadcast by commercial television casts doubts upon its mass appeal. Variations in the availability of the telephone cricket score service undermine this as a guide to interest in cricket but 5 million calls were made during one test match in 1977.

The financing of county cricket was revolutionised in the 1960s and 1970s. Membership subscriptions and gate receipts were the major sources of revenue until the 1950s but the relationship between them varied over time and between counties. Their inadequacies caused acute financial embarrassment just before the First World War when Gloucestershire, Northamptonshire and Worcestershire considered withdrawing from the County Championship and a crisis of less severe proportions occurred in the late 1930s. Some counties enjoyed generous assistance from aristocrats or other wealthy patrons but the scale and need for such help are unclear, though it could have been vital for a county such as Worcestershire which received £2,000 from Lord Cobham between 1908 and 1913[15] and whose regular income after being admitted to the County Championship in 1899 did not exceed expenditure until 1934. In the 1950s the rise of supporters' clubs and the organisation of football pools created alternative sources of income. Warwickshire's pool, the most successful, raised £2,000,000 between 1953 and 1972.[16] The distribution of test match profits and fees for televising them were also making vital contributions to the finances of county clubs and the increasing number of test matches played in the 1960s and 1970s can be seen as attempts to maximise these forms of revenue. By 1983 test match profits constituted 35 per cent of county clubs' total revenue.[17]

The stimulus for the introduction of the first one-day limited overs cricket competition, the Gillette Cup in 1963, was declining gate receipts at three-day matches. The greater spectator appeal of one-day matches led to the growth of this form of cricket. The Sunday League started in 1969 and the Benson and Hedges Cup in 1972. England first played one-day internationals in 1972 and World Cup competitions were held in England in 1975, 1979 and 1983. This expansion of one-day cricket caused the programme of three-day matches to be reduced by a quarter but the attraction of limited overs cricket meant that by 1980 the numbers watching one- and three-day county matches exceeded those who had watched the larger programme of three-day matches in 1963. Despite its financial advantages, one-day cricket has been blamed for hastening the decline of spin bowling and encouraging reckless batting, though higher standards of physical fitness and improved outfielding are listed among its benefits. Critics of the one-day game argue that its popularity represents a preference for an inferior form of cricket.

All the one-day competitions have always had sponsorship though that for the Gillette Cup in 1963 was only £6,500.[18] By 1978 £175,000 was paid to sponsor test matches, £175,000 the County Championship, £175,000 the Benson and Hedges Cup, £100,000 the Gillette Cup and £250,000 the World Cup.[19] As all but one of these competitions were televised, such sponsorship could be called indirect television advertising. In the 1970s county clubs made great efforts to present their facilities as locations where businessmen could entertain clients and by the 1980s sponsors for individual matches and equipment were providing nearly a fifth of the counties' total revenue. By becoming an adjunct of advertising, cricket had reached an accommodation with, and indeed become dependent upon, the consumer capitalism that had deprived the game of so many of its paying spectators. Yet although county clubs had become more attuned to market forces by 1980, they did not become fully commercialised. All remained members' clubs with the maintenance of a successful side being their major priority. Poor playing results rather than finance created animosity at annual meetings.

In the late 1970s the more commercialised ambience of first-class cricket saw earnings of leading cricketers rise but this was further encouraged by the need to offer higher rewards as a counter to those presented by Kerry Packer's rival version of first-class cricket and by the rise of the Cricketers' Association, a trade union for county cricketers established in 1968. In 1963 England test players received £100 per match plus expenses, perhaps less in real terms than the £27. 10s. plus rail fares paid in 1924.[20] In 1976 test pay became £200, £1,200 in 1979 and £1,400 in 1980. Salaries for run-of-the-mill county players rose less spectacularly though winning bonuses and higher pay for capped players make it difficult to determine when average real wages were lowest. In the 1890s professionals in London earned up to £2 per week but this could be doubled by tips from members for net practice bowling. The MCC paid £3. 10s. for home and £5 for away matches but not living expenses. Surrey paid winter retainers of between £1 and £1. 10s.[21] The agreed maximum wage for a county professional between the Wars was £440 but in 1933 and 1935 only two Essex professionals received over £400 and none in 1934. In 1974 Essex were paying players with three years' capped service £1,600 but match bonuses could be added to this.[22] By 1982 Middlesex players were considered the best paid with salaries between £6,500 and £8,500 but perks and expenses brought these to around £10,000 and £12,000.[23] In the 1980s it would appear that most county cricketers worked during winter with playing or coaching overseas being the most common occupation.

Benefits may have added to the attractions of playing county cricket but for much of this century professionals had no automatic entitlement to a benefit and the value of benefits differed considerably between counties. In 1953 Godfrey Evans, perhaps England's greatest wicket-keeper, received a benefit of £5,259, then a record for Kent, but John Ikin of Lancashire, at best a moderately successful test cricketer, received £7,175. In the late 1970s the value of benefits rose spectacularly. At Lancashire, where benefits tended to be high, they increased from £26,519 in 1976, to £63,000 in 1979 and £128,000 in 1980. Lancashire's highest benefit before 1914 was £3,111 and £2,458 between the Wars.[24] The most famous stars have always been able to exploit their celebrity. Grace most certainly did even though he was an amateur. In more recent times Botham probably heads the earnings list.

It has been claimed that higher financial rewards caused the spirit in which matches were played during the 1970s and 1980s to deteriorate. Objective measures of fair play are impossible but in test matches the average numbers of overs bowled per day were much lower in the 1970s than the 1930s and complaints about verbal abuse between players and about the greater use of short-pitched fast bowling increased. Yet the novelty of such tactics can be exaggerated. Bodyline bowling of the early 1930s, which was used in county cricket as well as on the Australian tour of 1932–3, could be described as physical intimidation and in the 1950s England sides slowed down over rates against Australia. But until the 1960s most counties had little prospect of winning the County Championship and the lack of alternative competitions may have curbed aggression and reduced temptations to employ questionable tactics.

III

You do well to love it, for it is more free from anything sordid, anything dishonourable, than any game in the world. To play it keenly, honourably, generously, self-sacrificingly is a moral lesson in itself, and the class is God's air and sunshine. Foster it, my brothers, so that it may attract all who can find time to play it; protect it from anything that would sully it, so that it may grow in favour with all men.
    Lord Harris's message to half-day and youth cricketers, 1931

Calculating the numbers who played cricket for recreation is complicated by the absence of a centralised body with responsibility for registering players and organisations. Surveys of leisure in England and Wales taken in 1965–6, 1974 and 1977, though based on relatively small samples, show that cricket was declining as a participant sport but holding its position as the team ball game with the second highest number of participants. In 1965–6, over 7 per cent of males aged over 16 participated in cricket at least once a month, 6.3 per cent in 1974 whilst the Sports Council in 1983 reported that only 1.5 per cent of adults played. On the other hand, the NCA estimated that between 1973 and 1985 regular participants increased from 400,000 to 500,000 but this does not tally with a study of the United Kingdom sports market which found that 800,000 adults and 800,000 children participated regularly in 1980.[25]

Crude guides to the extent of cricket-playing in England before the 1960s can be based upon localised calculations of the number of teams but too few of these have been completed to support conclusions about when participation at the national level reached its highest point. By 1939 more than half of the 1,100 or so clubs affiliated to the Club Cricket Conference, which were overwhelmingly from the Home Counties, had been established since 1918 but in 1983, of more than 2,200 affiliated clubs from a slightly broader geographical area, 135 had been founded between 1900 and 1913, 470 between 1919 and 1939, 410 between 1946 and 1960 and 555 between 1961 and 1983. The number of teams playing regularly in Bolton and its environs, with a population of about 350,000 in 1931, reached peaks of over 170 between 1930 and 1936. In 1900 the number was about 130 and 120 in 1980.

In the St Helens area of Southwest Lancashire, where far less cricket was played, the number of teams reached a modest peak in the 1930s, declined in the 1940s but rose sharply in the 1970s with the establishment of a mid-week cricket league. Around Doncaster in the West Riding, the number of sides playing regularly between the Wars was greater than before 1914 whilst the Doncaster and District league and the Infirmary League had most teams after the Second World War. However, it is not clear when the total number of sides in this locality reached its maximum.[26] In the early 1970s more than 80 per cent of village teams from 32 counties entered in the Haig National Village Championship had been established before 1939.[27] Evidence about scratch or occasional sides is even more sketchy. Matches between guests at country houses probably reached their peak in Edwardian times.[28] Between the 1920s and 1950s many clubs in Lancashire organised knock-out competitions for scratch sides which provided large numbers with opportunities to play occasionally. Around Bolton the most sides entering one competition was 64 but this was for sides of eight players. In 1925 and 1926 more than 40 sides entered the competitions for the Farnworth Social Circle CC.

Throughout the twentieth century a far higher proportion of adult males in England have played cricket than in Wales though the Welsh proportion has probably been greater than that of Scotland, with Ireland having an even smaller proportion than Scotland. In the mid-1980s almost 300 clubs were affiliated to the Welsh Cricket Association but the number of clubs playing regularly was perhaps twice as high. At the more humble levels of Welsh cricket, leagues rather than individual clubs tend to affiliate to the WCA. Clubs representing the major towns of the north coast and the industrial south were established by 1900. Between the Wars, works sides tended to be the strongest clubs in South Wales. The shortage of localised studies makes it difficult to estimate when cricket-playing reached its highest point in Wales although newspaper reports of cricket, admittedly a far from infallible guide, indicate that in Swansea probably more than 20 sides were playing regularly in 1900 but by 1914, with the apparent collapse of the Swansea and District League, fewer were playing. In the 1930s at least 30 sides played regularly. After 1945 this number may have fallen slightly but rose in the 1980s when the Swansea Central League had four divisions plus two indoor sections.

In Scotland over 300 sides were competing in leagues and competitions listed in *The Scottish Cricket Guide* during the mid-1980s and the Secretary of the Scottish Cricket Union estimated that perhaps 350 clubs played regularly. The Scottish County Championship, though not always representative of the highest standard of Scottish cricket, began in 1902 but for many years the competing counties came only from the east coast. The Western Union, a league for clubs primarily from southwest Scotland, was established in 1893. The North of Scotland League began in 1893 and the Border

League in 1895. The Glasgow and Edinburgh districts in the 1980s each had more than 80 sides playing regularly but of the SCU's four regions, the north had more clubs than either the west or east which included Glasgow and Edinburgh. The major league competitions of the Glasgow and Edinburgh districts were established in the 1950s.

Cricket has been played more extensively in the eastern half of Ireland but this largely reflects the distribution of population. The Northern Cricket Union was established in 1886 and the Irish Cricket Union in 1923. It is thought that very little cricket is played in Ireland outside the auspices of the ICU. In 1966 the Guinness Cup, an inter-provincial competition, was launched but Connaught does not enter a team and in the 1980s Galway had only one club. By the mid-1980s around 150 clubs existed in Ireland but the number of small clubs had declined since the 1960s though the organisation of more teams by larger clubs perhaps meant that the overall number of players had not declined. In Ulster the number of clubs affiliated to the NCU was around 27 in 1900, over 40 in 1920, around 80 in 1950 but about 60 in 1970.[29]

The spread of cricket overseas has been less extensive than that of soccer, tennis, golf or even rugby football and almost exclusively restricted to what was the British Empire. Only eight countries have played test cricket. England and Australia are usually regarded as having first played test cricket in 1877, South Africa in 1889, the West Indies in 1928, New Zealand in 1930, India in 1932, Pakistan in 1952 and Sri Lanka in 1982. By the 1980s, 18 other countries whose game was 'firmly established' but not sufficiently strong to justify test status were associate members of the International Cricket Conference. All test match countries and all but Argentina, Denmark, Israel, the Netherlands and the USA of the ICC had belonged to the British Commonwealth. In the United States cricket had been so firmly established around Philadelphia in the late nineteenth and early twentieth centuries that American touring sides played against English counties, however, the game declined in the 1920s.

In the 1970s more than half of those playing cricket regularly in Britain belonged to social classes I and II and more than three-quarters to social classes I, II and III[30] but oral evidence from the Bolton area suggests that there may have been greater working-class involvement in the first half of this century. From the late 1920s until the 1950s most recreational cricketers around Bolton were manual workers with some degree of skill. Not surprisingly many were employed in cotton factories. Most sides contained at least one teacher or clerk. Few labourers played and no doubt the demands of Saturday work excluded transport workers and shop assistants though often northern England Wednesday and Thursday Leagues catered

4.3 Searching for the ball, a perpetual frustration of much recreational cricket. As so many shrubs and so much long grass grew in the outfields of clubs, a rule of the Radcliffe Sunday School League prevented more than four runs counting when a ball was lost within the boundary

for shop workers and other groups not able to play on Saturdays. Works sides usually contained one or two managers. By the 1930s Sunday school sides began to contain a sprinkling of young men with secondary education and who were entering professional employment, but they tended to be from respectable, aspiring working-class families. In the 1960s and 1970s the number of manual workers playing for Bolton League clubs dropped and this could have been connected with the greater encouragement given to cricket at selective schools and comprehensives which had been selective. Cricket literature celebrates the social mixing of village sides in rural England where squires and parsons played alongside craftsmen and farm labourers but it is not clear how far the expansion of commuting in southeast England has affected the social background of village cricket. In Scotland village sides tend to represent the full range of local society. In the Irish Republic cricket has been a game of the better off but there is a much stronger working-class presence in Ulster.

For much of this century all parts of Britain have had what were perceived locally as socially exclusive clubs where working men would have felt out of place. Levels of subscriptions given in the annual handbooks of the Club Cricket Conference suggest that the Home Counties possibly had the greatest concentration of clubs with players from relatively privileged backgrounds and this was probably associated with London's greater professional and commercial opportunities. Since the 1950s players at the leading Merseyside clubs, many of whom had previously been educated at leading public schools, were recruited from a broader social spectrum and though this could be connected with the decline of Liverpool's cotton broking and related mercantile interests, it could also reflect a more widely diffused egalitarianism.

Cricket overseas has not been played by similar social groups in all societies. In Australia cricket was a well-established working-class recreation long before 1900 and all sections of West Indian society played by the late nineteenth century, whereas in India leading players tended to be recruited from the social elites. In Philadelphia cricket was a game primarily for 'gentlemen' by the early twentieth century, whilst in Argentina the game appears to have been encouraged among those of British descent by schools modelled upon English public schools. In general cricket abroad has been played by a wider section of society in those countries which received larger numbers of British working-class emigrants, but this is not true of the United States and Canada nor does it explain the game's popularity in the West Indies.

Not surprisingly oral evidence indicates that enjoyment of playing was the prime motivation of recreational cricketers but the companionship of other players is often mentioned as a major attraction. Around Bolton most sides playing at the humbler levels of local cricket during the first half of this century consisted of players in their late teens or early twenties. The few players in their middle thirties or forties were regarded as the old men of their sides. Teams playing at a higher level had more players in their late twenties and thirties whilst a tiny majority over fifty were able to hold their own. A nationwide sample in the late 1970s found that just under a half of recreational cricketers were aged over 30 but 40 per cent were aged between 30 and 44. When men stopped playing was also related to marriage and family commitments. In the late 1970s 58 per cent of players were married[31] but oral evidence reveals that wives and girl friends caused many to stop playing.

Almost all recreational cricketers learned to play as boys. Interviews with those who played in the Bolton area between the Wars and after 1945 recall that large numbers of boys and youths played knockabout games of cricket on fine evenings but Caradog Jones's *Social Survey of Merseyside*

4.4 Cricket remained popular among boys in industrial Lancashire as late as 1963 when this picture was taken in Mumps, Oldham

claimed that only 10 per cent of boys about to leave school in the early 1930s listed cricket among their interests. More were interested in reading, the cinema, football, fretwork, swimming and music. How far schools fostered enthusiasm for cricket-playing is uncertain. Until after 1945 cricket was a compulsory activity for most boys at public schools and though cricketing success contributed greatly to the prestige of such schools in the first half of this century, it seems likely that after the Second World War, with an economic climate where even those from privileged backgrounds had to earn their livelihoods, academic attainment came to count for more than cricketing success though such schools still possess excellent facilities for playing and practice.

Only the barest outlines of cricket playing in public sector education for most regions have been established. Selective schools, especially after 1918, were usually provided with playing fields which encouraged cricket-playing but until 1944 the overwhelming majority of working-class boys

4.5 Schoolboys played organised cricket too and, as this picture of a team drawn from schools in Huddersfield shows, 'whites' were unnecessary. They lost the Yorkshire cup-tie to Brighouse in May 1930

attended elementary schools. By the late 1890s at least 29 towns had inter-school competitions but these were far less than for soccer.[32] Elementary school cricket became more organised and widespread between the Wars but the reasons for this have not been investigated. Inter-school competitions in Manchester began in 1919 when 51 teams competed in seven leagues. By 1939, 149 teams were competing.[33] At Oxford in the 1920s elementary schools were allowed to play on the grounds of University colleges. Matches between sides selected from elementary schoolboys of different towns also expanded between the wars. In 1922, for instance, the Lancashire Schools Cricket Association was formed but most affiliated towns were from the eastern half of the county. Liverpool did not join until 1937[34] though its own inter-schools competition started in 1891. In the late 1940s the administrative structure of schools cricket was extended further. Discussions between the MCC and ACCC resulted in the establishment of the MCC Youth Cricket Association which concentrated upon coaching. Though all counties had school cricket associations affiliated to the English Schools Cricket Association by the 1980s, cricket in public sector schools has been ailing in the recent past. In the late 1970s fears that cricket was a declining school sport led the NCA to launch a special

4.6 Neither did adults have to be conventionally attired to enjoy the game. This is Friarmere CC from Delph near Oldham early this century

campaign to revive it. In the mid-1980s the Welsh CA Development Plan commented on the decline of cricket-playing and coaching in schools whilst the Scottish CU coaching convener reported that teachers' disputes had hit cricket in local authority schools during the mid-1980s.[35]

For most of this century the lack of playing fields restricted opportunities for working-class boys to play cricket at school. Some municipal authorities, such as Liverpool and Manchester, allowed schools to use parks for sports but Bolton was reluctant to do this in the 1930s. The enthusiasm of teachers could also be decisive. Bolton demonstrates that adult cricket could thrive even where little was organised in schools. A founder member of the English Schools Football Association, Bolton Schools Athletic Association had no cricket section until 1933. A Bolton youth cricket league fizzled out after two seasons in 1930.

For many regions uncertainties surrounding the social backgrounds of recreational cricketers make conclusions about connections between cricket-playing and economic fluctuations speculative. The 650 clubs founded between the Wars and which joined the Club Cricket Conference can be interpreted as a consequence of rising affluence in southeast England yet around Bolton, the number of sides playing regularly reached a peak in the early 1930s when local unemployment figures were highest. Playing cricket was not costly in Bolton between the Wars. Outside the tiny number of socially exclusive clubs subscriptions were usually five or six shillings and clubs provided all equipment except clothing. Even at the humblest levels of Bolton cricket in the 1930s almost all players wore white flannels and shirts although a rule of the Walkden League in 1914 that bowlers had to wear a white shirt or sweater suggests that this had not always been the case. Nevertheless white flannels could often be acquired second-hand or made from the bottom halves of white overalls. *The Times* found three types of teams playing in Regent's Park on Sundays in 1922. Some had players with neither white flannels nor pads, others had just one pad and a few with flannels whilst others had each player correctly attired.[36]

For talented players around Bolton and probably other northern and midland strongholds of league cricket there were economic incentives to play cricket. A tiny minority could become club professionals. Even the poorest paid professionals in the 1920s and 1930s received £3 a week during the cricket season, which compared favourably with skilled workers' wages, and although their duties occupied Saturdays and most evenings, these could be combined with a weekday job. Leading league clubs of the Bolton area paid 'amateurs' to play for them and it is an open secret that this persisted into the 1970s. Talented players in the 1930s and even the 1950s were likely to be offered employment at firms with cricket teams whilst employers who patronised non-works clubs used offers of jobs to persuade amateur players to change clubs. In the 1930s collections for outstanding performances could exceed £10. Yet most recreational cricketers played at a level without financial inducements. In the 1930s unemployment did not stop them playing in Bolton and many of the unemployed passed their time tending grounds. It was said that the club with most unemployed players had the best-kept pitch in the Horwich Sunday School League.[37]

The sale of cricket grounds to housebuilders, especially after 1918, restricted opportunities to play cricket. Between 1924 and 1934, 17 clubs in the Bolton area disbanded because their grounds were sold to housebuilders. Most were small clubs but ground difficulties caused the collapse of four clubs from the First Division of the Bolton and District Cricket Association. Only two clubs which lost grounds found alternatives and the second ground of one was sold for housebuilding within three years. For landowners, the profits of selling to housebuilders could far exceed the rents that cricket clubs were able to pay. In 1939 part of Whittlebrook Methodist CC's ground was sold for £600. The club had been paying an annual rent of £15. By 1939 great differences in the numbers of cricket grounds existed between English localities. The National Fitness Council found the number of cricket pitches to population in towns varied from one to every 5,500 to one to every 14,000 and local authorities differed in their enthusiasm to provide land for cricket. In 1926 35 towns with a combined population of over 1,500,000 had on average one publicly-owned cricket pitch for every 25,595 persons. Gateshead had none but Manchester had provided 88 and the LCC 336. In 1932, however, when pitches could be hired on Sundays as well as weekdays, this latter met only a third of the demand.[38] Even where playing fields associations brought more land into public ownership, opportunities for cricket clubs to hire grounds on municipal land sometimes scarcely increased. In the 1930s grants from the National Playing Fields Association and the Carnegie Trust allowed Bolton Corporation to develop nearly 40 acres of recreational land but no more than two or three clubs were able to use municipal land each season before 1939. In England by the mid-1960s 44 per cent of recreational cricket was played on publicly-owned land compared with 58 per cent for soccer.[39] The Welsh CA stressed in 1985 that poor maintenance of public cricket pitches was discouraging cricket playing whilst the reduction in the number of smaller clubs around Dublin has been attributed to the difficulty of finding fields.[40]

The nature of institutions spawning cricket clubs also determined opportunities to play. Usually clubs playing at the higher levels of cricket were independent entities though many established bowls and tennis sections. While the rural south of England village clubs do not appear to have been part of other organisations, in northern England many small clubs belonged to churches. The strength of the church presence within Bolton cricket at the start of this century suggests that even before 1900 it was expected that cricket clubs would be associated with churches or Sunday schools. By the early 1930s around 90 teams in the Bolton area were formally connected with places of worship. Denominational affiliations more or less reflected the number of each denomination's places of worship, with Anglicans and various Methodist sects having most though none of the five church clubs that played in the BDCA's First Division was Anglican. The number of Catholic clubs was disproportionately small. Although interviews have revealed that many who played for church sides did not attend church regularly, few 'boozers' and 'roughs' played in the Horwich or Radcliffe Sunday School Leagues and the strength of the church presence may have discouraged the formation of pub teams. The number of church teams in the Bolton area began to fall in the 1930s mainly because smaller clubs had difficulty retaining tenancy of their grounds. The Radcliffe Sunday

4.7 In the first half of this century cricket leagues in Bolton paid sickness benefit to those who missed work because of cricket injuries. No payments were made for repairs to false teeth

School League collapsed during the Second World War and the Walkden League, whose clubs were predominantly church teams, disbanded in 1948. The Horwich Sunday League has survived but in 1961 began to admit works welfare teams.[41] By 1980 only two clubs in the BDCA were affiliated to churches. Scattered evidence from other northern towns suggests that the church presence dropped massively after 1945 but how far this represents a decline of religion in urban culture requires further investigation. Until 1939, church support for Sabbatarianism in northern England limited opportunities to play cricket on Sundays although the LCC had permitted cricket to be played in its parks since 1922.

The church presence in recreational cricket at Swansea was always far less marked than in Bolton. In 1938 only one church side and two YMCA teams were among the twenty-eight entries for the Swansea Central League's knock-out competition and none with a church affiliation belonged to this

League in 1979.[42] By the mid 1980s the church presence in Scottish cricket was little more than negligible though there are a few old boys' sides of denominational schools. Church cricket clubs have been equally rare in Irish cricket. Possibly seven church clubs were affiliated to the NCU between the Wars and a few Boys' Brigades sides for short periods.[43] Yet religion has influenced the extent of cricket-playing in Ireland. Within Ulster the game is played predominantly by Protestants but this could reflect the greater encouragement given to cricket in schools attended by Protestants whilst throughout Ireland, but especially in rural areas, the Gaelic Athletic Association's prohibition upon the playing of English games, is thought to have discouraged participation in cricket.[44]

It is not known when cricket clubs associated with workplaces reached their peak but in most urban areas of England and Wales their numbers expanded rapidly between the Wars. Paucity of information about the formation of works clubs does not indicate whether the initial impetus came from workers or the growth of Taylorite industrial welfare schemes linked with the belief that providing sports facilities could discourage trade union militancy. The two works clubs with the best playing records in the BDCA during the 1930s had managers who were cricket enthusiasts, and their desire to be connected with successful sides led them to offer employment to players of other clubs and to play those not employed by their firms. Works clubs probably increased opportunities to play cricket though it would seem that among industrial concerns a labour force of at least 300 was needed to sustain a cricket club. Only very large firms could maintain interdepartmental competitions. No firm in the Bolton area appears to have had an internal competition but for the 1930s Pilkington Brothers at St Helens was able to sustain an interdepartmental league with usually about a dozen sides. In Swansea local government departments have played in the Guildhall League since the 1930s. Only one works club played in the Bolton League during the 1930s but seven competed in the First Division of the BDCA whilst the South Wales and Monmouthshire Association, arguably the major league competition in Wales, became dominated by works clubs.[45] Yet in Scotland and Northern Ireland the impact of works sides upon recreation cricket was less marked. By and large works cricket teams have reflected the industrial structure of localities. The decline of cotton and mining saw a vast reduction in the number of works clubs around Bolton in the 1970s whilst in the 1980s the Welsh CA found that works closures and reduced expenditure had caused grounds owned by firms to deteriorate.[46] However, even in 1974, cricket throughout the United Kingdom had more facilities provided by employers than any other sport.[47]

The significance of cricket in local culture has influenced participation in the game. Areas where cricket was played extensively before 1914 have remained comparative strongholds of the game. In the late 1970s it was calculated that among English regions, Greater London and the southeast had the second highest number of recreational cricketers but the smallest proportion of population who played. An estimate in 1980 that 14 per cent of all cricket clubs were concentrated in Yorkshire suggests a symbiotic relationship between cricket-playing and the county side's success for so much of this century. The admission of Glamorgan to the County Championship in 1921 and a desire to improve its playing record have been seen as major reasons for the creation of the South Wales and Monmouthshire Cricket Association in 1926 whilst it could be argued that the comparative weakness of recreational cricket in Scotland and Ireland could be related to the tiny amount of first-class cricket played in these two countries. N. G. R. Mair has suggested that climate, and the strength of golf and football being played almost all year have been further discouragements in Scotland, though the opinion of a Scottish sociologist that in Glasgow, working-class culture cricket is often 'not regarded as a game for real men' suggests there are other possible explanations but these require more systematic study. The English connotations of cricket have been thought to have limited participation in Ireland.[48] Since the 1950s overseas immigrants from countries where cricket was strong in popular culture have tended to play cricket in England. By 1980 two West Indian and two Asian clubs were playing in Bolton.

IV

Competitive cricket . . . tends to crush out every ounce of the real sporting spirit of cricket and introduces the contentious side . . . it leaves the real English spirit of amateur sport to be brushed ruthlessly aside for the more dangerous and unwholesome sport of competitive adventure in which two league points, or some piece of silverware . . . becomes more cherished in the end by the players than the actual game itself.

The Club Cricket Conference's Annual Directory, 1923

Geographical location and social status have largely determined the local organisation of cricket and the spirit in which the game was played. In southern England few socially exclusive clubs played in league or knock-out competitions before the 1960s. In 1923 the Club Cricket Conference prohibited its affiliated clubs playing in such competitions. A cynical interpretation of such opposition to leagues is that it stemmed from a desire to maintain social exclusiveness. The levels of subscriptions paid at many clubs affiliated to the Club Cricket Conference in the early 1920s suggests, however, that they were predominantly middle-class. Fear of relegation to a lower division could lead to the recruitment of players on ability rather than social background. League competitions were found predominantly in the north and midlands but even there socially exclusive clubs belonged to organisations such as the Liverpool Competition or Manchester Association which for the first half of the century showed a marked reluctance to adopt a league structure where clubs surrendered autonomy to a central authority. Though sides playing only friendly matches tried to win, many games between socially exclusive sides were not played in an intensely competitive spirit. In the Liverpool Competition during the 1930s few players objected to drawn matches provided that all who wished to bat had done so.

The Birmingham League, established in 1888, was probably the world's first cricket league and by 1914 most of what are still the major leagues were organised. There is no obvious explanation for the greater emphasis upon league cricket in the north and midlands though the dates of their formation and distribution suggest that the example of the Football League could have been important, but leagues may also have reflected and strengthened greater working-class involvement. By the early twentieth century even the humblest levels of clubs from the north of England were competing in leagues.

Recreational cricketers who played in the Bolton League during the middle decades of this century have recalled that matches in Sunday school leagues were just as fiercely contested. Even the lowliest leagues between the Wars found it necessary to engage neutral umpires and to have complicated regulations to prohibit the playing of unregistered players and the poaching of players, which in turn involved the establishment of sub-committees to adjudicate upon breaches of rules. In Bolton lists of those registered to play for each club were displayed at a sports shop whilst in the West Riding clubs advertised registrations of new players in the local press. The competitive edge to matches in the Horwich Sunday School League was so sharp in the 1930s that clubs could play enthusiastic but ungifted players only in emergencies, though in the Radcliffe Sunday School League, where most clubs fielded two sides, those prepared to commit themselves to a club could be more or less sure of a regular game.[49]

In the major leagues of northern England, playing success depended largely upon having the finances to engage skilful professionals and possibly to play 'shamateurs' or persuade them to change clubs. To raise cash between the Wars fund-raising events such as carnivals, gala days, rose queens, dances, whist drives and concerts were organised and by becoming major contributions to local social life helped to consolidate links between clubs and local communities. Clubs both exploited and strengthened local loyalties. By the 1960s and 1970s such events had largely disappeared but revenue from one-armed bandits and licensed bars more than compensated for the dwindling of gate receipts into virtual insignificance. In the Bolton area clubs with bars situated close to major roads have tended to become the most prosperous and bar income has enabled clubs to improve facilities and employ professionals with international reputations.[50]

V

Though the hardy few have been playing on and off (chiefly off) for the past couple of centuries, fewer still, let us admit it, have emerged to endow the game with real distinction.
    Nancy Joy, *Maiden Over* (1950) p.13

Cricket mythology attributes the skills of W. G. Grace to coaching from his mother but it would appear that less cricket was played among women in the Victorian period than during the eighteenth or early nineteenth centuries. In 1887 the White Heather Club was formed for ladies wishing to play after taking part in light-hearted matches at country houses, and in the 1890s, the Original English Lady Cricketers had two professional sides who tried to popularise the game among women.[51] During the early twentieth century some cricket was played at the more socially prestigious girls' boarding schools and training colleges but few clubs existed for those who had completed full-time education. In 1926 the Women's Cricket Association was founded by hockey and lacrosse players who wanted an alternative summer game to tennis and golf. Within a decade 120 clubs and 100 schools had affiliated to the WCA and 20 county associations were established.[52] The first women's international matches were played during the WCA tour of Australasia in 1934–5. The first women's test match in England was played in 1937. The International Women's Cricket Council was established in 1958, its founding members being England, Australia, New Zealand, South Africa and Holland. The first women's World Cup competition was held in England in 1973.[53]

At no time since 1926 has cricket playing been among the more popular women's sports in Britain. In 1974 it was estimated that two out of every thousand women played at least once a month whereas 50 per thousand played tennis, whilst in 1965–6, not one from a sample of 300 girls at either selective or secondary modern schools had played.[54] By 1954 nearly 200 clubs plus 100 schools and colleges were affiliated to the WCA but the lack of documentation about cricket played outside the auspices of the WCA makes it difficult to calculate when cricket-playing among women was most extensive. In the north of England perhaps most women's cricket was played in the 1930s when many clubs belonged to the Women's Cricket Federation which had county federations in Lancashire and Yorkshire. Six teams played in the Deane Valley League in 1927 and 21 in the Bradford Women's Cricket League in 1932.

By 1969 only 49 clubs, 22 colleges and 56 schools remained affiliated to the WCA and in the early 1970s the Sports Council considered that women's cricket as a participant sport was dying. A National Officer was appointed to promote the game and to encourage school cricket. A six-a-side version of the game was publicised but the results were not startling. By 1974 the number of clubs had remained constant but rose to 60 by 1980 though fewer colleges and schools were affiliated.[55] The geographical distribution of WCA affiliations was broadly similar to the distribution of men's clubs. In the early 1970s the game was centred overwhelmingly on England with Yorkshire having the greatest concentration of clubs but East Anglia, Lancashire, Cheshire and Middlesex each had slightly more schools. Women's cricket has never been strong in Scotland or Wales and in 1974 each country had only one club affiliated to the WCA. In Ireland women's cricket appears to have been relatively strong in the 1930s, declined sharply in the 1940s and collapsed totally in the 1960s but has revived with vigour in Leinster since the 1970s. By the mid- to late 1980s around 40 women's teams played regularly in Ireland with three-quarters of these being from Leinster. Probably around 1,000 women and girls now play cricket regularly in Ireland and are recruited from all social classes. In Leinster most women's clubs are the women's sections of men's and the revival of women's cricket in Ireland appears to have resulted from a desire among women who were supporters of men's clubs to play. No women's club has its own ground. There are more women's clubs in Munster than Ulster though a small but growing number of women play for men's teams in the north.[56]

Most of those who played under the auspices of the WCA belonged to the better-off social groups. Almost all affiliated schools were private though the expansion of higher education after 1945 perhaps gave more students from working-class homes opportunities to play at specialist physical education colleges. Very few girls' elementary and secondary modern schools played cricket but Nancy Joy has suggested that mill girls played for sides connected with the WCF in the 1930s. In 1945 four of seven sides which played in Bolton belonged to organisations whose male teams were predominantly working-class.[57] Admittedly fragmentary evidence indicates that the majority of players and officials in women's cricket were unmarried. All who played on the Australasian tour of 1934–5 were single and scorecards of matches in the Bolton area during the 1930s printed in the press show

4.8 A Women's Cricket Federation team from the West Riding in the 1930s. The Women's Cricket Association, however, insisted that all who played under its auspices wore skirts of a specified length

that almost all players were single. In 1969 only two of the 35 officials and coaches of the WCA, two of its 26 registered umpires, three of its 37 scorers and six of the 66 regional coaches were married. In Leinster in the 1980s about half the officials were married but the players, mostly aged between 20 and 22, tended to be single.

More women and girls have watched rather than played cricket. During one month in the mid 1960s 4 per cent of all women over fifteen were estimated to have watched a cricket match and in 1977 it was calculated that over a third of all spectators at cricket matches were female though the types of matches attended are not clear. County clubs have had lady members throughout the century but they were not always accorded the full privileges and voting rights of membership and in the 1980s were still not admitted during the hours of play to the pavilions at Lord's and Old Trafford. Lady members exceeded 10 per cent of Essex's total membership before 1914 and 25 per cent of Lancashire's in the late 1920s. By the mid-1980s some counties made no distinction between the sex of members whilst others had joint husband and wife membership. Nevertheless for most counties estimates for the proportion of lady members rarely exceeded 20 per cent. The biggest crowd at a women's cricket match in Britain was probably 10,000 for the England versus Australia match in 1951.

Though it has been highly unusual in England for women to be included in sides composed predominantly of men, ladies committees have been essential in recreational cricket to men's clubs. In addition to preparing teas, ladies in the Bolton area helped to raise funds by organising dances and other social events. By 1964 that of Little Lever CC had built up an account of £4,500 through bingo, whist and domino drives, jumble sales and spring fairs.[58] Most members of ladies committees were wives or mothers of players and perhaps involvement with club activities neutralised potential hostility to their menfolk's cricket-playing. Interviews reveal that in Bolton many women enjoyed opportunities to socialise with other women though this view is expressed more often by husbands than wives and invariably examples are quoted of men who stopped playing through pressure from wives or girl friends. But the comment of a wife of an enthusiastic recreational cricketer in Lancashire sums up the attitude of many wives and expresses much about how cricket was regarded for much of the twentieth century, 'Ah were a cricket wider, oh yes, for 30 years... but 'e could 'ave bin doin' a lot worse.'

NOTES

1 Only in May 1947 did the Imperial Cricket Conference define 'first-class' matches. The MCC was given the authority to specify which matches played in Britain should be regarded as first-class. County and international one-day matches are not officially defined as 'first-class' but it can be argued that in the mind of the general public such games are first-class. This essay treats one-day matches as part of first-class cricket. The current definition of what matches in the UK are accorded first-class status can be found in *Wisden Cricketers' Almanack*.

2 E. W. Swanton (ed.), *Barclays World of Cricket. The Game from A to Z* (1986), p. 51. Further details of the increase in the numbers of MCC members are provided in T. Lewis, *Double Century. The Story of MCC and Cricket* (1987).

3 K. A. P. Sandiford, 'The professionalization of modern cricket', *British Journal of Sports History*, vol. 2, no. 3 (December 1985).

4 C. Brooks, *English Cricket. The Game and its Players Through the Ages* (1978) discusses the relationship between the changing nature of the governing classes and authority within cricket since the late seventeenth century.

5 I am grateful to Mr B. Langley of the TCCB for providing lists of members of TCCB sub-committees.

6 M. Marshall, *Gentlemen and Players: Conversations with Cricketers* (1987).

7   A. W. Carr, *Cricket with the Lid Off* (1935), p. 70.

8   ACCC Minutes, 27 November 1945.

9   K. A. P. Sandiford and W. V. Vamplew, 'The peculiar economics of English cricket before 1914', *British Journal of Sports History*, vol. 3, no. 3 (December 1986).

10 Yorkshire CCC Annual Handbooks record match attendances. The Essex figures are calculated from gate receipt income provided in the annual reports of Essex CCC.

11 *Athletic News*, 10 April 1922, *Bolton Evening News (Buff)*, 17 February 1923. *South Wales Cricket Association Official Handbook*, 1986, p. 30.

12 K. K. Sillitoe, *Government Social Survey. Planning for Leisure* (London, 1969), p. 236; A. J. Veal, *Sport and Recreation in England and Wales. An Analysis of Adult Participation Patterns in 1977* (Centre for Urban and Regional Studies, University of Birmingham, 1979), p. 78.

13 J. A. Schofield, 'The demand for cricket: the case of the John Player League', *Applied Economics*, no. 15 (1983).

14 *Daily Mail*, 12 August 1966.

15 *Athletic News*, 28 July 1913.

16 L. Duckworth, *The Story of Warwickshire Cricket* (1974), p. 338.

17 D. Kirkby, 'The financing of county cricket clubs', *Journal of the Cricket Society*, vol. 13, no. 3 (1987).

18 G. Ross, *The Gillette Cup 1963 to 1980* (1981), p. 13.

19 M. Down, *Power, Money and Politics in Cricket since 1945. Is it Cricket?* (1985), pp. 144–5.

20 *The Times*, 29 April 1924.

21 C. Booth (ed.), *Life and Labour of the People in London. Volume VIII: Population Classified by Trades* (1896), pp. 146–7.

22 Essex CCC Notes on Annual Salaries. Essex County Record Office, D/Z 82/1/32, Essex CCC Minute Book, Essex County Record Office, D/Z 82/1/42.

23 G. Moorhouse, *Lord's* (1983), p. 150.

24 N. Preston (ed.), *Wisden Cricketers' Almanack 1954* (1954), p. 402; R. Warburton, *Lancashire Cricket 1982 Yearbook* (Manchester, 1982), p. 160.

25 Sillitoe, *Government Social Survey*, p. 120; I. P. C. *Sociological Monographs 12 Leisure* (1975), p. 20; W. H. Martin and S. Mason, *The U.K. Sports Market* (Sudbury, 1980), quoted by B. S. Duffield, J. P. Best and M. F. Collins, *Sports Council. A Digest of Sports Statistics* (1983), p. 19; *Sports Council: A Digest of Sports Statistics for the United Kingdom* (1986).

26 P. L. Scowcroft, *Cricket in Doncaster and District. An Outline History* (Doncaster, 1985).

27 J. Fogg, *The Haig Book of Village Cricket* (1972), p. 33.

28 Swanton, *Barclays World of Cricket*, pp. 605–6.

29 I am grateful to Mr D. Scott, Secretary of the Irish Cricket Union and to Mr W. J. McCarroll, General Secretary of the Northern Cricket Union, for information about cricket in Ireland. *Northern Cricket Union Centenary Brochure 100 years of Ulster Cricket 1886–1986* (Portadown, 1986).

30 *I.P.C. Sociological Monographs*, p. 20; Veal, *Sport and Recreation*, p. 68.

31 Ibid., p. 68.

32 *Education Department Special Reports on Educational Subjects*, vol. 2, (1898).

33 H. F. B. Thomas, *Schoolboy Cricket in Manchester. A Short History of the Manchester Schools Cricket Association* (Salford, 1947), p. 2; *Manchester Schools' Cricket Association Handbook 1939*.

34 *Lancashire Schools' Cricket Association Handbooks*, 1933–52.

35 Welsh Cricket Association Development Plan, January 1985; *Scottish Cricket Guide Season 1987*, p. 71.

36 *The Times*, 21 August 1922.

37 J. A. Hester, E. Ward and L. E. Perry, *1922–1972 Horwich Churches Welfare League* (n.d., n.p.) p. 11.

38 *The Times*, 4 June 1926, 18 November 1932, 12 June 1939.

39 Sillitoe, *Government Social Survey*, p. 146.

40 Welsh CA Development Plan 1985; information supplied by Mr D. Scott.

41 Hester, Ward and Perry, *Horwich Churches Welfare League*, p. 14.

42 *South Wales Evening Post*, 21 May 1938, 23 June 1979.

43 *NCU Centenary Brochure*.

44 Information from Mr D. Scott and Mr W. J. McCarroll.

45 *South Wales Evening Post*, 10, 12, May 1938.

46 Welsh CA Development Plan 1985.

47 *I.P.C. Sociological Monographs*, p. 21.

48 Swanton, *Barclays World of Cricket*, pp. 554–9, Information supplied by Mr Joe Sim.

49 Interviews with Messrs A. Burnham and J Pickstone, 2 April 1987 and Mr S. Webb, 14 September 1987.

50 Interview with Mr B. Taylor, 30 October 1987.

51 N. Joy, *Maiden Over* (1950), p. 28.

52 *The Times*, 23 April 1927, 25 May 1937.

53 Swanton, *Barclays World of Cricket*, p. 612.

54 *I.P.C. Sociological Monographs*, p. 20; Sillitoe, *Government Social Survey*, p. 139.

55 Women's Cricket Association Future Policy and Plans. Unsigned Typescript Memorandum, *c.* 1972; *Women's Cricket Association Year Books*, 1969 and 1974.

56 I am grateful to Miss Mary Craddock of the Women's Irish Cricket Union for supplying me with information.

57 N. Joy, *Maiden Over*, p. 44; *Buff*, 12 March 1932, 4 May 1935; Scowcroft, *Cricket in Doncaster*, p. 35.

58 *Club Cricketer*, August 1985.

5 FOOTBALL

TONY MASON

I

> In fact most of the boys' lives appeared to be devoted to football. They played
> football on weekdays; on Saturday they played or watched football; they said
> that they preferred football and when asked what they would like to do more
> of out of school they did not hesitate to put football.
>
> *Out of School: Second Report of the Central Advisory Council for Education* (England),
> 1948, p. 36

For most of this century football in Britain has been the working man's game. Most of the players at all levels were working men. Most of the spectators at all matches were working men. But an important middle-class element both rationalised the game and dominated its bureaucracy. By 1900 it had already become an important part of British popular culture. Today an enthusiasm for football is something shared by people of widely differing backgrounds and opinions. Henry Kissinger and Den Xiaoping, Daniel Cohn-Bendit and Roy Hattersley, Placido Domingo and Rod Stewart, the late Dmitri Shostakovich and A. J. Ayer all share love of football. It is one of the sports guaranteed to be found almost anywhere in the world. And it was made in Britain.

The modern game had regional origins in Scotland and in the English north, midlands and southeast. The English Football Association, formed in 1863, was the product of ex-public school and university players working in London, who hoped to produce some order out of the different varieties of football spawned in different schools and geographical locations. The aim was to produce one game. They failed in the sense that supporters of the Rugby variety determined to maintain its distinguishing features of hacking and handling and went their own way. But the activists of the early FA succeeded in that the association game, with one set of laws recognised by all players and administrators in these islands, had become well established by 1880.

An important factor both reflecting the growth and spread of the game and contributing to it was the Football Association knock-out cup competition first competed for by 14 clubs in 1871–2. It remains the nation's most popular sporting competition and the final at Wembley Stadium each

May has become a powerful national ritual particularly following the attention of radio and television. It was a competition which was rapidly imitated both in the counties and in the other three home countries: the Scottish Cup began in 1874, the Welsh in 1877 and the Irish in 1881. The coming of the cups did much to stimulate interest in football but it also brought with it a more competitive edge. The urge to win, especially against local rivals in Lancashire and the midlands, led firstly to some clubs poaching the best players from their rivals and soon to offering inducements in the form of jobs and money. Many of the first professionals were artisans from the west of Scotland where the game was well developed by the 1880s. A strong body of opinion within the game, well represented in the Football Association, wanted to maintain it unsullied by the paid player. It should be a pastime, not a living; a way of maintaining physical fitness in a sociable context. A good many of the more ambitious northern and midland clubs, however, had committees of local business and professional men determined to pursue the best talent for their teams paid for by the crowds of largely working men eager to watch. In order to keep the game under gentlemanly control, the English FA legalised professionalism in 1885. Three years later, the Football League was born in order that the leading clubs could have a more significant and predictable series of home and away matches with each other. The Scottish FA was somewhat more reluctant to grasp the nettle of professionalism but did so in 1893, two years after the first Scottish League season.[1]

The 1885 agreement preserved the idea of one game in England run by one authority but it ushered in a long period of struggle between the amateur and professional ethos which echoed and re-echoed down the corridors of committee and dressing rooms through much of the twentieth century. The supporters of amateur values fought a spirited rearguard action. One of the spearheads in the early 1900s was the Corinthians, a representative team, chosen from the best available amateur players, largely from the London area. In the early days of full-time training and practice they could still hold their own with professionals in friendly matches and beat the FA Cup holders, Bury, 10–3 in 1904. Every change of law was carefully scrutinised, none more so than the penalty kick, introduced in 1891. Gentlemen did not deliberately commit fouls and for some years the Corinthians would neither attempt to score with a penalty nor attempt to prevent their opponents scoring should the referee decide that the Corinthians had conceded one. A special knock-out cup for amateur clubs was established in England in 1894; in 1907 a group of diehards – mainly, but not entirely, from the south of England – broke away to form the Amateur Football Association. The FA, they said, was only interested in business football.

The values of the professional game were infecting the pastime side by encouraging defensive tactics, offside traps and fouls. They returned to the fold in 1914 to fight the old battles from inside.

Two aspects of the amateur–professional argument spelt trouble for the FA after 1914–18. One was that many secondary schools, especially grammar and public schools, preferred rugby to football for their boys because it had no truck with professionals. The second area of difficulty was the definition of amateur. Following an anonymous letter to the Durham FA in 1927, Crook Town, an amateur club in the Northern League, were suspended for having illegally paid a player over and above his legitimate expenses. Crook then named another 20 northern clubs which they alleged had had improper dealings with amateur players. A Football Association commission investigated in 1928 and suspended 341 players until the end of 1929. Several clubs were fined and officials suspended. There was a local outcry, with the Durham FA claiming that far from the bulk of these players being 'shamateurs' or clandestine professionals, it was simply a convention to pay a known flat rate in expenses, or tea money, as it was popularly called. The FA were criticised as pseudo-Mussolinis and told bluntly that their toughness had more to do with their arguments with FIFA than the ruling of football life in Durham. What was clear was that many amateur clubs kept very inadequate books, much to the FA's annoyance. But London had to retreat as gracefully as it could and most of the amateur players who wished to be reinstated eventually were.[2]

Suspicions of illegal payments to amateurs persisted. As late as 1963 an FA committee said that there was no doubt that amateur players were receiving payment but no one was able to produce proof. The amateur remained a privileged person in the eyes of the Football Association. Apart from jobs as scouts, trainers and managers, former professionals could not easily take part in the running of clubs, leagues or football associations; there were no restrictions on amateurs. This was discrimination and snobbery and it did not formally end until the word 'amateur' was deleted from the FA rules in 1975. The last FA Amateur Cup was competed for in 1974.

Social critics of the game, of course, regularly charged it with having too few players. The sneer at the 'looker-on' was usually coupled with the charge that the level of participation was low. But that was a charge that was increasingly inaccurate as opportunities to take part increased. It was not until 1906 that games periods became an officially sanctioned part of the curriculum in British state elementary schools. Until then, drill with the aim of promoting obedience was the training for the children of the working classes. Individual elementary school teachers did, however, organise football teams in their schools and several cities had schools football associations before 1900. By 1914 there were national organisations for England, Scotland and Wales. The number of schools playing football continued to grow despite the fact that during the 1920s and 1930s some grammar and public schools replaced football with rugby union. By 1968 over 14,000 schools in England, Scotland and Wales were playing football.[3]

Certainly the twentieth century has seen a continuous rise in numbers of players, even though there were never enough clubs or playing fields to meet the potential demand. Numbers of both did rise as local authorities, individual firms and voluntary bodies such as the National Playing Fields Association provided playing areas. The expansion of works football during the First World War and beyond is especially notable. In 1936 the Sheffield and District Works Sports Association claimed 80 firms in membership with 86 football teams and by 1946 25 per cent of all Sheffield clubs were works clubs. The Ashington Coal Company in Northumberland had 27 football teams attached to its welfare club in the 1920s. In the same period the National Council for the Pottery Industry was organising football competitions for employees with the explicit aim of improving relations both between employers and employed and between workers in different factories. The national trend towards organised participation in football seems upwards in England and Wales. About 10,000 clubs were affiliated to county football associations by the end of the 1930s and afterwards the growth is clear: 17,973 affiliated clubs in 1948, 25,217 in 1964, 30,862 in 1967 and 41,069 in 1985.[4]

The explosion of organised football on Sundays is the great participatory change of the last thirty years. Before the Second World War the FA had vigorously discouraged it. There were some successful attempts to have council-owned recreation grounds opened for play on Sunday, notably in London in the 1930s, but to play Sunday football was to risk excommunication by Lancaster Gate. Teams winning amateur cup games were expelled from the competition if it could be proved that they had included players who had taken part in Sunday football. During the Second World War servicemen and munitions workers were allowed to play on Sunday since many of them worked on Saturdays. But the FA refused to recognise Sunday play until 1960, by which time Sabbatarian sentiment was a good deal weaker and the phenomenon of Sunday play a good deal stronger. There are several small ironies involved in this change. Many of the Sunday clubs appear to be based on pubs. Consumption of drink per capita has been rising since the 1960s. Yet, earlier this century, one of football's few advantages, for some social observers, was that it kept players and spectators out of public houses.

In the 1980s, then, the number of players has never been so large –

5.1 This match on Blackheath in 1953 took place seven years before the FA finally accepted Sunday football. Sunday games were already allowing a dramatic growth in organised participation

1.6 million according to one Sports Council report. *Social Trends* in 1979 calculated that 20 per cent of the males between the ages of 16 and 24 actively take part in football. A higher proportion of males between the ages of 11 and 40 participate in the south than in the north.[5] Some sports centre managers cannot allow local football teams to train at the centres on weekday evenings because no one else would get a look in.

Football has always been popular on an unorganised level. It is not a game that requires equipment or even soft ground in order to play. Nor is it essential to have eleven players a side in order to fuel fantasies and generally have an enjoyable time. Street football was common throughout most of this century although in many places policemen and local magistrates would periodically attempt to curb it. The autobiographies of professional footballers often stress that it was in practice in the streets or casual games in the lanes and playgrounds that they picked up their skills. The 'tanna ba' player of Glasgow was not just a figment of journalistic imagination.[6]

5.2 Football could be played anywhere at any time until the traffic increase of the last decades. This is a London street in the 1950s

II

What we had in common – and he now turned to me to discuss one of the players – was that we were both Tottenham Hotspur supporters who had seen Willie Hall and George Hunt in their heyday. You could scarcely have a closer bond.

Alan Ross, *Blindfold Games* (1986), p. 207

But we have to return to the professional game because it was in that form that the game was at its most socially visible with its large stadiums, big crowds and spectacular weekly performances through a long season lasting from August until April. It was this apex of the game on which the newspapers and, later, radio and television focussed their attention.

After the First World War the Football League joined the Southern League to produce the organisational pattern that has changed so little. The 1920–1 season saw three divisions: divisions one and two and a third division south, each comprising 22 clubs. A third division north of 20 clubs was added in 1921–2 made up to 22 in 1923–4. In 1958–9 the two regional third divisions were transformed into third and fourth divisions with 24 clubs in each. There was tinkering with the number of clubs in the Scottish League – the first division of which curiously played throughout the war of 1914–18 – with fluctuations from 16 to 22 in the first division, and between 14 and 20 in division two before the major reorganisation in 1975–6 to a ten-club Premier Division and a first and second division of 14 clubs each.[7]

Crowds turned up in even bigger numbers in the inter-war decades than they had before 1914.[8] Even before the war it had become a regular occurrence to have over 100,000 at the English Cup Final at the Crystal Palace. In the inter-war years 36 clubs recorded their record attendances, often for Cup matches like the 67,037 at Huddersfield for the visit of Arsenal in 1932, the 47,428 at St Mirren against Celtic in 1925, the 28,281 at Hamilton Academicals for the visit of Hearts in 1937 and the 75,038 who were registered as having entered Tottenham's ground for their tie with the Cup holders Sunderland in 1938. League matches too could be big drawers and records never now to be surpassed included 51,380 at Stoke for the visit of Arsenal in 1937, 49,838 when Partick Thistle entertained Rangers in 1922 and 49,335 at the second division game between Fulham and Millwall in 1938.

Prices of admission had always varied according to the accommodation offered. Standing was cheaper than sitting; standing under cover was usually more expensive than standing in the open; and standing on the side, often in special enclosures or paddocks, was usually more expensive than standing behind the goals. Before the 1914–18 war the minimum price for admission to league grounds was sixpence (2½p) for adult males. In the inter-war years the most popular price was 1/– (5p) whereas since 1945 it has risen steadily to 5/– (25p) by the end of the 1960s and £1.00 in 1981. The Chester report in 1983 estimated that the popular price had multiplied seven or eight times in the previous fifteen years as against a four or fivefold rise in the retail price index.[9]

In the years after 1918 there was not too much anxiety about how these large crowds were crammed into league football grounds. Certainly the football ground had become a common feature of the urban landscape. Like Topsy most British grounds had just growed, along with the clubs, although some had been, and in the case of Bramall Lane, Sheffield, for example, remained, cricket grounds. In the 1870s and 1880s they had often been completely open to the weather, surrounded by ropes or palings. A pavilion would often be the first structure to be erected, somewhere for the players to change, perhaps, and for the committee or better-off supporters to sit under cover on match days. The first major grandstands were built in the 1890s after professional league football prospered. Much

5.3 'Amazing Crowds at Highbury'. This was Arsenal v. Tottenham in 1934. Was it better to be locked out and keep your money or pay to get in and not see anything?

of the early building on British football grounds was the work of a Glasgow engineer, Archibald Leith. He began at Parkhead and Ibrox, built Hampden Park in 1903 and his last major stand, completed in 1936, remains to provide style and solidity to the east side of Tottenham Hotspur's stadium.

Most British grounds were basically the same but had sufficient physical differences to suggest individual character. By the 1920s most would have a grandstand taking up one side of a rectangle plus three lots of open terracing. These terraces were commonly wooden framed on an earth banking. Dressing and board rooms would be located under the main stand. Increasingly a standing enclosure would be provided in front of the grandstand. The terracing behind the goal was often steep and high, commanding a dramatic view of the game. Several of these constructions were christened Spion Kop after the hill for which a battle was fought in the Boer War. There were few changes in this basic design until the 1960s, by which time concrete terracing and the cantilever stand had appeared. The first

5.4 Many British grounds were improved early in this century. This is Villa Park about 1900

of the latter was built for Scunthorpe United at their Old Show Ground and has already disappeared with the move to a new ground. The one at Sheffield Wednesday, erected in 1961, merited a mention in Pevsner's *Buildings of England*.[10]

What can be said about the game the people came to see? It is interesting to look at the progress and changing styles of play on the field through the careers of three wing forwards – outside rights as they were once known – whose careers did not quite overlap but who covered the bulk of the years from 1900 to 1977: Billy Meredith, Stanley Matthews and George Best. Meredith, who played for Manchester City and Manchester United between 1894 and 1925, saw the penalty area restricted to that immediately around the goal in 1902. Previously it had stretched across to the touchlines. From 1903 a goal could be scored direct from a free kick awarded for one of the seven penal offences of tripping, pushing, holding, kicking an opponent, jumping at an opponent, charging from behind and handling. Striking an opponent was added in 1914. The goalkeeper's privileges were being redefined too. From 1901 he could not be charged except when holding the ball, obstructing an opponent or when venturing outside the penalty area. After 1927 he could only be charged when in his own goal area and when holding the ball. From 1905 he could not advance from the goal line at a penalty kick and from 1929 he had to remain rooted to his line until the penalty was struck. His privilege of being able to use his hands outside the penalty area was removed in 1912.

Perhaps the most crucial difference in the laws of the game between the time when Meredith played and the forty years or so embracing the careers of Matthews and Best was the different offside law. Until 1925 you were offside if three opponents were not between you and their goal line when the ball was passed to you in their half of the field. After 1925 the number was reduced to two. The impact of this change on the nature of the game still provokes argument.

During the many seasons which Meredith played most teams adopted a 2–3–5 formation. The two wing half backs marked the opposition wings while the two full backs dovetailed inside to cover the centre. There was no third back, or defensive centre half. The centre half was a much freer utility player; he had defensive duties but was also free to move up in support of the attack. The offside law in Meredith's day made long forward passes relatively unproductive, especially as some teams adopted deliberate offside tactics which sometimes involved playing one full back in a deep defensive position. This put a premium on dribbling past opponents and making progress by short passes, either between forwards moving up together or in triangular patterns between half back, winger and inside forward. Meredith's role as the winger was to take on half back and full back and make progress to the corner flag, thence to cross the ball into the middle. If the attack moved up the opposite wing, then his role was to move inside to meet any ball that might arrive at the far post. Meredith himself was not so keen to cut inside nor to drag the ball back from the goal line although we are assured by contemporaries and later critics that he could do both. His control was good, he passed and dribbled well and regularly scored goals. He was not the fastest player and clearly slowed over a long career, but he was strong enough to withstand the quick tackling and heavy shoulder charging that was a feature of the game in his time.

Meredith had a somewhat controversial career off the field. He was an

early activist in the player's union in Manchester and a firm believer in
the idea that the top players should receive top wages. He was also convicted
by the FA of offering a bribe to an Aston Villa player in an attempt to
fix the result of a match and of accepting illegal payments, doing both
while with Manchester City. The club was punished and he was suspended
for the whole of the 1905–6 season.[11]

By the time Matthews first played for Stoke in 1932 the change in the
offside law had begun to make an impact on the game. Not everyone had
seen the need for the change. It appeared to be yet another example of
the FA truckling to business football – the League had been worried about
the decline in the number of goals as a result of deliberate use of the offside
trap. They were anxious lest the spectator should be discouraged. The
change appeared to have the desired effect. Most club and individual scoring
records in the English and Scottish Leagues came from the next 15 years.
But it also provoked a defensive realignment. The centre half's freedom
was revoked. He was pulled back to play between the two full backs as
a third back, either marking the opposing centre forward or being responsible for a zone around the front edge of the penalty area. The other
defenders were supposed to play around him. He was the pivot of a new
defensive system. In order to replace the centre half in midfield and attack,
one of the inside forwards began to take on the responsibility of linking
defence with attack. The W formation of forward play was born with
two wingers and a centre forward pushed well up the field and two inside
forwards joining two half backs in the midfield, some being given more
attacking, some more defensive, responsibilities. Not all teams changed
overnight and throughout the rest of the 1920s and the early 1930s some
teams played with three full backs, some two, some with both wingers
very wide and deep, some with them as far forward as they could be without
getting offside. But the success of Arsenal ensured that the new system
with its concentrated defence and rapid counter-attacks often based on
a couple of long passes and the speed of the forwards, would soon be
universally adopted. According to the veterans of a previous age it meant
that thrills had replaced frills. It seemed a reflection of the faster pace
of life.[12] Even in Meredith's day critics had argued that the game was
becoming too fast with no time to indulge in skill or artistry. There seemed
more justification for such opinions in the inter-war years as the players
got bigger and younger and the speed went up another few miles per hour.
To some people who saw both, the football of pre-1914, like the cricket
of the same period, seemed like a Golden Age. A contemporary critic
damned the game after watching the 1920 Cup Final: modern professional
football was like modern war, months of boredom, punctuated by moments
of intense fight, he said.[13]

Matthews broke into a game in which the professional foul, especially tripping from behind and deliberate hands, had long been a persistent irritant. It *was* also faster than ever before. But it was a game that still valued the wingman's contribution which in Matthews's case was far from inconsiderable. As a young man he was very quick, especially over the first ten yards, and this gave a tremendous impetus to his dribbling ability. He was quite a goalscorer in his early years, once getting a hat-trick for England in a fortunate victory over Czechoslovakia in 1937, but his aim became increasingly to reach the goal line and then to pull back a pass to a colleague running in. Meredith later claimed that Matthews would not have been given the time to play had he been active in the Meredith era, but this seems doubtful particularly as one of the Matthews's hallmarks was his ability to tempt the defender into the rash and often rushed challenge but not to be there when he arrived. Moreover Matthews's impressive acceleration over the first ten or fifteen yards took him clear of many would-be assassins.

Certainly, Matthews, like Meredith before him, was a star. The knowledge that he was playing would add considerably to the gate at home and away. Crowds wanted to see him deceive by skill, wit and pace, or to be played out of the game by a no-nonsense full back. In two senses he became a marked man but does not appear to have complained about it.[14] He gave immense pleasure to the people of Stoke, for whose team he played from 1932–47. When it appeared that he might leave for another club in 1938, a packed public meeting convened by local industrialists, probably helped to prevent it. Does such an episode tell us something about the geographically and culturally isolated, one-industry Potteries, or does it indicate something more about inter-war British society and football's place in it? The war both interrupted Matthews's career and emphasised his exceptional talent as he starred in a series of wartime games, several being internationals at Wembley. In 1947 he did move, to Blackpool, where he had bought a small hotel. At the age of 38 he helped his new club win the 1953 Cup Final. Like Meredith he played until he was 50. In 1965 he became the first footballer to be knighted, roughly 12 months before England won the World Cup without playing any wingers at all. In 33 years of the professional game Matthews had never even received a caution from the referee. By the time Matthews finally retired in 1964, a young winger from Belfast was entering a changed football world.

Neither Meredith nor Matthews ever had defensive duties. When their own team was defending they would usually be seen perhaps in their own half, more likely hanging about the half-way line, waiting for a clearance to come their way in order to initiate another attack. By the mid-1960s the relatively rigid W formation which had produced a clear division of labour between the players in the team was being replaced by more fluid and defensive systems. The football coach had become the dominating figure in the professional game. The true battlefield was identified as the midfield area where the struggle for possession of the ball took place. In the 1950s the Hungarians had removed their centre forward from the central prong of the W to a more withdrawn position and sorely confused the English and Scottish defences. The midfield area began to be congested whether the playing system was 4–2–4, the more cautious 4–3–3, 4–4–2, even 5–4–1. With these changes came a greater emphasis on physical condition and speed, especially in the English League. Best, who first played for Manchester United in 1963, began life as a winger, but the changing nature of the game forced him into a more centrally attacking role, with some freedom to move up, back and across in the search for openings. Best had all the skills of a Matthews and a Meredith and he needed them in a game which seemed to become faster by the season with space and time at a premium. He could dribble, pass and finish. He was also expected to tackle back and not to neglect defensive duties. Tightly marked and often harshly treated on the field he was the focus of press and television attention off it. He was a star whom the media would not allow to live a quiet life even if he had wished to. He was El Beatle, the pop-star football player of the 1960s, with more money and more opportunities to consume than Meredith or Matthews had ever had. There was never any chance that Best would play until he was 50. He had given up by 28. Meredith would have recognised the football of the Best era but have been astonished by the changes since his day. It was not only that balls and boots were lighter, shorts briefer, shirts thinner, and hair longer; nor was it that there was now shirt numbering, floodlights and substitutes. It was also that the whole career structure of the professional player had undergone a dramatic change.[15]

III

Week by week, in the widest variety of climatic conditions and against all sorts of physical and mental intimidation, he submits himself to vigorous and merciless public scrutiny. It is an ordeal that few of us need face, and an excellent reason for according our respect to those who must do so.

Bob Crampsey, *The Scottish Footballer* (1978), p. 48

Like other spectacular callings with an opportunity to achieve glory or at least a brief notoriety, the professional footballer's life has seemed an attractive one for many generations of schoolboys and young men. Surely

5.5 In 1965 Arsenal had just signed this Blackburn 13-year-old. Here his parents
admire his 'exceptional talent'. Unfortunately Philip Isherwood didn't make it.
Arsenal have no record of him

it must be better than office, factory, train or mine. But since 1900 only
about 3–4,000 of each generation have attained the cherished ranks and
even for those it was not always a life of beer and skittles. Even if things
went well the career could barely hope to survive for twenty years, while
injury, loss of form or the misfortune to play in teams badly managed
could bring it to a close long before that. Ex-footballers could then find
themselves short of friends, capital, work and, above all, psychic satisfaction. As Billy Meredith's biographer so understandingly put it when referring to his life after football: 'like a precious possession that he had let
fall into someone else's hands, football was a source of anxious concern
to him and he suffered a mixture of heartbreak at its loss and jealousy
of its new owners'.[16]

But the material rewards of football have undoubtedly grown. If Billy
Meredith could return today he would be very gratified at the earnings

of the top players. Sir Stanley Matthews too must occasionally reflect on what his salary might have been in the 1980s. All of Meredith's and most of Matthews's career covered the nearly six decades of the maximum wage. Before 1914 it was fixed at £4 all the year round but in the first years of peace a combination of inflation and player pressure pushed it up, briefly, to £9 a week. The maximum was £8 per week for most of the inter-war years and gradually rose after 1945 to reach £20 per week during the playing season and £17 in the summer by 1961. Not all players received the maximum, of course, even with the bigger clubs. West Ham, for example, had only seven players on the £8 maximum in 1925. Perhaps 10 per cent of players were on the maximum in the 1930s and about a quarter in the 1950s. Some players obviously did much worse than the maximum, especially in the close season. There were also signing-on fees, benefits after five and ten years with a club and, perhaps, business help from club directors. Some of the bigger clubs began providing houses between the wars. A number, certainly relatively small before 1945, might earn extra cash by journalism or for advertising products, as George Camsell did in 1928 when he praised Phosferine as the greatest of all tonics. And then there were the under-the-counter payments, rumoured to be widespread but rarely surfacing in the company of sufficient evidence to allow the FA to prosecute offenders. We saw that in 1905 they did find Manchester City and Meredith guilty of illegal payments. A successful case was also brought against Sunderland in 1956 but it is not clear how large was the iceberg under this tip.[17]

The maximum wage, together with the retain and transfer system, was an attempt by the men who ran football both to control the professional and to prevent a small number of rich clubs monopolising all the talent. One reason why such a system lasted so long was the weakness of the players' union. The individual made his own bargain and even under a maximum wage the better paid did not always see the need to belong to a collective organisation. Before 1914 £4 per week was still double the wage of the skilled worker and much higher than the earnings of the unskilled or labourers. Moreover, although we have pointed to the job's essential insecurity it was probably as secure a job as most of the working class could hope to get. As the late Dick Walker, who played for West Ham from the late 1930s until 1952, told Chuck Korr, 'we didn't think a lot about money ... but we were doing a lot better than most of the people we knew'.[18]

There was some feeling in both press and public at the end of the war, and inside the game itself, that footballers should be better paid. They had had a good war, many of them in front-line positions, others helping to maintain the morale of troops and munition workers at home. Radio and press attention continued to exalt the status of the top players, contributing to the growth of a tendency among that group to compare their wages and conditions with other members of the entertainment industry with whom they occasionally came into contact. Moreover, during the massive boom in attendance in the immediate post-war years it was easy to feel that the players should have a greater share in the profits. One sign of this new feeling was a discussion of footballers' wages at the National Arbitration Tribunal in 1947. Two years later the Ministry of Labour set up a joint committee of themselves and the various interested parties.[19]

As we saw earlier, wages did rise after 1945 but the maximum wage was not abolished even though the Association Footballers' and Trainers' Union, led by former Portsmouth player Jimmy Guthrie, was pursuing a new deal for footballers. But not forcefully enough for some members and by 1958 the name had been changed to the Professional Footballers Association and a new and publicity-conscious chairman elected. Jimmy Hill organised a successful strike ballot during the 1960–1 season. If the maximum wage was not abolished, then footballers would strike, something which they had only come close to doing once before, in 1909. In the event, their demands were met without the necessity of a strike.

But the retain and transfer system remained, in many aspects a more powerful symbol of management's hold over the professional player. Each April League clubs made two lists. One comprised all those players who were to be retained and on what terms. The other listed those players who were not to be retained. If a player was on list one, but did not like the terms offered, he had some not always palatable choices. He could appeal to the League Management Committee. He could give up the game, because while he was retained by one club he could not find employment with another. In theory he could not be transferred to another club unless he agreed but in such situations pressures doubtless built up. It was often pointed out that longer contracts would serve one of the purposes of maximum wage plus the retain and transfer system which was to prevent the bigger and richer clubs obtaining all the best players, but clubs were reluctant to provide players with such security.

It took the courts to abolish it. In December 1960 George Eastham, Newcastle United's English international inside forward, asked for a transfer. His request was refused and in April 1961 the club informed him that he would be retained in 1961–2 on the same wages as in 1960–1. Eastham refused to re-sign. A further transfer request was rejected, Eastham took a job in the south and appealed to the League Management Committee. They said it was a matter between club and player and refused to intervene.

Table 5.1

Average annual earnings (£)	1955–56	1960
Skilled manual workers	622	796
Semi-skilled	469	581
Unskilled	435	535
League players	713	923
Division One players	772	978
(Division One) First team players	832	1,173

Sources: PEP, English Professional Football, XXXII, 496. *Planning*, June 1966, p. 131. Chester (1968), p. 35 and J. C. Routh, *Occupation and Pay in Great Britain 1906–79* (1980), pp. 120–1.

By this time, as he had not re-signed he was not being paid. But Newcastle refused to allow him to move elsewhere. In October 1961 he issued a writ against the club alleging that they were depriving him of the opportunity to earn a living as a professional footballer. This was an unlawful restraint of trade and he claimed damages. In 1963 Mr Justice Wilberforce found in Eastham's favour. A system of two-year contracts for players was agreed the same year.[20]

The average earnings of skilled manual workers had probably been rising marginally faster than those of footballers between the mid-1950s and 1960 (see Table 5.1). With the abolition of the maximum wage this rapidly changed. Between 1959 and 1962 the average earnings of first team players in the first division almost doubled and between 1955 and 1964 League players' average earnings showed an increase of 148 per cent. Average industrial earnings had gone up by 62 per cent during the same period. Bob Crampsey found that the wages of the average division one player in Scotland remained double those of the skilled artisan there throughout the period 1910–65.[21] New possibilities had been opened up for all professional players, especially those with the top 40 clubs. By the end of the 1960s the basic pay of players in the first division was between £3,500 and £5,000 a year and it was boosted by a variety of incentive schemes tied to results and drawing power. These were the years when television, both in advertising and its wider exposure of the game, embraced leading players as fellow workers in the entertainment industry. They were the years when George Best could commission an architecturally adventurous house in the Cheshire stockbroker belt and drive a Rolls Royce Silver Cloud. In 1968 the rules of the FA and the Football League still forbade players to have agents. But by 1978 no top player was without a financial entourage of agent, accountant and bank manager. And something close to freedom of contract had arrived. Players could sign contracts for any number of years and move at the end with no hindrance, the transfer fee being fixed by a tribunal. Signing-on fees and a percentage of the transfer fee were other boosts to the earnings of the football elite. The rush to get leading players to endorse products meant that they could make more outside football than directly from the game.

Kevin Keegan signalled the arrival of the modern footballer-businessman. He signed contracts to promote Fabergé Toiletries, Harry Fenton Suits, Mitre Sports Goods, Patrick UK (Ltd.) Boots, Nabisco Shredded Wheat and Heinz Baked Beans. He formed companies registered in tax havens such as the Isle of Man: Kevin Keegan Investments Ltd., Kevin Keegan Enterprises Ltd., and Kevin Keegan Sport and Leisure Ltd. He also had a four-year contract with BBC television worth, it was reported, £20,000. We noted earlier that more players were participating in organised football than ever before and they were buying £23 million worth of football boots each year. *Sports Trader* has characterised the 1980s as a 'veritable soccer boom'. It was a boom which enabled Bryan Robson to sign a contract for £25,000 a year to wear Balance Boots and Gary Lineker to endorse a boot for a 3 per cent royalty on sales which, his accountant hopes, will net one million pounds. In 1951 Stanley Matthews received £20 per week for endorsing football boots made by the CWS.[22]

Professional footballers do have relatively short careers and they do give some pleasure to millions. Between 7 and 10 million people watch a televised match even if attendances at the grounds have been falling. The wages of the leading players are no more irrational than those paid to leading bankers or company chairmen. It is also salutary to remind ourselves that in 1985–6 40 per cent of the 1,950 registered English League players earned less than £10,000 a year. On the other hand, 32 players earned over £60,000 and another 55 in excess of £50,000. Even those 227 earning over £20,000 a year on 1 January 1985 were earning 25 times the 1961 maximum wage when prices and average earnings have risen only six or seven times since then. Footballers' wages actually rose 45 per cent between 1979–80 and 1980–1 when the price level only went up 20 per cent. The other side of this coin shows that 3,022 players were retained by English League clubs in 1960–1: in 1985–6 that number had fallen to 1,950. All this suggests that professional football has entered a new business age.[23]

IV

Football still offers the best sponsorship there is . . . it is demographically unbeatable.

Barry Gill of CSS, 'The business of sport', *The Observer*, 10 April 1988

As we have noticed already, opponents of professional football have long stigmatised it as a business. The need to make money meant win at any cost and to hell with the *spirit* of the laws. Get away with what you can. Buy and sell players as if they were sheep. Prejudices often contain small grains of truth and those manifested by the critics of the professional game are no exception. Of course there had to be a business element to football played between two teams of paid players on an enclosed ground, with an entrance fee to watch, and run by a limited liability company. But the game's rulers, in England especially, had always tried to control the business side: directors could not be paid, dividends were limited to 5 per cent before 1914 and 7½ per cent thereafter. The competitive aim did not include eliminating all rivals as in normal commercial operations. A football club cannot survive alone. This was recognised by the Football League's adoption, from the beginning of this century, of a strategy of income redistribution between the clubs. Home teams took the bulk of the gate receipts but paid a small per capita sum to the visiting team which by the end of the 1960s was fixed at one shilling (5p) for each adult and 6d (2½p) for every schoolchild, the minimum payment being £100. After 1945 a 4 per cent levy on total gate receipts was pooled and divided between the clubs and the money from television and the football pools was similarly administered. In Scotland gate money from the standing terraces, but not the seating accommodation, was shared from 1905.[24] Interestingly, as there had been no maximum wage in Scotland, neither was there an official limitation on the payment of dividends. Not that many Scottish clubs appear to have paid any at all, except Celtic and Rangers. They are particularly notable exceptions, however. Celtic paid 20 per cent in their first year as a company and in 1913 each of their senior directors received £50. In the three seasons 1963–6 Rangers paid out £93,000 in dividends – four times as much as was paid by all the English League Clubs taken together.[25] Similarly shareholding in professional clubs in both England and Scotland, certainly up until 1945 and probably long after for many of the clubs, appears to have been an extension of the supporters' role. Many clubs had considerable numbers of working-class shareholders who each owned a very small number of shares, often only one. Their motives were clearly not financial.

The motives of directors were usually very similar to those of shareholders. The aim was to win football matches rather than make money: although if the club managed to do one they could generally rely on doing the other. But when profits were made they were usually ploughed back into reserve funds, to be used for ground improvements or strengthening the team or to meet expenses in the less successful years which eventually came to every club. Football clubs were utility rather than profit maximisers whose sole aim could not be 'to make profits, for persistent losses on their football activities are tolerated by the large majority of them'.[26] But in the 1980s these losses became so severe that the word 'crisis' began frequently to be associated with football in discussions which often seriously questioned its future.

It is well known that attendances at League football matches in England peaked in 1948–9 when they reached 41.2 millions. These had fallen to 29.6 millions by 1969–70 and 24.6 millions a decade later. In 1984–5 they had declined to 17.8 million, a fall of nearly 28 per cent. The biggest falls over the period 1959–60 to 1984–5 had been in the third and fourth divisions but no club had escaped. Declining crowds were not entirely matched by falling gate receipts – because of increases in the price of admission and the rise in the number of seats – but the costs of running the clubs had escalated dramatically. Players' wages, VAT from the 1979–80 season onwards, ground improvements following the Safety of Sports Grounds Act of 1975 – which often involved borrowing at high rates of interest – and the costs of policing on match days, swallowing about 9 per cent of gate receipts by 1984–5: all these combined to force clubs both to search for new sources of revenue and to look at the way they were run.[27]

Up to 1914 directors ran football clubs, often picking the team that a trainer and perhaps a secretary prepared during the week for match play. The club office was a very small affair. During the inter-war years many League clubs began to appoint managers or secretary-managers to run them, often with quite wide business as well as footballing responsibilities. The success of Herbert Chapman, first at Huddersfield and then at Arsenal, gradually persuaded more and more boards of directors to appoint a football expert to run the playing side. Even so the team manager did not become universal until after 1945 and directors' interference in team matters has probably never quite disappeared.[28] Increasingly the manager became identified as responsible for the success or not of the club and a recipient of the bouquets should it be the one and the brickbats and the sack should it be the other. In the last decade the size of the managerial team has grown perceptibly and although the number of players employed by the clubs has fallen, the bureaucracy has increased. Most leading clubs now have one paid director / chief executive but, in addition, they will almost certainly have a club secretary, a youth development officer, an advertising and promotions executive, a catering manager and a commercial manager as well as team manager. The Football League itself appointed a commercial director in the spring of 1987. What this reflects is the desperate search for alternative sources of income to meet increased costs.

Sponsorship found football in the 1980s. By 1982 Northern Ireland had two cup competitions and the Irish League sponsored by three drink companies, Morans, Hennessy's and Smirnoff. Skol adopted the Scottish League Cup in 1984-5 and Fine Fare the Scottish League in the following season. The Football League itself became the Canon Football League in 1983-4 and, after a brief liaison with the *Today* newspaper, the Barclays League in 1987. Each of the 92 League clubs receives a share of a million pound pool and there are an additional number of merit and incentive schemes. Individual clubs have been able to sign lucrative shirt sponsorship deals since 1983. Tottenham, for example, signed a three-year contract with Holsten worth £750,000 to the club and Wang agreed to pay Oxford United £300,000 over three years so that their name could appear on Oxford shirts. Sponsors also support individual matches, match balls (a long tradition) and the kit of individual players. At the grounds of the more prestigious clubs, executive boxes can be let to companies interested in entertaining clients on big match days. At Manchester United in 1986 such facilities cost around £3,000 a year and they had a waiting list. Some 3,000 companies were estimated to have taken part in football sponsorship during 1984-6. Shirt manufacturers have proved another lucrative source for several clubs. Adidas supplied the kit for Manchester United in exchange for the right to sell replicas of the first team strip. Aimed mainly at young supporters it was a market with a reputed £1 million annual turnover. Adidas gave the club £600,000 as a 'loyalty' payment over four years with an additional percentage when sales hit a certain figure. Umbro and Hummel UK, a Tottenham Hotspur-owned subsidiary of a Danish company, are competing for a replica market worth £7 million by paying clubs to change their shirts every two years. In 1987-8 51 out of 92 clubs did so, including cup holders Coventry City. The club tried to prevent their supporters learning about the new shirt deal before the Cup Final in which they were to appear in the 'old' shirts.[29]

A further important sign of economic pressure is the new breed of football club director. Increasingly drawn from the worlds of finance, advertising, property development, entertainment and newspaper ownership, they often appear to have little previous connection with either club or community. Some of them, such as Irving Scholar and Paul Bobroff, who wiped out the Tottenham debt by making the club a publicly quoted company on the Stock Exchange, claim that football and business can have a mutually beneficial relationship. But the motives of the newcomers have certainly aroused suspicions. In 1984 newspaper owner and publisher Robert Maxwell tried to buy Manchester United for £10 million. His money instead saved Oxford United from bankruptcy although his attempt to merge

Oxford and Reading foundered on the rock of popular feeling. He then bought Derby County and would have also purchased Watford had not the Football League remembered its rule about directors having an interest in only one club. Mr Maxwell claims to like football but what seems also germane is his involvement in a circulation struggle with the Murdoch papers.

Fulham was bought by Marler Estates for £9 million in May 1986. Marler may not have had much interest in the game of football but it did have interests in two other clubs very near to Fulham. It owned the Chelsea ground at Stamford Bridge, though not the club, and had recently purchased Queens Park Rangers. It was soon apparent that the plan was to merge Fulham with QPR and develop the former's riverside ground at Craven Cottage. Only opposition from supporters and other business interests together with the local authority's refusal to grant planning permission destroyed the scheme. Most football clubs do not occupy such valuable land as these three London clubs. But many football grounds are ideally located for megastores or shopping malls. The price of survival may be external vigilance.[30]

It remains to be seen what football's relationship with business will produce. It may still be that so far as the playing side is concerned, directors' hearts will continue to rule their heads and that the new generation of entrepreneurs will not expect to make profits directly from what some people now call the football industry. On the other hand, the bigger clubs may insist that the structure and financial arrangements of professional football in England change. Already, since 1983, the distribution of television money has been made less equal. In league matches home clubs no longer share the gate with visitors and the League's constitution has been changed to give more power to the big clubs. Professional football remains a peculiar business but it is less unrecognisable in 1988 as business than at any other time in its 100 year existence.

V

Severe stands the little referee.
Around him howls the angry multitude.
They dance with rage.
He is not hurried, his voice is neither high nor low.
If you throw things at me, he says, composedly,
I will close the ground for a month.
And the crowd is awed silence.

William Pickford, referee and FA administrator, *The Listener*, 19 September 1937

Of the three star players mentioned earlier only Best played in the current period of football crowd violence that has transformed football stadiums. 'Most football grounds in England and Wales are now built like medieval fortresses, with pens at each end, with barriers designed to prevent spectators from climbing over; with gates, fences and protective wire to prevent rival fans bombarding each other; and with the use of what is called a sterile area – a no man's land. The pens are built so as to ensure that the rival fans are, for practical purposes, locked in during the course of the game, so that they are not able to get at the opposition.'[31]

Stanley Matthews presumably is and Billy Meredith almost certainly would have been disappointed by these developments. Of course, football crowds have always aroused mixed feelings. On the one hand they were spectacular and exciting but they could also be unfair, dangerous and potentially destructive. An article in *Fry's Magazine of Sport* in 1913 found them unattractive. 'A magnificently fought out game ending in a goalless draw will leave the crowd sullen and morose; they will wend their way home from the ground with black looks, cursing the bad luck of the home side. An undeserved victory for their own team will leave no regrets as to the result... There is no sportsmanship in a football crowd... Partisanship has dulled its idea of sport and warped its moral sense. It cannot enjoy a game that has been won by the visiting team. A referee is good or bad (with adjectives), according to the manner in which his decisions affect the home side... It lives and thrives on success. Defeat disheartens it, and rather than watch its club get defeated it will stay away.'

Seventy years later the fascination with the beast was little diminished and the excitement of membership stressed: 'The cheering and the singing and the chanting from a crowd big enough to fill several hundred lecture theatres could not fail to have a profound effect upon him. He was as sentimental as Hitler about applause and crowds. As the stand rumbled and thundered around him his flesh thrilled and the spirit within was elevated and chastened. He felt the pain of his own isolated individual life' (Howard Jacobson, *Coming From Behind* (1985 edn), pp. 61–2.

Football crowds doubtless shared many of the mysterious qualities of other crowds but in Britain by 1900 no other crowds regularly gathered in such size. Moreover because most matches were won by home teams and the great majority of spectators were home supporters the role of the crowd in the outcome was thought to be important from professional football's earliest days. Watching football was a far from passive experience and not dissimilar to that of the Victorian music hall crowd before drink disappeared from the auditorium and a new breed of theatrical entrepreneurs cleaned up the performance.

As the popularity of the game increased, the size of football crowds rose dramatically. In 1908–9, for example, 6 million people watched first division matches, an average crowd per game of 16,000. By 1937–8 14 million saw the season's first division games with the average crowd up to 30,000. The FA Cup was an enormously popular competition. In 1905–6 63 matches from the first round proper to the final attracted 1.2 million spectators. In 1935–6 the same number of matches saw just over 2 million people go through the turnstiles from the third round to the final. Important league games, local derbies and cup ties often attracted more spectators than grounds could comfortably accommodate. Working out ground capacities was far from an exact science and crowds often spilled onto the pitch as overcrowding became unbearable. In the crush of spectators who often swayed down the terraces it was remarkable that more did not receive serious injuries to ribs or ankles. It could be a frightening, as well as an exciting, experience and on five occasions proved a disastrous one. At Ibrox Park in April 1902, a wooden stand behind the west goal collapsed during the Scotland–England international and 26 people fell 40 feet to their deaths. Over 500 more were injured. On 9 March 1946 an estimated crowd of 80,000 turned up at Burnden Park, Bolton to see the FA Cup match between the local Wanderers and a Stanley Matthews-less Stoke City. One corner of the terracing became heavily overcrowded, in part because some 1,500 people got in by climbing over turnstiles and a number of crush barriers collapsed: 33 people died and 400 were injured. At Ibrox Park, again, on 2 January 1971 a crush on a stairway near the end of a match between Rangers and Celtic resulted in the deaths of 66 people.[32] On 11 May 1985 a fire destroyed the main stand at Bradford City during a game against Lincoln with the loss of 55 lives. The fifth and most serious accident occurred at Sheffield Wednesday's Hillsborough ground on 15 April 1989 when 95 people, mostly from the Liverpool district, were crushed to death.

The Bolton disaster had been followed by a Home Office inquiry which repeated many of the findings and suggestions of the Departmental Committee on Crowds of 1924, itself established following the serious overcrowding at the first Wembley Cup Final the previous year. Closer examination of grounds, licensing, the construction of smaller sections on the terraces had all been suggested in the past but had never been enforced by any central authority, football or governmental. The Wheatley Report on the 1971 Ibrox disaster strongly recommended that stadia with a capacity of 10,000 or more should be licensed by the local authority. The 1975 Safety of Sports Grounds Act introduced a system of certification with the local authority listing the improvements which must be made if a ground

Crowds from the past

5.6   On the Stretford end of Old Trafford, 1936

5.7   A *Picture Post* article in October 1949 entitled 'Glasgow's Football War' included this photograph of a policeman waiting for Celtic and Rangers to take the field

5.8 Pre-hooligan youth at Charlton for a cup-tie against Scunthorpe United in 1962

was to be used for a given capacity. The operation of the Act was limited
to designated stadia which meant grounds on which international cricket,
football and rugby was played and all first and second division football
grounds. After the fire at Bradford City in 1985 the definition of designated
stadia was extended to all football league grounds with a maximum capacity
of over 10,000 which meant all but Torquay and Scarborough. The 1987
Fire Safety and Safety of Sports Grounds Act strengthened the legislation
and extended certification to all stadia with a capacity of 7,500. Unfortunately, this did not prevent the disaster at Hillsborough.

By the 1970s, of course, it was crowd behaviour which appeared to be
the most important issue facing football, in England at least. From the
1960s, descriptions and photographs of unruly activities both before, during
and after football matches and both inside and increasingly outside the
grounds began to appear on the news as well as the sports pages of the
newspapers and increasingly to be featured on television. Football hooliganism had arrived.

In 1983 an American social psychologist, Jeffrey Goldstein, classified violence at sporting events into five main categories: frustration disorders, outlawry, remonstrance disorders, confrontation and expressive riots.
Frustration disorders may occur when spectators' expectations about access
to the game or how it will be played are not met. Unfair behaviour by
the opposition or incompetence by the referee as perceived by the crowd
may also spark such disorders. Outlawry disorders occur when groups
of violence-prone spectators use sports events to act out their anti-social
activities by attacking officials or rival supporters and damaging property.
Such violence is seen as the mark of a delinquent element. Remonstrance
disorders take place when some of the crowd use a sports event as an
opportunity to express political grievances. Confrontation disorders break
out when spectators from rival religious, geographic, ethnic or national
groups come into conflict. An expressive riot can be produced by the intense
emotional feelings generated by victory or defeat especially if the circumstances are particularly exciting or unexpected.[33]

The great majority of disturbances on British football grounds before
1960 seem clearly to fall into category one. Matches abandoned when some
of the crowd thought they should have been completed, foul play by the
visitors and, in particular, referees identified as unfair or incompetent provoked most of the trouble. A typical example was the match between
Wolverhampton Wanderers and Bury in October 1919. Three minutes from
the end, with Bury leading 1-0, the referee awarded them a penalty. The
crowd came onto the field, the referee fled, and the match was abandoned.
At the FA inquiry the ground was closed for a month.[34]

Expressive riots do not appear to have been very common in British sport but it may be that those Scottish supporters who pulled down the Wembley goalposts in 1977 after the victory over England were taking part in such a riotous celebration.

Remonstrance and confrontation disorders clearly overlap. Both seem to have been rare on British football grounds although there are examples from Northern Ireland. In September 1912, when Carson was urging Ulster to prepare to fight against Home Rule, there was a riot at the Belfast Celtic–Linfield match. Sixty people were treated in hospital, five with gunshot wounds. In 1920 shots were fired into the crowd by the security forces at a cup replay between Belfast Celtic, a team identified as representative of Catholic and Nationalist sentiment, and Unionist Glentoran. The trouble began after Celtic supporters waved banners and sang in support of an independent and United Ireland. The year before, an Irish Cup semi-final between the same teams had been abandoned when, with Glentoran two goals ahead, Celtic supporters invaded the pitch. Although, according to *The Times*, Irish Republican songs were sung, it seems clear that, on that occasion, it was the combination of political feeling and impending defeat which set off the trouble.[35]

For four years in the 1920s Belfast Celtic withdrew from the Irish League. Their success, on their return, clearly did nothing for the self-image of Protestant Unionists and matches with Linfield, who, like Glasgow Rangers, only recruited Protestant players, were often characterised by vicious fighting among the spectators. The climax to years of hostility came during a match in 1948. A Linfield player accidentally sustained a broken ankle. At the end of the game Linfield supporters invaded the pitch and broke the leg of the Celtic player they held responsible. Belfast Celtic thereupon disbanded.[36]

Confrontation disorders also occurred in Scotland and especially in Glasgow. There seems little doubt that religious sectarianism was at the root of it. Glasgow Celtic were a Catholic foundation with strong Irish associations. Glasgow Rangers were an exclusively Protestant club with firm relations with Ulster. The supporters of most of Glasgow's teams in the early part of this century often organised themselves in brake clubs. Based on districts, public houses or churches, between one and two dozen men would travel to the matches in a horse-drawn conveyance, known as a brake, before 1914 and in a motorised version after the First World War. Colours were worn and elaborate banners displayed. It was in the 1920s, in part reflecting the changing political situation in Ireland, that Glasgow magistrates and police waged a successful campaign to rid the streets of the brake clubs who, they claimed, deliberately set out to confront each other and provoke serious breaches of the peace. But although the brake clubs had been tamed, violent confrontation between the supporters of Rangers and Celtic certainly had not and most of the 60 years since the 1920s has been punctuated by incidents, the last major one at the televised Scottish Cup Final in 1980.[37]

That leaves us with the category of outlawry disorders. It seems clear that many of the incidents labelled football hooliganism in England in the last 20 years could be characterised as outlawry disorders. Examples would be the fighting between spectators and police at Luton v. Millwall and Birmingham v. Leeds in 1985 and the attack on Chelsea supporters by a group of Cambridge United fans in 1984. Which brings us back to Justice Popplewell's description of the grounds as fortresses. Football hooliganism became a political problem. The state increasingly interfered in the world of football not only by increased numbers of police at matches but by special police units, the use of surveillance equipment and enhanced police powers. Crowd behaviour at football matches became part of the law and order issue on which the Conservative Party placed a high priority in three successful general elections. The liberty of the individual to go to a football match when and where he liked was severely if patchily curtailed. Luton Town banned all followers of the game from their ground except those living in the Luton district who held identity cards.

Popplewell had been asked to look into the operation of the Safety of Sports Grounds Act of 1975 with particular reference to the fire which destroyed the main stand at Bradford City and crowd trouble which resulted in the death of a spectator at the ground of Birmingham City. It was also agreed that he should take account of any lessons arising from the disturbances at the European Cup Final of May 1985. At that match in Brussels, Liverpool supporters broke into a section of the terracing containing Juventus fans and in the confrontation which ensued 39 people, mostly Italians, died and 400 were injured, crushed and trampled when a wall collapsed as they tried to escape. He confessed to a lack of success in reaching what he felt was an adequate explanation for football hooliganism.

He said that there had always been a small group who found violence attractive. The football ground is a convenient theatre for them at the moment though it could just as easily be somewhere else. Their main target is opposing fans. They do not only come from the rougher elements among the working class. Many have reasonable jobs and earn a proper living. A second group imitates the first group. The feeling of anonymity in the crowd produces loss of inhibition and self-discipline and membership of an enthusiastic and partisan group further contributes to an atmosphere in which violence can be produced. A third group have more 'rational' reasons for violence such as failure to get into the ground quickly or finding their habitual place occupied by others. Popplewell emphasised that the vast majority of spectators abhorred violence and just wanted to see the football.

He could offer nothing save further preventive measures: the unfettered right of the police to search those who are either entering or trying to enter a football ground to be made statutory; a new offence of disorderly conduct at a sports ground should be created for England and Wales; the power to arrest under Section 5 of the Public Order Act 1936 should be widened; the banning of the sale of alcohol in grounds should be reviewed for executive boxes; and all Football League clubs in England and Wales should adopt some form of membership scheme.[38]

VI

One might almost, in unsympathetic mood, call Association football a weed of the industrial field. It has run riot over a large part of the globe.
  Edward Shanks, *My England* (1938), p. 232

One result of the Heysel Stadium disaster was that English clubs were banned from taking part in the lucrative European competitions. This was a particular irony in that it was the British in general and the English and Scots in particular who did so much to introduce the game to Europe and further afield and to establish it as the world's most popular game in the first half of the twentieth century. The spread of the game was due to its basic simplicities and satisfactions but also, no doubt, to Britain's world power status and the ubiquitousness of her international commercial and trading connections. British communities sprang up in many parts of the world. There were 30,000 British nationals in Buenos Aires by 1877, for example. The British presence often meant schools and part of the curriculum was almost certain to be British games. On overseas fields it was unlikely that football would remain the exclusive possession of the expatriate for long. Engineers, sales representatives, clerks and manual workers of all kinds began football in Europe, Latin America and in the Empire, often aided by employers and entrepreneurs. One of the latter awarded a cup for competition between local teams in St Petersburg in 1907 and Sir Thomas Lipton gave a trophy for competition between Uruguay and Argentina in 1902. The British soldier usually carried a football in his knapsack and ships of the Royal Navy visiting friendly ports often organised football matches too. Once the process began it accelerated in a remarkable manner, a phenomenon helped by the number of British tour-ing teams, amateur and professional, prepared to venture on summer excur-sions abroad and by the wandering British football coach. Largely ex-professionals, they were already teaching the basic skills throughout western and eastern Europe and in far off Montevideo well before 1914.[39]

Britain, with its high standards, domination of the 1908 and 1912 Olympic football competitions, professional leagues, and international prestige was the country to whom the growing numbers of European football enthusiasts looked for leadership. Britain was, of course, gracious enough to provide it, but did not want to get mixed up in international committees or fed-erations. When FIFA was born with just seven members in 1904 none of the four British football associations joined. But the accelerating contact between footballers from these islands and the European mainland necessi-tated a reappraisal and in 1906 Britain not only joined but had D. B. Woolfall elected president. The 1914–18 war disrupted football as it did much else and a dispute over how quickly the footballers of Germany, Austria and Hungary should be allowed to play with teams of the former allied and neutral nations led to the British, who were against an early resumption, withdrawing from FIFA in 1920. The British associations rejoined in 1924 but differences as to what constituted an amateur meant that it was another short stay. The core of the dispute was the European insistence on broken-time payments. If a player missed work and therefore lost income by playing football he should be compensated: such compensation should not jeop-ardise his amateur status. The home countries demanded their own severer definition: only legitimate travelling and hotel expenses should be allowed; anything else turned the recipient into a professional. The British Associ-ations did not mince words as they pulled out of FIFA. Broken time would not work. Most of the football associations which made up FIFA were of recent formation 'and in consequence cannot have the knowledge which only experience can bring'.[40]

It might have been some consolation to those on the receiving end of such arrogance to know that the FA also refused to have anything to do with the Home Office Departmental Committee on Crowds set up after the pitch invasion of Wembley in 1923. No one could tell them anything about football. FA hauteur was even more strikingly shown by the response to Uruguay's invitation to take part in what became the first World Cup in 1930. Sir Frederick Wall's letter, dated 30 November 1939, deserves com-plete quotation:

Dear Sir

The letter of the 10th ultimo from the Associacion Uruguaya De Football inviting a Representative Team of the Football Association to visit Uruguay in July and

August next to play in the Worlds Championship in Montevideo has been considered by our International Committee.

I am instructed to express regret at our inability to accept the invitation.

The Uruguayans were so keen to have a British team in the tournament they even asked the Foreign Office if there was anything they could do. The Foreign Office declined to become involved.[41]

Nonetheless as football became an international phenomenon it could not fail to gather political significance and therefore Foreign Office interest. By the end of the 1920s it was expressing some anxiety that British professional sides on close season tours to Europe were neither behaving well nor playing well and in consequence doing nothing to improve the prestige of this country abroad. As late as 1938 the Foreign Office aimed 'to discourage the staging of football matches with foreigners and that on more than one occasion we have drawn attention to the embarrassing situation created as the result of the visits abroad of poor teams'.[42] On the other hand the use of culture to further foreign relations could not neglect sport and sport meant football as British diplomatic representatives in Greece and Portugal, for example, pointed out.

The 1930s was a period when Germany and Italy in particular saw sport as war by other means. Both the FA and the National Government had resisted TUC-led attempts to abandon an international football match with Germany in November 1935, and the Foreign Office were so anxious about the return in Berlin in May 1938 that Robert Vansittart sent a letter to the secretary of the FA reminding him of the England team's responsibilities. The Consular Report of Current Events in Berlin summed up a great victory in the prestige war: 'the splendid game played by the English team was thoroughly enjoyed by the huge crowd and it is now recognised that the excellence of English football is still something to be admired and coveted. The game undoubtedly revived in Germany British sporting prestige which had previously been discounted owing to disappointing displays by British professional teams in former years.'[43]

The British belief that their football was best remained a plant of sturdy growth despite unpredictable frosts. Our failures in the Olympics after the Second World War could be explained by the fact that the opposition from eastern Europe were professionals allowed to compete as amateurs by a supine International Olympic Association. Defeat in the World Cup of 1950 by the United States could also be forgotten in a pre-television era as an inexplicable aberration. Even the famous defeat at Wembley in 1953 by Puskas's Hungarians, whose manager turned the knife by insisting that not only were they amateurs but the players had given up their annual holidays to come over and play the match, seemed to matter less than the home victories under the new floodlights and on BBC Television, of Wolverhampton Wanderers over Moscow's Spartak and Budapest's Honved. British claims to superiority at club level provoked *L'Equipe* into initiating the moves which led to the establishment of the European Cup in 1955. It was twelve years before a British club won it.

Britain remained an important influence in FIFA particularly during the presidency of Sir Stanley Rous 1961–74.[44] He had been Secretary of the FA for 30 years and was firmly of the opinion that only ill-disposed persons brought politics into sport. He did much to encourage the game in those newly independent countries of Africa and Asia who saw sport as a relatively cheap and relatively speedy method of winning international prestige and who boosted FIFA's membership by 63 per cent between 1959 and 1984. But by 1974 he was 79. He took a 'European' view of the World Cup preferring a small competition comprising most of the elite teams from Europe and Latin America with token representatives of those nations whose football was improving but whose standards clearly placed them in the international fourth division. Europe had by far the largest number of registered players: it contributed the bulk of FIFA's income. With all due respect, could the tail be allowed to wag the dog? In 1974 he was defeated by a Brazilian multi-millionaire on a platform of a larger World Cup, with more places for the newer Afro-Asian countries, the glossy package to be paid for by world-wide television and multi-national sponsorship. It was a symbolic moment. Britain was not only no longer a great power but part of a European bloc which was itself outnumbered by former colonial dependants. It was a political victory as well as a triumph of the new commercialism over the remnants of the old amateur ethos. The game which Britain had exported to the world had finally cast off British tutelage.

Football in Britain has been a man's game in its literal sense: *a game for men*. The FA Council made it quite clear in 1921 that they thought it unsuitable for women who should not be encouraged to play.[45] Women *had* played, increasingly during the 1914–18 war and throughout the 1920s in some areas, but it is only in relatively recent times that organised football for women has really developed. There are now some 10,000 women players in some 300 teams, mostly in the south of England. Moreover the Sex Discrimination Act of 1975 has led to a small, but growing number of women refereeing men's matches.

But if football has been a game closely tied up with notions of masculinity it has also been associated with northern-ness. This is especially true of the professional sector. The Football League was originally made up of twelve northern and midland clubs and its headquarters were in Preston for years and even now has only moved as far south as Lytham St Annes.

John Bale found that in spite of economic changes which appear to have shifted the power and wealth of Britain inexorably to the south, more clubs and players per head of population were found north of the Trent and the dominant flow of talented footballers was from north to south. The strongest concentrations of the production of professional players in 1979 were in northeast England and in the northwest, especially Merseyside. South Yorkshire was another fertile district for footballers and so was central Scotland, a traditional recruiting ground for English, as well as Scottish, clubs.[46]

Football certainly has an extraordinary hold on the Scottish public. Attendances at Scottish League and cup games have risen each year since 1982 and in 1974 as many as 26 per cent of the adult population in Scotland paid to watch football. But football seems to have had an added role in the cultural life of the Scots, becoming the main medium of expression of a dislike of England and the English. The annual international between the two countries gave the smaller, poorer nation the opportunity to show its dominant neighbour that the British national game was played best of all by Scots. Such a view was buttressed by the knowledge, which provoked feelings of both pride and irritation, that the English League was heavily staffed by Scottish players.[47] Few English players played for Scottish clubs, a fact underlined by the notice attracted by the change in policy of the new management of Glasgow Rangers in 1986. The biannual visit to London for the Scotland–England international has seen many of these expressions of national feeling from 1913, when the *Manchester Guardian* described the Scottish supporters as demonstrating 'racial defiance' with their chants of 'Scot-land Scot-land' and the *Daily Express* match report was headlined 'Scots looters repelled', to 1977 when the celebrations of the Silver Jubilee of Queen Elizabeth II coincided with a rise in support for nationalist politics and a 2–1 Scottish victory at Wembley. At the end of the game the pitch was invaded and the goalposts pulled down. Some writers such as Stuart Cosgrove have linked the inconsistency of Scottish football to a national schizophrenia; 'the reality of being a small dependent country set against the desire to be independent and of monumental importance'.[48] But if football has often been characterised as the people's game, by which is meant northern, Scottish, male working-class people, there is evidence to suggest that, at least in England, it is less working-class than it once was. Although most recreational players still live in the high-rise districts of Britain's major cities and the main areas of council housing, significant concentrations have been identified in high status neighbourhoods with relatively young age structures. A survey of the changing face of football in 1982 noted that the vast majority of the 3 million adults who had stopped watching the professional game between 1970–1 and 1980–1 came from the lower class socio-economic groups. While those in C2 and DE fell respectively 42 and 41 per cent and those in C1 dropped 26 per cent, the ABs lost only 4 per cent.[49] There were other signs of a growing middle-class interest in the game. *The Observer* and *The Sunday Times* greeted the opening day of the 1950–1 season with one match report between them. By 1960 it was seven plus a review and a welcoming article. Clubs have increasingly sought to increase the size of the audience who will pay more and for seats as against the traditional standing places. They have been concerned with improving their image in order to attract commercial sponsorship and sponsors seek their customers from the better off.

Football in Britain is undergoing a commercial revolution. In 1960 gate receipts accounted for about 85 per cent of all the income of the average league club. By the end of the 1970s this had fallen to 75 per cent, and the trend is clear. At Aston Villa, for example, gate receipts in the four seasons between 1978–9 and 1981–2 were respectively 62, 64, 58 and 62 per cent of total income.[50] This will not result in any drastic change in control of the clubs because professional football has never been the people's game in that sense. Most club supporters have always had about as much influence on policy as the unenfranchised had on Victorian parliaments. The supporters' club has never been an alternative power base. Their heyday, like that of the professional game itself, was probably in the decade after 1945. Even in 1960 some 350 were affiliated to a National Federation claiming half a million members. Their main function was to raise money for the clubs and to run social events and match excursions. Their reward was not power within the club but controlled access to the players who by the 1950s had lifestyles some distance removed from that of the traditional supporters. Only shareholders could vote at the annual general meetings of league clubs. The frustrations which such powerlessness produced in a minority of fans, allied with modern technology had two interesting effects in the 1970s and 1980s. One was an explosion of fanzines in which small numbers of supporters, sometimes focussing on a particular club, sometimes analysing the problems of the game more generally, have their say.[51] The second effect was the establishment of a national Football Supporters Association, whose main aim is to claim a place in the game's governing circles. Perhaps this too is a sign of a developing middle-class involvement outside the board room.

England won the World Cup in 1966 – one of those moments, like the Kennedy assassination – when everyone in England remembers where they were. The victory was thought to have helped Labour win the general election later that year. In 1970, England's quarter-final defeat in Mexico

(An enthusiasm that cannot be damped)

FOOTBALL

BY THE

UNDERGROUND

HUMOURS OF LONDON Nº 3

5.9 Still an enthusiasm which cannot be damped?

was supposed to have contributed to the Labour government's loss of the election. Football is probably of less importance to fewer people in Britain now than at any time this century. Traditional football values of loyalty and sociability are under threat from a fickle and volatile local support. A variety of counter-attractions compete for the time, money and energy of the potential supporter. This decline in popularity has had the result of putting the professional game at the mercy of media and sponsor. In the 1950s football was thought to embody the limited but essentially decent side of traditional, masculine, working-class culture. The attachment of the street gang to football has tarred the game with the scandal of the pathology of working-class life. Yet there remains a world of knowledge and a memory of games and players, referees and famous victories, good seasons and bad. One enthusiast need only utter two words to another to betray the vast amount of sharing that is possible for them both, the product of a long involvement of time, attention and money. Perhaps therein lies the meaning of football. Mary Douglas called this a culture.[52]

NOTES

1 For the early history of the organised game in Britain see A. Gibson and W. Pickford, *Association Football and the Men Who Made It*, 4 vols. (1906), James Walvin, *The People's Game* (1975), Tony Mason, *Association Football and English Society 1863–1915* (Brighton 1980), John Hutchinson, *The Football Industry* (1982), Brian Lile and David Farmer, 'The early development of Association Football in South Wales, 1890–1906', *Transactions*, Honourable Society of Cymmrodian, 1984, pp. 193–215, Bob Crampsey, *The Scottish Footballer* (1978).

2 *Durham Chronicle*, 13 January, 3, 24 February, 2 March, 3, 17 August, 7 September 1928.

3 Scotland had two organisations: one for under-18s and one for under-15s. Department of Education and Science, *Report of the Committee on Football* (HMSO 1968), hereafter Chester (1968), pp. 15–22. By 1957 84 per cent of Public Schools played Rugby Union as the principal game whereas over 90 per cent of secondary modern schools played soccer. Grammar schools were split more or less equally between the two sports. *World Sports*, November 1957.

4 On Sheffield see Nicholas Fishwick, *From Clegg to Clegg House. The Official Centenary History of the Sheffield and Hallamshire County Football Association 1886–1986* (S&H CFA, 1986). The number of affiliated clubs in the Sheffield Association rose from 400 in 1914 to 700 in 1930, 897 in 1948 and 1,303 in 1983. The number of member clubs of the Birmingham & District CFA rose from 1,182 in 1925 to 2,424 in 1967, to around 3,000 in 1980. Michael Dintenfass provided the Ashington reference. Pamphlet, Ashington Coal Co. Ltd. (1924), p. 62–5 in Northumberland County Record Office 538 / 250 / 1. Richard Whipp provided the Potteries reference from minutes, National Council of the Pottery Industry, Football Competition Sub-committee, 28 March 1923.

5 Peter McIntosh and Valerie Charlton, *The Impact of Sport for All Policy 1966–1984 and a Way Forward* (Sports Council, 1985), p. 118. M. Shaw, *Sport and Leisure Participation and Lifestyles in Different Residential Neighbourhoods* (Sports Council, 1984), p. 45.

6 Two girls were among seven young people summoned for playing football in the street in Highgate in 1922. *The Times*, 12 April 1922. Offenders were

sometimes sent to prison although when that happened to seven Glasgow youths in 1933 it provoked a question in the Commons for the Secretary of State for Scotland. H. C. Deb, 280, Cols 2404-5, 25 July 1933. Street football teams playing on Sundays and run by the players themselves were a regular feature of at least one area of Liverpool in the decade after the war. J. B. Mays, *Growing Up in the City. A Study of Juvenile Delinquency in an Urban Neighbourhood* (Liverpool, 1964), pp. 169-77. Mays concluded that football should be used in the 'anti-delinquency drive to a much greater extent than it ever has been.' By 1988 tentative steps to follow that advice were being taken in Birmingham. See *The Independent*, 13 April 1988.

7 Scottish professionals were paid a maximum of £2 during the First World War and were expected to have another job. One of the most famous of them, Patsy Gallagher of Celtic, was fined by a munitions tribunal for absenteeism and later suspended for six weeks by the Scottish League. Gerry Rubin M/S (1984). There was no automatic promotion from the Scottish Second Division to the First before 1918.

8 Crowds are not the only measure of the influence and attraction of the game. Many workmen and youths would not have been able to go, due either to lack of money or time. But they could read about the game in comics and newspapers, talk about it with their workmates and, later on, listen on radio. The football pools had further widened the game's appeal by the 1930s. Many boys were introduced to football by their fathers. Both as a pastime and a job and, like many other cultural phenomena, from trade unionism to gardening, football ran in families. Even women might have a place behind the scenes of the junior club. For their important role in the affairs of one village club in North Wales, Ronald Frankenberg, *Village on the Border. A Social Study of Religion, Politics and Football in a North Wales Community* (1957), ch. 4.

9 The Football League, *Report of the Committee of Enquiry into Structure and Finance* (Lytham St Annes, 1983), p. 14, hereafter Chester (1983). Boys under 14 have generally been allowed in at half price. Women were often allowed in free before 1900 but by 1962 the Management Committee of the Football League was blaming them for falling gates. They remain a largely untapped source of support. At the end of the 1960s about a third said they were interested but less than 10 per cent went. Chester (1968), p. 52.

10 Liverpool's Kop opened in 1906 and was first covered in 1928. Famous Kops at Villa Park and Hillsborough were both open to the elements until comparatively recent times. The authority on football grounds is Simon Inglis, *The Football Grounds of England and Wales* (1983).

11 There is an excellent biography of Meredith: John Harding, *Football Wizard. The Story of Billy Meredith* (Derby, 1985).

12 *The Times*, 19 January 1925.

13 *The Times*, 26 April 1920.

14 See his autobiography *Feet First* (1948) and *Feet First Again* (1952) and also A. Davis, *Stanley Matthews CBE* (1962). He was never cautioned or sent off.

15 Best tried 'come-backs' with Hibernian and Fulham between 1974 and 1977. He also cooperated with journalists to produce bizarre biographies, *Best of Both Worlds* (1968), *Best: An Intimate Biography* (1975), Michael Parkinson,

and a third *Where Do I Go From Here?* (1981) with Graeme Wright, in which he denied much of the content of the second. Best appears to have suffered from Manchester United's failure to replace manager Matt Busby with an equally strong character, *The Sunday Times*, 9 December 1984. Shirt numbering was not made compulsory in League matches until 1939. Floodlights were allowed for Cup and League games from 1955–6 and substitutes for one injured player from 1965.

16 John Harding (1985), p. 207.

17 Phosferine helped cure a variety of conditions from maternity weakness to brain fog. *Durham Chronicle*, 20 January 1928. A former chairman of Manchester City had suggested the League declare an amnesty over illegal payments in 1950 but received little support. On the Sunderland case see Arthur Appleton, *Hotbed of Soccer* (1961), pp. 213–14 and Simon Inglis, *Soccer in the Dock* (1985), pp. 116–39.

18 Charles Korr, *West Ham United* (1986), p. 178.

19 A Committee of Investigation under the Conciliation Act of 1896 reported on the terms and conditions of professional players in 1952. On this and an economist's view of the footballer's pay and contract in the two decades after 1945 see Peter J. Sloane, 'The labour market in professional football', *British Journal of Industrial Relations*, 7 (1969), pp. 181–99.

20 On the Eastham case see George W. Keeton, *The Football Revolution* (1972), ch 8.

21 Crampsey (1978), p. 20.

22 Keegan's contracts were listed in *The Sunday Times*, 16 November 1980. For Robson see *The Guardian*, 21 May 1986 and for Lineker, *The Observer Colour Supplement*, 16 August 1987. *Sports Trader*, 24 February 1983.

23 Chester (1983), pp. 19–21. *Digest of Football Statistics*, The Football Trust, (1985 edn), pp. 47–8.

24 Chester (1968), p. 55.

25 Chester (1968), p. 54.

26 N. C. Wiseman 'The economics of football', *Lloyd's Bank Review*, January 1977, pp. 29–43.

27 Chester (1983), p. 18, *Digest of Football Statistics* (1985), pp. 3–16.

28 On the career of Chapman see Stephen Studd, *Herbert Chapman, Football Emperor: A Study in the Origins of Modern Soccer* (1981). Interestingly four shareholders held 35 per cent of the shares at Arsenal in 1937. *The Economist*, 17 April 1937.

29 See *Marketing*, 28 May 1987, *The Independent*, 14 August 1987, *Business*, March 1986, *Coventry Evening Telegraph*, 8 May 1987 and *The Times*, 20 August 1986.

30 On the Fulham and Chelsea affairs see *The Observer*, 1 March 1987 and *The Guardian*, 26 January 1988. On the Football League's decision to prevent Robert Maxwell buying Watford see *The Guardian*, 16 December 1987.

31 Home Office, Committee of Inquiry into Crowd Safety and Control at Sports Grounds, Interim Report, Cmnd. 9585 (1985), p. 41. Policing inside football grounds was expected to cost clubs £3.4 million in 1987–8. The Football Trust will pay about 35 per cent. But the cost of policing outside grounds on match days could be as much as another £16 million. In some areas it has been estimated

that 10 per cent of police strength was needed to cover sport on Saturday. *The Independent*, 18 January 1988.

32 Inglis (1983), p. 33.

33 Quoted in Home Office, Committee of Inquiry into Crowd Safety and Control at Sports Grounds, Final Report, Cmnd. 9710 (1986), p. 58.

34 *The Times*, 8 November 1919.

35 Alan Bairner and John Sugden 'Observe the sons of Ulster: Football and politics in Northern Ireland' in Alan Tomlinson and Gary Whannel (eds), *Off The Ball* (1986), pp. 146–57. *The Times*, 10 March 1919.

36 See John Sugden and Alan Bairner, 'Northern Ireland. Sport in a divided society' in Lincoln Allison (ed.), *The Politics of Sport* (Manchester 1986), pp. 90–117.

37 The best account of the good business which the 'Old Firm' has made out of sectarianism can be found in Bill Murray, *The Old Firm. Sectarianism, Sport and Society in Scotland* (Edinburgh 1984). See also Colm Brogan, *The Glasgow Story* (1952) pp. 175–7. The emotional commitment and identity which Celtic and Rangers attract is also explored in Tom Gallagher, *Glasgow: The Uneasy Peace* (1987) and Callum Brown, *Social History of Religion in Scotland* (1987). Ironically the sectarian identification of the clubs delayed the acquisition of sponsorship in the 1980s. To sponsor one club ran the risk of boycott by supporters of the other. In 1984 one firm agreed to sponsor both but by 1988 each had separate sponsors. Tom Campbell and Pat Woods, *The Glory and the Dream. The History of Celtic F C 1887–1987* (1987), p. 326.

38 Popplewell (1986), p. 60-4. A group of sociologists at the University of Leicester have made a long study of football hooliganism. Their findings are presented in Eric Dunning *et al.*, *The Roots of Football Hooliganism: An Historical and Sociological Study* (1988). In a later article they suggested that anti-hooligan measures such as heavy policing, fences and blacklists, may have produced groups of well-organised 'super hooligans'. *The Guardian*, 17 May 1988.

39 An introduction to the spread of football overseas can be found in Willy Meisl, *Soccer Revolution* (1955), John Arlott (ed.), *The Oxford Companion to Sports and Games* (1975) and Tony Mason, 'Some Englishmen and Scotsmen abroad: the spread of world football' in Tomlinson and Whannel (1986), pp. 67–82.

40 Quoted by Alan Tomlinson, 'Going global: the FIFA story' in Tomlinson and Whannel (1986), p. 93.

41 Public Record Office F.O. 395 / 434.

42 P.R.O. F.O. 371/22591. On Greece and Portugal see F.O. 395 / 555 and 395 / 556. The Foreign Office was firmly opposed to British teams visiting Latin America or South American teams coming to these islands as late as 1945. F.O. 371 / 45052.

43 P.R.O. F.O. 395 / 568. Ireland and Wales did not play international matches against non-British countries until after 1945.

44 His own version of these events is set out in Stanley Rous, *Football Worlds: A Lifetime in Sport* (1978).

45 *The Times*, 6 December 1921.

46 J. R. Bale, *Sport and Place: A Geography of Sport in England and Wales* (1982), p. 43.

47 In the 1960s one writer calculated that family outings to football matches in Scotland were twice as popular per head of population than in England.

D. E. Allen, *British Tastes* (1968). On the other hand, average attendances at Premier League games in 1986–7 at 11,721 were still some way behind the English First Division average of 19,794. The number of Scottish professionals with English clubs appears to have reached a peak in 1929 with 362. By 1965 it had fallen to 258, was down to 198 in 1975 and a rough calculation for 1987–8 suggests that only 115 are currently registered. Crampsey (1978), p. 32.

48 Stuart Cosgrove, 'And the Bonny Scotland will be there: football in Scottish culture' in Tomlinson and Whannel (1986), p. 102. *Manchester Guardian*, 7 April 1913. *Daily Express*, 7 April 1913. H. F. Moorhouse is currently leading a one-man campaign for the wider understanding of the cultural role of football in Scotland. See his 'Professional football and working class culture, English theories and Scottish evidence', *Sociological Review*, 32 (1984), pp. 285–315, 'It's goals that count? Football finance and football subcultures', *Sociology of Sport Journal*, 3 (1986), pp. 245–60. 'Repressed nationalism and professional football: Scotland versus England' in J. A. Mangan and R. B. Small (eds), *Sport, Culture, Society* (1986), pp. 52–9 and 'Scotland against England: football and popular culture' in *The International Journal of the History of Sport*, 4, 2 (1987), pp. 189–202. Brogan (1952), pp. 173–5. The Conservative Government insisted that the match be switched from Wembley to Glasgow in 1985 because it wished to prevent public disorder on a holiday weekend.

49 Quoted in *The Observer*, 19 September 1982. The survey was produced by Target Group Index, a branch of the British Market Research Bureau.

50 See A. J. Arnold and G. Stewart, 'Financing and management in the football industry', *Managerial Finance*, 12, 1, 1986, pp. 11–19.

51 On the fanzines see *New Statesman*, 30 October 1987, *The Independent*, 10 December 1987. On the other hand thirteen local councils have helped to rescue League clubs in financial difficulties but without any noticeable change in the way they are run. *The Guardian*, 20 April 1988.

52 Mary Douglas and Baron Isherwood, *The World of Goods* (1980), pp. 75–6.

GOLF 6

J O H N   L O W E R S O N

Golf . . . is the Great Mystery.
> P. G. Wodehouse, *The Heart of a Goof* (1926, 1928 edn), p. 15

Golf is widely held to be one way of ruining a good walk in the country, a cause of apoplexy and a prime factor in heavy drinking, and a tendency to waste time amongst the affluent male middle classes. It is certainly not a mass sport, although the recent impact of television has widened its spectator appeal enormously. In England, at least, it has been generally assumed to be a preserve of the snob and social climber, a significant rung on the ladder of status. The Welsh have often disliked it because it is associated with English invasions, with the alienation of native common lands and the disruption of the Sabbath. Amongst Scots, who like to think that they invented it, the hoary myth that it is a game for all classes still exists and there is a considerable feeling that its export to England and its consequent trivialisation was one of the sadder disasters of modern times. The very fact that one can write in this vein, drawn from an extensive literature of golfing humour, marks something of the game's singular importance in the last hundred years or so. It can be argued, as I will here, that golf represents *par excellence* a number of major strands in modern British society – the tension between spare time and active recreation, the frequent confusion between the idea of a game and the assumptions of a sport, and the parallel strands of exclusiveness and extension which the development of sophisticated signs of social class has necessitated. It also has a core of values which reflect the absorption into recreational activities of the ethics of utilitarian individualism, however much the activity and its followers may seem to be at odds with that.

I

Golf is only a game.
> P. G. Wodehouse, *The Heart of a Goof* (1926, 1928 edn), p. 102

The first issue is one of scale. Because golf has been a 'private' game for much of its modern existence the very extent and national impact of its

provision is rarely realised. The very figures are fluid; although it is unusual
for clubs to go out of existence in the way that they did earlier in this
century new ones are being added steadily. At the time of writing there
are some 2,101 clubs in the British Isles; 1,286 in England, 456 in Scotland,
116 in Wales and 243 in Ireland as a whole. They play over 1,994 courses
of an average size of 100 acres. Put another way, a total area greater than
that of the Isle of Wight is now devoted to the playing and servicing of
this one game, land which has been extracted steadily from agricultural
production and, occasionally, other recreational uses since the late nineteenth century. It is doubtful whether any other sport, with the possible
exception of game shooting, is quite so ravenous in its demands on the
landscape. Of those clubs, 1,224 (58 per cent) date from before 1914, 373
(18 per cent) from the inter-war period, and the rest have been created
since. Before 1879, there were 72, 52 of those in Scotland; the key decades
were the 1890s and early 1900s when 512 clubs were founded in England
alone and another 192 in Scotland.[1] If any game can be said to have 'boomed'
then golf is that one. Like most modern sports it has supporters who have
tried to give it a spurious place in antiquity, usually as a medieval Dutch
game called 'Kolve', a sort of individual hockey played on ice. Certainly
it appealed widely to that other Protestant race, the Scots, whose burgesses
and divines (as well as the occasional aristocrat) played it on the sandy
links of the eastern shore. Rudimentary rules, windswept discomfort and
a grim endurance seem to have characterised this development. That it
became a risk to the lives of the innocent is evident from the adoption
in some areas of red golfing coats and the alarm cry 'Fore!' as a means
of warning that players were approaching. Much repeated claims that this
was a 'democratic' game need to be tested against the evidence of the cost
of early hand-made implements and of balls stuffed with feathers, let alone
against diary accounts that show middle-class players setting off for the
links at times when local artisans had been at work for several hours.
It was pan-class in the sense that by employing helpers, poor 'caddies',
it did introduce some artisans to a game in whose growing popularity
they were to share as exiled demonstrators of the required skills, the golf
professionals. The wholesale export of what had often been dismissed as
'Scottish croquet' until the later Victorian period owes much to the nostalgia
of exiled Scottish commercial and professional men but probably more
to the holidaymaking habits of the English as the chances for travel offered
by railways were underpinned by a soft myth of Caledonia and her virtues.

Golf was imported by the English middle classes because it admirably
fitted a number of their late Victorian needs. Concerned about physical
health, self-persuaded that the demands of office work were a real risk
to mental wellbeing and anxious to extend into the middle and older years

some sense of the manly athleticism that the public schools they attended
or emulated had acquired as a cult, upper- and middle-class men found
an apparently perfect answer in golf. It could be played at almost any
age, it demanded exercise in the open air, it was apparently easy to learn
and it could be pursued for much of the English year, without the distinct
seasonal restrictions of almost all other alternatives. But it had other charms
as well. It did not seem to demand the rushing about of its contemporary
in popularisation, lawn tennis, and also it was not initially tainted with
the presence of women whose participation could only be expected to limit
the manly appeal of any activity in which they joined. Although few articu-
lated it as such, the structure of achievement in the game appealed considerably to the expanding commercial and professional middle classes. Its scoring
was mathematical and it offered several modes of competition: against one's
opponents in a match, against 'bogey' the abstract notion of excellence
on a particular course, and against one's own previous best performance.
Although it was rarely played singly, golf was a singularly personal game,
well suited to the consciousness of 'inner-directed' individualism offering
another set of possible targets for proving virtue.

Yet this was eventually far less significant than the opportunities it offered
for social differentiation, the measurement and assertion of status and the
display of achievement and acceptance in the class-ridden world of late
Victorian urban life. Clubs matched suburban needs, even when in smaller
market towns there were no identifiable suburbs as such. The colonisation
of the rural fringes which developed both from population pressures and
from the romanticised 'Englishness' of a singularly rootless society produced
a demand for tame rural recreational space, but space only to be shared
with people of like minds, like income and from a similar social band.
Clubs which were instrumental as syndicates in acquiring such space were
also devices for excluding people who would not fit, for encouraging emulation and the necessary degree of deferent patience which would prompt
an urge to join. Golf also brought with it an arcane language – Scottish
slang, 'cleek', 'baffie' and so on – that could easily be used to prop up
local snobberies.

Although there were several million potential consumers, virtually anyone
with an annual income of over £100, by the time of golf's first great popularity, the 1890s, the initial number of followers was much smaller: perhaps
60,000 or so by 1900 in the United Kingdom as a whole. The essentials
were available cash and available time. A likely average annual cost of
playing in Edwardian England was about £18, a sixth of an established
clerk's wages. A round of 18 holes took about three hours. For the many
who worked part of Saturdays there was considerable pressure on the afternoon and, increasingly, on Sundays despite the countervailing assumptions

6.1 You do not need to be young to play golf. When professionals retire they
can still compete in senior professional tournaments. This one was held at Fulwell
in April 1957. The driver was 72-year-old George Duncan and his partner the 82-
year-old James Sherlock.

of Sabbatarianism. In fact, golf became one of the wedges used by middle-
class men to break a hole in the restrictions on Sunday recreation. Inevitably
the lead was taken by the English, 40 per cent of whose clubs had adopted
Sunday play by 1913. Nonetheless just as important was the cohort that
had not, overwhelmed in percentage terms by much more intransigent
Welsh and Scottish customs. With such popularity it was weekday play
that dominated most players' thinking and it was the ability to choose
how to spend one's time that meant that the early players were usually
the younger retired, successful professional men and businessmen with a
commercial base sufficiently firm to be left to underlings. With the lingering
impact of the doctrine of work such absenteeism was soon garbed in the
distinctly untestable justification that golf offered an unparalleled opportunity for the conduct of private discussions, and the opening up of new
commercial contacts. It also drew down the accusation that playing the

game obsessively both lessened its recreative values and actually contributed considerably to the perceived decline in national moral fibre and competitiveness which resulted in paranoia over German-made imports in the 1890s and the reverses of the Boer Wars. Perhaps more than any other game golf became a sounding board for the moral dilemmas of an affluent middle class uncertain about its own specific social place and its future.

Although golf has very probably been played in Scotland since the fifteenth century, the oldest continuously extant club in the world is generally held to be the Honourable Company of Edinburgh golfers, dating from 1744. Arguably the single most significant date in the game's history is 1754, that of the founding of the St Andrews Club, later the Royal and Ancient, which remains the arbiter of golfing standards, rules and etiquette. Although the end of the nineteenth century saw both the refinement of regulations and attempts to set up various bureaucracies, golf has retained some of the anarchic localism of its roots. Influential though the Royal and Ancient might be, its place in the general hierarchy is honorific, its sanctions generally those of disapproval, although the growing twentieth-century importance of commercially sponsored tournaments played by professionals has led to regulatory patterns which exist alongside and intertwined with the older forms, and these have reinforced that authority.

Golf effectively came to England when Scottish exiles began to play in Manchester in 1818. But its spurt of growth can be traced to its connections with another burgeoning Victorian activity, the seaside holiday. In 1864 the North Devon Club (later 'Royal' – as in yachting the prefix became a necessary cachet) was founded at Westward Ho! and Englishmen played by their own sea for the first time. Close on followed the (Royal) Liverpool Golf Club at Hoylake. Oxford and Cambridge formed University clubs in 1875 and played the first university match three years later, claiming to have founded the first match between clubs, as distinct from within clubs or between separate individuals, in the world. From then on, although a substantial Scottish input remained, at least in terms of personnel, it was the English urge for and attitudes to sport which determined its growth. Whilst making money from offering advice, many Scots seem to have felt that their offspring had been spirited away and that the real virtues of the game were being distorted by the English.

By the 1880s individuals returning from their holidays north of the border or in the few favoured seaside resorts would often buy a few implements and one of a steadily growing number of instruction books and hit balls around suitable local land. As others watched and copied them small clubs were formed which then used the accumulated business skills of their members, as well as their bargaining power, to rent land. Golf's popularity coincided with the agricultural depression when marginal land was initially easy to come by at either very low rents or even low purchasing costs for the more ambitious. Only after a couple of decades was there a pressure from speculative builders around some of the larger towns, which forced some of the less firmly based clubs either to fold, or to begin a process of leapfrogging with housing estates until they could find a suitable and permanent site. By that time, however, the more prescient and prestigious builders were operating with club developers as they realised the value of a club's presence in raising the social tone and desirability of their offerings. In the 1890s a club was formed once a fortnight in England. Despite the assumptions that golf is a 'suburban' game it was one that flourished equally rapidly in market towns – Market Harborough in Leicestershire acquired a club in 1898, Newark in Nottinghamshire in 1901. Although there were obvious regional concentrations, particularly around the northern industrial towns and most especially in the south-east, golf reflected the general tastes and clubbability of a middle class that, if hardly homogeneous, claimed more in common than it recognised internal differences. The only significant regional variation in English golfing style was determined by whether a club played on seaside links or one of the increasingly popular inland courses. Whilst many, not least the Scots, would proclaim the eternal superiority of the former it was the latter which allowed the greatest opportunities for golf's anglicisation in terms of social rigidities, 'popular' emulation and conspicuous expenditure.[2]

In many senses it was this framework of providing for the game as much as the game itself which dominated its pre-1914 growth. I shall discuss the nature and developments in play shortly but there can be few sports which have so rapidly seen their fairly simple origins swept up by and encased in an apparatus of facilities far greater than its pursuit actually needed. Whilst a few northern clubs, such as Furness with its home-made course, held out for the simple style and the East Brighton had its royal membership playing from deceptively rudimentary club huts, most were caught up in the pressures for self-awarded signs of social achievement. The seaside resorts were very influential in this since golf became an integral part of their competition for a 'nice class' of visitor. In 1887 Eastbourne, the 'Empress of Watering Places', acquired a club with the patronage and practical help of its landlord and prime developer, the Duke of Devonshire, who leased it some downland sheep pastures. It soon attracted 500 members and a 'Royal' adjective, as could only have been expected. For a game so assuredly class-specific, golf acquired the unusual distinction of becoming a significant weapon in the first forays of municipal socialism as resorts entered into open battle by virtually any means to keep their place in the seaside hierarchy. Bournemouth began this in 1893, Brighton took until

1908. Municipally owned they may have been but they reflected little of the 'democratic' sense of socialism: pricing and leasing ensured that these courses were kept firmly in the grasp of those whom their developers wished to attract. In the long term the idea of public provision was to be a major focus of argument about the need to extend golf's participants in social as well as numerical terms, however those issues were well shrouded in the early days.

Many of the pioneer clubs played on such land as they could find, favouring the sandy heath and scrub of the coast and inland outcrops. This was often land that older communities had dedicated to common use. Two tensions emerged. Because of some uncertainty about ownership players often assumed that their game could be slotted into the gamut of uses which common land had allowed by custom. But, unlike the older playing of cricket or football, golf took up much greater areas of land and interfered more obviously with other users. Graziers found their cattle herded away and workers seeking breathing spaces found their walking and playing areas both blocked and dangerous. Lincoln was only one of a number of places where farmers destroyed golf tournaments by driving cattle into the middle of matches. There, at least, they won but in many areas it was the golfers' fiscal and legal clout that carried the day. On Mitcham Common in Surrey, it took over a decade of court cases before a compromise to protect the spatial demands of all three groups was thrashed out. Much of the traditional hostility between ramblers and golfers dates from the 1890s and is still very much alive in many areas.

Common land, heath and rented pasture which could not be played over before haymaking gave way fairly quickly to the dedicated course. Here two forces were at work; changes in golfing technology and skill levels related to challenging play were always important, but there was another major influence, the aesthetic sense of landscape. By the turn of the century the latter was increasingly significant and much of the game was pursued in surroundings derived from the inspiration of Capability Brown. The interrelationship between fairway, rough and woodland seems to have owed as much to the joy of the eye as to techniques and players' endurance. Golf developed into a mixture of game and convivial walk in a romanticised countryside, preserved for privileged syndicates. The Calvinistic purity of the Scottish wilderness often had less appeal to the English than their emulation of the gentry. This was reinforced by a growing emphasis on the '19th hole', a clubhouse with many more facilities than lockers and washrooms. The Royal Liverpool was prepared to lay out £8,000 on a new clubhouse in the 1890s: Leeds, which began with a cottage adapted for £3 in 1896 spent £3,500 on a replacement in 1909. Occasionally the more ambitious clubs took over estates from the impoverished aristocracy, converting instead of emulating manor houses. The Shirley Park Club at Croydon was created around Lord Eldon's former house in 1914 and the Royal Automobile Club was prepared to spend £75,000 at Epsom. Occasionally there was irony in this as when a proprietary group bent on attracting an 'exclusive' clientele spent £25,000 in 1912 on founding the St George's Hill Golf Club at Weybridge on land symbolically cultivated by the Diggers during the Civil War. The Club seems to have kept this link rather quiet.

Growing popularity and social pretensions of this nature pushed the cost of golf development up. Sample rents gave way to extended leases or even demands for land purchase. An unexpected slowing in death rates led the London Necropolis and National Mausoleum Company to lease land it had intended for interments in Woking, Surrey, to the local club. With such pressures there was an increasing tendency for clubs to protect themselves and raise money by forming limited liability companies. Occasionally, as at Leeds, this prompted a mild exodus of older members who felt that simplicity and spontaneity had been sacrificed to that commercialism which they hoped to escape in their sport, but by 1910, with new developments costing £200 a hole, there seemed to be little alternative. Simple 9-hole courses gave way to 18 holes and most larger towns acquired several distinct clubs to cope with the level of demand: such clubs often reflected the local status ladder within the middle classes. Historical lists make this difficult to reconstruct, but local discussions can usually produce an order of preference, and rivalry, fairly quickly.

It was not just the framework for the game which changed by 1900, so did the essential nature of play. The wooden clubs developed by the Scots for basic play were augmented steadily by a bewildering range of iron-headed ones for close play, the product of secondary casting techniques in the metal trades. Virtually the only thing they all had in common was the use of seasoned hickory shafts which offered the right combination of firmness and flex. Initially hand-produced by golf teaching professionals as a sideline in their sheds by the course they gradually moved, in the lower price ranges at least, into workshop manufacture by firms such as Spalding's and Slazenger's, as well as into anonymous products sold under department store brand names by Gamages, the Army and Navy and so on through their burgeoning sports departments. Feather-packed balls gave way in the mid-nineteenth century to those filled with gutta percha; this speeded up production but seems to have made little difference to the style of play. A major change came in the United Kingdom in 1902 with the introduction from the United States of the Haskell ball. This had a machine-wound core of rubber strips with a degree of elasticity which greatly increased the actual distance an average golfer could drive a ball. One almost immediate effect was upon courses which had to be greatly increased in length. Despite Scottish laments that such developments reduced the real skill of playing, the Haskell dominated the game within a couple of years and pushed development costs up considerably. With the pneumatic tyre fostered by the 1890s bicycle boom, the spread of motoring and the much lower-key production of the condom, the new golf ball built up the status of leading firms in the rubber industry. By 1914 golf balls were selling £2,000,000 worth a year, roughly the same level as banana imports. Yet, despite this growth, unit prices stayed firm: no large firm seemed willing or able to go below the half-crown limit until well after the First World War. This dominance meant a high level of failure for smaller firms which tried to break into the Edwardian market.

II

A professional is one who carries clubs for hire or receives any consideration, either directly or indirectly, for playing or teaching the game (with the exception of instruction by writing) or playing in a match or tournament. All others are amateurs.

> Ladies' Golf Union, 1938, in *Golf Illustrated*, 5 February 1938

Golf's first and most consistent appeal was as an amateur game, onto which much of the *corpus* of late Victorian notions of ethical purism was rapidly grafted. Much of the early writing on technique concentrated as much on style as on efficiency, the stroke was to be viewed as an art form. Occasional eccentrics such as the sporting journalist and amateur champion, Horace G. Hutchinson, were allowed to get away with play which was distinctly unconventional but the general emphasis was towards elegance of swing, and this was reinforced when photography became a standard component of instruction books and golfing magazines in the Edwardian years. That it was better to play well than to win was transferred to golfing expectations just as readily as it was taken up elsewhere by the English. The very way in which the Royal and Ancient was left to change rules very slowly, despite occasional grumbles and abortive threats to provide a 'democratic' and representative national federation indicated a considerable fear that over-regulation would actually benefit the professional and the development of marginal foul play in an all-out effort to win. Many golfers cast a nervous glance at the rows which beset the Football Association. Yet the game avoided the rank social discrimination which permeated rowing: there was none of the bland assumption that only a gentleman could teach another one how to play properly. Much of this was undoubtedly due to the way in which the game was imported from Scotland, together with Scots artisans who, if they were halfway competent, found a ready employment market amongst the instruction-hungry English. Like real tennis but on a much larger scale golf developed as a game where it was perfectly acceptable to play regularly against a professional, both as instructor and as another measure of the development of individual skill. Yet the servant nexus was never very far distant, since the average club professional rose through the ranks rather like a superior domestic employee. Hours of bedraggled observation as a caddie could lead up to ground care, clubmaking and beginning to play with members. The path usually lay south where an ordinary professional could expect to earn about the same as a skilled foreman, albeit working far longer hours. Yet Scots dominance did not last long: by 1900 over half of the 300 English club professionals were natives. Job security was limited – Tom Williamson, the Nottinghamshire Golf Club pro for 54 years never had more than a 'temporary' appointment.[3] For many, a major part of their income came from the equipment shop they were normally expected to run at their own risk and this was repeatedly threatened by clubs, which saw sales as a means of reducing their own liabilities, or by members, who bought in bulk as syndicates. There was also considerable bitterness when many paid club secretaries and players such as Hutchinson, who made a considerable income from journalism, still claimed the right to play in amateur tournaments whilst the usually far superior professionals were excluded. The longer-term outcome was the emergence of the 'tournament pro' who now dominates many people's perception of the golf scene, free in all but name of being tied to clubs.

Playing with the pro was still very different from mixing with him and most ordinary golfers seem to have exhibited the same degree of social blindness with which they treated servants in general. If they were prepared to allow their workers to play and to be condescended to in the way that English fishermen treated Scottish ghillies, they were rarely ready to allow English or Welsh artisans onto their courses as equals. There was a slow movement to found some artisan clubs, led by the Royal Ashdown Forest when it founded the Cantelupe Club in 1897, an example Hoylake copied with its Village Play Committee. This was prompted less by a sense of equality than by a calculated coming to terms with local opposition to the loss of common land by effectively buying it off, and by the instrumental offering of free or low cost play to artisan members in return for maintenance work on the greens and buildings. Artisans were only allowed to play when most members did not want to, although deference and patronage usually came together in an annual competition for which the middle classes provided both the prizes and the refreshments. Yet these artisan clubs became

6.2 You can play golf in all weathers too. This is one of the few artisans to reach
the top, first as an amateur and then as a professional, Abe Mitchell at the Amateur
Championships of 1912, Westward Ho!

one source of great English players, as well as club pros. One of the greatest,
Abe Mitchell, revealed just how bitter a path this could be when he became
a tournament pro just before the First World War. He expressed his frustration at the way in which he was repeatedly treated as a very second-class
citizen by amateurs with whom he competed in supposedly open tournaments until he made the final break in which his skill could be recognised
for its own sake as well as considerably boosting his winnings.

As the game developed, play for its own sake became caught up in the
general move towards club and then inter-club tournaments. It is perhaps
a mark of golf's quintessential individualism that early on it developed
a means of identifying overall 'champions'. Initially, and paradoxically,
this was a Scottish and a professional honour. Prestwick inaugurated the
Open Championship in 1860, hosting it until 1870 when it was shared
with the Royal and Ancient and the Honourable Company from Edinburgh.
This rota persisted until two English clubs were admitted in 1893. The
initial prize, a trophy belt, was replaced by a cup in 1872. Played at first

over two rounds in one day, it was extended to four over two days in 1892. Because of the growing pressure of entries it was limited to 80 players on the eve of the First World War, those being sorted out by two qualifying rounds. Although its early decades were dominated by Scottish professionals the rewards were essentially honorific, with tiny money prizes until a prize fund was established in 1893, offering £100 in prize money, of which the winner received £30 and a gold medal. Clearly some of the new English players found both the standard of play daunting and the professionalism slightly suspect, so in 1885 the Royal Liverpool informally inaugurated an Amateur Championship persuading the Royal and Ancient to recognise a general one formally the following year. It moved between England and Scotland on alternate years, with a steady increase of the number of participating host clubs. Although the St Andrews doyens recognised the championship, control lay in the hands of the participating club oligarchy, 26 by 1914. Its history reflected the continued tension between the Royal and Ancient and the burgeoning English golfing world in which 'tradition' and the honorific continued to be expressed in deference to the former. It was as if the very newness of the game needed validation by an almost spurious attribution of tradition to its conduct.[4]

The first Englishman to win the Open was John Ball, a Royal Liverpool Amateur, in 1890, but it remained essentially a pro's tournament. The first winner of the Amateur was A. F. MacFie in 1885 but it was Horace G. Hutchinson who won the formal inaugural in 1886. Entries for the Amateur ran at a consistently higher level in the early decades, but the late Edwardian period saw a considerable upsurge in the number of professional entries for the Open Championship when prizes started to rise in value and a new species of pro emerged, the super-player whose link with a club often became nominal. The key figures in this became legendary: Harry Vardon, James Braid, J. H. Taylor and Ted Ray. These men set standards of golfing style and performance which were eagerly followed by thousands of envious amateurs in the popular and specialist press. Although the sheer consistency and expertise they displayed, together with regular practice, took them well outside the league of most of the leading amateur players, by 1910 they continued to offer, often through popular ghost-written manuals, standards which amateurs could hope to emulate. It took golf as a game and these players as a group well outside the normal amateur–professional divide of British sports.

But golf did not escape the ethical crises of sport in general. Whilst many golfers and club committees welcomed their professionals winning regional and national tournaments, as advertisements for the quality and status of the clubs, there was a persistent division of opinion over the extent

6.3 One of the first great professional tournament players. Harry Vardon in 1912

to which tournaments should feature in club life. Constructing seasonal rituals and ascribing playing as well as social and financial precedence within and between neighbouring clubs made the development of tournaments virtually inevitable, but there remained a strict emphasis on the symbolic in prizes and a deep fear of the motives of 'pothunters', whether motivated by an urge for gain or just a hunger for fame. Developing club teams was one way in which this was partly contained, but there was no escaping the significance of individual championship rounds, however scoring was measured, and the developing of handicapping systems (not fully worked out before the 1920s) both aimed for fairness and actually increased the problems as it offered further ground for argument.

III

Golf courses and golf rules should be made to consider the average rather than the experienced player.

A. K. Padgham in P. Lawless, *The Golfer's Companion* (1938), p. 85

The game which had been condemned by various Edwardian writers as sapping the English will to fight and opening the country to the risk of German invasion managed to continue through the First World War. 'Business as usual', amongst the group to which golf primarily appealed kept it going, though not without some inconvenience. The military requisitioned Blackpool's course for the duration and Bridlington lost its greens both to defence works and the plough when the County Agricultural Committee took it over. Elsewhere, self-denial was more apparent – the St George's Hill Club handed over its clubhouse to the Red Cross which used it as a hospital, treating 3,000 patients through the hostilities. The mid-Surrey Club subscribed £1,300 to war work and entertained 20,000 soldiers to tea between 1915 and 1919.[5] Despite the demand for rubber, Dunlop kept 2,000 women making golf balls, claiming that they would otherwise lose all employment.[6] It was some time after the war that the half-crown ball barrier was breached, although general inflation had actually cut the price very effectively. A country tired from war found in golf one of the pleasures by which memories could be blocked out, although we shall see that it also became another one of the means by which Britain's continued decline could be measured.

Golf and its fashionable accessories, baggy plus-four breeches and loudly coloured Argyle socks, are frequently identified as part of the parrot display of the affluent between the wars. This was sedulously fostered both in fashion magazines and in contemporary fiction. Since the 1890s there had been a golfing literature which strayed far from mere instruction. There were love stories, even a utopian work: J. A. C. K.'s *Golf in the Year 2000*. None of these, however, reached the popularity of three inter-war works, A. G. McDonnell's *England, Their England*, P. G. Wodehouse's, *The Heart of a Goof* and Agatha Christie's *The Murder on the Links*. For these, golf was not only the setting, but its pursuit offered an incisive humorous insight into middle-class snobberies – the real irony being that they were designed to be sold to those at whom they poked fun. Golf became an apparently inseparable component of the continued expansion of Metroland, north London's suburbia, part of middle-class England's huge land hunger. But the picture is partly an illusion. Between the Wars some 239 clubs were founded in England, fewer than in either of the decades surrounding the turn of the century. The trend towards luxury continued, perhaps epitomised by the opening in 1938 of the new club at Radlett, Hertfordshire, 15 miles or so north of London; 'Another of the stately homes of England is no more', as the old Newberries' family mansion became the local club.[7]

The problem of how far participation should be extended remained a particular question for the English. There were two issues – the availability of space and of clubs which could attract a more popular membership. In a sense the artisan movement led the way but found it difficult to break out of the patterns of deference built into its origins. By 1921 12 clubs had been formed, with a total of 350 members: the numbers grew rapidly after 1927, reaching 172 with 15,000 members by 1937. The growth was fostered after 1921 by the Artisan Golfer's Association, founded by J. H. Taylor and Lord Riddell. They produced some legendary figures, not least Abe Mitchell who moved from artisan play to being a tournament pro, and William Sutton of the West Cheshire Artisan club who was the English amateur champion in 1929. The Association assumed that, if all clubs founded a dependent body, 200,000 new working-class golfers could be recruited. But the symbiosis put many artisans off, just as the snobberies of existing golfers kept most clubs firmly barred to such a wide new member-ship.[8] The other much-vaunted possibility was that of extending municipal courses: by 1929 London had only two, at Richmond, which were badly overcrowded. Development was slow but the possibility of some artisan membership allowed some clubs, such as the Royal Eastbourne, to use it as an excuse to break local taboos on Sunday play.

Golf's directions between the Wars were determined less by a social con-science than by technological change and a growing concern with the top levels of play. The key factor was the steady supersession of the hickory shaft. Messrs Hardy of Alnwick, the leading fishing tackle makers, had tried to achieve greater flex and drive by making built-cane shafts but the idea did not catch on, not least because of cost. The real break came with the product of tubular steel shafts, which were finally recognised as legal by the Royal and Ancient in 1929. A surprisingly large number of amateur players continued with hickory but the new clubs and the established ball design combined to raise the performance of the best amateurs and pros, virtually demanding that ordinary players needed even blander courses to feel adequate when playing a round. The tension between technical possi-bilities and what most members can do has remained a constant in the game, reiterated once again with the development of carbon fibre shafts since the 1970s. What steel allowed for the average player, which only the most expensive craft production had offered before, was the matched set of clubs with all its theoretical advantages for balance. Limitation to 14 clubs per player eventually reduced the insane combinations of the collector-player as well as the load on caddies: the decline in the availability of the latter also prompted the reduction. What did proliferate were accessories and golfing fashion, replacing the near-universal and rather scruffy Norfolk jackets and breeches which had allowed the Edwardians to imagine them-selves guests at a country house party. The utilitarian demands of British weather fought a long battle with styles derived from the Prince of Wales. Women players made even greater demands on golfing fashions in the 1930s.

The issue, however, that obsessed golf writers and, willy nilly, their readers was the apparent decline in performance amongst top-class British golfers. It appeared as yet another instance of the dictum that, having developed a sport to a fine art and exported it wholesale, the British were apparently incapable of continuing to dominate its play. A country which had just won a major war and now had an empire larger than at any previous time nonetheless continued Edwardian recriminations about finding itself outclassed in world sporting terms. In golf, it was the Americans who had clearly seized mastery, and very largely in the world of the tournament professional. Immediate post-war claims that amateur golf was such fun to watch because it was so inconsistent rapidly gave way to warnings about the approaching 'desperately youthful' Americans who dominated English professional tournament play for a decade or more.[9] Abe Mitchell could win the first *News of the World* tournament to be revived after the First World War, but in international competition there seemed little hope of breaking the dominance of Americans which spread into the amateur game as well when a US team won the first amateur international at Hoylake in 1921. It caused some surprise when a British team won the first international professional match in 1926. What the Americans had behind them, apart from an earlier adaption of the steel-shafted club, was a professionals' association, started in 1916, which did a great deal to prepare promising talent for the tournament circuit. The British still wallowed in a widespread ambivalence to professionals, who were widely regarded as little more than the talented servants of amateurs. When the American, Walter Hagen, was runner-up in the 1923 British Open he refused to attend the award ceremony in a clubhouse that had been banned to professionals during the week of play.[10] In a real sense it was the inter-war period which saw the emergence of the parallel golfing networks, professional and amateur. The former dominates popular attention but, apart from providing an impossible model for the latter, there is relatively little interaction between the two. In limited terms, top-class golf now became a spectator sport, restricted by the weight which could be borne by courses never designed for it and by the use of gate money not only to meet expenses but to exclude social undesirables.

In a decade where golf looked to America for leadership, it found it in Walter Hagen and, contrastingly, in the amateur player Bobby Jones. When their compatriot, Jock Hutchinson, won the British Open at St Andrews in 1921, he began a run of American successes rarely broken by British players. Arthur Havers won at Troon in 1923 but it was 1934 before

Henry Cotton demonstrated that there was a serious British alternative. Even the amateur championship was won by Americans in 1926, 1930, 1934, 1935 and 1938. But there at least the British could produce three players who fitted an earlier mould of the gentleman amateur capable of very high standards of play. Ernest Holderness, a career civil servant later knighted, provided an elegance of style and achievement much at odds with the increasingly 'scientific' or 'mechanical' golf of the steel club, and the standardised ball, whose size had been fixed at 1.62 inches by the Royal and Ancient in 1921. Holderness, 'the beau-ideal of an amateur' had to fit practice into the weekends and holidays the Civil Service allowed him: as he rose in the echelons he was effectively lost to the game by the 1930s.[11] He was followed closely by two other great Oxford golfers, Cyril Tolley and Roger Wethered. One key British amateur player, T. P. Perkins, the 1928 British amateur champion, followed the path of Abe Mitchell and others who, without the economic and social security of Holderness and Wethered, turned professional to make the most of the potential they had shown. It was the pull of adequate, or even grander, financial rewards on the emerging tournament circuit, with its manufacturer's sponsorship of individuals and other business links only open to the professional, which many commentators deplored. The threat to open a totalisator at the tournament at Frinton-on-Sea in 1929 provoked agonies which other potential mass sports had already faced and partly absorbed. 'Do we want our golf courses crowded with a set of raucous-voiced thugs whose ideas on sportsmanship are as far removed from the ideals as the earth is from the moon?'[12]

British hopes were restored partially in the 1930s with the appearance of Henry Cotton, the first public-school educated son of the professional classes to take golf seriously as a career. In 1934 he became the first British winner of the Open for eleven years, including a second round of 65 that was not bettered until 1977. He won again in 1937 and then again in 1948, one of the few inter-war British professionals who could match American consistency of play. Ironically, his first victory was as the professional of a Belgian club, but it brought him back to England, for Ashridge in Hertfordshire. Although he obviously brought prestige to the club, Cotton had to bridge the uncertain ground between employment and that of being a public entertainer. The latter he certainly became when he appeared as a variety act at the London Palladium in the 1930s, with demonstration strokes sandwiched between the more conventional offerings of vaudeville.[13] It would clearly have been impossible twenty years earlier and was a long way from the threatened strike by professionals at the 1899 championships over inadequate prize money, an action only stopped when Harry Vardon set himself up as go-between. It was that which had led to the formation of the Professional Golfers' Association in 1901 which founded its own matchplay championship with £200 in prizes, prompted by backing from the *News of the World*. Most professionals remained as combined instructors and shopkeepers, and it was to face the increased pressures on this from sports manufacturers that the PGA formed the Professional Golfers' Cooperative Association Ltd in 1921 as a central wholesale body for its members. The links with industry grew and there was a steady rise in the importance of the domestic tournament circuit for professionals. It was almost a symbol of the economic consumer revival of the mid-1930s that the PGA tournament was augmented by another sponsored by the *Daily Mail* in 1936 with £2,000 in prize money. In the same year, as part of the newspaper war, the *News Chronicle* started a tournament worth £1,000 and golf manufacturers chipped in with the Silver King tournament of similar value. For all the prestige of the Open Championship it only reached that figure after the Second World War. Even the most consistently successful professional would hardly make much money on his British play alone.

For all the attractiveness of professional tournaments, some now appearing on newsreels, their actual visibility was strictly limited. It was the written word of the journalist which brought them to most golfers' attention. There was little doubt that the run of players had other objectives for the game to fulfil. As Henry Longhurst noted in 1934, almost with rueful admiration, the ordinary club was primarily a place for social intercourse amongst people who played at the weekends, who never practised nor bothered to take lessons from the club pro, and who plodded round in brown Harris Tweed plus-four suits, with the main aim of arriving at the nineteenth hole, 'Where his conversation turns on motor-cars, his day's play, income tax, his day's play, the Minister of Transport and his day's play.'[14] The game was a major prop for the self-esteem of the urban yeoman.

IV

Women's golf is very different now-a-days from what it was when the Ladies' Golf Union was first instituted. It was a pastime then, it is a business now.
Englishwoman's Yearbook and Directory (1915), p. 253

It was ironic that the first English broadcast of a golf game, in 1927 on 2LO was by a woman, reporting on a woman's game: Miss E. E. Hulme giving her version of the Ladies' London Golf Foursomes tournament at Addington.[15] The initial growth of golf had been powerfully anti-feminine as the game offered men yet another escape from domestic demands. In many areas the idea that Sunday morning was for men's golf and women's churchgoing was well established by 1914. But women encroached early into golf, producing a grudging but very segregated acceptance. Objections centred on their supposed weakness, inability to drive a ball far and slowness of play, made worse by chatter; to which was added a concern about de-feminisation and the potential for distracting male play that a shapely feminine swing could produce. But the initial linking of golf's popularity with holiday resorts meant that women often accompanied their husbands. So, after being confined to small putting greens, they gradually developed their own clubs. Usually this meant playing from a shorter tee over 9 holes of a men's course, the 'hen runs', or more rarely on a separate one with separate club facilities. If a course was shared women were usually barred from weekend play and during local tournaments. But younger middle-class women took to this new open air game almost as rapidly as their men and, when the Ladies' Golf Union was formed in 1893 by 20 Ladies Clubs, they absorbed many of the assumptions of bureaucracy that characterises modern sport. It still operated in tension with the women's committees of so many men's clubs, whose concern was not with regulating play but with providing refreshments for tournaments. It was the presence of women as much as anything else that prompted the move towards luxurious Edwardian clubhouses.

Golf appealed to many younger women as yet another limited step in their liberation, although some of their sisters chose to pour acid on greens in the suffragette direct action of 1913. The development of handicapping actually allowed the sexes to play together, so that the foursome was added to the range of respectable matrimonial stalking grounds of the more affluent middle classes. But there were other standards which helped foster some sense of feminine achievement. The Ladies' Golf Union instituted an amateur championship in its first year and this was won for three years in succession by the first of the great women golfers, Lady Margaret Scott, whose style was a model for many men. She then gave up playing. Golf at this standard tended to attract women who were also seeking some freedom in other sports, although few reached the level of Charlotte 'Lottie' Dod, the 1904 Ladies' champion who also skated, played hockey, was an Olympic archer and a Wimbledon singles lawn tennis champion, as well as an alpinist of note.[16] She was much freer than the Orr sisters who were rumoured to have been forbidden by their father to play in tournaments when he heard that people were betting on the results.[17] As the game was established it produced women of even greater quality. Twenty-one years after Lady Margaret Scott's first victory the legendary Cecil(ia) Leitch, a doctor's daughter, won the championship in 1914; her 'masculine' style was formidable. The war and strikes then prevented a repeat until 1920 when she won again, and again in 1921. The following year she was runner-up to Joyce Wethered, arguably the finest woman golfer ever: Miss Wethered could never drive as far as a man but her short game was of a standard that few men could match. She had been introduced to the game by her brother Roger, whom we have already encountered. She won again in 1924 and 1925 (beating Cecil Leitch at Troon in one of the great matches of history), and then retired, re-emerging to defeat the American Glenna Collett in another celebrated final at St Andrews in 1929.

Many women players had no ambitions at this level but golf passed as powerfully into their vocabulary as into their husband's and it was made a good deal easier by the freer styles of clothes that followed the First World War. The old fears of 'rational dress' faded away, to be replaced by good solid tweeds, Argyle pullovers and stout golfing brogues. It was 1934 before Miss Gloria D. Minoprio marked another stage by appearing in trousers at a championship – 'slacks' were still frowned on in many conservative circles.

Women's golf was dogged by being widely regarded as a pale imitation of the man's game, however much the few individuals we have mentioned gave it a separate respectability. On the whole, until the Second World War, British women sedulously avoided the professionalisation of the game. It was widely held that the Ladies' Golf Union's obsession with handicapping and with score rather than matchplay actually inhibited players of Joyce Wethered's calibre from developing faster. Certainly most women depended on men for instruction, although a few of their own number added to the spate of handbooks for beginners. Most clubs shared a pro with the local men or hired their own. Prince's Ladies' club, playing on Mitcham Common, employed Mrs Gordon Robertson as their pro before 1914, and in 1911 Sunningdale Ladies employed as theirs Lily Freemantle, the daughter of a well-known male professional. One woman followed Abe Mitchell's path to professionalism before the First World War, Miss D. M. Smyth, who became the pro for the Le Touquet Ladies' Club after some years of amateur play in England.[18] The essential difference was that these few women had to remain as teachers, as there was no cash prize tournament circuit for them to latch on to. Amateurism remained a key issue at the heart of women's golf and the greatest of the late-1930s players, Pam Barton, fell foul of powerful taboos when she published *A Stroke a Hole* (1937) as a clear profit-making book. Yet she was only following a track well-trodden by the Wethereds and by numerous male 'shamateurs'.[19] The symbolic separation of the women's game as a clearly second-rate activity, however much nominal deference might have been paid to Joyce Wethered, became only too clear when a match was arranged in 1938 with that other

6.4 Women broke into golf early, producing a grudging but very segregated acceptance. This is the formidable Miss Cecil Leitch in a ladies' open meeting in 1913

6.5 By 1938 their style was being featured on the cover of the only weekly golf journal in the world

subordinate group, the artisans. The Prince's Ladies played the Prince's Artisans at Sandwich; Lady Astor and Mrs Menzies were drawn against R. Watson (a railway porter) and W. Moat (a butler).[20] The men won, but in one sense neither team did. Yet this is, perhaps, an unnecessarily pessimistic picture. The quality of British women's golf had been recognised by the Americans when the Curtis Cup, an international match played every two years, was established in 1932. The match, like its male equivalents for the Walker and Ryder Cups, was played alternately in Britain and the United States, with similarly disappointing results for the British side, although the latter did achieve both the first halved match (in 1958) and then (in 1986) the first ever outright victory by any British team, male or female, amateur or professional, on American soil. Nonetheless for much of its early life the Curtis Cup was a clear index of the dichotomy between the two countries' approach both to 'amateurism' and womens' sport in general.

V

Blind Hove golfer says U.S. will stand by democracy.
  Brighton and Hove Gazette, 3 September 1938

This typified many reactions to approaching war in the late 1930s. Golf seems to have offered little sense of the claims to be found in football or rowing that meeting over the sport would foster international understanding. Nor had anyone gone far in developing the late Victorian utopian notion that golf tournaments could act as surrogate wars. But the sense of 'carry on regardless' was already well developed. By the time of Munich golfers were exhorted to carry gas masks with them and clubs were asked to provide slit trenches alongside the greens in case members were caught in an air raid. No one seems to have asked why the Germans would waste expensive bombs on attacking golf courses. Despite the wartime demand for rubber and steel which virtually killed the production of tackle some managed to play on; one of London's two municipal courses at Richmond was kept open. But courses in general fell to the demands of agriculture and the realisation that they provided possible landing grounds for the feared gliders and paratroops expected to follow wholesale German bombing. So the golf course and the right to play the game became another of the freedoms for which the British were fighting; for a while an image compounded of pastoralism and solidarity replaced the quintessential snobberies of the inter-war period.

Golf came slowly out of Crippsian austerity – land and materials were still too valuable for too much to be released quickly. Yet the Open was played again in 1946 as was the Amateur. For all this, the game grew very slowly over the next quarter century. From the war's end until 1970, 134 clubs were founded, only 13 more than in the single decade of the 1930s. Scarce materials, post-war inflation, high land costs and a primary concern for reconstruction seem to have offered little incentive for golf development.

It is clear, however, that there was a steadily growing demand to play the game which the inherited facilities could not cope with. Waiting lists grew and the game became one, together with flyfishing, which appealed to the high mass consumption society that emerged in the apparent prosperity of the 1960s. Golf attracted many of the newer house and car owners of the 'property-owning democracy'. Generally speaking, the sense of an achieved social status may have had less to do with this than the appeal of a perceived life-style, the lip-service at least given to the much-trumpeted concept of an emergent 'leisure society' and also to the televising of the game. Golf is singularly telegenic, both in terms of focusing on the tensions of close-up play, and in the wider portrayal of the idealised landscape which relatively few had seen before. The end result was that the 1970s saw the biggest boom for 50 years, with 208 new clubs coming into existence, a rate which dropped sharply with the onset of the economic recession at the end of the decade. One late-1960s estimate put the number of golfers at about a million, 1 in 50 of the population, and the figure was estimated to have doubled since the mid-1950s. At that level, it was assumed that 500 new courses would be needed in the 1970s to meet the demand: as we have seen, that was not met. The chief problems were the chronic land shortage of much English development and an ambivalent attitude amongst country planners to course provision, particularly in 'Green Belt' areas.[21] The other was pernicious inflation: in 1975 development costs for an average 18-hole course were estimated at up to £200,000, just over ten years later it was put at £900,000.[22] At this level there was still some tendency towards exclusivity and very high membership fees. Some private developers responded well to this, particularly where golf was incorporated into an imported American 'Country Club' mode with squash and tennis courts as well as good restaurants. Perhaps the oddest example of this was the PL London Golf Club Ltd, founded at Bedwell Park, Hertfordshire, in 1976. 'PL stands for Perfect Liberty, a state of mind which recreation is intended to foster', a state well intended by the parent company, Fuji Kokusai Ltd, which sought to meet the needs of golf-hungry Japanese businessmen in London and to give them an opportunity to conduct negotiations with the British in a deceptively softening environment.[23]

Far more significant, however, was the 1970s emphasis on public ownership as the answer to popular demands. Local authorities were often very sceptical about this and unwilling to enter into partnership with private developers. Golf was often most successfully sold when it could be coupled with a pride in urban renewal: it fitted particularly well into the real as well as municipal socialism of many northern urban authorities, who were sold the game as an answer to the problem of derelict land. Bedlington in Northumberland opened its public course in 1972 on the site of a former opencast mine. Where clubs like this opened, the degree of use, at up to 80,000 rounds a year, was often twice what a private club would have considered reasonable but it indicated the level of demand. This was, however, not so much an extension of golf to manual workers as a sign of the bulging prosperity of lower-middle-class groups. Golf became a major feature of the new generation of new towns and cities that late-1960s planners anticipated: for them the capital costs were only a small part of their overall infrastructure. Abbey Hill in Milton Keynes was opened in 1975, following the new city's private club Windmill Hill, of 1972, with its neighbouring public course. Delapre in the expanding Northampton was opened by the development corporation in 1976, Washington, Co. Durham followed in 1979. Their availability and cheapness of play has formed a constant theme of the advertising that is used to lure people away from the costly south-east. This overall expansion would have been impossible without the steady real drop in the price of golfing equipment brought by international mass production. As with fishing, the lowest point of pricing was reached in the later 1970s when Woolworth's began to sell clubs: matched half-sets, imported from abroad and ready bagged, could also be obtained from multiple discount stores such as House of Holland. The paradox was that the prices probably fell too far for the assumed sophistication of many of the new players – it became important to be seen with good equipment whatever the quality of play.

Golf's latter-day boom owes much to its increasingly high public profile; it has developed as one of the handful of sports whose major results are regularly reported in the mass media. For a game which has owed much of its modern history to its being identified with both individualism and social exclusiveness this has not been an easy transition. But it has learned to cope by operating at many levels, some with surprisingly limited overlaps. The key development has been that of the professional tournament, both as spectator sport and as advertising vehicle. Golf courses, by their very nature, were not intended to cope with large numbers of spectators, yet by 1968 the Open Championship attracted a crowd of 50,000. One answer which the host clubs and the Royal and Ancient together had to provide were temporary grandstands at the major holes. Film and radio reporting gradually extended the numbers who could follow the major tournaments 'live', or at least acquire rather more of the flavour of play in peak newscasts. But the real change came with the advent of outside television broadcasting on a large scale. Whereas the first sports to attract this type of coverage, football, cricket, lawn tennis and racing, take place on limited spaces that can be covered easily with a few cameras, golf course layouts make particular demands that became easier to meet as portable equipment and sophisticated relays were developed. The runner bringing news back to the radio commentary box was a creature of limited life. The BBC gave live television coverage to the Open for the first time in 1955. Now the presence of television is a standard feature of at least eight British championships a year, often deliberately created to be part of a mass publicity event.

The tournament circuit has become inextricably entangled with high levels of commercial sponsorship. This had actually begun in 1903 when the *News of the World* sponsored the PGA World Match Play tournament, something it did until 1969, when it gave way to tobacco, whisky and insurance companies in succession. Golf manufacturers, who had long supported professionals with equipment, saw the value of advertising their products further. Dunlop sponsored the Masters' Tournament from 1946–1972. But the key role in high profile sponsorship has been that of tobacco and drink firms. Benson and Hedges began a successful international in 1971, Dunhills took over the Dunlop/Silk Cut Masters in 1979. Suntory took over from Piccadilly and Colgate in 1979 to underwrite the World Match Play Championship at Wentworth. Hotel and insurance companies have also been lured in alongside the major equipment firms, all acutely conscious of the considerable visibility of their trademarks in the inevitable close-up shots. Amateur tournaments are less attractive, but Ford has supported a club golfers' tournament since the mid-1960s as well as a boys' championship, together with the *Daily Express*. They also sponsor 'the girls' [their words], fostering the Women's Professional Golf Association, and provide the courtesy cars for the Open.[24] With a commercial involvement at this level, the prizes have moved from the modest rewards designed to boost the earnings of club professionals to being a major and highly regulated series of standard fees for a very limited number of players dedicated entirely to an international tournament circuit. Prize money had been creeping up from the 1920s: for the Open it reached £1,000 for the first time in 1946, with a first prize of £150. By 1955 the first prize was £1,000, the total £3,750. Twenty years later, the winner collected £10,000 out of £100,000. Inflation trebled both figures by the early 1980s. With gate money at the Open reaching over £500,000 by 1981, it had moved far from the low-cost early days, with their threats of players' strikes.

THE GREATEST CORPORATE HOSPITALITY OPPORTUNITY
OF 1989 IS APPROACHING.
TO RESERVE YOUR PLACE IN SPORTING HISTORY, APPLY NOW

6.6 Not only is golf a favourite sport of the sponsors. It is also frequently used
for corporate hospitality. It is the Ryder Cup which is the hospitality opportunity
of 1989

Professional golf tournaments attract 'national' players and are often
followed by media and public in terms of national pride. But it is largely,
like motor racing, a repeated demonstration of individual professional
skills: appearance money and personal retainer fees are as important as
prize money at this level. From a British point of view the history of golf
in the post-war period has largely been one of dominance by foreigners,
either from the old Dominions or the Americas. In these circumstances,
the emergence of native 'star' golfers has been limited and there have been
few of top world class. The first, almost 30 years after Henry Cotton,
was Tony Jacklin, whose victory in the 1969 Open was the first British
triumph for 18 years. Jacklin, a working-class boy turned professional at
the age of 18, went on to hold both the British and US Opens at the same
time. He also played for Britain in the Ryder Cup, an annual transatlantic
professional match inaugurated in 1927. Britain has rarely won this, with
repeated US victories at a ratio of roughly 1:6. In 1985 Jacklin, as non-
playing captain, finally led Britain, now reinforced by players from con-
tinental Europe, to its first victory for 28 years. The overall picture has
been even worse in the amateur equivalent, the Walker Cup. There have

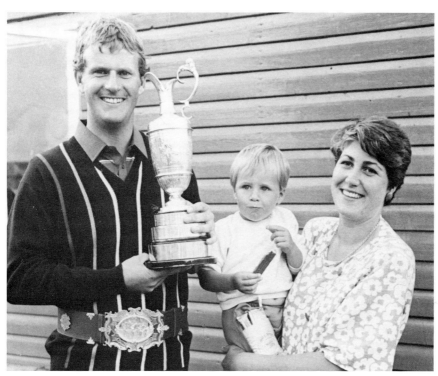

6.7 A Scot who plays like one but has an English accent. The modern millionaire sportsman, Sandy Lyle

been occasional compensations. Jacklin's mantle has passed in the mid-1980s to two players: 'Sandy' Lyle, and Nick Faldo, Open champions in 1985 and 1987 respectively. Behind these men are a number of steadily competent players, men and women, but few who can compete successfully with the American or European best.

In many senses the progressive elaboration of 'Scottish croquet' has come to symbolise the ways in which sport in Britain both reflects and reinforces widespread assumptions about national attitudes to achievement and performance. The very spread of the game has done much to reinforce a fundamental sense of social division. Although it has provided a means of signifying mobility it has also operated to encourage a host of petty snobberies. It has emphasised gender divisions and inequalities. It has pandered to a suburban romanticism about controlled nature and it has encouraged the segregation of land use. Bumbling amateurishness rather than ruthless competition seems to have characterised many of its management's attitudes and it has fostered deference to traditions of dubious antiquity. But it has been exported wholesale and it has given hours of pleasure in the open air to millions. It may even be that the activity has done more to restrain than foster the ill-health so frequently caricatured in cartoon and novel. In Bernard Darwin's works it fostered some of the most elegant sports prose writing of the mid-twentieth century.[25] When Sandy Lyle won the US Masters in the spring of 1988 it also demonstrated that the British could still occasionally surprise their bumptious offspring.

NOTES

1   This information, and factual records throughout this essay are taken from *Benson and Hedges Golfer's Yearbook 1986.*
2   This is an extension of my 'Scottish croquet, the story of the English golf boom,' *Golf World*, August 1983, p. 101ff.
3   Geoffrey Cousins, *Lords of the Links: The Story of Golf* (1977), pp. 42–3.
4   See Geoffrey Cousins, *Golfers at Law* (1958) *passim.*
5   *Golf Illustrated*, 9 May 1919.
6   Ibid.
7   *Golf Illustrated*, 2 July 1938.
8   Peter Lawless, *The Golfer's Companion*, p. 399ff.
9   *Golf Illustrated*, 11 July 1919.
10 Donald Steel, *The Guinness Book of Golf Facts and Feats* (1982), p. 37.
11 Peter Lawless, *The Golfer's Companion*, p. 138ff.
12 *Golf Illustrated*, 12 April 1929.
13 Donald Steel, *The Guinness Book of Golf Facts*, p. 229.
14 *Evening Standard*, 21 December 1934; article by Henry Longhurst, 'The average golfer'.
15 P. Lawless, *The Golfer's Companion*, pp. 238–9.
16 Donald Steel, *The Guinness Book of Golf Facts*, p. 237.
17 Ibid., p. 233.
18 Robert Browning, *A History of Golf* (1955), p. 192ff.
19 *Golf Illustrated*, 5 February 1938.
20 *Golf Illustrated*, 24 September 1938.
21 See J. A. Patmore, *Land and Leisure* (1970, 1972), pp. 74–80 and A. W. Davidson and J. E. Leonard (eds.), *Land for Leisure – Golf Courses* (1975).
22 *Benson and Hedges Golfer's Yearbook*, 1986, p. 7.
23 Davidson and Leonard, *Land for Leisure*, p. 37.
24 *Benson and Hedges*, p. 13.
25 See, for instance, his *Golf Between Two Wars* (1944).

HORSE-RACING 7

WRAY VAMPLEW

I

> Betting is the manure to which the enormous crop of horse-racing and racehorse breeding in this and other countries is to a large extent due.
> R. Black, *The Jockey Club and its Founders* (1891), p. 349

The history of horse-racing in Britain is one of a rise and subsequent decline as a spectator sport, but of a permanent association with gambling. For most of those interested in racing the quality thoroughbred was, and still is, little more than a betting mechanism. Even the minority who attend race meetings are unusual among watchers of elite sport in that they have no knowledge of the sport derived from personal participation at a lower level. Horse-racing has no real recreational version for participants: pony clubs and gymkhanas are not the equine equivalent of backyard cricket or playground soccer.[1] To racegoers, almost as much as to the betting shop *habitués*, the horse is an agency for gambling. Possibly in Victorian times there was a greater appreciation of the thoroughbred as an animal, since many race spectators and betters would have had at least a passing acquaintance with horseflesh in the form of pit ponies, ploughing teams, omnibus haulage, or, higher up the social scale, perhaps as hunters or carriage horses. Nevertheless the *raison d'être* of horse-racing has always been gambling: organised racing began as matches for wagers between owners of quality horses and three to four centuries later it provides an almost daily opportunity for betting, the turnover of which in 1985–6 topped £2,500 million from off-course facilities alone.[2]

II

> Racing is wholly dependent on the continued interest of the public.
> Benson Report on *The Racing Industry* (1968), p. 9

At the time of Victoria's accession racing was a national sport carried on at the local level because of the difficulty in transporting horses long distances. Few courses held more than one meeting a year and most of these were associated with local holidays. Travelling shows, beer tents, gaming booths, open-air dancing and, for a privileged few, balls and dinner parties all contributed to a full day's pleasure. Newmarket was a major exception for here, at the home of the Jockey Club, racing was a serious business and there was no room for the fun of the fair. Everywhere, however, unless they wished to use the grandstand – not that there always was such a structure – no one needed to pay to watch the races. Entry fees to the stand could be collected without much difficulty as access could be relatively easily restricted: two or three burly custodians could see to that. For the racecourse as a whole restriction was not so easy a task. Enclosure would have been necessary and this was not possible where racing took place on common land. Elsewhere it was legal but expensive and the returns might not have justified the outlay considering the low disposable income of most potential spectators.

The first agent of change was the railway which enabled owners to send their horses the length and breadth of Britain both quickly and safely. More than this the railways revolutionised passenger transport and, from that first racing special run by the London and Southampton Railway Company to the 1838 Derby, eager racegoers took advantage of the new mode of travel. All racecourses within proximity of a station found their spectator catchment area both widened and deepened by the speed and convenience of railway communication. Generally the race committees welcomed the excursionists as their spending on food, alcohol and the gaming tables allowed booth rentals to be raised which in turn boosted the prize fund. The one great exception was again at Newmarket for the Heath was regarded as the preserve of the privileged with no place for the pleasure-seeking holiday racegoer. To thwart the invasion of the masses advantage was taken of Newmarket's many courses to start races literally miles apart so that only the mounted gentry could adequately follow proceedings. Whether in or out of favour spectators still did not pay at the gate: despite rising incomes as the fruits of industrialisation trickled down to the mass of the population, no race committee of any significance moved to charge a general entrance fee. At some of the roughest courses brute force collections were attempted, but the general practice was to charge only those racegoers who viewed from the stands or the comfort of private carriages.

Not until April 1875 did Sandown Park, situated 13 miles from Hyde Park Corner, attempt to make money out of the metropolitan racegoing market by opening its turnstiles as the first enclosed racecourse in Britain, entry to which required a fee from all spectators.[3] Such was its financial and racing success that it changed the character and structure of British racing. Throughout the nation racecourse entrepreneurs hastened to follow where Sandown had led and by the end of the century racing was taking place at enclosed courses all over Britain. The majority of the new enclosed meetings were also successful and many of the older established fixtures were forced to follow suit and rebuild stands, create enclosures and charge for public admission. Primarily this was done to preserve the quality of their racing: they could only hope to entice the best horses by increasing their prizemoney to a level commensurate with that of the enclosed courses. The best way to ensure this was to charge at the gate and this involved some form of enclosure. Even Newmarket, despite its acknowledged racing reputation, found that the quality of horses being attracted to the Heath by the prizemoney on offer was such as to leave the Jockey Club with no option but 'to substitute the white rails of modern civilisation for the old-fashioned ropes of our forefathers'.[4]

For most courses the choice was simple: either you erected fences or you went to the wall. Most unenclosed meetings, if they did not disappear altogether, struggled along with racing of an inferior character. A few open meetings, however, did more than merely survive: at Ascot, Epsom, Good-wood, Doncaster and York racing flourished. The charisma of traditional prestige events may have helped – though the prizemoney for the Derby had to be raised to a level comparable with the major prizes at the enclosed courses – but their real protection lay with their position in the social rather than the racing calendar. Members and would-be members of high society felt a social obligation to put in an appearance at these meetings and their spending produced ample funds which kept the courses viable.

Sandown had originated as a partnership but became a limited company in 1885; most other enclosed courses adopted company status from the beginning. Although the Jockey Club set a dividend limitation of 10 per cent this was still a worthwhile target for the racing companies: indeed even the average dividend of 7.5 per cent paid in 1913 compared more than favourably with the consol rate of 3.4 per cent.[5] Their financial good fortune stemmed from their ability to persuade substantial numbers of racegoers to become paying spectators. Although no comprehensive crowd statistics are available for nineteenth-century racing, contemporary comment suggests that at the turn of the century racecrowds of 10–15,000 were not uncommon; double this could be expected at a leading fixture; and perhaps 70–80,000 at a major public holiday event.[6]

The marketing policies of the racing companies were aimed very much at the working man who was encouraged to attend by the offer of Saturday afternoon racing, a leisure time-slot of increasing importance. A new style of race programme was also promoted; one dominated by two-year-olds, sprints and handicaps, all of which had a sufficient degree of uncertainty

7.1 It cannot be denied that racing draws people from all walks of life, and it showed. This was Ascot in 1907

about their result to make for exciting racing and an attractive betting market.[7]

Women also attained increased significance as spectators. Unlike on the participant side of racing where their role remained severely constrained, by the turn of the century several thousand women were being attracted to the major gatemoney meetings. Prior to the establishment of the enclosed course relatively few women went racing. The aristocrats frequented Ascot where there was the Royal Enclosure to accommodate them; Epsom and Goodwood too were part of the elite social season. Elsewhere, however, ladies were rarely seen except for a few in carriages or in private stands: respectability inhibited them from utilising the free space or even the public grandstands. This social parameter was accepted by the racing companies who encouraged the attendance of 'ladies' by the formation of racing clubs whose membership was carefully vetted. Such clubs were not new but the earlier ones at Epsom, Stockbridge and Lewes had not admitted women at all whereas, although membership of the new clubs was still a male prerogative, subscribers obtained ladies' badges or could be accompanied by ladies on the payment of an extra fee.

Racegoers attend meetings for reasons different to those of the team

7.2 And this was York in 1955

supporter; not for them the intense identification or fanatical, even maso-
chistic, commitment to a club. Hence confrontation riots between groups
of rival fans are unlikely to occur at racetracks. Nevertheless crowd disorder
was not unknown at mid-Victorian race meetings. Indeed trouble was commonplace at several London courses in the late 1860s: at Bromley a pitched
battle was fought between angry punters and welshing bookmakers; at
Streatham a rioting mob tore up railings and attacked a jockey whom
they felt had not tried to win; and at Enfield a similarly suspected rider
was allegedly saved from lynching only by the intervention of armed racecourse officials. Disturbances at some metropolitan meetings became so
bad that in 1879 parliamentary legislation was used to suppress them. Provincial meetings too had their disorder, particularly when backers felt that
they had not had a fair run for their money or when bookmakers welshed
on winning bets. No doubt too the uninhibited holiday atmosphere associated with many meetings, the ready availability of sex, alcohol and gambling, and the activities of the criminal fraternity – pickpockets, coiners
and the like – contributed to many a fracas.

The proprietors of the enclosed courses had much to lose if such behaviour
continued for they had undertaken substantial investment and this property

had to be protected.[8] Hence, in order to reduce the propensity to disorder, gambling and drinking became more stringently controlled. Drink was an accepted British sporting tradition, but, with booth rentals becoming less important as a source of revenue, access to alcohol, while not eliminated, was certainly restricted. Racing, of course, had a symbiotic relationship with gambling and could not afford to do without it, but it became restricted to betting on the races and the cardsharps, thimblemen and the operators of the evens/odds tables were no longer tolerated. Like known criminals and prostitutes they fell victim to a more strictly enforced segregation policy. Traditionally this had been a matter of employing a few pugilists to keep the 'riff-raff' out of the stands but now the lower elements of the racing world were not even allowed on the course. Gatemen became subject to Jockey Club licence and the best of them were employed at many meetings and, by travelling the racing circuits, were able to familiarise themselves with defaulting bookmakers and other *personae non gratae*. Yet it was not only potential troublemakers who were excluded: itinerant entertainers, tipsters and traders all found themselves less welcome than before. Indeed the whole holiday atmosphere was dampened down. Symptomatic of this was the more efficient use of time: the employment of professional starters and, from the late 1890s, the use of the starting gate enabled meetings to adhere to a stricter timetable than the traditional races where the starts of the afternoon events often depended on the quality of the race committee's luncheon.

Such a combination of repressive and reformative measures seems to have improved racecrowd behaviour – at least on the enclosed courses – but the racing boom which followed the First World War saw the reappearance of serious disorder, though the problem lay with racetrack gangs rather than with the crowd. Record attendances meant record betting and thugs moved in to seize their share by robbing bookmakers or operating protection schemes. Racing hit the front pages as territorial disputes between the gangs were settled by violence. Caught in the crossfire, almost literally, was the racing public. Many racecourse executives seemed unable to cope with the problem. Bookmakers organised their own defence through local protection associations and the fact that some of these groups employed bodyguards may have influenced a Jockey Club decision to appoint officials whose duty would be to protect the public and supervise racecourse security arrangements, matters previously left to the racecourse management. The new policing force did not begin operations until 1925, but it was swiftly effective: within a year the Jockey Club could claim that it had 'already attained in many directions the objectives for which it was formed'.[9] On unprotected parts of courses, such as the Downs at

Epsom, unpleasant experiences still occurred and even in some enclosures there were occasional outbursts of violence, but generally, if spectators were willing to pay for their racing, then they could expect it to be trouble-free. However, the time was rapidly approaching when such expenditure would not be so easily obtained: racing's crowd problem was to become one of attendances not behaviour.

By the 1930s many racegoers (and ex-racegoers) were complaining that the consumer was no longer king. The *Ilchester Report* of 1943, an internal Jockey Club inquiry, revealed that courses which had been modern in the late nineteenth century were now antiquated, often with poor catering and inadequate betting facilities.

Certainly racecourse attendances were on the decline in the 1950s; from an average of 11,964 per day per meeting in 1953 to 9,168 in 1961.[10] Poor amenities, high travelling and parking costs, competition from other leisure activities and the rising volume of televised meetings, from 27 to 183, all played a part. The situation was aggravated in the 1960s by the opening of thousands of licensed betting shops which, by offering convenience and cheapness – at least as regards entry costs! – seduced the marginal racegoer and encouraged regular attendance at the shop rather than occasional visits to the track. By 1967 aggregate race crowds were down to 3,234,971 (from 4,287,345 in 1953), an average crowd of only 7,530.[11] The decline in racegoing drastically undermined the profitability of the racecourses. In 1966 15 of the 63 courses made losses and only 17 made profits of over £5,000; total profits before tax were £286,000, a meagre return compared to the almost £6 million invested. These figures were based on book values but, for 1967, current value data are available for 30 courses which suggest an effective rate of return on capital employed of only 1.4 per cent.[12] Such a performance did not encourage further investment and this put attendances on a downward spiral as a failure to improve spectator amenities naturally dissuaded even more from spending a day at the races.

The development of the enclosed gatemoney course had allowed increased prizemoney to be underwritten but now the reverse occurred. Racecourse executives could not maintain real levels of prizemoney which by 1967 had fallen to slightly over half that of 1937.[13] Most certainly British courses could not match the money being offered to race winners and place-getters abroad. The low levels of prizemoney at home discouraged owners from purchasing the best British bloodstock which increasingly was exported to those who could afford it. Consequently foreign-owned, and increasingly foreign-bred horses, began to capture the top prizes in British racing which seemed to be on an inclined plane, if not to oblivion, then clearly to a low-standard, small-scale sport.

III

You now see before you the spectacle of a once proud sport reduced to utter
dependence on public money.

> David Robinson's 'Gimcrack Dinner Speech' (1969)

Yet this has not happened. Admittedly attendances have continued to
decline and, although in 1985 the crowds were the highest for three years,
they totalled only 2,388,598, an average of merely 5,148 at each flat or
mixed meeting.[14] Other indicators, however, suggest that British racing
has turned the economic corner. Prizemoney for flat racing has increased
from £6.99 million in 1976 to £16.95 million in 1985 with an almost equivalent proportional rise for National Hunt from £2.97 million to £7.45 million.
Even allowing for inflation this represents a remarkable rise, though the
money available per race still lags behind other leading racing nations.
Two positive effects of the rise are the 15.3 per cent increase in the number
of runners at flat races (10.8 per cent over the hurdles and jumps) and
a record high of 9,348 in the number of live foals born.[15]

The industry has been rendered viable by a combination of public and
private enterprise. On the one hand, from the late 1950s commercial sponsorship once again began to inject funds into racing. Some railway companies had done this in the mid-nineteenth century in gratitude for the traffic
which racing generated; publicans, hoteliers and others in the drink trade
had done likewise; but now the motive was advertising pure and simple.
In 1967 such sponsors provided £99,000, some 8 per cent of all prizemoney;
by 1985 the sum had risen to £3,420,000 and the proportion to 20 per
cent.[16] Even the Classics had succumbed to the need for funds to underline
their prestige and the 1984 season witnessed the General Accident 1,000
and 2,000 Guineas, the Ever Ready Derby, the Gold Seal Oaks and the
Holsten Pils St Leger.

The other major injection of funds has come from the gambling sector
which, via the Horserace Betting Levy Board (HBLB), pumped £195 million
into racing between 1961 and 1985, signifying a major change in the financial
relationship between horse-racing and betting.[17] Prior to the enclosed course
gambling made little direct contribution to the balance sheets of the racing
industry. Bookmakers and the proprietors of gaming booths might pay
a fee to the clerk of the course, but that was all, apart from the successful
wagers of winning owners, and generally gambling was more likely to
increase than offset the costs of ownership. With the advent of the enclosed
meeting the structure of racing was shifted towards those types of races
most likely to appeal to the gambling spectator, who, of course now paid
at the gate. However, it was not until the establishment of the on-course

totalisator in 1929 – many years after its introduction in France and Austra-lasia – that racing really began to dip its bucket into the financial stream flowing from the betting on the sport.

Run by a statutory authority, the Racecourse Betting Control Board (RBCB), the objective of the tote was to make a financial contribution to racing by the deduction of a percentage from the pool of bets before the money was distributed to winning betters. The initial results were disap-pointing as the tote was caught in the pincers of overestimated revenue and underestimated expenditure: the worsening economic climate reduced attendances and the decentralised nature of British racing inflated operating costs. Moreover, as it operated on a cash not a credit basis, the tote found it difficult to tap off-course betting. In 1931, however, an arrangement was made with the private enterprise Guardian Pari-Mutual Ltd. (later Tote Investors Ltd.) for credit bets made in the latter's offices to be transferred to the tote on a commission basis. By 1938 totalisator betting totalled just over £9 million of which £2.5 million came from off the course. This con-trasted with the estimated legal off-course betting of £85 million, and the unrecorded, but no doubt even greater, illegal off-course betting, neither of which made any contribution to racing at all: a parasitic relationship to be sure. The tote captured only a fraction of the total betting on horse-racing and only 2 per cent of its turnover was being returned to the sport to aid in such measures as the improvement of racetracks and spectator amenities. Nevertheless the principle of assisting racing from the proceeds of gambling had been established.[18]

Apart from the TIL arrangements no attempt was made before 1960 to obtain any funds for racing from off-course betting, the vast amount of which was illegal anyway. The Betting and Gaming Act of 1853 had made it an offence for bookmakers to operate either in the streets or in betting houses. Although the rich man's betting clubs, such as Tattersalls, which operated on a credit basis were exempt from the legislation, the working man's access to legal betting was drastically curtailed. Racecourse betting was a permitted alternative but few workers had the resources to attend more than their local meetings. Ready-money postal betting – initially to Scotland to which the 1853 Act did not apply but from 1873 to the continent when the northern avenue was closed – was another option, but it was risking one's money in more ways than one. It was simply easier to resort to the illegal street bookmaker who, unlike the postal operator, generally did not welsh on his clientele and offered starting price odds which the backer could check in his racing paper.[19] Such betting increased in the last quarter of the century and led to a Select Committee whose recommendation of tougher penalties on both the street bookmaker and

THE AFTERMATH OF THE DERBY.

7.3 That's what racing is all about, Peter, or the punter's view of the turf
accountant, drawn by Tom Webster

his clients was endorsed in the Street Betting Act of 1906. Neither bookie
nor backer were swayed and another Select Committee in 1927 reported
that 'the business is . . . of such dimensions and . . . steadily increasing in
volume'.[20] It could not be put down yet it was not to be tolerated.

Eventually, following the *Peppiatt Committee Report*, reality was faced
and, to save police time and maintain some respect for the law, ready-money
betting shops were sanctioned under the Betting and Gaming Act of 1960
to come into effect from 1961. The black economy was whitened though
the restrictions imposed to prevent the offices becoming too attractive
ensured a continuing sepulchral tinge: only as recently as 1984 were toilets,
comfortable chairs, cable television and light refreshments allowed.
Nevertheless the shops still attracted a large clientele because of their convenience and broadcast commentaries. By 1968 there were over 15,000
shops, a clear sign of the latent demand for such gambling outlets. This had
fallen to just over 10,600 by 1985 due to consolidation and rationalisation:
34 per cent are owned by Ladbrokes, William Hill, Coral and Mecca. The
fall was certainly not because of a decline in betting which rose from £1,161
million in 1971 to £3,706 million in 1985.[21] Although there is still an overwhelming preponderance of betting with bookmakers – more than in any
other country – the tote has shared in the growth by expanding its own

7.4 But it was not all sunshine especially on May Day 1929 at Kempton Park

off-course facilities and by promoting its credit betting facilities so that it has become the largest credit bookmaking service in Britain with some 47,000 credit customers. *En route* it has also become the largest individual commercial sponsor of racing in Britain.[22]

It has been public money which has thrown the lifeline to racing. Tied in with the legalisation of betting shops was the formation of the HBLB charged with functions similar to the RBCB which it replaced. These included the promotion of technical services, the modernisation of racecourses, improvements in veterinary science and contributions to prizemoney. The objectives were to be attained by the institution of a levy on the tote and on bookmakers. Initially the levy fell disproportionately upon the totalisator which between 1962–3 and 1966–7 paid 32 per cent of the total despite having only 5 per cent of betting turnover. A more equitable policy was introduced so that when the levy of 1972–3 raised over £6.2 million – in contrast to the £1.8 million of the first levy – some 97 per cent came from the bookmakers, a much fairer reflection of the betting scene.[23]

A major policy of the HBLB has been to preserve racing as a genuine national sport, as countrywide live entertainment. During the nineteenth century many race meetings came and went as local enthusiasm and the ability to raise prizemoney waxed and waned. In addition Jockey Club legislation of 1877 requiring a minimum of £300 added money per day's racing put paid to many small-scale events, and from the early 1880s the Club showed a reluctance to license new courses and schedule further meetings. The result was that the last quarter of the century saw 32 new meetings but the loss of 95 others.[24] No new courses have been opened since the 1920s but several have closed. By the 1960s many racecourses were under threat as the low rate of return on their capital made the offers of the developers very tempting: indeed seven yielded between 1963 and 1965 including the once famous Manchester and Hurst Park. Many suffered from part-time management which failed to perceive opportunities to utilise the courses for revenue-raising activities such as shows, golf driving ranges, exhibitions, etc., which were taken up by more enterprising executives. Although the decentralisation of British racing contributed to the under-utilisation of resources, both the Jockey Club and the HBLB were determined to maintain the number of courses, partly because one of the great attractions of British racing is the great variety of tracks on which bloodstock is tested. Some run clockwise, others counter; some have hard uphill finishes, others have a downhill sprint to the line; some have more bends than the Cresta Run, others possess straights with seemingly endless horizons. This lack of standardisation adds to the unpredictability of racing: here indeed are there 'horses for courses'. Some racecourses were assisted by cheap loans and grants which enabled their executives to update facilities and thus provide a reasonable standard of amenity for the public. Although some courses continue as profit-oriented enterprises with shareholders hoping for dividends, many are now in the hands of local authorities who subsidise them for the benefits which accrue to the area through racing. Others have actually been taken over by a holding company of the HBLB with all profits being ploughed back into racing: ironically one of the courses to which this occurred was Sandown Park, the pioneer enclosed gatemoney course of a century ago. Ultimately all meetings are dependent upon public money. Many of them, especially mid-week ones, are still directly unprofitable, but they serve to sustain the public's interest in racing and, of even more importance, provide a daily betting market from which the HBLB can divert funds to the courses.

British racing has been saved by an acceptance that Britain is more a nation of punters than of racegoers. Whereas the *Ilchester Committee* refused 'to encourage the stay-at-home backer – a person who contributes nothing to the business of racing nor to its finance', the HBLB has a stated policy of tilting 'racing in a direction which helps to generate betting turn-over'.[25] Times have changed. In the eighteenth century, and even on occasions in early Victorian times, paternalistic race committees provided races for the free enjoyment of the local community. Now the gambling activities of the working man (and woman) help finance the racing ambitions of owners and provide employment for professional race-course executives.

IV

The racehorse is now one of the first destinations of the newly acquired wealth of a prosperous financier.
     G. H. Strutfield, 'Racing in 1890', *Nineteenth Century*, 27, (1890), p. 925

Few owners can have considered racing as a money-making concern for in aggregate racing has been, and remains, an economically irrational pursuit. Although the development of the enclosed course enabled a greater volume of prizemoney to be offered – from £413,066 in 1882 to £511,734 in 1910 – it also encouraged greater horse ownership with the result that prizemoney available per horse in training actually declined from £216 to £132; this at a time when the pressure of demand was forcing up training fees, jockeys' retainers and bloodstock prices.[26] Moreover, race entry fees and forfeits meant that owners were racing mainly for their own money. In 1913, the first year for which comprehensive data are available, English owners supplied 63 per cent of all prizemoney, as compared to the 23 per cent of their French counterparts: at no course across the Channel was the proportion higher than 28 per cent, whereas at Manchester owners contributed 50 per cent, at Hurst Park 62 per cent, at Kempton Park 66 per cent, at Newbury 69 per cent and at Sandown Park an astonishing 82 per cent.[27] No wonder that some owners felt that the *pari mutuel* should be anglicised as soon as possible. The eventual introduction of the totalisator, however, did not ease the position all that much as, unlike on the continent, it was given an on-course monopoly of betting. Hence it was no surprise that the *Ilchester Committee* reported in 1943 that 'the owner is called on to make too great a contribution to stakes', a view echoed by the 1968 *Benson Inquiry*, even though by the mid-1960s the proportion coming from the owners had fallen to 24 per cent thanks to the betting levy and commercial sponsorship.[28] Unfortunately, despite the continued increase in funds from these sources, the parlous economic plight of most racecourses, the main provider of prizemoney in the 1960s, has forced an upturn in the owners' percentage which, over the past decade, has averaged 26.9 per cent and is rising.[29]

There has never been any chance that owners in aggregate could cover their costs. In the 1880s it was estimated that about £300 was required to keep a horse in training but, as shown above, only just over two-thirds of this was available as prizemoney. During the inter-war years every race-horse needed around £650 before it paid its running expenses, yet in 1928, the high watermark of stakes in the period, less than a third of this was available per horse. By the 1960s prizemoney contributed only 23.8 per cent of the total costs of ownership and, even with the increased subsidisation of the industry since then, only 6 per cent of horses in 1980 covered their racing and training costs: in fact at a time when the average costs of ownership were about £8,500 per annum 53 per cent of horses won less than £100.

Most owners lose money and most are prepared to do so. For the majority horse ownership veers towards the consumption – conspicuous in some cases – rather than the investment end of the racing spectrum. In this they resemble many other upper- and middle-class sportsmen in that, within limits, they are prepared to pay for their pleasure: they are of the same ilk as the yachtsmen who would spend a small fortune to win a trophy or the shootingmen whose game costs well in excess of the shop price.

For most owners racing was a hobby, albeit sometimes an expensive one, but for some it involved other motivations. Traditionally there has been prestige and status associated with being a racehorse owner: it may be inflationary to label racing as the sport of kings but in the 1830s perhaps a third of owners were titled and half a century later the figure was still at least an eighth. This attracted those who invested in bloodstock primarily in search of social returns. If they too became owners of high quality thoroughbreds then, not only might their names appear on the racecards alongside those of the nobility, but there was also the chance that introductions in the paddock might lead to invitations elsewhere, an aspiration given support by Edward VII, both when Prince of Wales and when monarch, who accepted several of the *nouveaux-riches* into his social circle.

There is probably still a degree of social emulation involved in horse ownership, though the social and economic changes of the past three or four decades have broadened the base of ownership. Most recently two distinct features have emerged. First, as the costs of racing have increased, multiple ownership has enabled the industry to maintain, and indeed increase, the number of horses in training: by the mid 1970s about 20 per cent of racehorses were the property of partnerships, syndicates or companies, the latter often using their animals as a form of advertising. Second, the past decade has seen a move into British racing by international owners to whom the costs appear to have been immaterial. The Maktoum brothers and Khaled Abdulla, men whose weekly incomes are counted in millions of pounds, have invested heavily in the British turf with, in 1984, 350 and 135 horses in training respectively. At the highest level horse-racing in Britain now relies on such wealthy foreign owners: indeed in 1984 only three of the twelve leading owners were domiciled in Britain.

V

It is good to breed Derby winners because they will in time beget other horses capable of the same splendid and useless triumphs.

Bentley's Quarterly Review (1859), p. 281

The economic position of ownership is complicated by some owners being involved in the breeding side of the industry. For many of the aristocracy and gentry in the nineteenth century horse breeding was intimately associated with ownership: anyone with money could purchase a good horse (or what they thought was a good horse) but it took talent to give Darwinism a helping hand and breed a classic winner. Most breeders, however, had an eye on the yearling sales and even in the 1870s, prior to the changes brought about in racing by the enclosed course, nine-tenths of thoroughbreds were produced for sale. Most provided a useful income supplement for farmers operating with one or two brood mares; some were the 'inferior' or surplus stock of the aristocratic stables; yet others came from the studs of large-scale breeding companies, a development which began in the early 1850s with the Middle Park and Rawcliffe Studs and which was stimulated in the later nineteenth century as increased prizemoney and new, *nouveaux-riches* owners made their presence felt in the bloodstock market.

Until the Second World War and beyond it was the studs of the great owner breeders – dominated in the inter-war years by the Earl of Derby and the Aga Khan – which set the pace for the breeding industry. Even as late as 1953 the 14 leading owners (in terms of winnings) all relied on horses which they had bred themselves.[30] Since then increased taxation, especially death duties, and substantially increased costs have forced the break-up of many large private studs. They have been replaced by a proliferation of small breeders – by 1980 7,182 of the 10,484 breeders in Great Britain and Ireland possessed only a single brood mare[31] – and, more significantly, by commercial establishments who almost alone could finance the purchase of the best stallions. The international enterprise has also hit the racing scene. Robert Sangster, for one, has brought the concept of the multinational firm into racing and in 1984, besides 421 horses in training, world-wide he had an interest in 34 stud farms, owned 278 brood mares and had 76 horses standing as stallions.[32]

In the late nineteenth century owners of brood mares on average could sell their produce for around £270 which would appear to be a profitable activity given that to bring an animal to the yearling sales would cost somewhere between £200 and £225.[33] However, up to a third of the mares covered might not fall pregnant; death rates among foals could be as high as 20 per cent; and there was perhaps a further 25 per cent wastage rate before the sales. Certainly few owners would make money from sending their stallions to stud, for, whereas with mares even maidens of the track were allowed to lose that title off the course, only stallions with good racing records were given any chance to be sires. In the early 1900s, for example, there were just over 300 stallions registered for thoroughbred breeding (about two-thirds of which would actually sire foals in any one year) but there were well over 1,500 mares being serviced each season.[34] Although some stallions would cover only a few mares, others could be in high demand and, if their offspring had the right conformation and some of them performed well on the racetrack, then their owners could anticipate substantial returns. In the 1890s a good stallion, serving the traditionally accepted maximum of 40 mares, could bring his owner between £2,000 and £4,000 per annum. An outstanding animal such as *St Simon* could make even these sums seem insignificant. He first went to stud in 1886 at a fee of 50 guineas which had risen to ten times that amount a decade later: during his stud career he serviced 775 mares and earned his owner at least £250,000.[35]

Horse breeding, then, appears to be more economically rational than horse ownership. However, a recent doctoral thesis at the University of Cambridge has suggested that in fact there is considerable irrationality in the breeding sector.[36] The rationale of breeding is that the racehorse is not a standardised commodity and that race-winning ability is inheritable, but as currently assessed – by conformation and by pedigree (including ancestral racing performance) – this is not so obvious. In her study of modern British racing Dr Macken found only very weak positive correlations between these variables and racing ability. If market price can be taken as a reflection of perceived quality, then historically her work is supported by the fact that between 1883 and 1892, 227 well-bred yearlings were each sold for over 1,000 guineas but only two in five of these expensive animals repaid their purchase price.[37] There may, of course, be a stronger relationship between pedigree and performance than these figures and those of Dr Macken suggest: it may just be disguised by other factors including the ability of trainers and jockeys. Success on the racecourse cannot be guaranteed and therein lies one of the attractions of racing.

Horse-racing, more than any other sport, has been subject to state inter-

vention. In the breeding sector this began in the mid-nineteenth century
with the institution of government-subsidised Queen's Plate races, long-
distance events whose winners would have demonstrated the possession
of both strength and stamina, qualities which could then be passed on,
via breeding, to army remounts and halfbred farmhorses. It should not
be forgotten that, although the horse was no longer the fulcrum of Britain's
transport system, it remained vital for military and agricultural purposes.
Most thoroughbred breeders, however, responded instead to the structural
changes within racing and two-year-old races, sprints and handicaps had
little to offer farmers or GHQ. Immature horses were too susceptible to
break-down; sprints hid stamina deficiencies; and handicaps gave weak
horses the chance of beating stronger ones. Consequently in 1888 the
Queen's Plates were abandoned.

A more permanent market intervention came with the establishment of
the National Stud which was set up in 1916 when Colonel Hall-Walker
offered his entire stock of thoroughbreds to the nation conditional only
on the government purchasing his stud farm at Tully, County Kildare and
his training establishment at Russley Park, Wiltshire. Under pressure from
the Army Council, who hoped that the high-class thoroughbreds would
form the basis of the army's light horse stock, the government agreed to
pay £65,625 for the properties for which they received gratis horses valued
at £48,040. The nation gained a valuable asset and Hall-Walker a peerage,
becoming Lord Wavertree, and, perhaps of more significance in this era
of bought titles, he was elected to the Jockey Club.

Much criticism was levied at the Stud by proponents of private enterprise
who claimed that government involvement would lead inevitably to poor
management with consequent further demands on the public purse. In practice, however, the enterprise seems to have been run on strict commercial
lines and between 1919 and 1939 made an average annual net profit of
£4,268, not outstanding but reasonable given the economic circumstances
of the time.[38] Its viability was attributable to racing rather than military
demands for, although the Stud had been established professedly on strate-
gic considerations, by the mid-1920s it was clear that the future of the
army lay with mechanisation.

Even in an age when privatisation has become the catchword, the National Stud has survived. Indeed the recent *Sparrow Report* into its future
recommended that it should be retained in public ownership and developed
for the national benefit as a 'centre of excellence'.[39] Its activities are actually
to be widened to include the standing of National Hunt stallions.

Another form of market intervention has come from the Jockey Club
itself. Towards the end of the nineteenth century, there were fears that

Racing is an industry

7.5 The horses are bought and sold, after a selling plate at Manchester in 1901

And people are employed to do a variety of jobs

7.6 Some are skilled, like this breaker-in

7.7 Some are not, like these muckers-out

7.8 And we must not forget the trainer

7.9 Morning exercises, Newmarket

the new structure of racing, exciting as it was to spectators, would be detrimental to the bloodstock industry. This led the Club to impose curbs on the number of two-year-old races and to attempt to make longer distance racing more attractive to owners by forcing race committees to divert more of their funds away from sprints. More recently in the 1960s the Club had emulated foreign practice in establishing a system of pattern racing by which major races have been graded into classic, prestige and feature events so as to provide a comprehensive series of tests over various distances for the best horses of all ages. By offering higher levels of prizemoney than non-pattern races they are designed to set the standard for British racing and encourage the breeding of the highest grade of thoroughbred. Breeders' premiums, by which part of the prizemoney is given to the breeder of the winning horse, have also been introduced. The *Ilchester Committee* recommended against these on the grounds that the breeder had already obtained the market value of his horse when he sold it. However, by the time of the *Benson Inquiry*, they were considered to be a useful incentive, especially if combined with pattern racing, to encourage breeders to further improve the quality of their animals.

VI

In all probability the three principal jockeys of England will earn, or at any event receive, more money in a year then the whole professional staff of a modern university.

L. H. Curzon, 'The horse as an instrument of gambling', *Contemporary Review*, 30 (1877), p. 391

Other things being equal, and often when they are not, it is the skill of the jockey which determines the race result. In the early days of racing, owners generally rode their own animals but soon some of them realised that their chances of winning could be increased by employing specialist jockeys, though until the early nineteenth century most of these were nothing more than riding grooms, liveried servants beholden to their employer. However, as commercial attitudes strengthened within racing, more independent jockeys emerged and by the late nineteenth century the leading riders were able to pick and choose for whom they rode. Rewards to the most skilled of these diminutive men became as large as they were small. Although scheduled riding fees were only £3, with £2 extra for a win, presents and retainers – ample compensation for a restriction on the choice of employer – could lift annual incomes to a level 'before which 2,000 guineas in bare riding fees shrinks into insignificance'.[40] Coincident with this, but no coincidence, was the development of celebrity status: whereas riders in the earlier part of the century rarely even gained a mention in the race results, five or six decades on leading jockeys became cult figures. The sporting press quoted their opinions, chronicled their activities and created identities for them both on and off the racecourse. When Fred Archer, champion jockey for 13 successive seasons, married in 1883 special trains were run to bring the crowds to cheer their hero.

Most aspiring jockeys never gained such adulation. Of the 187 apprentices registered in 1900 only 75 became licensed jockeys and a mere 48 of these rode as such for more than one season.[41] Although racing was unusual among sports in having formal appenticeships, if a boy was small then it was easy enough to obtain one, for few trainers objected to taking on cheap stable labour who, if they had the talent to win races, could also supplement the establishment's income. Unfortunately for too many, particularly those from an urban background, their size owed more to nurture than to nature and a few months of country food and fresh air soon ruined their chances of a riding career. Training gallops weeded out others. Even those apprentices who showed promise might not secure many opportunities to ride in races as owners were reluctant to offer them mounts until the institution of an apprentice weight allowance in the early twentieth century. Nor could those who graduated from the racing stables be guaranteed employment as the demand for jockeys was generally one for established riders. The market for jockeys was one of permanent excess supply: rarely were there more than a score of runners in a race but there were 20 times this number of riders seeking a mount.

At least they did not face serious competition from amateur riders. Indeed the amateur–professional debate never really surfaced in flat racing once lighter weights became the norm. Most amateurs could not make the low weights required for flat racing so they preferred National Hunt races where the heavier weights carried demanded far less of a sacrifice of the good life.[42] In any case from 1879 the Jockey Club insisted that all gentlemen who wished to race against professional jockeys had to be licensed and this was not granted readily: horseflesh was becoming too valuable to be put at risk by unskilled amateurs. Moreover there were many races over fences which were restricted to 'gentlemen riders'. Up to the formation of the National Hunt Committee in 1866 the term was somewhat elastic, but, from then on, a qualified amateur rider had to belong to one of a select list of clubs or be an officer of either service on full pay, a magistrate, a peer or bear a courtesy title. Persons of lower social standing could be balloted in, but they had to be nominated by men holding the club or commission qualification. There were some modifications to these rules, particularly after the reorganisation of the Committee in 1883, in that the list of approved clubs was extended, and farmers (and their sons) of at least 100 acres became eligible, though those seeking entry by ballot now had to be proposed and seconded by members of the Committee itself.

Training was not hard, though there was the problem of adapting to new technology such as the starting gate or the monkey-on-stick style of riding introduced with such devastating effect by the American jockeys during their invasion of the 1890s. Injuries were not uncommon but the Jockey Club attempted to assist those riders who literally and figuratively fell by the wayside. Although a compulsory insurance scheme was not introduced until 1923, the establishment of the Bentinck Benevolent and the Rous Memorial Funds in the nineteenth century served as a paternalistic effort to help distressed jockeys and their families. The jockey's greatest enemy was weight. During racing's close season many riders lived too well and then had to shed several pounds or more. For many masochism was almost a professional necessity: today nutritional research has enabled jockeys to follow a sensible, if restricted diet, but in the nineteenth century most had to rely on eating very little and combating even that with Turkish baths and purgatives.

The existence of Jockey Club assistance to those riders in need weakened any move towards unionism for welfare purposes. In any case jockeys, like most other professional sportsmen of the time, were reluctant to institutionalise their industrial relations.[43] Certainly racing was a highly competitive industry in which the star riders achieved their economic rents and saw little point in joining any union; and without the champions the bargaining position of a union would be seriously undermined. It took a long time for wider societal pressures to be felt and not till 1966 was a Flat-Race Jockeys' Association finally set up.

By this time the 'present' to winning jockeys had become so customary as to be regarded as a recognised charge of 10 per cent of the prizemoney. Race fees had risen to £7 for flat races and 10 guineas for National Hunt, the latter a recognition of the lower prizemoney and greater dangers over the hurdles and fences. Despite the increase, so skewed was the distribution of earnings that perhaps only 40 of the 170 licensed flat-race jockeys could say that they were doing well financially.[44] As always owners preferred to offer rides to those who had proved their ability. Stable staff often received up to 5 per cent of prizemoney, but, unlike with jockeys, this had not yet become an established practice. Moreover as owners, and consequently trainers, felt the financial pinch of racing in the early 1960s, wages for stable lads fell behind national earnings trends. This resulted in more girls taking up stable work, perhaps with their love of horses providing a psychic supplement to their meagre wage packet. For some, however, there would soon be an opportunity to become jockeys as in 1972 the Jockey Club allowed women – initially called 'jockettes'! – to race at recognised meetings; initially only against each other, but from 1973 in open competition.

VII

'The public don't count.'
  Lord Rosebery quoted in J. de Moubray, *Horseracing and Racing Society* (1985), p. 93

For most of its time as an organised sport British horse-racing has been controlled by a self-appointed group of socially elite owners. Founded in the early 1750s as one of the first formally organised sporting bodies in the world, by the mid-nineteenth century the Jockey Club had become acknowledged as the preeminent authority in racing matters. Local race committees had increasingly turned to the Club to settle disputes and had voluntarily adopted the Club's *Rules of Racing*. Compulsion replaced volunteerism in 1870 when the Club ruled that neither the programme nor the results of any British flat race would be published in the Club's official organ, the *Racing Calendar*, unless the meeting was advertised as being run under Jockey Club rules. Adding bite to the regulations was a further proviso which declared that any owner, trainer, jockey or official who took part in any unrecognised meeting would be disqualified from participation in authorised events. By the end of the century the Club had complete control over British flat-racing.[45]

No official list of members was published till 1835, but, judging from the names attached to entries in Jockey Club Plates and to the resolutions printed in the *Racing Calendar*, membership from the beginning appears to have been predominantly aristocratic. Generally it has remained so with a place in the club being guarded as carefully as other family heirlooms. The policy of the club has been to elect 'its own members from those who are interested in racing and whom members consider suitable to exercise authority and jurisdiction in such matters'.[46] During the nineteenth century two black balls from a minimum of nine votes were sufficient to exclude any aspiring members: the Earl of Glasgow used to blackball a certain Colonel Forester with unfailing regularity, once hiring a special train from Scotland in order to arrive in time to perform his self-appointed duty. New owners drawn from industry and commerce came on to the turf but not into the Club. In 1870 both Sir Joseph Hawley and Lord Durham raised the issue of rendering the Club more representative of racing interests but they gained little support. The exclusive nature diminished a little after the First World War and some industrialists and businessmen managed to secure election, though usually only after they had secured honours and belated acceptance into high society: Lord Glanely, who began his working life as a shipping clerk and eventually purchased a peerage from Lloyd George for £100,000, was the first self-made man to be elected to the Club in 1929. Yet these were only chinks in the otherwise impenetrable armour of the Club. At one time in the inter-war years there were only two commoners listed in the membership and, although a few ageing businessmen might gain entry, there was no room for the small owner or for those who made a business out of racing. Social position and hereditary influence still remain the best way of gaining a place. Even though there has been some broadening of the membership base, in 1985, 52 of the 113 members held titles and a further 13 were high-ranking army officers.

However, although democracy has had no place in the portals of Jockey Club power, the winds of change have blown through racing and certainly the establishment of the HBLB has undermined the ultimate authority of the Club. When the Turf Board was set up in 1965 by the Jockey Club and the National Hunt Committee to coordinate and direct racing policy (as opposed to the day-to-day running of racing and the administration of its rules) the representatives of the HBLB were excluded from permanent membership on the orders of the then Home Secretary. However, in 1967, Lord Wigg, the newly appointed chairman of the Levy Board refused to accept this and three HBLB members then received standing invitations to attend Turf Board meetings and in 1968 the Joint Racing Board was set up as a policy-making body of the Turf Authorities and the HBLB.

The challenge to the Jockey Club by the HBLB stimulated other interest groups to lobby for changes in racing, among them the National Sporting League (founded in 1902), the Racecourses Association (1907), the Thoroughbred Breeders' Association (1917), the National Association of Bookmakers (founded as the National Bookmakers' Protection Association in 1932, but with antecedents back to 1921) the Racehorse Owners' Association (1945), the National Hunt Trainers' Association (1962), the National Trainers' Association (1964), the Professional National Hunt Jockeys' Association (1964), the Flat-Race Jockeys' Association (1966) and, of course, the Transport and General Workers' Union which had represented stable workers in negotiations with the Newmarket trainers since 1937. Most of these bodies had had little, if any, influence on Jockey Club policy in the past, but, now, they saw a chance of getting a hearing and indeed pressure exerted on their behalf by the HBLB has resulted in other racing interests being considered in the decision-making process. To protect itself the Club sought, and obtained, a Royal Charter in 1970 which enshrined its powers such that an Act of Parliament is required in order to modify its authority. Thus the Club remains the titular head of British racing but its power to direct overall policy has been eroded by the influx of money from the betting levy: the HBLB now calls many of racing's tunes. Nevertheless the Club has changed some of its old practices and attitudes. It has accepted that to preserve its power it must share it and it has developed an awareness of the necessity for good public relations. No longer can the Club adopt the view of Lord Rosebery, doyen of the Club for many years, whose apparent motto was 'the public don't count'.[47] Now its overt policy is 'actively to promote the attraction of live racing by making the spectator once more the focus of our sport'.[48]

The club has also changed its attitude towards women in racing. For a long time there was a reluctance to see them as anything more than adornment in the enclosures and for most of the nineteenth and early twentieth centuries many female owners felt obliged to disguise their gender by the use of male pseudonyms. No wonder the suffragettes attacked racecourse grandstands and eventually found a martyr at a race meeting when Emily Davison threw herself under the king's horse at the 1913 Derby and was killed. Now, with no recorded cases of apoplexy within Jockey Club ranks, women own, train and even ride racehorses.

Racing needed rules and a court of appeal and initially the sport – it was not yet an industry – benefited considerably from the monopolisation

7.10 Lady jockeys in 1925 and 1972. Giving a toast to equal opportunity perhaps?

of power by the Jockey Club which used its authority to codify and cleanse racing. Something was rotten in the state of racing when, in the horseflesh version of mutton dressed as lamb, the 1844 Derby, the classic race for three-year-old horses was won by a heavily disguised older horse. The Club took steps to stamp out such corruption and ensure that the rules of racing were enforced. By the later nineteenth century they had instituted a system of specialised, professional racing officials whose use they 'recommended' to other meetings; they had developed the use of licences for trainers, jockeys and even racecourses which could be instantaneously revoked should there be a whiff of corruption or incompetence; and, of course, their distinction between recognised and unauthorised meetings was a powerful weapon in the war against turf criminals. Yet more could have been done. Towards the end of the century there was growing and sustained criticism of the Club. Too few members were attending the business meetings and even the stewards were being castigated for their timidity and their reluctance to take action unless an abuse was so flagrant that it could not be ignored. In particular they were accused of doing nothing to combat the growing menace of drugs which were making a farce of the formbook and a mockery of the professed rationale of racing, the improvement of thoroughbred bloodstock. Eventually in 1904 the eyes of the Three Blind Mice – as the triumvirate were being labelled in some irreverent circles – were opened by the Hon. George Lambton, the trainer brother of Lord Durham, a leading member of the Jockey Club. After informing his brother of what he intended to do Lambton doped five of his own horses which had shown no previous form, but which, under the influence of drugs, gained four first places and a second. Doping was then made a turf offence. Thereafter open doping ceased and even covert drug usage must have decreased after the development of the saliva test in 1910.

Warning-off was the ultimate punishment meted out by the Club to turf offenders in the nineteenth century. This has remained the basic major weapon in the Jockey Club armoury, but from the 1920s there has been less reluctance to go further and institute legal proceedings. That imprisonment might result if found out has acted as a greater deterrent to turf corruption than any warning-off. The latter was more a social stigma and perhaps only really deterred those potential criminals in the higher echelons of racing. It had been preferred to the courts as, unlike in legal proceedings, Jockey Club trials put the onus on the accused to prove themselves innocent.

Writing in the 1930s one turf commentator observed that 'it is generally conceded that the English Turf today, if not altogether immaculate in its many phases, is as clear an institution as one could reasonably wish to find it. The system of control was never tighter. Acute misdemeanours

are few and far between.'[49] This could not have been written a century
before. Racing still has the taint of corruption; this is almost inevitable
because of its association with gambling which tempts some to follow the
crooked track. Doping still occurs, horses are still pulled and illegalities
are still attempted. Yet the problem is much less than many losing punters
might infer. The high priority given to racecourse security services by both
the Jockey Club and the HBLB has seen to that.

VIII

> Racing is a multi-million pound sporting industry; there is a tension between
> its sporting and industrial aspects. But it is saved by being a sport.
>   C. R. Hill, 'Charting a course for compatibility', *The Times*, 17 February 1988, p. 44

Horse-racing has become a major sports industry. It provides entertainment
for millions, commoners more than kings, via the racetrack, television and
betting shops and employment for thousands in the studs, stables and gambling outlets. Investment in thoroughbred bloodstock in the late 1970s was
estimated at some £160 million and sales of such animals made a positive
contribution to the British balance of payments.[50] Betting turnover in 1979–
80 topped £2,393 million, of which £173 million found its way into government coffers thanks to the lucrative betting tax.[51] A decade further on
the figure for government revenue tops £300 million.[52] Nevertheless economics alone has not determined the industry's fortunes: indeed, as has
been shown, its economic efficiency has often been circumscribed by social
factors. Moreover, the markets associated with racing have not always
been allowed to operate freely. Even the Jockey Club, that bastion of right-
wing privilege, interfered with the right of nineteenth-century capital when,
in the interests of owners, it limited racecourse dividends to 10 per cent
thus forcing surplus funds either to be reinvested into facilities or to be
added to prizemoney. Most market intervention, however, has come from
the state, though generally with Jockey Club approval and support. Queen's
Plates, the National Stud, and the totalisator were all accepted as assisting
the racing industry; and, of course, the betting levy has proved to be the
salvation of the British turf. In return the government has imposed its own
betting tax and has insisted on other interests besides those of the Jockey
Club having a say in the running of racing in Britain.[53]

NOTES

1 In 1985 only 548 amateur riders' permits were issued by the Jockey Club.
2 *Report of the Horserace Betting Levy Board (HBLB)*, (1986), p. 30.

3 An enclosed course had been tried in London in 1837 when John Whyte, an entrepreneur before his time, erected a barrier around his Hippodrome circuit in Bayswater. It was a financial disaster as insufficient spectators were willing to pay the shilling minimum entrance fee. J. Rice, *The History of the British Turf* (1879), pp. 202–5.

4 Earl of Suffolk, *Racing and Steeplechasing* (1886), p. 211.

5 *Bloodstock Breeders Review*, 4 (1914), p. 282.

6 C. Richardson, *The English Turf* (1901), p. 213.

7 For a discussion of the role of uncertainty in attracting crowds to sports events see W. Vamplew, *Pay Up and Play the Game* (Cambridge, 1988), pp. 77–153, 174–80.

8 For example £34,000 was raised to finance Haydock Park and £80,000 for Newbury. *Shareholders Register of Haydock Park Racecourse Company*, 1898; *Prospectus of Newbury Racecourse Company*, 1905.

9 Quoted in E. Rickman, *On and Off the Racecourse* (1937), p. 266.

10 These figures are for flat racing. When mixed and National Hunt meetings are included the decline is from 8,594 to 7,340. *Report by the [Benson] Committee of Inquiry into the Racing Industry* (1968), Appendix 1.

11 For all meetings the figures are 4,665,762 (5,955,797) and 6,271. *Benson*, Appendix 1.

12 *Benson*, pp. 68–70.

13 *Benson*, p. 66.

14 For all meetings 3,749,811 and 4,185. *Report by the [Jockey Club] Stewards* (1985), p. 66.

15 *Report by the Stewards*, pp. 66–7.

16 *Benson*, p. 92; *Report by the Stewards*, p. 65.

17 *Report of HBLB* (1986), p. 33.

18 In 1962 the Totalisator Board acquired all the share capital of the TIL, *Benson*, p. 138.

19 By the end of the nineteenth century starting prices were determined, with universal consent among press and bookmakers, by representatives of two leading racing papers, the *Sportsman* and the *Sporting Life*. For further detail see W. Vamplew, *The Turf: A Social and Economic History of Horse Racing* (1976), p. 223.

20 *Select Committee on Betting Duty*, 1923, 5, p. xiii.

21 *Benson*, p. 138; *Reports of H.M. Customs and Excise Commissioners*.

22 *Report of Horserace Totalisator Board* (1986), pp. 85–6.

23 *Benson*, p. 140; *Report of HBLB* (1973), para. 5.

24 Calculated from data in the *Racing Calendar*.

25 *Report of the Racing Reorganisation [Ilchester] Committee* (1943), para. 53; *Report of HBLB* (1986), p. 5.

26 Calculated from data in the *Racing Calendar*.

27 *Bloodstock Breeders Review*, 7 (1918), pp. 18–19.

28 *Ilchester*, para. 12; *Benson*, p. 92.

29 Calculated from data in *Report of the Stewards* (1985).

30 S. C. Macken, 'Economic aspects of bloodstock investment in Britain', PhD, University of Cambridge (1986), p. 33.

31 Macken, p. 40.

32 J. de Moubray, *Horseracing and Racing Society* (1985), p. 119.

33 For a fuller discussion of the economics of breeding in the late nineteenth century see Vamplew (1988), pp. 107–10.

34 In 1978 there were 1,205 active stallions and 15,862 brood mares. Macken, pp. 40, 50.

35 D. Craig, *Horse Racing* (1982), p. 55.

36 Macken.

37 Calculated from data in Richardson, pp. 273, 276.

38 Calculated from data in *Reports and Accounts of the National Stud*.

39 *Report of HBLB* (1986), p. 9. In 1922 the Irish provisional government claimed ownership of the Stud. Eventually it was agreed that the British government would retain the stock and pay £21,300 in lieu of rent. In 1943 Tully was given up and the Stud was transferred to Newmarket.

40 T. A. Cook, *A History of the English Turf* (1905), p. 521.

41 Calculated from data in the *Racing Calendar*.

42 The heavier weights probably stem from National Hunt's association with owners riding the horses on which they also went hunting. There may also be a link with breeding for army remounts as officers were unlikely to be of flat-race jockey proportions.

43 W. Vamplew, 'Not playing the game: unionism in British professional sport 1870–1914', *British Journal of Sports History*, 2 (1985), pp. 232–47.

44 D. Malcolm, 'Jockeys and riders', *New Society*, 1 July 1965.

45 Not till 1866 was a body, the Grand National Hunt Steeplechase Committee, formed to control National Hunt racing. It became known as the National Hunt Committee in 1889. Eighty years later it was merged into the Jockey Club.

46 *Select Committee on Betting Duty* (1923), 5, p. 1443.

47 Cited in de Moubray, p. 93.

48 *Report of the Stewards* (1985), p. 4.

49 A. W. Coaten, 'The evolution of racing' in Earl of Harewood, *Flat Racing* (1940), p. 127.

50 Macken, Appendix B.

51 Macken, Appendix A.

52 *The Times*, 17 February 1988, p. 44.

53 The present tax was first introduced in 1966. An earlier imposition between 1926 and 1928 fell victim to the strong resistance of the National Sporting League. For details see Vamplew (1976), p. 207.

LAWN TENNIS 8

HELEN WALKER

I

> The scene should be laid on a well-kept garden lawn. There should be a bright warm sun overhead... Near at hand, under the cool shadow of a tree, there should be strawberries and cream, iced claret mug, and a few spectators who do not want to play but are lovers of the game... If all these conditions are present, an afternoon spent at lawn tennis is a highly Christian and beneficent pastime.
>
> Robert D. Osborn, *Lawn Tennis – Its Players and How to Play* (1881)

Lawn Tennis was imported to England as a consequence of the incarceration in Wingfield Castle of Prince Charles d'Orléans, grandson of Charles VI of France, taken prisoner at the battle of Agincourt. A keen player, he is said to have taught the game to the young nobles of his gaoler's family. Henry VIII is reputed to have risen at 5 a.m. to play tennis in the enclosed court at Hampton Court Palace. He kept his own professional playing partner Anthony Ansley, who supplied balls and rackets. *The Oxford Companion to Sports and Games* notes that Queen Elizabeth I was once entertained by ten Somerset men, servants of the Earl of Hertford, who played their game of handball in a square court marked by hanging lines, with a centre line crossing. 'In this square they played, five to five, with handball, with bord and cord, as they term it, to the great liking of Her Majesty.'[1]

Games of what is now known as Real or Royal Tennis were a regular feature of the European courts through the fifteenth and sixteenth centuries. Stemming from the French *tenir* 'to hold', the name of the early game had many variations, tenes, tennys, tennise or tennys, all of which were corruptions of the call given by the server at the point of the delivery of the ball.[2] The French version of the game, *jeu de paume*, was extremely popular. The first championship, recorded as being won by a woman named Margot, took place in Paris in 1427, and by the end of the sixteenth century, Paris had 1,800 courts for its quarter of a million population. A chill caught after such a game is said to have contributed to the death of Valois King Louis X.

The *Sporting Magazine* of 29 September 1793 predicted the popularity of a version of tennis in relation to that older game: 'Field tennis threatens to bowl out cricket.' Eighty years later a reference to 'long tennis', presumably similar, occurred in *Games and Sports* (1873) which is amongst the earliest compendiums of pastimes to contain a mention of the game.[3] Several years before this publication Major Gem, clerk to Birmingham Magistrates played a form of outdoor tennis on a rectangular court with a Spanish friend, Perera, and in 1872 they, together with two local doctors, established the first lawn tennis club at the Manor House Hotel in Leamington Spa. It is however Major Walter Clopton Wingfield JP, retired army Colonel, member of the corps of Gentlemen-at-Arms at the court of Queen Victoria and direct descendant of the gaoler of Charles d'Orléans, who is credited with the popularisation of the game as we know it today. A book of rules was published by him in December 1873 and the following July his application to patent 'A New and Portable Court for Playing the Ancient Game of Tennis' was granted. Five guineas bought a painted box containing poles, pegs and netting for creating a court, four tennis rackets, twelve 'rubber cored and flannel covered' balls, a mallet, brush and book of rules. Designed to be played on an hourglass-shaped grass court, the Major recommended it for frosty days when the best of the shooting was over and the ground too hard for hunting.[4]

Wingfield named his game *Sphairistike* after the Greek for 'ball-game'; however so great was his dislike of the popular corruption 'sticky', within a short time he began to promote it as 'lawn tennis'. The earliest use in print of the latter term occurred in an enthusiastic and prophetic report contained in *The Army and Navy Gazette* of March 1874:

A new game has just been patented by Major Wingfield, late 1st Dragoon Guards, which, if we mistake not, will become a national pastime. Lawn Tennis – for that is the name under which the game makes its appearance – is a clever adaptation of tennis to the exigencies of an ordinary lawn piece of ground.[5]

The *Morning Post* of 4 May the same year repeated the *Gazette*'s prediction adding that the game might be both seen and played the following week at either the opening day of the annual cricket match between the Household Brigade and the Royal Engineers at the Prince's Cricket Ground, Brompton Road, or at the Polo Club, Lillie Bridge.

Lawn tennis was soon being played overseas. Its first appearance in the United States was probably on a wet Massachusetts afternoon in the summer of 1874 when James Dwight and F. R. Sears played with a set of net, rackets and balls which had been imported from England. The game caught on rapidly; only six years later the first lawn tennis tournament of the Staten Island Cricket and Baseball Club was held at New Brighton and the United States Lawn Tennis Association formed in 1881. Lawn tennis was introduced to Brazil and India in 1875 and the latter's first tournament, the Punjab Lawn Tennis Championships, was held in 1885.[6] In the 1870s tennis became established in Germany and France; by 1883 Hamburg had three courts and the first national championships were held four years later. Australia's first court was constructed in asphalt and laid at the Melbourne Cricket Club in 1878, the venue of the first championships, which were held two years later.

Following the promotion of the game in society magazines such as *Vanity Fair*,[7] the rapid ascendancy and status of lawn tennis as an extra diversion to be provided by the hosts of weekend house parties was guaranteed and 'no afternoon party was complete without it'.[8] A year before the first reference to the game in *The Times*,[9] while staying in 1876 at Bingham Rectory in Nottinghamshire, Oscar Wilde wrote to a friend, 'We have had some very pleasant garden parties and any amount of lawn tennis.'[10] The à la mode position occupied by the game was shortlived however, and by the 1890s some commentators were predicting its demise. In 1903 N. L. Jackson noted that 'the game [had been] dropped as an adjunct to fashionable parties some ten years ago', but compared this domestic decline with 'the Continent and America [where] the game has taken a great hold ... and players and spectators follow it with great keenness'.[11] While no longer in favour at the weekend house parties of the middle classes, lawn tennis nevertheless became, in addition to cricket, an established favourite with the new suburbanite, and was especially favoured by women.

The literature published in the 1880s had enthused about the emergence of the new outdoor game, and included a number of instruction manuals published in the French language which indicated its link with *jeu de paume*, and also, up to the turn of the century, demonstrated an increasing preoccupation with the codification of the rules. In addition to the MCC and LTA Rules published in successive editions, R. C. Hope's *Lawn Tennis Code* and *The Perfect Score Sheets* (1885) and *Lawn Tennis Tournaments* (1883) by C. L. Dodgson (author Lewis Carroll), which set out 'the true method of assigning prizes with proof of the fallacy of the present method', some dozen publications related to this, while the format of the various handbooks and manuals, well established by 1900, testified to the continued interest in the game by this date.[12]

The comprehensive *Outdoor Games and Recreations: A Popular Encyclopaedia for Boys* was published by the Religious Tract Society in 1892. 'No mere *réchauffé* of the conventional boy's handbook – "scrappy and indigestible", but a veritable recreative textbook, prepared by experts ... and treated with sufficient amplitude of detail and thoroughness of exposition to prove of very real and permanent value', the book's stated intention was to inculcate 'both manly and Christian' virtues. Whether the extent of the coverage of different sports was an indication of the degree to which each could help achieve this aim was not stated, but the 150 pages on model yachting, boating and canoeing, compared to 38 pages on cricket would seem to indicate the greater suitability of the former pastimes. Whereas 83 pages were devoted to winter and ice sports, which included long-distance and fen skating, lawn tennis was given a mere 16. While an obvious explanation was its relative newness, the captions accompanying the illustrations of the various tennis strokes possibly provide an alternative answer. Implicit in them is the suggestion that tennis might encourage the development of characteristics other than those manly and Christian. The overarm lob for example, is described as 'showy form, but bad', and blatant competition might deter boys from becoming the 'strong, erect, full chested, broad shouldered men of vigour, constitution, high animal spirits and dauntless courage . . . wanted by the Church today'.[13]

The promotion of Christian values was not an ethos motivating the residents of the 'salubrious suburb' of Bedford Park in the founding of a tennis club soon after the completion of the estate in the late 1870s. An 'aesthetic' community of artists and poets, amongst whom lived the poet W. B. Yeats, the estate was at that time located on the western edge of London. For an annual subscription of half a guinea family membership of the tennis club could be bought and the asphalt courts rented by the hour. The club was an active social centre but characteristic of the unconventional style of the suburb the actions of its members in playing tennis on a Sunday brought an unsuccessful petition and irate letters to the editor of the local press. An editorial of 28 May 1880 presented the position of the *Acton, Chiswick and Turnham Green Gazette*:

If lawn tennis on Sundays is right at the Bedford Park Club, may it not be claimed that billiards, bagatelle, bowls and even skittles would be proper at the surrounding public houses ... That is the legitimate outcome of such reasoning and surely every Englishman would deprecate such an influx of Sunday amusements.[14]

No such moral breach of the sabbath was countenanced by the members of the Pussellawa Lawn Tennis Club in Colombo. Their Book of Rules, already in its ninth year of publication by 1893, stated that the tennis courts would be closed during the hours of (English) divine service in Pussellawa parish church. Even early this century the orthodoxy of the Lord's Day Observance Society prevailed as far as tennis on Sunday was concerned. Visits by the young Osbert Lancaster to his grandfather meant the playing of croquet rather than tennis on that day because: 'Whereas the tennis court was visible from the road and the vicar feared that the spectacle of the gentry at play might lead the villagers into sin, the croquet lawn was concealed by a dense shrubbery'.[15]

With its codification of the rules, the inauguration and development in 1877 of the Wimbledon Championships, considered in detail in a later section, provided the fundamental impetus to the game. Two years later the first Irish Open Championship was held, which, unlike its English counterpart, featured a women's championship. Ireland also won two tennis medals in the first Olympics held in Athens in 1896. A century later there are 170 clubs affiliated to the ILTA and 20,000 people known to be active in the sport in the Republic.[16]

Through the last two decades of the nineteenth century the *Field* published an annual *Lawn Tennis Calendar* containing a list of clubs and secretaries together with the rules of the game. From the late 1880s to the turn of the century the rising curve of interest in lawn tennis flattened off in terms of both entries and spectators for championship matches. The first Wimbledon champion, Spencer Gore analysed the reasons for this, writing in 1890 that,

Whether anyone who has played really well at cricket, tennis or even rackets will ever seriously give his attention to lawn tennis beyond showing himself to be a promising player is extremely doubtful, for in all probability the monotony of the game as compared with the others would choke him off before he had time to excel in it.[17]

But in fact the young had turned to other diversions, principally bicycling, a craze for which it was said 'had infected society'.[18] Notwithstanding Gore's view, lawn tennis resisted this shift in fashion and by 1900 in excess of 250 clubs had affiliated to the LTA. One such was the Honor Oak Cricket Club founded in 1866, whose members had formed a Lawn Tennis section 'productive of much success' in 1884. An exclusive entrance fee of five shillings and subscription of half a guinea allowed the men access to the club and either sport all year round but women were allowed access only during the tennis season. A successful club, by 1887 it boasted 51 tennis members both male and female and 61 cricket players. As the final event of 1890, following a season when the tennis team had won its entire fixture list, the tennis section organised an evening's fund-raising entertainment in the form of a smoking evening at the Grove Tavern, Lordship Lane, an event popular with widely differing types of clubs at this time.

The steady growth in membership continued until the First World War and beyond, particularly as the club increasingly fulfilled an important social function for the community. Club play was introduced on Sundays in 1925, and two years later the first all-year hard courts were built. In 1931 the club moved to a new site on Dulwich Common and the evenings of the August bank holiday week saw a Ladies' Invitation Doubles Tournament held in conjunction with cricket matches and social functions of various types. After the outbreak of war in 1939 the closure of the tennis section was followed by the dereliction of the courts: the championships were only revived in 1949 and some of the earlier triumphs regained in the South London League in the later 1950s and 1960s.[19]

The Innellan Bowling and Tennis Club held its first 'Grand Tournament' on 27 July 1889 for which the local laird donated a silver cup each for bowls and tennis. Originally founded by the local clergy as two separate clubs intended for the younger members of the community, funds were raised by concerts and steamer parties to the bathing station at nearby Ferry Rock. A decade after the inaugural tournament a crisis in the funds of the club led to the sending of individual letters to each household in the community stressing the importance of the facilities offered by the club especially in view of Innellan's emergent role as a holiday resort for Glaswegians. However, in common with the wider experience, the fortunes of the club continued to decline producing a widespread drop in membership around the turn of century, although the effort to reverse this slump led in 1904, on payment of an annual subscription of five shillings, to the admittance of women members for the first time.[20]

Immediately before and following the First World War there was a steady rise in the rate of tennis club affiliations to the LTA. After a slight drop in 1924, 1,620 clubs were affiliated in 1925, the total reached almost 2,500 by 1930 and peaked at 3,220 in 1938. Through the 1920s the *Daily News* published the *Tennis Annual* giving details of the tournaments for each year; the edition for 1927 lists 'a record number' with 55 tournaments planned for July and 60 in August, while the five proposed as early as March were to be played on hard courts. The position of the tennis club as an essential component of the social life of the provincial suburb was by this period well established. Marshington and the role of its tennis club in the transition to adulthood of Muriel Hammond during the First World War is carefully drawn in Holtby's *The Crowded Street*. Muriel's experience of 'coming-out' was common to a generation of young women for whom, as the necessity for chaperoning began to recede, membership of the local club provided opportunities for social contact with the opposite sex to an extent hitherto unknown. While playing her first match in a state of nervous anxiety lest she should play badly or worse expose the safety pin holding the waist band of her skirt, Muriel realised with horror that 'the other courts were deserted. The whole of Marshington was there on the veranda. The whole of Marshington, finishing its tea, had nothing better to do than watch the set. Muriel felt fifty eyes boring holes into her humiliated back.'[21]

As the faster and more aggressive game played by professionals permeated club play so, according to one observer, the average age of the club member lowered. Writing in 1949 Macqueen-Pope recalled an earlier era when lawn tennis

was a much gentler, more leisurely game than it has now become and nothing like so strenuous. The speed came from abroad. Young men did not devote themselves to it as they do today. It was the more middle-aged men who were the backbone of the numberless clubs. If young men played, they did so as a change from cricket, or to please their sisters and fiancées.[22]

Any history of lawn tennis will inevitably centre on middle-class involvement in the game with the cost of equipment and the need for a court underpinning its social exclusivity but also ensuring its synonymity with class privilege. For Gwendolen Freeman, a 1930s insurance collector in the poor areas of Birmingham, the fact that she spoke what the residents termed 'lawn tennis' precluded her from acceptance by the local community.[23] For the poorer and/or urban player the provision of open space for a variety of leisure uses had increased around the turn of the century and had been given a particular impetus by, for example, the 1905 unemployed Workmen's Act, which authorised local authority employment schemes, such as road-building and also park improvements. Under this Act tennis courts were set out in two of Bristol's three main parks and in Manchester's ninety-acre Platt Fields no less than 46 tennis courts together with 2 bowling greens, 13 football pitches and 9 cricket pitches were created. Employers also made provision. In 1893 the employees of the Bristol tobacco company W. D. and H. O. Wills founded the Wills Association Football Club with facilities for cricket and lawn tennis. Three years later the London Business Houses' Amateur Sports Association was founded with a lawn tennis section formally and separately constituted in 1920.[24]

In her *Lawn Tennis for Ladies*, Mrs Lambert Chambers, Wimbledon Champion for a total of seven years, only barely acknowledged the existence of the player of moderate means:

Exercise in the open air and exercise of a thorough and engrossing character carried out with [sic] cheerful and stimulating surroundings, with scientific methods, rational aims and absorbing chances, surely that is the foundation of a healthy culture ... [Lawn tennis] is more or less within the reach of all, rich or poor. It can be played on one's own lawn ... or even in some of the public parks.[25]

The lack of land available for tennis courts in the older local authority schools had inevitably barred thousands of children from access to the

8.1 Tennis was marvellous for meeting members of the opposite sex. Off court was probably as important as on court in Regent's Park, April 1924

game and, within the ethos of reconstruction after the Second World War, this factor, together with the failure of the game to attract young players of calibre, was linked with a continued concern at Britain's inability to produce top quality players. In 1946 Slazenger promoted a professional tournament at Scarborough and the following year at their invitation, three times Wimbledon champion Fred Perry returned from the United States with a brief to revitalise the game in the post-war period. With Dan Maskell, Perry toured Britain giving a series of exhibition matches at local tennis clubs, donating the proceeds to club funds. 'Focus on Tennis' was organised by the Central Council of Physical Recreation in 1948 and for the next three years, using equipment supplied by Slazenger, Maskell and Perry took tennis to the schoolchildren of Britain through the months of June, July and August. In 1949 the LTA also began a coaching programme which was reputed to be the most comprehensive in the world, although it ran into criticism almost from the outset for perpetuating the elitism of the game.[26]

8.2 This looks a more serious affair in Matlock, June 1921

With a brief to examine the factors affecting the development of games and sports so that 'these activities may play their full part in promoting the general welfare of the community', the Wolfenden Committee reported in 1960.[27] *British Lawn Tennis* wrote off its proceedings as 'nine wasted years' but its recommendations as far as the establishment of a Ministry of Sport was concerned were overdue and provided a stimulus to the training programme in several sports, including lawn tennis. With nearly 1,000 schools affiliated to the Junior Development Scheme in that year, the LTA claimed that 'no matter where a promising youngster may live, the machinery exists to have him discovered, tested and according to his capabilities trained or rejected'. However, despite these claims, as *British Lawn Tennis* pointed out in an editorial, there had been no domestic Wimbledon champion since Fred Perry and as a testimony to the relative unpopularity of the sport in this period, a rise in the number of children who declined the offer of a place at a training school.[28]

No more effective at producing home-grown champions as its forerunner, today the LTA Prudential Grass Roots scheme involves some 35,000

8.3 Not a handicap but schoolgirls learning their strokes at Barn Elms School, 1959

children each year in basic tennis coaching. In addition, 'short tennis', lawn tennis in miniature, is played by children under 12 years of age on a court the size of that used for badminton, using a light plastic racket and yellow foam balls with a slow flight and consistent bounce. Organised through a regional and county tournament structure the first short tennis national championship held in 1983 attracted 480 entrants; five years later the game involved 100,000, is taught by 1,000 schools and the under-8 national competition attracted 3,000 entrants.[29]

Despite the efforts of those organising the various training schemes to open up the game, its early exclusivity is carefully maintained by the older tennis clubs: London's Queen's Club and Vanderbilt Indoor Racquet Club are both patronised by royalty, the rich and famous. The former is partly

8.4 1918 at Queen's Club. A reminder that tennis in Britain has mostly been for the toffs

owned by the LTA and has a membership of 2,500, the Vanderbilt is smaller with 800. Always full, the waiting period for membership of Queen's is six or seven years, nevertheless having the right sponsor expedites an application to pay entrance fees of £600 and £650, and annual subscriptions of £396 and £500 respectively. The Queen's Club has 38 courts, two real tennis courts, two rackets courts, two squash courts, a billiards room and a bridge club and court fees range from £12 to £15. Popular with peers, Hurlingham is an all-round club set in sixty acres of parkland. There is a six-year waiting period to join a membership numbering 6,000 allowing play on one of 39 courts, use of the cricket ground, squash courts, croquet lawns and bowling greens for an entrance fee of £500 and an annual subscription of £327.75. In contrast, typical of local authority provision is Craiglockhart Sports Centre in Edinburgh. Council-owned, no membership subscription is charged but there is a court fee of £3.75 for play on one of 19 tennis courts. In addition to a gymnasium the centre has also provision for squash, badminton and yoga.[30]

II

A tennis ball does nothing without reason.
> W. T. Tilden quoted in M. Robertson (ed.) *The Encyclopaedia of Tennis* (1974), p. 125

The *Field* of 2 November 1895, contained a description and estimated costs for the construction of a 'Surrey tennis lawn' out of one and a half acres of rough meadow, and indicated 'the very small sum for which a moderately good court could be constructed'. The ground could be excavated, levelled, harrowed and sown with good quality grass seed all for less than six pounds, although maintenance costs were not estimated. While grass was advocated as the most suitable playing surface, the *Field* also costed other court finishes. A gravel court, was regarded as 'first rate', and depending on the rate for cartage, would cost between £25 and £50. Brickdust, 'the best yet devised for winter use' required the ground to be levelled at a depth of eight inches, some 60 loads of burnt brick rubbish costing 3s 6d per load raked and levelled and 40 loads of finer material rolled over the surface gave a total cost, including labour, of under £40. A cinder court, 'cheap and easily constructed', cost £20, whereas asphalt, 'the most expensive and the most enjoyable hard court', required the digging of foundations and was estimated to cost in the region of £200. A wooden floor laid for an indoor lawn tennis court was estimated to cost between £500 and £3,000.

In his *The Cost of Sport* published in 1899, F. G. Aflalo also insisted that lawn tennis was 'among the pastimes that cannot easily be made the pretext for heavy expenditure', maintaining that the expenditure fell into 'only four categories':

(a) The building or making of a court, as above.

(b) Belonging to a club, which might obviate the need for (a). Here 'little or no expense is incurred beyond one guinea as entrance fee and one or two guineas annual subscription which sometimes includes the use of club balls'. For the use of private courts, for example at seaside resorts, an average charge of 2 shillings per hour with players providing their own balls and rackets was thought likely.

(c) Engaging professional instructors. Here, despite his preface Aflalo, in a rare reference to the elite nature of the game, admits that this 'is almost impossible for a player of only average means'. However, he did note that certain clubs offered the services of a professional at a nominal charge of 3d per set; 'outside these there is no recognised tariff, but a very general arrangement is half a guinea per hour plus expenses'.

(d) Entering tournaments. The fees may vary upward from 2s 6d to 10s 6d for each event. Balls are generally supplied.

Quite apart from the financial implications there were physical costs incurred in the playing of the new game. The first of many articles referring to 'lawn tennis leg' or 'knee' appeared in *The Lancet* in 1883, while the following year the 'Pathology of lawn tennis' was debated in the columns of New York's *The Medical Record*. 'Tennis arm' or 'elbow' seems to have been a problem since the development of the smash and overarm service; it prevented the defence of his Wimbledon championship in 1887 by William Renshaw, winner from 1881 to 1886 and again in 1889.

There are not at present nor have there ever been any rules limiting the size or shape of a lawn tennis racket; those used in the earliest days were adaptations of rackets designed for real tennis. The head was curved with a comparatively small area of gut and the shaft disproportionately long for such a small head. The ball used in real tennis was heavier than its lawn tennis counterpart and more wood was used in racket construction to provide weight and spin to shots. The first steel-framed rackets were introduced in the 1930s but were not favoured. Re-introduced into the North American and European markets in the late 1960s by Lacoste, both steel and aluminium rackets have become fashionable in the belief that a more powerful serve can be obtained. However, apart from wood, beech for cheaper rackets, hickory for racket shafts and ash with its pliability for the oval head, inlaid and veneered with mahogany and walnut, rackets are now mostly made of metal, fibre-glass, graphite and various composites. The weight and balance of the racket is also critical. The most significant trend in rackets in recent years has been a move away from the conventional head size of 70 sq ins to the mid-size of 85 sq ins and oversize 100 sq ins in order to provide a larger 'sweet spot' or hitting area, and greater power. Since before the Second World War, players using Slazenger rackets at Wimbledon have had available an overnight restringing and repairs service. A sophisticated record kept of the racket requirements on different surfaces of the individual player enables the company to supply replacement rackets at a few hours' notice.

Most top-class players use rackets strung with gut. Favoured for its great elasticity sheep gut is also the most expensive, requiring the gut of six or more sheep to string one racket. Beef and hog gut are also used, but at club standard most players use rackets strung with one of a variety of nylon-based materials. The tension used by players is very much a matter of personal taste and assessment of the playing conditions. Between 60 and 70 pounds pressure is the norm – Fred Perry used 65 pounds tension; however Bjorn Borg is reputed to have had his rackets strung at 80 pounds pressure.

The balls used in lawn tennis were originally hollow and made of un-covered india rubber. The rules of the game specify neither rubber nor cloth covered balls but the 15 dozen balls which were made especially for the first Wimbledon championship were given white cloth covers, sewn in the pattern still in use today. The thread used was unbleached carpet thread; the dyed thread, used by certain makers 'for the sake of prettiness' was barred. In 1901 balls made by Slazenger were used for the first time at Wimbledon, a contract which the company has fulfilled since that year.

Better quality modern balls are covered with a mixture of 70 per cent wool and 30 per cent nylon and are required to have stitchless seams, weigh between two and two and one-sixteenth ounces, have a uniform outer surface and measure between two and one-half and two and five-eighths inches in diameter. Bounce and hardness tests were introduced in the 1920s and as the game developed in the 1930s the preferred ball became harder and faster and serves of around 130 mph were recorded. At present, when dropped onto a concrete surface from a height of 100 inches, the bound of the ball must be between 53 and 58 inches. Pressureless balls are produced in Italy and Sweden but are less popular than the standard 10lb per sq ins ball in general use. Until 1970 white balls were stipulated for all match play, but the increase in indoor first-class tennis led the Inter-national Lawn Tennis Federation to experiment with the use of red- and yellow-coloured balls to improve their visibility by player and spectator alike, and their use is now commonplace. In match play new balls are offered after every nine games or seven in the first instance since they are used in the pre-match knock-up.

III

It is its want of variety that will prevent lawn tennis in its present form from taking rank among our great games.
    Spencer Gore quoted in R. Brace, *Tennis* (Newton Abbot 1984) p.7

The salient fact about lawn tennis, and therefore about Wimbledon, which is its capital, is not its age but its youth. Compared with the veteran of cricket or the patriarch of golf, lawn tennis is part of recent history. Lawn tennis had been invented before 1877 but the first Wimbledon champion-ships held in that year gave the new pastime a style and a status, clarifying conflicting codes and lending form and substance to conditions of play.

The All England Croquet Club had been inaugurated in 1868 at a meeting hosted by J. H. Walsh, editor of the *Field*, at his offices in the Strand, and it was he who introduced lawn tennis into the programme at Wimbledon and induced the proprietors of the magazine to offer for competition a silver challenge cup to the value of twenty-five guineas, later won outright by William Renshaw. Prior to the organisation of this first meeting no tournament nor even an important match had been played under the code drawn up in 1875 by the Tennis Committee of the MCC who had adopted the hourglass-shaped court, claimed by Major Walter Wingfield as part of his invention of the game of Sphairistike.

The MCC code excited controversy among the adherents of the new game. Most were players of rackets and tennis and the methods of scoring these two games had their advocates in lawn tennis. Nor was there unanimity over the size of the court, height of net, position of service line or the question of faults. The tennis sub-committee of the All England Club might have based the championship on the existing code but instead framed what was virtually a new set of rules; three of the principles laid down by them in 1877 have stood the test of time and are still law:

(a) A rectangular court 26 yards long by 9 yards wide, the net being suspended from posts placed 3 feet outside the court.

(b) The adoption of tennis scoring in its entirety.

(c) The allowance of one fault without penalty, whether the service has dropped in the net, in the wrong court, or beyond the service line.

Reputed to have been organised in part to raise money for the repair of a pony-roller, the advertisement for the first championship meeting, signed by Henry Jones, honorary secretary of the Lawn Tennis sub-committee, was contained in the *Field* of 9 June 1877, 'The All England Croquet and Lawn Tennis Club, Wimbledon propose to hold a lawn tennis meeting, open to all amateurs, on Monday, July 9th, and following days. Entrance fee, £1 1s. Two prizes will be given, one gold champion prize to the winner, one silver to the second player.' It was added that 'players must provide their own rackets and shoes without heels', and that intending competitors could obtain balls for the purposes of practice 'on application to the gardener'.[31]

The names of the 22 men who responded to the advertisement were drawn at the offices of the *Field* two days before the opening of the meeting. Tennis histories claim that the familiarity with tennis scoring of the majority of the entrants 'prevented any marked dissatisfaction with the rules'. However, the first champion, Spencer Gore, and one or more others, disagreed: 'We detested the tennis scoring, which was then for the first time introduced and which puzzled us "pretty considerable".'[32] Gore, one of several old

Harrovians playing in the championship, had the advantage of expertise in both rackets and real tennis, but was one of the earliest players to employ the technique of forcing one's opponent to the service line while remaining at the net. Despite his win Gore remained unconvinced that the game had any future, writing over a decade later in 1890 that, 'It is its want of variety that will prevent lawn tennis in its present form from taking rank among our great games.'[33]

By 1879 the field entering the Wimbledon championships had increased to 45 men, only nine of whom had competed earlier. By this date Oxford University had established a doubles championship and Ireland a national championship, both for men and women. The Wimbledon runner-up that year, Irish champion baronet's son Vere St Thomas Leger Gould, was later to be the subject of considerable scandal when he was involved in a particularly grisly murder case.[34]

The increasing success of the club led in 1880 to the leasing of the Worple Road ground for a further 12 years, additional dressing room accommodation was provided in a new clubhouse costing £450, a substantial number of new members attracted and a balance of £230 reported, together with profits of £300. F. H. Ayres, the developing manufacturer of outdoor games, supplied improved balls to replace the earlier hand-stitched type and on Saturdays the club now provided ball-boys to assist players. Twelve courts were available for use and the championship entry numbered 60 men competing under the revised set of rules introduced that year. These increased the entry charge for competitors from one shilling to a half-crown, lowered the net at the posts to 4 feet, brought the service line in to a distance of 21 feet from the net and imposed limitations on the size and weight of the ball.

While the ascendancy and then unassailability of the Renshaw twins led to a halving of the list of competitors during the early 1880s, their success and innovative style of play resulted in 2,000 or more spectators paying to watch a challenge round between the two brothers. For those travelling to the championship by train the South Western Railway Company stopped its special trains at a halt by the ground and it was said that late-comers would pay a half-sovereign for a brick on which to stand for a better view of the game. Reflecting the extent of this popularity the All England Club removed the term croquet from its title. However, concern at this negation of the origins of the club resulted in its restoration 7 years later.

The inauguration of a Ladies' Singles Championship at Wimbledon in 1884 drew a field of just 13, and the ladies had to await the conclusion of the men's singles before starting their matches. In the same year the

8.5 Clothes have been known to attract more attention than the play. Miss G.
E. Tomblin became the first lady to play tournament tennis in shorts at Chiswick
Hard Court Club in March 1932

doubles championship, together with its trophies, relocated from Oxford
as a consequence of waning interest in that venue. Although by 1885 the
number of entries for the Men's Singles had increased by only 10 to 23,
public interest had grown to the point where no less than 3,500 spectators
watched the challenge round in this year.

  1887 was the first of six years of the supremacy within ladies' tennis
of the 'incredible Lottie Dod'. A winner at 15 years of age she won the
championship with the loss of only two games. However, as with successful
women players who came later, her achievements on court were frequently
overshadowed by comment on her style of dress. Extremely avant-garde
for the period, her looped-up skirt and pinafore set a pattern of media
interest in women players which anticipated Lenglen's bandeau or the furore
generated in the age of austerity at the sight of 'Gorgeous Gussy' Moran's
lacy knickers in the 1949 Wimbledon.[35]

In 1888, the All England Club abdicated its legislative functions in favour of the newly formed Lawn Tennis Association, retaining however, complete administrative control over the championship meeting. Amongst the most exclusive in the world, there are 325 male and 75 female members, excluding the champions who become honorary members and 90 temporary members elected on an annual basis. Its independence is still maintained although the management committee includes members representing the council of the Association and the LTA receives a share of the net profits from the gate.

The date of the championships was altered in 1893. Wimbledon's growing position in the social calender meant that the event needed to create its own niche clear of the Henley Regatta and Varsity cricket match, but the change also reflected the fact that the crowds of the 1880s had still not returned. Three years later continued concern at the low entry for the championships led to the introduction of the All England Plate as a consolation prize for those eliminated in the first or second rounds, and the waiving of the fees for members of LTA-affiliated clubs wishing to compete; nevertheless despite these incentives only 31 names were drawn.

1900 saw the inauguration of the International Lawn Tennis Championship known as the Davis Cup. Britain and the United States were the two original contenders for the trophy which had been donated by the father of Dwight Davis a Harvard undergraduate and US state player.[36] Other than in wartime and 1901 and 1910 there have been challenges for the Cup in every year. The form of the competition has not altered since its inception and consists of a team of four who play a series of singles and doubles matches over three days; however, changes made to the structure of the competition have not diminished the domination of American and Australian teams.

The early years of the new century were dominated by the Doherty brothers whose play, together with the international focus initiated by the American ambitions to recover the Davis Cup in 1905, helped revive the interest of both players and public in the Wimbledon Championships. By 1911 the field for the men's singles had reached around 100, an entry which began to force into focus the issue of whether the draw should be seeded or remain 'blind', a debate which was to remain unresolved throughout wartime and for more than another decade. In 1919 the first Wimbledon championships to be held since the outbreak of war received royal patronage with visits from George V, Queen Mary and the Princess Royal. The release from wartime privation ensured the success of the championship and this was borne out in the gross receipts which amounted to £9,390 compared with £7,000 for the last pre-war event in 1914, £4,555 in 1913 and £3,468

8.6 20 July 1935 on Wimbledon Centre Court. This was the scene following the
announcement that rain would prevent any further play in the Davis Cup Final
between the USA and Germany. The middle class threw cushions

in 1912.[37] 8,000 spectators saw the *début* of the first female 'star' of the
game, French champion Suzanne Lenglen, soon to become a household
name and one of the first sportswomen to be referred to in the press by
her first name. The 20-year-old Lenglen's startling defeat of 40-year-old
Mrs Chambers, seven times Wimbledon Ladies' Singles champion, assisted
by the contents of a tiny silver cognac flask thrown onto court by her
father, generated a furore in the press. Worse, however, was the shock
caused through the adoption by the champion of a liberated style of dress
which included a short calf-length skirt and the audacious dispensation
with stiffened foundation garments allowing a 'brazen' display of her figure.
The women's dressing room at Wimbledon and elsewhere contained a rail
near to the fire-place on which players could dry the steel-boned corsets
which were a desperately uncomfortable but nevertheless essential dress
convention both on or off court. 'It was never a pretty sight', recalled
Elizabeth (Bunny) Ryan, 'for most of them were blood-stained.'[38] In 1920

8.7 Wimbledon was not built in a day. In April 1922 building was a very labour-intensive industry

Lenglen returned to stun Wimbledon with the new 'bobbed' hairstyle dressed with two yards of brightly coloured silk chiffon wound tightly around her head. The famous 'Lenglen bandeau' was copied by young women within days and the constant press interest in both this and her 'natural' mode of dress contributed much to the post-war revolution in women's fashions.

1921 was the final year in which the Wimbledon championships were played in the original wooden court at Worple Road, and for many this marked a break with the pre-war, essentially English, vicarage tea-party atmosphere of the game. The advent of Suzanne Lenglen had ensured the demise of the venue. The excitement she generated resulted in the receipt of 5,000 applications for the 500 bookable seats. This unprecedented demand led to the Wimbledon Committee commissioning a design for a stadium with a court capable of seating more than the existing 7,000. Designed by Stanley Peach, at an overall cost of some £140,000, the new stadium at Church Road included a centre court built in concrete to seat up to 15,000 spectators. The Worple Road buildings and courts became the sports pavilion and grounds of Wimbledon Girls' High School, and the new complex was opened by the King on 26 June 1922 at the beginning of the wettest Wimbledon fortnight ever. Both the centre court and court no 1 which housed 5,000 had been fitted with rain covers, however the two outside courts in which the stands of the original championship court had been reused, were out of commission for most of the event. The men's singles final between the Australians Patterson and Anderson was disrupted not only by rain but also by the former player calling for a change of shoes and by the need to wait for a plane to pass out of sight before play could be resumed.

The seeding of the draw was introduced for the 1924 Wimbledon following its sanction by a general meeting of the LTA. While not adopting the American and European practice of seeding by merit until 1927, this innovation guaranteed that two nominated players of the same nationality would not clash in the same quarter of the draw. In the same year the title of 'The Championship of the World' was dropped from use; nevertheless Wimbledon remained a meeting recognised by the International Federation and as such, overseas governing bodies were permitted to send representative teams to compete in it.

Wimbledon's fiftieth jubilee in 1926 represented a milestone in the development of the game but in the controversy surrounding Lenglen's participation that year, a more fundamental break with the amateur origins and ethos of the game. On the first Monday of the jubilee championships, King George V and Queen Mary presented commemorative gold medals to every past and current champion of Wimbledon's 50 years, and on this occasion the patronage of royalty extended to participation; the Duke of York, later King George VI played in the men's doubles with Sir Louis Greig, later chairman of the All England Club. They were eliminated in the first round.

Live radio broadcasting of the Wimbledon championships began in 1927 and a decade later the development of outside broadcast techniques to enable the televising of the Coronation in May 1937 were utilised for the Wimbledon championship that year. *The Listener* commented that 'as in the news films, it has seldom been possible to watch the progress of the ball itself', but nevertheless felt that the exercise, which had 'aroused universal interest', was worthwhile.[39] The BBC has retained its monopoly of the coverage of the event with 16-times winner of the British Professional title, ex-All England Club coach Dan Maskell, the principal commentator since 1951.[40]

Any account of Wimbledon fortnight produces details of the prodigious amounts of food and drink consumed. But lesser known statistics include

8.8 In the 1930s you could pay messenger boys to queue in your place at
Wimbledon

Woodward's of Cheam who hold the lucrative contract for supplying and
bedding out the 1,500 hydrangeas, 1,000 marigolds, 3,600 antirrhinums
and 1,000 petunias which are watered in a regime which begins at 5.30
a.m. The 10,800 square yards of grass originally laid with virgin seaside
turf from Cumberland proved too lush and soft after rain and a special
mix of seed was developed to provide the resilience necessary for constant
use over the fortnight. The cutting and mowing of the courts is still done
entirely by hand and the 'old horse roller' (as it is known), which weighs
2,500 pounds, throughout the championship is daily drawn across the turf
by five men.

    While acknowledging the need for Wimbledon to retain its primacy in world tournament terms, in 1960 *The Economist* was predicting that the Wimbledon championships of that year would be the last in which all the players were 'amateurs'; 'Experience suggests that there is rarely a middle course in professional sport . . . players are grossly exploited and overpaid.' It would, the writer predicted, be the ordinary spectator who suffered as ticket prices were inflated to cover the increased costs incurred. That the demand for tickets was not wholly inelastic had been indicated by the recent failure of the Wimbledon debenture issue which had offered an annual entitlement to centre court seats in lieu of interest.[41] The ladies champion María Bueno, received £20 in prize money that year. Wimbledon became an open tournament finally in 1968, and at the first championship in 1969 Rod Laver won prize money of £2,000 and Billie Jean King £750.

Inordinately long matches such as the 112-game contest at Wimbledon between Gonzales and Pasarell in 1969 led to pressure for the introduction of the tie break. A nine-point method introduced for the US Open in 1970 was rejected in favour of the less dramatic 16-point tie break first used at the 1971 Wimbledon championship, in turn replaced by a 12-point system in 1979.

For the first time in 1984 all five Wimbledon titles were retained by the defending champions and prize money reached an all time record level: John MacEnroe won £100,000 for the men's title, Martina Navratilova £90,000 for the women's.

IV

Martina Navratilova, Hana Mandlikova, Jo Durie . . . Gabriela Sabatini . . . Zina Garrison . . . none of them wore a skirt or a tennis dress for practice. Why . . . have the pros allowed shorts to become a thing of the recent past? . . .

   Far more important than ease of movement, or comfort, or personal preference . . . is, so it seems, being comfortable with one's image. Or rather, one's sponsor being comfortable with one's image.

   Adrianne Blue, *Grace Under Pressure. The Emergence of Women in Sport* (1987), p. 13

The professionalism of lawn tennis has generated controversy since the Second World War; references made at the turn of the century suggest that at that time it was by no means regarded as a problem. In 1897 the United States Lawn Tennis Association had offered a contribution of £40 towards the steamship fares and a further £10 towards the rail fares of the British team invited to cross the Atlantic that summer. Fund-raising efforts the following year enabled £160 to be contributed to the costs of the American team travelling to Britain for a return encounter. In 1903 in Aflalo's *The Sports of the World*, N. L. Jackson noted that there 'are a few professionals at lawn-tennis, all of these being ground men or court attendants, employed by clubs'. However, he also described 'an attempt' at Nice to encourage professional players, where 'handsome prizes' had been offered for matches between them. A tournament was also arranged so that 'the best amateurs and professionals ... shall meet to decide which is the superior player'. Rather than compromise the status of the amateur, the contest was not to be for any prize, only 'the honour of winning'.[42]

This type of event persisted until the 1920s. In a sport which was fundamentally amateur, leading lawn tennis players were invited to appear in tournaments and would receive only their expenses. From the outset there had been both patrons and players of independent means, but the demands of the game, travel costs and opportunities for profit led inexorably towards the professionalisation of the sport, although its pursuit in the years following the First World War brought an unprecedented set of problems, not least because the majority of organisers world-wide were unpaid volunteers. Notwithstanding the fact that tennis had been an Olympic sport since 1896, the failure of the ILTF and the International Olympic Committee to agree a definition of amateurism led to its exclusion from 1924 – until 1988 at Seoul. Through the 1920s and long before the tennis revolutions of the late 1960s both Tilden and Lenglen, although still theoretically amateurs, regularly confronted the USLTA and the French Federation with their professional postures. While at the outset rejecting the concept of payment for sport, 'Big Bill' Tilden did not refuse the considerable sums offered by newspapers for 'exclusives', and even at times wrote his own feature articles.

There is little doubt that Tilden, who in 1931 was credited with the fastest serve ever recorded at 163.6 mph, was an able self-publicist whose image was promoted to the point of synonymity with his 'fuzzy bear' sweaters in as calculating a publicity exercise as the Lenglen bandeau. In addition to his overt disobedience of the USLTA amateur code, there is no doubt that Tilden's homosexuality inflamed the US authorities anxious, according to Tinling, to obliterate the effete image with which American men's tennis had been tainted since its earliest days.[43] When, over an article given to the press, the USLTA suspended Tilden in Paris on the eve of the 1928 Davis Cup semi-final against Italy, the ensuing débâcle threatened international relations between France and the USA and was resolved only after the personal intervention of US President Harding.

Madison Square Garden, New York, provided the venue on 9 October 1926 for the first lawn tennis tournament in which former amateurs played for a fee. Following Wimbledon that year, Lenglen had been persuaded by the American impresario, known as 'Cash and Carry' Pyle, to turn professional for a sum reputed to be $100,000. An unsuccessful tour across America followed but it was only after Tilden in conjunction with the USLTA failed to persuade the ILTF to hold an open tournament in Philadelphia in 1930, that he turned professional and several players of different nationalities joined the Tilden circus. A pattern of the great players, notably Cochet, Vines, Perry, becoming professional at the height of their careers became a well-established feature of the 1930s. In 1938, in an attempt to stem the steady flow of amateur talent to the professional circuits, the Cumberland Club moved at the AGM of the LTA the 'eight-week rule' which would have allowed amateurs to receive travelling and hotel expenses but only for a maximum of eight weeks in any one year. Although unsuccessful it paved the way for post-war practices. During the war pro-am exhibition matches to support the work of, for example, the Red Cross bridged the widening gulf between the two flanks of the sport; thereafter the earlier segregation was resumed. In the immediate post-war period there were renewed efforts to secure realistic and workable rules on amateurism. In 1947 the Cumberland Club successfully represented their 'eight-week rule' motion leading to what the magazine *Lawn Tennis* later described as 'farce' persisting until 1951. The decision of the LTA in 1956 to sanction expenses for the whole year was modified in 1958 to 240 days of which not more than 150 could be spent abroad.[44]

After winning the Wimbledon championship in 1947, the American Jack Kramer turned professional the following year. Rapidly assuming the role of promoter while still playing first-class tennis, by 1952, according to an increasingly critical press, Kramer was following the current amateur champion Frank Sedgeman from event to event offering inducements to persuade him to join the Kramer 'circus'.

However, despite massive promotion and a virtual monopoly of talent, both press and public anticipated the predictability of the 'pay for play' fixtures and ensured that they remained an uncertain risk. Subsequently Kramer was to write: 'The craziest thing about tennis during these years was that the fans continued to be attracted to the traditional amateur "fixtures", even though they knew that the pros had the best talent.'[45] In 1957 Kramer promoted a major event at Forest Hills, New York to be held during the week after the Wimbledon finals. Alongside such stars as Gonzales, Sedgeman, Trabert and Rosewall, who were earning some $50,000 per year, the newly signed Lew Hoad, correctly predicted by Kramer as the Wimbledon champion of that year, was billed to appear. In the event only a small crowd was drawn and a large and unspecified sum of money lost.

Through the late 1950s waning public interest inevitably hit the professional players harder than the amateurs. In 1959, the Wimbledon men's singles champion, Peruvian Alejandro Olmeda, accepted just £12,500 for a 12-month professional contract from Kramer, but in the same month Neale Fraser turned down an offer of £A18,000 not simply because of his stated desire to play again in both Wimbledon and the Davis Cup, but because he had 'good prospects' with his current employers, Slazenger and cigarette manufacturers W. D. and H. O. Wills and also 'an offer from a P.R. firm'. A variety of devices such as a three-bounce rule and an extra long service court were introduced to revive interest in the game but between the late-1950s and mid-1960s, in both the pro and amateur forms, large crowds were only to be found at the principal national tournaments such as Wimbledon, although even there attendances, already falling off in 1959, dropped further to 20,171 the following year and to 19,680 by 1963.[46] Such was the desperation of the promoters that in the same year the organisers of the United States Singles Championships spent £10,000 in an endeavour to attract an overseas entry of calibre. At a cost said to exceed £6,000 a jet airliner was chartered to bring 75 foreign players from 27 nations to Forest Hills. The £45 per day received by each player, amateur or professional, to cover board and lodgings during the tournament contrasted starkly with the £1 per day paid to competitors in the professional championships at Eastbourne to defray both accommodation and meal costs.[47]

There was a slight upswing in the fortunes of the game in the late 1960s, although the Dixon American professional tour collapsed after only 87 spectators turned out at one of the venues. In 1968 Australian Margaret Court turned down £23,000 to turn professional stating that the offer 'had not proved as interesting' as she had expected and that it would have meant 'spending nine months in the USA and playing 167 matches'.[48] Nevertheless, a greater mass appeal resulted from increased televising of matches, particularly with the arrival of colour; training programmes were initiated even in eastern European countries and with the ending of the cold war, players from Communist countries began to participate to a much greater extent in tournaments in the west. At the forefront of the campaign for open lawn tennis, Britain, supported by the professional organisations and public opinion, pressed for reform. Following a meeting of the LTA in December 1967, it was announced that the distinctions which existed between amateurs and professionals were to be removed and henceforth all participants would be known as 'players'. Implicit in this decision was an open Wimbledon for 1968, a proposal that led the ILTF to contemplate Britain's expulsion until a meeting in Paris the following March agreed a compromise of open events for a trial period. Three categories of player were distinguished, firstly the amateurs who were not to play for money, secondly registered players who received prizemoney but were under the control of their national associations, and finally, contract professionals who were controlled by the promoters. The first tournament to be held under this ruling was played at Bournemouth in April 1968, followed two months later by the first ever open Wimbledon.

The major men's professional tennis circuit, the Grand Prix, came into being in 1970. Developed from an idea originally proposed by Jack Kramer, there was to be a money bonus pool allocated on the basis of a cumulative point system designed to encourage the best players to compete regularly and qualify for a special championship tournament, the Masters. For the first seven years the tournament, involving the 12 leading players, was held at different international venues, but since 1977 it has been permanently fixed at New York's Madison Square Gardens.

Seeking a comparable organisation to the Professional Golfers' Association, the contract tennis players formed the Association of Tennis Professionals in 1972 and immediately took issue with the ILTF over the nine-month ban imposed on Nikki Pilic for failing to play in a Davis Cup match. Their action obtained a reduction in the ban but, as it still extended over the 1973 Wimbledon fortnight, the ATP withdrew 79 players from the tournament in support of Pilic. Despite the non-appearance of 13 of the 16 seeds Wimbledon that year attracted over 300,000 spectators. The authority of the ILTF has been challenged regularly since, not least by Lamar Hunt's Dallas-based World Championship Tennis. However, in November 1983 the WCT agreed to adhere to the Grand Prix arrangements for five years, while still committing $13.7 million dollars to its own 22-event circuit for that year. Grand Prix prizemoney in 1983–4 amounted to $15 million, with an additional $3 million in the bonus pool which offered $600,000 and $150,000 to the leading singles and doubles players respectively, the remainder being shared by the top 32 singles players and 16 doubles players.[49]

While tennis players now number among the world's most highly paid sportsmen and women, their wealth is not just derived from match winnings. The principal source of income of the tennis superstar results from the lucrative endorsements of widely differing products ranging from clothes to tea and photocopiers. By no means an automatic outcome of a player's position in the world's 20 top-ranking players, promotional agents are concerned to discover players with 'on-court talent and off-court appeal': 'Players, especially women, have to be attractive, articulate and intelligent to make good marriages with potential sponsors.'[50] Jack Kramer's endorsement of Wilson rackets began in 1947 with a 2.5 per cent commission on each sale; in his autobiography, *The Game*, Kramer noted that during his professional playing career his income from this source had averaged $13,000 annually, reaching $160,000 by 1975.[51]

A tennis star of the calibre of Chris Evert has been described as 'a perfect vehicle' to promote products off-court.[52] Winner of some 155 tournaments, 18 of which are Grand Slam events over the seventeen years up to 1988, her on-court earnings alone have reached $8 million. However, this figure represents a small percentage of her estimated total earnings of $60 million gained through both off-court endorsement and exhibition matches. In addition, Evert has run a world-wide coaching series and won some 15 cars as bonus prizes. The calculation of her off-court earnings constantly exerts the minds of sports commentators and the figures quoted are their estimates:

Exhibition matches	$500,000
Chris Evert Active Line hair products	$500,000
Boca Raton tennis club	$500,000
Ellesse tennis clothes	$500,000
Wilson tennis rackets	$250,000
Lipton tea commercials	$200,000
Wheeties cereal	$150,000
Rolex watches	$100,000
TV commercials	$150,000
Synchronised tennis coaching	$100,000
Converse shoes	$50,000[53]

In 1982, Martina Navratilova, backed by a team of advisors including a coach, a nutritionist and a motivator, became the first tennis professional to earn $1 million in a single year when she won 15 out of 18 tournaments and 90 of 93 matches. West German Steffi Graf, snapped up in 1985 at the age of 15 by Advantage International, a dollar multimillionaire at 17, had won prize money in excess of two million dollars by early 1988. Her principal endorsements include Opel cars and BASF, which together yield $750,000 per year, however she receives in addition an estimated $1 million each year from Adidas.[54]

Off the court, although male tennis players earn considerably less than female players, their overall winnings exceed those of their female counterparts. When as an unseeded 17-year-old player, West German Boris Becker won the Wimbledon Championship in 1985 and again in 1986, he became a millionaire overnight. A tax exile in Monte Carlo, in 1988 his total career winnings approximated three million dollars; his off-court earnings some $20 million, including $500,000 from Coca-Cola.[55]

Writing in 1979, Jack Kramer argued that tennis now had world-wide appeal and that its stars were international celebrities. He expressed the hope that the game would be reinstated as an Olympic event and that tennis would come to be regarded as *the* world game.[56] Almost a decade later tennis attained a place in the 1988 Seoul Olympics; its progress towards Kramer's second wish is still a matter for conjecture.

NOTES

1   J. Arlott (ed.), *The Oxford Companion to Sports and Games* (Oxford, 1975), p. 604.
2   G. Robyns, *Wimbledon: The Hidden Drama* (Newton Abbot, 1973), p. 19.
3   J. Arlott (ed.), *The Oxford Companion*, p. 604.
4   R. Brace, *Tennis* (Newton Abbot, 1984), p. 5.
5   *Army and Navy Gazette*, 7 March 1874.
6   In 1949 India hosted the first Asian championships at the famous Calcutta South Club. For a more detailed investigation of the early years of lawn tennis and in particular its growth in American see T. Todd, *The Tennis Players* (1979) especially chapters 13 and 14.
7   *Vanity Fair*, 24 October 1874.
8   F. G. Aflalo, *The Sports of the World* (1903), p. 402.
9   *The Times*, 6 July 1877, p. 11.
10 J. Arlott (ed.), *The Oxford Companion*, p. 604.
11 F. G. Aflalo, *Sports of the World*, p. 404.
12 For example, W. J. Blevin, *Tennis Players' Handbook* (Liverpool, 1885); J. Marshall *Tennis* (1890). See also F. W. Foster, *A Bibliography of Lawn Tennis, 1874–1897* (1897).
13 G. A. Hutchinson, *Outdoor Games and Recreations: A Popular Encyclopaedia for Boys* (Religious Tract Society, 1892), pp. 558–76.
14 M. J. Bolsteri, *The Early Community at Bedford Park* (1977), p. 109.
15 O. Lancaster, *All Done From Memory* (1953), p. 152, quoted in J. Lowerson, 'Sport and the Victorian Sunday: the beginnings of middle-class apostasy', *The British Journal of Sports History*, vol. 1 (September 1984), no. 2, p. 212. The members at Wimbledon voted two to one in favour of play on Sunday afternoons in 1888. T. Todd (1979), p. 92.
16 N. Carroll, *Sport in Ireland* (Dublin, 1979), p. 65.
17 A. Wallis Myers, *Fifty Years of Wimbledon* (AELTC, 1926), p. 35.
18 Ibid.
19 M. B. Alexander, *A History of Honor Oak Cricket and Lawn Tennis Club* (1965).
20 E. J. Jennings, *Innellan Bowling and Tennis Club, 1854–1944* (Glasgow, 1945).
21 W. Holtby, *The Crowded Street* (1981 edn), p. 51.
22 W. Macqueen-Pope, *Twenty Shillings in the Pound* (1949), p. 283. See also J. G. Smyth, *Lawn Tennis* (1953) for an account of the changes through this period.

23 G. Freeman, *The Houses Behind. Sketches of a Birmingham Back Street* (1947), quoted in C. Chinn, *They Worked All Their Lives* (Manchester 1988).

24 H. E. Meller, *Leisure and the Changing City* (1976), p. 117.

25 D. L. Chambers, *Lawn Tennis for Ladies* (1910), p. 5.

26 See F. Perry, *An Autobiography* (1984) and successive editorials in *British Lawn Tennis and Squash* and *British Lawn Tennis*. There were some suggestions that the LTA were not enthusiastic about broadening the game's social base. 'It was quite apparent from this trip that people felt the LTA were not terribly concerned with the development of the game. Park superintendents felt that they were being neglected, some schools felt much the same and all too often some of the counties were not really trying to spread the game to a new generation of players ... despite my reports at the time and the similar views of other experienced individuals since, the LTA is only now, in the 1980s, beginning to ... widen the base of the playing pyramid.' Dan Maskell, *From Where I Sit* (1988), p. 192.

27 *Sport and the Community*, the Report of the Wolfenden Committee on Sport, Central Council of Physical Recreation (1960).

28 *British Lawn Tennis*, February 1960.

29 *The Observer Colour Magazine*, 19 June 1988. The number of players affiliated to the LTA has increased from 202,000 in 1977 to 251,000 in 1986, *Social Trends*, 18 (1988).

30 Ibid.

31 A. Wallis Myers, *Fifty Years of Wimbledon*, p. 8.

32 Ibid., p. 9.

33 R. Brace, *Tennis*, p. 7.

34 In 1907 Vere St Thomas Leger Gould was found guilty of the murder of a Danish widow after attempting to ship her dismembered body in two trunks from the south of France to London.

35 T. Tinling, *Tinling: Sixty Years in Tennis* (1983) provides a fascinating insight into tennis fashion. It has been suggested that as Miss Dod was little more than a schoolgirl in 1887 she was allowed to wear a skirt about ten inches above the ground thus facilitating her aggressive game. T. Todd (1979), p. 132.

36 Costing some £160, the trophy is a punch-bowl made from 217 ounces of solid silver lined with gold, standing 13 inches high with a diameter of 18 inches.

37 A. Wallis Myers, *Fifty Years of Wimbledon*, p. 63. H. L. Doherty's death in 1919 prompted a leading article in *The Times*, 23 August 1919.

38 T. Tinling, *Tinling*, p. 24.

39 *The Listener*, 30 June 1937.

40 D. Maskell, *From Where I Sit* (1988).

41 *The Economist*, 2 July 1960, p. 24.

42 F. G. Aflalo, *Sports of the World*, p. 405.

43 T. Tinling, *Tinling*, p. 71.

44 *Lawn Tennis*, February 1968, p. 15.

45 J. Kramer, *The Game* (1981), p. 240.

46 *British Lawn Tennis*.

47 Ibid., October 1963.

48 *Lawn Tennis*, April 1968.
49 R. Evans, *Open Tennis* (1988).
50 *The Observer Colour Magazine*, 19 June 1988.
51 J. Kramer, *The Game*, pp. 135–6.
52 *The Observer Colour Magazine*, 19 June 1988.
53 Ibid.
54 Ibid.
55 Ibid.
56 J. Kramer, *The Game*, p. 305.

9 ROWING

CHRISTOPHER DODD

I

... there is *nothing* – absolutely nothing – half so much worth doing as simply messing about in boats.

> Kenneth Grahame, *The Wind in the Willows*, (1908)

How extraordinary that *The Sportsman* should publish in 1916, deep into the First World War, a lavish volume on *Yachting and Rowing*, part of its series on *British Sports and Sportsmen*.[1] How fortunate for later generations that it did. Large enough to be a cushion in a punt, weighty enough to substitute for a cox in a pair-oar, austere enough to render it to a little-disturbed corner of the library, it nevertheless gives insight into an Edwardian world of privileged leisure. In it Walter Bradford 'Guts' Woodgate, the man who cribbed a self-steering device from a crew of Nova Scotians at the Paris International regatta of 1867 and persuaded the Brasenose four-oared crew's steersman Weatherley to jump overboard in a race at Henley in 1868, leading to disqualification on the day and eventually to much unemployment among coxswains, skiffs through reminiscences of great oarsmen he has known.

And the judge knew them all, including the common law branch of the Court of Appeal whose judges – Lords Esher, Smith, Chitty, and Macnaghten – were all rowing men, three of them Blues. He knew the Poet Laureate Bridges who rowed for Corpus and turned down a place in the Oxford boat in 1866 because of exams, surely an unusual occurrence at that time of muscular Christianity. He knew 'Skipper' A. P. Lonsdale who had 'two voices, one light and alto when speaking quietly, alternating with basso profundo when objurgating a chum as partner in an eight for faulty rowing'. And among dozens he describes, unfortunately with little indiscretion, the founding fathers of amateur coxing Tom Egan and Arthur Shadwell and schoolmasters like R. S. Kindersley and Dr Warre of Eton.

In the same volume Alfred Davis outlines the regattas and the clubs of the Thames and Victor Mansell writes about the professionals, a class of oarsman that much of the rowing world would not acknowledge. There is no doubt what Mansell thought about the pro–am divide: 'They represent branches of oarsmanship run side by side, certainly not hand in hand.' It was an extraordinary state of affairs seen from afar when a sport should be so respectful of talent, so full of privilege and style, yet so divisive. The argument originally developed because of suspicions of cheating where stake money and betting were involved as well as confusion over technique and the benefits of fitness through manual work. Matters of class and snobbery were stirred in, followed later by xenophobia. Many influential rowing people were convinced that one way to beat foreigners at Henley Royal Regatta, by far the most important event, was to ban them. Henley, they argued – and this was true – was never designed as an international regatta. In 1901 Willy Grenfell (later Lord Desborough), supported by Dr Warre of Eton and Rudie Lehmann, a Cambridge man and one of the most influential coaches of the day, failed to persuade the Royal Regatta to ban foreigners, but the use of professional coaches was banned from 1902. In 1908, when the Olympic regatta was scheduled for the little Thamesside town, foreigners were banned from the Grand at the regatta so that they couldn't try out the course. Angry newspaper correspondence about this ended when the Belgians, holders of the Grand, wrote to say that they would not dream of entering just before the Games. In 1906 Vesper Rowing Club of Philadelphia were banned because the amateur status of their 1905 crew was suspect and because they had received money from public subscription to send them to Henley. As a result it was not until 1914 that American crews came again to Henley. And when Harvard ran off with the Grand Challenge Cup on 4 July as the storm clouds of war gathered overhead, England's rowing world mourned as it was about to mourn the loss of so many of its fine young men in France and Belgium. An ad appeared in *The Times* three days later which aped that which followed the loss of the Ashes. It said: 'In loving memory of British Rowing, which passed away at Henley on Saturday July 4th. Deeply lamented by many sorrowing followers, who hereby place their regret on record.' The *Pall Mall Gazette*, however, said it was not downhearted. 'We have just got to learn the lesson that we have no indigenous superiority in sport, and that, if we wish to retain or regain our position, we have got to work for it.'

The world described in *Yachting and Rowing* changed faster than the authors had no doubt expected. They had lived through the zenith of boating as a pastime and through one of the most affluent periods of Britain's history, particularly for their class of person. When Woodgate was a young man in the 1860s and 1870s professional sculling was at its height and getting a Blue, if not a ticket to high rank in the professions or public life, was certainly not a hindrance. There was little organised sport apart from rowing, and there was a leisure boom under way which made weekending on the river fashionable for the wellheeled and popular for the hoi polloi. The trains took Londoners out for the day or the weekend to the riverside hotels and houseboats of the Thames Valley, while every village had its regatta. Almost every river in England had boating activity on it,[2] skiffs and canoes for hire. The coastal resorts and the lakes became boaters' paradises and all the best great houses had boats on their private lakes. If you didn't have a boating lake, best to build one. On the Seine the scene, captured by the Impressionists from their river haunts, was similar, and in Philadelphia Thomas Eakins began his outstanding career as a portrait artist by painting Max Schmitt in a *Single Scull* (1871) and following this masterpiece with a series of accurate paintings of rowers which reflected both boating life on the Schuylkill and his brush with Impressionism in Paris.[3] In Germany, in Italy, in Hungary, in Belgium, in Holland, in Russia, boating was the thing to do. In England, while Warre, Lehmann, Woodgate, and others were busy writing the 'How to do it' and the 'Whodunnit' books of rowing, Charles Dickens Jr published *Dickens's Guide to the Thames* in 1885, Jerome K. Jerome was tossing jokes into his traveller's guide to the Thames (*Three Men in a Boat*, 1889), and E. V. Gregory painted *Boulters Lock on Sunday Afternoon*, the picture which encapsulated the English way of leisure, in 1895. Kenneth Grahame unleashed Ratty and Mole to mess about in boats in 1908 in *The Wind in the Willows*, a work which quickly became a children's classic, and John Betjeman's poem 'Henley Regatta 1902' described it as 'the flowering heart of England's willow-cooled July'.

The period between the turn of the century and the First World War, then, was one of lackadaisical loafing in the elegant and affluent clubs and private boathouses of the Thames Valley, of passion for the river as the trains brought Londoners out for the weekend, and of exploring watery byways up and down the land. The second generation of gentlemen oars was dying off. Its way of life was already becoming a backwater as other team sports grew and provided the mass activity and spectator interest which rowing could not undertake. Professional rowing had passed its heyday but was still running vigorous world championship matches and exporting men to teach the world to row and to build the world's boats. Meanwhile the committee rooms raged, often with passion, about the inequities of the pro–am argument and Britain's international performance, and they managed to create a third class of oarsmen who were neither professional nor amateur. There were two governing bodies. Most clubs did not admit women, some hardly acknowledged their existence, and though books like

9.1 One recreational side of messing around on the river. The ice-cream boat
could have been found during any of the first four decades of this century. This
one is Kingston Regatta in July 1921

Yachting and Rowing and the weighty coaching manuals of the day by
Lehmann, Woodgate and others make no mention of them, they were sculling and rowing, though admittedly not in large numbers.

How did the oarsmen get into such a pickle? Competitive sculling was
established in London in the eighteenth century when wager matches and
'coat and badge' races developed between the thousands of watermen who
worked on the river. Doggett's Coat and Badge, started in 1715, is the
lasting remnant of this, now raced by amateurs but founded by the Irish
actor and sometime manager of Drury Lane Theatre, Thomas Doggett,
to commemorate the accession of the Hanovers to the throne. Handel's
'Water Music' is associated with it; it is a race from London Bridge to
Chelsea for watermen in their first year of freedom from apprenticeship
to the Watermen's Company, and the winner gets a handsome red coat
and breeches, a silver arm badge, a cap and buckled shoes. Huge crowds
would gather for such events, coat and badge races being held in several

boroughs along the Thames. In the first half of the nineteenth century wager matches between scullers and crews became very popular, and the sport, organised with backers and betters, was a development of rivalry between ferrymen and dockers. Between 1835–51 there were 5,000 sculling matches on the Thames, which works out at five per week for 16 years.[4] A few could make a good living, while others who worked at upriver trades like barge-building, dredging, and fishing could supplement their income too. Activity was not confined to the Thames, either. Newcastle upon Tyne was the large centre outside London. Competitive rowing also developed in coastal waters, particularly at Whitby in Yorkshire, along the south coast, and in Cornwall with pilot gig racing. But it was with the English and World professional sculling championships that it spread to the Empire and America, and the races attracted heavy sponsorship, heavy betting, great athletes, and considerable skullduggery.

Amateurs took to the river first at Westminster School whose boathouse was almost opposite the royal barge house and Searle's boathouse on the site of the present St Thomas's Hospital. There was also much water activity at Eton. At first the school authorities were not in favour of the exploits of their pupils, but rivalry developed between the two schools and was spread to the universities of Oxford and Cambridge by their graduates. Both places were again suited to rowing, having rivers meandering past the college doorsteps. Picnicking expeditions soon developed into races between college crews which developed into formal racing to uphold the honour of colleges. The university boat clubs emerged soon after the first University Boat Race was held at Henley in 1829. This attracted a large crowd and was influential in establishing a regatta there ten years later. The Boat Race became an annual event in 1856, while Henley, started by town people to boost trade at their fair, was quickly taken over by rowing interests and has been held each year since, except during the two World Wars. It was not the first regatta: Chester, Durham, and Tyne are older, but Henley quickly became the most prestigious in Britain and in some senses remains so in the 1980s. Despite or perhaps because of its unique features such as having a course longer than the Olympic or international distance of 2,000 metres, such as racing two-by-two, and such as being run by a self-perpetuating oligarchy with its own rules, and despite the existence of national championships since 1972, Henley's pots are both much sought after and difficult to win. Moreover, its setting on the longest straight stretch of the upper Thames in a magically beautiful valley is the place where every oarsman wants to row – at least once in his life. Except for two invitation years in 1981–82, it has never admitted women. An independent Henley Women's Regatta was started in 1988.

In its first few years, like many other regattas, Henley included races for professionals, but they never competed there against amateurs. The Boat Race permitted professional coaches in its early years. As the century progressed the amateurs, who were dominated by the Oxford and Cambridge set, turned more and more against professionals, except in so far as scullers would pay them to coach because it was recognised that pros knew more about sculling a single boat with two oars than most amateurs. But crew racing was pretty much the preserve of the amateur and the amateur coach. It was a curious state of affairs because the two were inextricably linked, the young college men buying and renting their boats from the men who made them and experimented with their design and construction.

II

Amateurs? There ain't none.
  Paul Gallico, *Farewell to Sport* (New York, 1938) p.108

Rowing people, in common with other sportsmen, were very good at determining what an amateur was not. But deciding what an amateur is has eluded them. The first specific rule concerning amateurism was Henley's in 1839 when it was decreed that 'every boat shall be steered by an amateur member of the club or clubs entering'. The first *Laws of Boat Racing* were codified in 1849 by a meeting of the Oxford and Cambridge University clubs and principal London clubs, and adopted by Henley in 1850.[5] In 1872 these were revised, mainly redefining fouling, but eligibility to race was left unwritten and up to the regattas. It was not until 1878 that things began to get difficult, although it was clear that the notion of the amateur already existed because the 1862 *Rowing Almanack* listed clubs under the headings 'Gentlemen, tradesmen, and watermen'. Woodgate considered that 'the old idea of an amateur was that he was a gentleman, and the two were simply convertible terms'. An amateur was defined by his differences from a professional, and a professional is a person whose livelihood depends to some extent on winning. A professional participates to earn, therefore trains and practises more, and therefore gains more skill. An American committee defined him in 1909 as 'one who enters or takes part in any athletic contest for any other motive than satisfaction of pure play impulses or for exercise, training and social pleasure derived, or one who desires and secures from his skill or who accepts of spectators partisan or other interest, any material or economic advantage or reward'.[6] Or more extremely, professionalism is 'the purpose to win a game by any means, fair or foul'.[7]

This introduces a prevalent problem concerning the professional, that of the possibility of cheating to satisfy backers and punters. In big contests much more than the stake money was at stake. Not all professional rowers were cheats, of course, but there were some spectacular cases of suspected misbehaviour, the most notorious being a contest sponsored by Rochester Hop Bitters in the US between Ned Hanlan and Charles Courtney. Jack Hopper, one of the last men to take part in the Christmas Handicap in Newcastle upon Tyne which fizzled out in the 1930s, said that cheating was one of the causes for the decline in professional sculling, and told tales of his experiences at the hands of cheats concerning both subtle interference with equipment and unlikely official decisions.[8]

If Woodgate was right, 'amateurism' developed to separate the gentlemen from the lower orders, exacerbated by the introduction of 'mechanics' clauses, as we shall see. The professional athlete was held in low regard, having questionable character as well as social inferiority. It was not necessarily his fault: his practices were seldom subject to uniform rules of sport. Clubs then flourished on degrees of exclusivity, and the view that skill and strength gained in a regular occupation rendered someone ineligible for amateur competition helped, particularly in rowing where the professionals were actually rowing boats as their livelihood. Competition was thus restricted on the basis of ability and social position, not on that of money earned from it. Cash prizes were common among amateurs in rowing in the mid-nineteenth century.

More than a century since this metamorphosis took place, however, it has been turned on its head. Now the Amateur Rowing Association, the sole governing body of the sport in England, conducts its affairs openly, democratically, and in fierce defence of what it considers to be amateur sport, while its chief proponents have increasing assistance from bodies which support them financially and those who give them time off to develop their skill and strength. The ARA employs full-time professional coaches, mainly to develop the sport and coach the coaches. The motivation comes from the Olympic movement which at the medal-winning end of its affairs puts more and more pressure on athletes to raise their standards while redefining 'amateur' in vague idealistic and unrealistic terms. Baron de Coubertin, founder of the modern Games, was taken with the ancient Greeks' ideas about the harmony of body, mind, and spirit, and he believed that people who earn money from participating in athletics will tend to 'give up their whole existence to one particular sport, grow rich by practising it, and thus deprive it of all nobility, and destroy the just equilibrium of man by making the muscles preponderate over the mind'.[9] He visited the Much Wenlock Games in 1890 and Henley Regatta as well as Rugby School before founding the Games and was much taken with the English

9.2 When the British travelled they took their sport with them. No problems about amateur status here

way of doing things. Then hear his successor Avery Brundage on amateurism in 1969: 'The felicitous phrase "religion of sport" used by de Coubertin ... was well chosen for the chivalrous amateur code of fair play, and good sportsmanship embraces the highest moral laws. It is a humanitarian religion – it, like the golden rule, stands for the right against wrong. No philosophy, no religion preaches loftier sentiments.'[10] So Brundage deems amateurism sacred, but the results of it at the modern Olympics would certainly toll a bell with Coubertin. To add to the confusion, the word 'amateur' has become a term of mild abuse, frequently heard in sporting circles. What many expect in amateur sport now is a 'professional' approach to the task in hand, not an 'amateur' one. As Oxford's first professional Director of Rowing, Steve Royle, said before the 1988 Boat Race: 'We are completely professional, only there's no money in it. We're not amateurs, we're sportsmen.' His graduate American president Chris Penny agreed: 'Sacrificing months of your life, that's damn serious. The amateur era has gone ... It's like the Olympics. Months and months of work for just a few moments of exhilarating joy, fantasy. It's only worth it in retrospect.'

But let us return to the Victorian rowers who were among the earliest to tackle the definition and see what they made of it.

On 10 April 1878 a meeting at the Leander rooms in Putney considered amateur status and wrote a definition which began 'An Amateur oarsman must be (*inter alia*) an Officer of H.M.'s Army, or Navy, or Civil Service ...' and went on to debar those 'employed in or about boats'. Henley that year saw its first cup won by foreigners, Columbia College taking the Visitors', and another American crew defeated in the final of the Stewards'. They were the Shoe-wae-cae-mettes, French Canadian watermen from Monroe, Michigan. The man from *Bell's Life in London* – probably the editor, ex-coxswain Tom Egan – was beside himself when he saw them: 'Their rowing was ... execrable, I never saw worse form in any crew having first-class pretensions; "bucketting" would be a mild term in describing their stroke ... some of the crew did not receive the plaudits bestowed on them with that becoming modesty which is generally inseparable from true merit.' The Stewards brought their rules into line with the Putney meeting's, and in 1879 the Shoes' entry was refused. Entries from outside the United Kingdom must be 'accompanied by a declaration made before Notary Public with regard to the profession of each member of the crew', and this must be certified by the British Consul, the mayor, or the chief authority of the locality. The Henley statement read 'No person shall be considered an amateur oarsman or sculler – (1) Who has ever competed in any open competition for a stake, money or entrance fee; (2) Who has ever competed with or against a professional for any prize; (3) Who has ever taught, pursued, or assisted in the practice of athletic exercises of any kind as a means of gaining a livelihood; (4) Who has been employed in or about boats for money or wages; (5) Who is or ever has been by trade or employment for wages a mechanic, artisan, or labourer.'

Further alarms were ringing, it seems. That year representatives of Oxford, Cambridge, Leander, London, Thames, Royal Chester, Kingston, Twickenham, and Dublin University met to found the Metropolitan Rowing Association to form representative national crews to meet foreign challenges at Henley or elsewhere. They never realised this ambition, but they saw Germania Ruder Club of Germany enter the Grand in 1880. Then in 1882 four store clerks from Hillsdale BC in Michigan, three times American amateur champions, were refused entry by Henley.

On 20 May 1882 the *Field* in a report headed Amateur Rowing Association said that 'this society, established in 1879 under the title of the Metropolitan Rowing Association, for the purpose of associating members of existing amateur rowing clubs, with a view of forming representative British crews to compete against foreign and colonial clubs, has adopted the above designation, and is controlled by a committee composed of the following members: J. Catty (Thames RC), H. J. Chinnery (London RC), F. Fenner (London RC), F. S. Gulston (London RC), J. Hastie (Thames RC), J. H. D. Goldie (CUBC), Rev. R. W. Risley (OUBC), S. le B. Smith (London RC), and Charles Charteris, hon. sec., plus, ex-officio, the presidents of OUBC and CUBC, and the captains of Dublin University BC, Dublin University RC, Leander, London RC, Kingston, and Thames'. They met again at the Red Lion on 21 June and made their first object to 'maintain the standard of amateur oarsmanship as recognised by the rowing clubs of the UK'. In June 1883 the ARA said that no person could be considered an amateur who (1) Had ever taken part in any open competition for a stake, money, or entrance fee; (2) Had ever knowingly competed with or against a professional for any prize; (3) Had ever taught, pursued or assisted in the practice of athletic exercises for any kind of profit; (4) Had ever been employed in or about boats, or in any manual labour for money or wages; (5) Had been by trade or employment, for wages, a mechanic, artisan, or labourer, or engaged in any menial duty; (6) Was a member of a boat or a rowing club containing anyone liable to disqualification under the above clauses.

The pig-headedness of the definition shone through even at a time when class structure and social attitudes were extremely polarised. In case the Establishment missed the point, though, *The Times* obligingly spelt it out – with irony, one hopes: 'The outsiders, artisans, mechanics, and such like troublesome persons can have no place found for them. To keep them out is a thing desirable on every account. Let no base mechanic arms be suffered to thrust themselves in here.' They had succeeded in identifying a huge class of oarsmen who were neither professional because they complied with conditions one, two, and three nor were amateurs because they were victims of four, five, or six. Thinking oarsmen wrestled with these clauses, but they failed to unravel definitions of conflicting ideas about sport and society. They failed to understand the difference between 'sport' and 'athletics', failed to understand that vague and divisive aims of clubs are unacceptable to large segments of the population, failed to understand why amateurism developed, and failed to realise that once confused notions of amateurism became accepted in clubs, colleges, and schools, organising them became an end in itself.

According to the *New English Dictionary on Historical Principles* (Oxford, 1888) 'sport' is derived from the Middle English and French words 'desport' and 'disport' meaning 'a pleasant pastime, entertainment or amusement; recreation, diversion'. 'Athlete' in the broad American sense of athletic activity is derived from the Greek verb 'athlein', 'to contend for a prize', or the noun 'athlos' which means contest, or 'athlon' which means a prize awarded for the successful completion of a contest.[11] Here lies the conflict according to Keating: 'In essence, sport is a kind of diversion which has for its direct and immediate end fun, pleasure, and delight and which is dominated by a spirit of moderation and generosity. Athletics, on the other hand, is essentially a competitive activity, which has for its end victory in the contest and which is characterized by a spirit of dedication, sacrifice, and intensity.' The first equates amateurism with the spirit of play; the second with the business of winning. 'The pursuit of excellence in athletics', Keating says, 'tends naturally and inevitably to some form of professionalism.'[12]

The ARA broke its back on the rocks of menial and manual labour on 15 September 1890 when the National Amateur Rowing Association was set up at the Old Bell at Doctors' Commons with J. J. Lonnon of Polytechnic as Hon. Sec. and F. Goodwin of City of London as treasurer. Dr Furnivall, founder of the Working Men's College, was behind it, and it gathered support from figures whose rowing pedigree sounded as pink and blue as the ARA's, as well as from clubs like Nottingham Brittania and Falcon, Oxford. Its first president was the Duke of Fife and its last, Lord Iveagh. Its rules were similar to the ARA's but made no reference to mechanics, artisans, or manual labour. It attracted many clubs, and set about running its own regattas. Some clubs kept a foot in both associations by affiliating to both under different names, so that Polytechnic was an NARA club and Quintin was an ARA club. Strictly speaking, they could not meet each other because they could not take part in the same regattas. There were engaging disputes as to why, say, a worker in the Post Office was an amateur but a postman was not. There were more serious causes of friction. The ARA would not recognise the NARA as having any role in international selection, even though the ARA turned its back on its second aim until after the Second World War. Indeed, in 1921, discussing a new constitution for the British Olympic Association, it commented 'that organized international athletic competitions to take place at regular specified periods, and the consequent expenditure of time and money, are entirely contrary to the true spirit of amateur sport'.[13] Good relations and cooperation are put down to the generosity and help shown to NARA clubs by ARA club members, while the serious conflicts arose between the NARA and Henley. At the 1919 Peace regatta for the King's Cup, presented by George V 'for any crew of amateur oarsmen' who were ex-combatants in the Allied nations, the Stewards decreed that an amateur was what prevailed on 4 August 1914 in the country of origin. The NARA entered a crew certified as amateurs 'according to the NARA definition'. The

Stewards invited them to certify each man as an amateur according to the ARA definition. The NARA declined and were forced to withdraw.

Then in 1936 the Stewards refused entry to the Australian eight from the Sydney Police who were on their way to the Olympic Games in Berlin. This time indignation carried the day, though not for the men from down under. There was a question in the House and Charles Tugwell, honorary secretary of the NARA, approached the ARA and the Stewards for a knocking of heads. The result was that in January 1938 the ARA and Henley dropped their references to manual labour, and the ARA dropped the whole of clause five (above). Crews could then mix, but it took a long while for the associations to merge. In short, the ARA was run by a committee which had 11 members nominated by founder clubs who then elected six more, three members for the remaining Thames, Lea, and Medway clubs, and half a dozen for the rest of the country. The NARA was organised in eight autonomous associations who ran their own regattas. Merging for the ARA meant a reduction in the entrenched position of founder clubs and sharing regional responsibilities with NARA regions, and for the NARA, disbandment. In 1948 both affiliated to the international federation (FISA), and in 1950 both talked with the Scottish ARA with a view to one British body. The ARA's 'nominating' clubs at first refused to give up their seats, but after Kingston, Twickenham and Molesey sacrificed one of their two committee places the way was open. The committee was enlarged, boundaries were adjusted, and nominated members reduced. The merger became effective on 1 January 1956. Charles Tugwell of the NARA achieved his ambition, helped by the chairman and secretary of the ARA, G. O. 'Gully' Nickalls and J. H. 'Freddie' Page.

III

As George Sims did it, the thing savoured of Turner's notion of perspective, a realization of what should be, without any knowledge of what must be. There was that strange sympathy in the boat builder which was in Matt Taylor, and the Claspers too, and which is outside all calculation.
Theodore Cook, *Rowing at Henley* (Oxford 1919) p.90

When amateur competition started boats were large and heavy, derivations of naval cutters, often built to carry passengers or cargo. Gradually they were honed down, the significant steps being the rediscovery of the outrigger, the development of shell construction, and the invention of the sliding seat. The outrigger, which the Athenians used for the top tier of rowers in their 'triērēs' warships, reduced the width and therefore the weight and the wetted surface of the craft by supporting the rowlock in which the oar pivots on a frame extended from the gunwhale instead of on the gunwhale itself. Shell construction started by bringing the keel inboard which further refined the hull shape, and for fine racing boats using a thin plywood skin instead of the overlapping planks of clinker. This reduced weight and water resistance. The Americans used a papier-mâché skin for some years, an example being the boat brought to Henley in 1878 by Columbia College, who eventually used their cedar boat for racing. The swivel rowlock was a controversial but significant development, being the replacement of thole pins by a 'gate' which held the oar in place. The sliding seat transformed the rowing stroke and changed the shape of the most sought-after oarsmen. Fat fixed-seat boats required brawny short-arsed men; lean sliding-seat boats required longlegged slim-limbed rowers.

Of course, none of this happened overnight. Each development required the genius to think it up, the marine architect to get it right, the engineer to apply the required technology, the materials scientist to produce and adapt substances to do the job, and the coaches and rowers to see the advances and how best they could use them. There are rival claims to the inventions, but it is generally agreed that the keel-less boat is the Derwenthaugh boatbuilder Harry Clasper's, a four built in 1847. Clasper and the Tyne boatbuilders were trying to design a boat with the narrowest possible beam while giving adequate leverage for the oars. The earliest claim for the outrigger is for 1828, made by Robert S. Hunter in *Rowing in Canada since 1848*. Wooden outriggers were experimented with on the Tyne from 1836.[14] The American George Steers, who was to design the yacht *America*, built an out-rigged four in 1838 which was not successful. In 1845 J. W. Conant of St John's College, Cambridge, introduced them to Henley on his sculling boat and in the same year Clasper solved the problem by developing the iron outrigger which he tried out in a four-oar. In the same year Searle built an eight with outriggers for Cambridge in eight days which was 60 feet long and 2 feet 10 inches wide, but they did not use it in the Boat Race because of inexperience and bad weather. But the Boat Race was out-rigged in 1846.

Theodore Cook in *Rowing at Henley* (1919) claims that Clasper used a cedar skiff with a keel-less hull when he raced Coombes on the Tyne in 1844, and that he had built several smooth-bottomed boats including one used by the Claspers in the Thames regatta of 1849. C. M. Pitman's *Record of the University Boat Race*[15] says that OUBC used an 1847 keel-less Clasper four to win the Stewards' at Henley in 1852. But it was Mat Taylor from Ouseburn to whom the keel-less hull has been mostly attributed. A ship's carpenter and experienced sculler, he was engaged as a trainer for 45 shillings a week by Royal Chester for the 1854 season. He built an out-rigged four-oared smooth-bottomed keel-less boat named *Victoria* which won the Stewards' and Wyfold cups for the club in the following year with considerable ease. The boat was given to the Science Museum in South Kensington in 1937. It was certainly Taylor who built the first keel-less eight in 1856 for Royal Chester, whose captain J. B. Littledale worked closely with the Geordie on design, bringing the lessons of his family's Liverpool shipbuilding concern to bear on the racing boat. The boat was about 55 feet long, ten shorter than the keeled eights popular at the time, and 25 inches wide at its greatest beam. Despite not being able to balance or 'sit' the boat properly even with Taylor demonstrating and coaching them, the inelegant Chester crew took the *Eugenie* to Henley and won the Ladies' Plate and the Grand. Taylor's reputation was made in an afternoon, and many similar boats were made, including one for the Oxford president A. P. Lonsdale at his own expense in which his crew walked off with the Boat Race in 1857. Oxford engaged Taylor 'not to instruct us in the art of rowing but to show us the proper way to send his boat along as quickly as possible'. Cambridge won in a Taylor boat in 1859 and Eton won the Ladies' six times in an 1861 Taylor model. The keel-less boats marked the beginning of the art of watermanship for the gentlemen-amateurs. The boats were inherently unstable, and now it was up to the crew to make them stable by getting the catch of the blade in the water right, by getting the pressure on their feet right, and by getting the pressure of the oar button against the thole pins of the outriggers right. In short, more skill was needed to row them.

Herbert Manchester in *Four Centuries of Sport in America*[16] credits the American professional sculler Walter Brown with the sliding seat, although oarsmen in Newcastle and St Johns, Nova Scotia, were experimenting with them. But the best claim, at least for a reliable slide, seems to be that of another American, J. C. Babcock of Nassau Boat Club. This important innovation was used by Yale in their race against Harvard in 1870. Many had tried to improve fixed seats by greasing with lard or tallow, including Tynesiders and boys at Bedford. The first reported use of slides was in Chicago in 1857; in England R. O. Birch used one in his sculling boat at King's Lynn regatta in 1870. Their introduction at the yardstick English rowing events was by London RC and Pembroke College, Oxford at Henley in 1872 and by both crews in the 1873 Boat Race. Tynesiders had shown the way, a sliding Taylor crew comprehensively beating a fixed-seat Chambers crew in 1871. Slides were treated with suspicion and caution because runners made of glass or bone were sometimes troublesome: material science lagged behind innovation. There were other problems, too, such as Guy Nickalls's alarming experience in the Diamond Sculls of 1888 against

W. Sweetman: 'Shortly after the start ... I heard a bang, and a shower of shrapnel fell around me; the balls from his bearings. I offered to start again and he paddled back to the raft and got another slide fixed.'[17] Babcock's sliding-seat six-oared gig used leather-covered wooden frames grooved at the edges to slide on brass tracks. His development threatened Mat Taylor's notion of hull shape because slides required larger state rooms for the oarsmen, and therefore longer boats.

The leather-covered metal button for oars was introduced in 1870, and in 1874 Mike Davis produced a swivel rowlock in America which was soon taken up by scullers, and more cautiously by sweep oarsmen to replace fixed or thole pins. The sliding seat introduced something new into the music of rowing, a 'swoosh' as the rowers returned up the slide while feathering to prepare for their next stroke. The swivel or gate removed the haunting beat of button against tholepin, described here by Theodore Cook: 'The rattle of the riggers at the finish, the music of the tide beneath her body as she shot between the strokes, the grim yet heartening sound of splendid and unbroken strength when all eight blades crashed in together – these are the things that no one who has heard and felt them will ever forget.'[18]

Developments since these have all been brought about by materials. Nylon has made slides better; alloys have enabled outriggers to be stronger and more aerodynamic; carbon fibre has made oars stiffer and lighter; plastics have introduced hot and cold moulding into hull construction. Hull and oar blade shapes continue to change, but the only real innovation in the twentieth century has been the development of the sliding outrigger. The seat is fixed while the outriggers slide, giving a smooth ride, an advantage to scullers with strong legs, and, it is thought, a few seconds over the international distance of 2,000 metres. First experiments were by two Britons at Bedford in the 1950s who were once more ahead of the materials game. The Germans succeeded in the 1980s, only to have sliding outriggers banned by the international federation on the grounds of their expense at a time when great efforts were being made to reduce costs and spread rowing in Asia and Africa. There have also been two developments which alter skin friction by acting on the water. Both are banned by the international federation. The first is a slurry called Polyox containing methylated spirit and is released from a tank under the bow canvas by the action of a sliding seat. Results of trials of this 'slippery water' conducted in the 1960s by Geoffrey Page, the ARA's technical officer, were spectacular. He reckons Polyox would be worth ten lengths of an eight over the Henley course of 1 mile 550 yards, and recommended banning the substance, which may be a pollutant, immediately.[19] The second is a ribbed coat dubbed 'clingfilm' developed by the Americans and used on the hull of their coxed

four at the 1984 Olympic Games, where they won a silver medal behind
Britain. Very fine grooves or riblets showed 6 per cent less drag than a
smooth surface according to researchers at the National Aeronautical and
Space Administration (NASA), and Boeing's Flight Research Institute tested
it on a sculling boat and said that speed was increased by 2 per cent or
four lengths over 2,000 metres.[20] Both finalists in the America's Cup used
it in 1987 and Oxford secretly applied it to their hull for the Boat Race
in that year, a move which helped them psychologically if not by reducing
drag resistance in the Wagnerian storm in which they raced and won. Shortly
after that, FISA and the ARA and Henley banned 'clingfilm'.

Most of these developments happened in fits and starts. When one looks
back on them it is easy to imagine them arriving overnight. But refining
and learning to use them took many years, particularly the sliding seat
which caused a profound change in the rowing stroke and led to a school
of orthodoxy, the long lay back at the end of the stroke and the excessive
lean forward at the beginning, against Fairbairnism which permitted fewer
extremes in more comfort, eventually to the same or better effect. Battle
between these lasted from the turn of the century to beyond the Second
World War and was not confined to polite exchanges of coaching manuals.
It fanned vitriolic correspondence in *The Times*, heated both exchanges
on the river bank and a sauceboat of prejudices to spice rowing's social
stew and to make and break reputations.

IV

Orthodoxy is particularly severe in keeping the eyes in the boat. This not only
turns the body into cast-iron, but also paralyses the mind.
  Steve Fairbairn on Rowing (1951) p.535

The period between the wars was regarded as a Golden Age of British
rowing. Having got over the shock of foreigners competing and sometimes
winning, the oarsmen set about beating them. At the Olympic regatta in
1908 all four events were won by British crews; by the close of the 1936
Games 12 gold and 6 silver medals had been wrested from 25 events in
seven Olympiads. The Amateur Rowing Association played very little part
in this, and the National ARA less, the former because they turned their
backs on their original purpose of forming crews to beat foreigners, and
the latter because they were not accepted as true amateurs. A NARA four
from Nottingham and Union was at the 1928 Games.

There were 60 clubs in existence when the ARA was formed, and 38
regattas. By 1890 there were 457 clubs including 301 in the London area.
By 1925 there were more than 200 clubs listed in the Rowing Directory
of which 100 were ARA clubs, 40 NARA clubs, and the rest unattached.

Two sides of the Boat Race

9.3 Popular identification with the crews. These children were buying favours in 1924

9.4 The exhaustion and exhilaration of the winner – Oxford in 1980

The decline is attributed not to a fall in numbers of oarsmen but to polarisation into fewer larger clubs to take advantage of increasing opportunities for competition. There was now rowing all the year round, which received a tremendous boost with the foundation of the Head of River Race in 1926. It was started by clubs on the Thames tideway at the instigation of Steve Fairbairn as a focal point to winter training and as an imitation of the Oxford and Cambridge bumping races, except that it was a time trial instead of a collision course. The formula was soon copied in many places. Long-distance time trials like the Head, which by the 1970s was attracting more entries than the permitted maximum of 420 eights, are the basis of autumn and spring competition, and autumn and spring more or less merge through the rowing winter.

Fairbairn was the name most upon rowing men's lips from the turn of the century until his death in 1938. He was known universally as Steve. He was an Australian who arrived at Jesus College, Cambridge, in 1881 and got his first Blue in the same year. Eleven of his relatives also pulled for Jesus. He managed to attend one lecture in six years there, but the college had a fine record on the river from 1875–85 and then declined sharply when Fairbairn returned to the family sheep station in Australia. He came back and began serious coaching in 1904, his ideas making Jesus great again and being exported to Thames RC where he coached from 1905–25, then to London RC when he was persuaded by Archie Nisbet to join Thames's deadly rivals in 1926 after a rumpus on the Thames committee. His ideas also infiltrated Cambridge college rowing and such unlikely places as Zurich Football Club who won the Grand in 1936 after their coach Arthur Dreyfuss translated much of Steve's coaching maxims into German. They were in effect coached by correspondence.

'No greater personality has ever devoted himself with such unflagging interest or such inexhaustible energy and patience to the promotion of the welfare of oarsmen!' said the authors of Jesus's history of rowing. The style caused outrage and passionate support. He summarised it as 'The whole job of rowing begins and ends in concentrating on working the oar to propel the boat', whereas orthodoxy was 'an endeavour to make oarsmen hold and move their bodies in what the coach considered ideal positions ... holding the body straight and making it move in a jerky position that caught the eye but did not move the boat'.[21] The styles differed in two main respects. First, the orthodox style caught the beginning of the stroke with the shoulders, opening up an angle between thigh and rib as quickly as possible when the blade was dropped vertically into the water. Steve advocated driving the blade into the water and letting the slide take care of itself, which should result in a swing of the body simultaneous with an even drive of the legs through the stroke, driving the boat through the water. Secondly, orthodoxy said that the blade was whipped out of the water to be followed by a swift recovery up the slide while the boat was running, while Steve said there should be a swift withdrawal of the blade from the water by means of a quick flick of the wrists down and away – the hands-away which feathers the blade automatically – but that the oarsman should lie back at the finish and take plenty of time in starting his recovery. Steve was a teacher who had time for all shapes and sizes – after all, Jesus was a very small college. He wanted oarsmen to think for themselves.

Orthodoxy, meanwhile, saw no merit in unorthodox methods. Steve's crews were ragged, sloppy, and lazy to orthodox eyes. Orthodoxy was straight-backed, eyes-in-the-boat, highly disciplined stuff, and its preachers and adherents were from rowing's top drawers of Eton and Oxford. Dr Edmond Warre, an Etonian who became president of OUBC before returning to teach at his old school, was asked to coach the eight by R. H. Blake-Humphrey in 1860 and did so by daily invitation for the next 25 years. When Gilbert C. Bourne was at Eton in the late 1870s he found the training and coaching unaltered since Warre had started. Warre was invited to lecture to OUBC on the elementary rowing stroke in 1907. By the mid-1930s the line-up on the orthodox side was Leander, Oxford, CUBC, and Trinity Cambridge, while Fairbairnism could claim London, Thames, and colleges like Jesus, Pembroke, and Selwyn. In 1935 the Cambridge president invited Nisbet to coach, which put not only Trinity's nose out of joint but also that of the CUBC priest of orthodoxy Peter Haig-Thomas, as described by George Drinkwater in *The Boat Race*: 'To a man like Haig-Thomas orthodoxy was a matter of faith far transcending allegiance to his old university, though while he was wanted on the Cam he did not, apart from sporadic help to college boat clubs, accept Oxford's invitations. Now, however, he gave his services willingly and completely.'[22] Two other Cambridge coaches went with him and Nisbet's Fairbairnist Cambridge won – as orthodox Cambridge crews had done for the previous eleven races. Style on the bank was maintained by both sides through this period. Haig-Thomas used to entertain his crews at his house in Goring and hire staff from Hurlingham Club and a bus to get the crew there.

It was also a period of individual feats, such as H. R. A. 'Jumbo' Edwards collapsing in the Boat Race in 1926, returning to it in 1930, and winning two gold medals in a day at the Los Angeles Olympic Games of 1932 where he was substituted into the pair and the four. He was one of rowing's great characters, an experimenter and eccentric who had a long but not very successful career as an Oxford coach. The most remarkable was Jack

9.5 A legendary coach, Jumbo Edwards, with crew and cigarette. He was probably demonstrating a 'Moriarty' derived from Sherlock Holmes

Beresford Jr, who sprang upon the Henley scene in 1920, a young man of Polish origin who had been invalided out of the army after joining up from Bedford School. He recovered from his leg injury by messing about in a dinghy at Fowey. Having won the Diamonds he lost the gold medal at the Olympic regatta by one second to Jack Kelly the American. Kelly had been refused entry by the Henley Stewards, legend saying that he fell foul of the manual labour bar by being a bricklayer. The real reason may have been that the 1906 ban on his club, Vesper of Philadelphia, was still in force. Whatever the truth, Kelly's son eventually avenged the

9.6 The sun did not always shine at Henley. This is 1939 and Jack Beresford (bow) and Dick Southwood are dead-heating with the Italians G. Scherli and E. Broschi in the Invitation Double Sculls

slur in 1947 by winning the Diamonds at his second attempt. His sister Grace visited the regatta before her celebrated screen career, and as Princess of Monaco she and the Kellys eventually became the regatta's own royal family. Beresford won the Diamonds three more times, the Wingfield Sculls, the amateur championship of Great Britain, seven times, and won medals at the next four Olympiads. His last Olympic appearance was in Berlin in 1936 when with L. F. 'Dick' Southwood, and coached by Eric Phelps, he won the double sculling gold medal. The same crew dead-heated for Henley's first double sculls event in 1939 with an Italian crew who were European champions and whose combined age was 24 years less than their own.

While what may be termed the elite of rowing, the relatively small group of families and their friends, maintained international success on the water and an inward-looking lifestyle at home which was somewhat in keeping with their fathers' generation, the effects of their aloof class structure were

9.7 Practical watermen. The Phelps dynasty, Eric, father Bossie and Ted

beginning to be felt abroad. The professional scene was fading to oblivion in the 1930s. Stake money was hard to raise, good professionals hard to find, and rumours of cheating easy to listen to. The few remaining fixtures such as the world championship and the Newcastle Christmas Handicap disappeared. The latter finally collapsed when Hitler's bombers hit the boat-house and the fleet. The former had a brief revival after the Second World War in Australia. But many of the protagonists were carrying English lessons abroad. The two sons of Aaron Pocock, boatbuilder to Eton College, had left for Canada to become lumberjacks on the proceeds of a professional win by one of them, and a chapter of pleasant accidents led one to be boatman to Yale University and the other to establish a company in Seattle which became the largest builder of racing boats in North America. Their uncles and their grandfather were boatbuilders too, and their maternal grandfather kitted out Stanley with portable craft in which to go and look for Livingstone. Eric Phelps, one of a dynasty of Putney watermen, was coach to von Opel in Germany, and the success of the Germans at the 1936 Olympic Games was largely due to English professionals who coached in and about their clubs. Lou Barry, from another clan of watermen in

West London, nephew of Ernest and brother of Bert, who were both professional world champions, coached in Ireland and then in Italy. There were men making oars and boats in Australia who learnt their trade in England. The economic climate and the shortage of opportunities to use professional coaching skills at home spread English professionals – and some amateurs too – far and wide. Their influence was to be felt in North and South America, Europe, and the Empire.

V

Mrs Daniell was most successful as coxswain, her extraordinary height enabling her to look clear over the head of the bow oar in an eight, while her knowledge of the river and her able manipulation of the rudder lines made her services much prized.

> *A Summary of the Records of the Calcutta Rowing Club 1858–1932*, compiled by L. H. Macklin, p.9

Women seldom get a mention in the man's world of rowing, but their participation is not a recent phenomenon. The above quotation is in a passage on the founder members of the Calcutta club which puts the phenomenal Mrs Daniell into the 1860s. It is unlikely, however, that she was actually a member like her stockbroker husband. Ann Glanville ran a Cornish pilot gig female crew on the Tamar that often beat men's crews and won Le Havre regatta in 1850 after rowing the English Channel to get to it. In 1880 Lady Greville's *The Gentlewoman's Book of Sports* said 'It is essential for every English girl to learn to row.'

Dr Furnivall did as much as he could to get women out in boats, encouraging both his students and the waitresses in his favourite ABC cafe to join Furnivall Sculling Club and indulge in great picnic expeditions upstream from Hammersmith to Canbury Island near Kingston at weekends. Jessie Currie remembered her introduction when she moved into a studio in Primrose Hill and the outgoing tenant said: 'Let me introduce you to Dr Furnivall. He will ask you if you can scull. If you say "No", he will take you up the river to teach you. If you say "Yes" he will take you up the river to keep you in practice. He will take you, anyhow.'

Furnivall was one of the begetters of the NARA as well as a great scholar and instigator of many literary societies such as the Chaucer Society. 'Few people would have known', Jessie wrote in *Memories of F. J. Furnivall* in 1921, 'that some of the greatest living scholars were often in the doctor's boat, as we sculled up from Richmond'. He invented the octuple by rigging an eight which he bought from New College Oxford for eight scullers and coxing it himself. After the girls performed well in it the first time,

Furnivall arranged a publicity outing: 'The next time they were afloat they were exposed to a battery of cameras belonging to the various newspaper reporters ... by this means the girls' eight became quite world-famous. The Doctor claimed it as the only sculling eight, which caused the girls of an American college to send over illustrations of their eights; but their style proved to be rowing, and so the Doctor's contention was maintained.'[23]

Lucille Eaton Hill, Director of Physical Training at Wellesley College, advocated rowing for women in 1903: 'The physical benefits which women derive from rowing cannot be exaggerated, provided they are willing to master the rudiments ... Correct rowing induces an erect carriage and finely poised head, a full chest and well-placed shoulders. Incorrect rowing disturbs all harmony of the figure.'[24]

The Women's Amateur Rowing Association was founded in 1926 and the Ladies' Boat Race between Oxford and Cambridge in 1927, the latter over half a mile on the Isis as a style contest. The idea of women competing rather than indulging in deportment was slow to be accepted. The race fell into abeyance but was revived as a competitive fixture between the universities' women's clubs in the 1970s and now takes place at Henley on the same day as the lightweight men's race between Oxford and Cambridge. Women rowed in a 'style' charity regatta arranged by the Belgians in aid of war cripples in 1925, the Dutch wearing long skirts which were tied up at the knees to prevent them catching in the slides. The WARA started regattas for women's crews and revived the sport after the Second World War. The French and Danes organised women's regattas before the men's European championships which they hosted respectively in 1951 and 1953. The European championships started in 1954 when Britain's coxed four won the bronze medal. The only other medal was Penny Chuter's silver in the sculls in 1962, the year before the WARA merged with the ARA, a move started by the holding of the European Championships in London in 1960. The next medal won by a British woman was Beryl Mitchell's silver in the world championship sculls in 1981, and then, sculling under her married name of Beryl Crockford, she won the lightweight world title in doubles with Lin Clark in 1985.

Domestically, there has been a rapid change in the number of women taking up the sport. Pauline Churcher, chairman of the ARA's Women's Rowing Committee in 1979, reported that mixed clubs increased from 41 in 1969 to 157 a decade later. Not only that, but many of the 41 did not actually permit women to row, and all the clubs which did were in the north, midlands, and west. None were in the south, the heartland of rowing. Twelve of the 41 were colleges or universities and four were schools – all in the Inner London Education Authority. Of the 157, 38 were colleges

9.8 Some great scholars and waitresses might have been in this eight coached and coxed by Dr Furnivall in 1907

and universities and 16 were schools with women members. There were seven women's clubs, two of which admitted males.[25]

Several factors have contributed to these changes. One is the introduction of national championships in 1972 which by 1979 were offering titles in all the internationally-recognised boat classes for seniors and juniors. Another is the admittance of women to the Olympics in 1976, and the start of an international junior championship for women in 1978. Events for lightweights were introduced in 1985, the same year as the distance

9.9 By 1981–2 a woman was coxing the Oxford boat, Susan Brown

for women was increased from 1,000 to 2,000 metres. Regattas have introduced or increased the number of events on offer, and in major rowing
centres like Oxford and Cambridge the popularity of the sport has shown
no decline as the proportion of female students has risen with the breakdown
of the male- and female-only colleges. In 1973 general training weekends

were introduced for women to provide basic coaching, and they have proved popular.

VI

All rowed fast but none so fast as stroke.
A popular misquotation derived from *Sandford of Merton* by Desmond Coke (1903)[26]

In 1947 both the ARA and the NARA affiliated to the international rowing federation,[27] and British crews entered the European championships for the first time. Merger of the two associations finally took place in 1956, with 296 clubs sheltering under the new umbrella. There have followed 30 years of enormous change, both in attitudes and structure, both organisational and social. The ARA introduced a closed shop in 1957, requiring all competitors to be members of clubs affiliated to the association or to an appropriate overseas federation. The first training film was released in that year; in 1960 a system of licensing umpires was introduced and the Women's European Championships were held on the Welsh Harp in Willesden, London. The first international selection board was appointed in 1961 and the Women's Amateur Rowing Association was incorporated into the ARA in 1962. In the following year the association appointed a professional trainer, Jim Railton, a former junior sprinter but not an oarsman. The Nautilus scheme was started in 1966, a first but not very successful attempt at a national squad. But, at a time when the international record of British crews was dire, the ARA was coming back to its original first purpose when the metropolitan clubs had begun to tackle the problem 90 years before. In so far as any one body had carried the international can from then it was Leander, with considerable support from the universities and clubs like Thames. But British crews had managed only one medal in four Olympiads, and only three in the seven European championships since the merger of the ARA and NARA. East European countries had entered the Olympic arena as well as the European championships, and it was already apparent that expecting club eights and maybe fours to reach finals, let alone win medals, would soon be a thing of the past in a climate of rising standards and, dare one say it, an increasingly 'professional' approach to preparation. Rowing, as never before, was becoming work. Only ten British crews reached finals between 1965–74 in European, world, or Olympic competitions.

In 1967 there was a major reorganisation when the committee was replaced by a council and the number of nominating clubs reduced to OUBC, CUBC, Leander, London, and Thames, while the regions were reorganised.

In 1971 Britain's first multi-lane 2,000-metre course became operational at Holme Pierrepont, near Nottingham, and this was to have as profound an effect on the calendar as the inspired appointment of Bohumil Janousek as full-time professional coach to the association in 1969. Janousek was christened Bob after arriving from Prague with no English. He was lent a flat and sent to language school in New Oxford Street. He was well-qualified to take on British rowing, having a degree from Charles University in physical culture and an Olympic medal as well as proven coaching ability, unbounded energy, and quick wit. His appointment was surprising coming from a group of people who were firmly entrenched in the rowing establishment. The ARA's president was John Garton, chairman of the Henley Stewards. It was inspired because only a foreigner with the advantage of setting out with no English could persuade the entrenched corners of the sport – the older universities, the colleges, the public schools, the provincial clubs, the large 'top-drawer' clubs, all of whom had axes to grind and traditions to stand on while grinding them – to at least give him enough rope to hang himself and his foreign ideas.

The social climate among the active oarsmen was on Janousek's side. Their generation was not fussed about accents or how long they wore their hair even if some of their elders were. Janousek devoted much time to listening, and then introduced courses for coaches (rowing being unrecognised as a specialism in British colleges of physical education), and turned round the international record by 1973 when Chris Baillieu and Mike Hart, two Cambridge Blues, came third in the European championships. In 1974 Janousek's eight, made up of Leander and Thames Tradesmen men, the latter coached initially by Railton, came second in the world championships and second in the Olympics two years later after one change of crew. In 1976 women's rowing entered the Olympic programme, and in 1986 women's lightweight rowing entered the world championship programme. From 1970–88 British crews have won 8 Olympic medals, 15 world championship medals, 16 lightweight medals, 4 women's lightweight medals, 1 European men's medal (this competition was discontinued in 1973), 1 women's world medal, 16 junior medals, and several successes in the Match des Seniors for under-23 crews.

Penny Chuter, an outstanding sculler, skiffer, and punter in the late 1950s and early 1960s, was the second professional national coach appointed, and after working under Janousek she became principal coach to the association when he resigned to become a boat manufacturer after the Olympics in 1976. In 1986 she became director of international rowing.

So new names both of people and clubs changed the map of British rowing. The Scottish merger mooted in the 1950s never happened, and

9.10 Penny Chuter in the 1960s before becoming the ARA's second professional coach. She became Britain's director of internationl rowing in 1986.

the Welsh broke away in the 1980s to form their own association. The purpose-built National Water Sports Centre at Holme Pierrepont made national championships and a full international regatta possible each year. The course hosted the junior championships in 1974 and two world championships in 1975 and 1986, giving Britain an unrivalled reputation for efficient organisation. The Commonwealth Games regatta of 1986 was held on Scotland's course at Strathclyde, which also hosted the world veterans' meeting in 1988. In 1987 500-metre sprint racing was televised, and the Serpentine regatta was revived. By 1988 there were several regattas on multi-lane courses and multi-lane courses at such places as Peterborough, London and Bristol Docks, Bewl Bridge on the Kent–Sussex border, the Rother Valley near Sheffield, and Coate Park near Swindon.

Problems arise as quickly as they are solved. The sport is growing in the number of participants and in diversification. Women's rowing in particular has had enormous growth and has enormous growth potential. A number of development officers have been taken on to spread the sport, particularly amongst youth who have access to water but who are not from traditional rowing schools. Rowing for the disabled is being encouraged. Random dope testing during winter training was pioneered by the ARA from 1981, the first rowing federation and the first sport in Britain to do so. The demands and cost of international competition seem to be ever greater and to involve more categories of people. Financial pressure is great, government money being called more to account, and sponsorship for such a low-profile team activity hard to come by. The Rowing Foundation, a charity to promote water sports, was set up by the ARA, as was the British International Rowing Fund to raise sponsorship for the international squads, and a group of enthusiasts have made the first steps towards setting up a national rowing museum and education centre.

The latest change in organisation began in 1986–8 when the international side of the sport was hived off into a 'wholly-owned subsidiary' called the British International Rowing Schemes, and a registration scheme was set up whereby various categories of rowers were offered membership of the association in exchange for racing season tickets, insurance, and a magazine. Thus the ARA has changed from a federation of clubs paying a sliding-scale of affiliation fees and regattas paying a per-entry levy to a mass-membership organisation. For the first time it will know how many adherents it has. Membership of the Stewards' Enclosure at Henley is restricted to about 5,000: in the first six months of the registration scheme, the ARA had attracted 10,000 members, and that was through the winter half of the season. There is also a strong move towards more autonomy for the regions and less centralisation of the Hammersmith headquarters of the association. There has also been a change in the hierarchy during the eighties. Far fewer of the executive, including the president and the executive secretary, are from the 'establishment' of rowing. The 'old' ARA casts less of a shadow than it did and there is more of the spirit of the NARA, less stuffiness and more goodwill.

The sport also recognises that it faces difficulties in its traditional areas of operation. The increase in leisure activities brings more rival users to waters which have been left largely to the rowers in the past. For all its success in obtaining more funds and sponsorship for some of its activities it has not yet found ways of attracting income that sports with more televisual appeal and company image association have come to enjoy. Both in its old haunts and new ones like redeveloped docks, it can get caught in battles over the use of water where the stakes are far higher than its resources, where influence, friends and its natural attraction as an activity are the only things on which it can rely.

The ARA's popularity with its members – regions, clubs, regattas, individuals – and with its relations like Henley, the Boat Race, the Skiff Racing Association, the Scots and Welsh remains, and will probably continue to remain, elusive. In spite of its attempts to improve the oarsman's and the oarswoman's lot, the association is often treated like a cox on a bad day – the target of moans, groans, and opprobrious epithets.

NOTES

1   *Yachting and Rowing, British Sports and Sportsmen, The Sportsman* (1916).
2   Neil Wigglesworth, *Victorian and Edwardian Boating from Old Photographs* (1988).
3   Elizabeth Johns, *Thomas Eakins. The Heroism of Modern Life* (Princeton University Press, 1983).
4   Wigglesworth, *Victorian and Edwardian Boating.*
5   Richard Burnell, 'The Amateur Rowing Association 1882–1982', *British Rowing Almanack* (1982).
6   Clark W. Hetherington, C. A. Waldo, and William L. Dudley, 'Report of the Committee on an Amateur Law', *American Physical Education Review*, 15 (March 1910).
7   Edward Mussey Hartwell, *Physical Training in American Colleges and Universities*, US Bureau of Education Circular of Information 5 (Government Printing Office, 1886).
8   Christopher Dodd, 'The bonny brave boat rowers', *Regatta Magazine* (December 1987), Amateur Rowing Association.
9   David Cort, 'The Olympics: myth of the amateur', *The Nation*, 199 (1964).
10 Avery Brundage, address at the 68th session of the IOC, *IOC Newsletter*, July 1969. Compare de Coubertin with the latest attempt at definition by the Henley Royal Regatta in 1981. 'An amateur is one who practises the sport of rowing without deriving, or having in the past derived, profit or material gain from so doing. An amateur shall not forfeit amateur status by receiving legitimate out-of-pocket expenses or loss of profits or salary, if they are specifically incurred in respect of training or of competition in regattas, and are received with the consent, and subject to the rules, of his national federation.'
11 James W. Keating, 'Sportsmanship as a moral category', *Ethics*, 75 (October 1964).

12 James W. Keating, 'Athletics and the pursuit of excellence', *Education*, 85 (March 1965).
13 Keith Osborne, *Boat Racing in Britain 1715–1975* (1975).
14 Burnell, 'The Amateur Rowing Association 1882–1982'.
15 C. M. Pitman, *The Record of the University Boat Race* (1909).
16 Herbert Manchester, *Four Centuries of Sport in America* (New York 1968) (reissue).
17 Guy Nickalls, *Life's a Pudding* (1939).
18 Theodore A. Cook, *Rowing at Henley* (Oxford 1919).
19 Christopher Dodd, 'Slimy Al and the riblets', *American Rowing* (March–April 1987).
20 Alec N. Brooks, Allan V. Abbott and David Gordon Wilson, *Scientific American*, vol. 255, no. 6 (December 1968).
21 F. Brittain and H. B. Playford, *The Jesus College BC* (Cambridge 1930).
22 G. C. Drinkwater, *The Boat Race* (1929).
23 Jessie Currie, Gwendoline Jarvis, and others, *Memories of F. J. Furnivall* (private subscription, 1921).
24 Lucille Eaton Hill, *Athletics and Out-door Sports for Women* (1903).
25 Pauline Churcher, 'Development of women's rowing 1969–79', *British Rowing Almanack* (1980).
26 See *Oxford Dictionary of Quotations*, 3rd edn (1981), p. 154. The actual quotation reads: 'His blade struck the water a full second before any other ... until ... as the boats began to near the winning post, his own was dipping into the water *twice* as often as any other.'
27 Fédération Internationale des Sociétés d'Aviron.

10 RUGBY UNION

GARETH WILLIAMS

I

> I remember William Webb Ellis perfectly. He was... generally regarded as
> inclined to take unfair advantages at football.
>
> Rev. Thomas Harris, a Rugby School contemporary of Ellis, quoted in *The Origin of
> Rugby Football* (Rugby, 1897), p. 21

The commemorative tablet erected at Rugby School in February 1900 in
honour of William Webb Ellis, who in 1823 'first took the ball in his arms
and ran with it, thus originating the distinctive feature of the rugby game',
tells us more about the late-Victorian mind than it does about the early
nineteenth-century beginnings of rugby football.

Ellis's piece of inspired illegality was resurrected during a flurry of public
correspondence between various Old Rugbeians in the wake of the formation of the Rugby Football Union in 1871. By the 1890s there were sound
reasons for explaining the birth of rugby in this way, especially for old
boys – in both senses – who viewed the abolition in 1871 of 'hacking'
(the vigorous and apparently character-building kicking of an opponent's
shins) as a collective bereavement and who felt aggrieved at the diluting
of their manly, mauling game by the effete innovation of passing; after
all, no one recalled Ellis actually having *passed* the ball. Their suspicions
that the drift towards a more open, faster spectacle would encourage entertaining the gallery rather than playing the game for itself were confirmed
within 20 years when its popularity among the working classes of the industrial north provoked a major crisis in the ranks of the RFU, culminating
in the breakaway of half the clubs in it to form the Northern Union in
1895. To memorialise W. W. Ellis, therefore, was to reassert the game's
public school amateur origins, and to perpetuate an act of creationism
reassuring to an age that found a Carlylean 'great man' theory of history
more to its taste than Darwinian evolution.[1]

In truth, it took several decades for rugby to evolve from diverse forms
of public school football, via the so-called 'Cambridge Rules', the FA rules
of 1863 and the RFU's counter-proposals of 1871, into the recognisably

modern game of the 1890s. It is also difficult to deny the sociologists Dunning and Sheard's argument that it is 'just not . . . plausible that a deeply entrenched traditional game could have been changed fundamentally by a single act', and even more implausible that the 'deviant' action of a low status day-boy should have been regarded as desirable rather than punishable. They follow through with a most cogent case for seeing rugby's separate development as the byproduct of a conflict between established and ascendent classes in the public schools. Older, impeccably aristocratic establishments like Eton, Winchester, Harrow and Shrewsbury could adopt a 'new' form of popular street football with impunity, but the headmasters of more recent foundations like Cheltenham, Marlborough, Wellington, Clifton and Haileybury, as well as re-endowed old grammar schools like Sherborne, Sedbergh and Tonbridge opted for the game they themselves had learned as masters or pupils at Arnold's Rugby, a school like theirs that had come into existence to cater for a thrusting industrial and commercial middle class anxious to put as much distance as possible between themselves and the lower orders from which they might be thought to have sprung.[2]

The origins of rugby, as of association football and most of the other organised sports of Victorian England, lay in the reform of the public schools. The cults of athleticism and muscular Christianity acquired a greater seriousness in the face of foreign threats to England's colonial and commercial dominance. What J. A. Mangan has dubbed the 'precarious fusion' of Christian gentility and social Darwinism produced a games-field rhetoric, 'a frame of reference and a rationale for action . . . for generations of public schoolboys'.[3]

The RFU was summoned into existence in 1871 out of an urgent desire to rescue the game of rugby from the confusion of unregulated modes of play into which it was slipping. The FA was formed in 1863 and the association game was growing in popularity: it was no coincidence that the RFU was established in the same year as the inaugural FA Challenge Cup Final. The Rugby School influence was pervasive in the early years: the RFU's first five presidents, the first captain of England, and seven of the 15 who constituted the RFU's first committee were all Old Rugbeians. There were 16 Rugbeians in the first Oxford XX of 1872, and 10 in the first English side of the previous year. The old boy network has always counted for a lot in English rugby because that is how it started.

What made the necessity for a unified code of rules even more pressing was the diffusion of the game from the schools and universities to wider society. The mechanics of the process of dissemination are not too hard to envisage. There is a Webb Ellis-like implausibility in the popular picture of clubs springing up overnight once the son of the local squire or factory-owner brought home from his public school an oval ball. Yet something not too dissimilar must have happened when several old boys of the same school living and working in fairly close proximity to each other wished to continue playing the game they had known at school. Old Rugbeians in mid-century Liverpool first selected teams from among themselves on an alphabetic basis, A to M versus N to Z, or by matching the Football Club against the Boat Club. When in 1857 the Gentlemen of Liverpool met the Gentlemen of Manchester at Edge Hill, it was advertised as 'Rugby versus the World'. The social composition of Manchester FC, founded that year, is instructive. Its early players were products of Rugby, Manchester Grammar School, Uppingham, Edinburgh Academy, Fettes, Cheltenham and Oxbridge colleges. Several went on to be capped and they stimulated enough local interest to justify holding seven international matches at their Whalley Range ground between 1880, when the England v. Scotland match drew 8,000 spectators, and 1892. The club, though, was socially 'closed'. The annual subscription was fixed at 10s. 6d. in 1886, when a skilled workman's average weekly wage in Lancashire was 33s. 6d.; the distinction between 'the old nobility' and lesser mortals was expressed in differentiated membership fees and separate stands. It was this social exclusiveness that enabled soccer, which arrived later, to become the popular game in Manchester.[4]

All the northern clubs had respectable origins. York FC was founded in 1868 by ex-pupils of St Peter's School, York, Leigh (1877) by a local surveyor, St Helens three years earlier by an industrial chemist at Pilkingtons. Hull was formed in 1865 by the head of a shipping company, a wine merchant, a solicitor and ex-public schoolboys from Rugby and Cheltenham; more significantly, in 1871 a plumber, a glazier and a gas fitter also became members. Rochdale had clear gentry origins in 1867 but by 1881 there were as many as 57 rugby clubs in the district, fielding 80 teams.[5]

Clubs, like the football codes themselves, were not created *ex nihilo*, they were often built on pre-existing formations like schools, churches, places of work and neighbourhoods. Just as Aston Villa, Bolton, Everton and Burnley soccer clubs were familiar offshoots of the church's missionary activity, so were Wakefield Trinity (formed in 1873 by the Young Men's Society of Holy Trinity Church) and Bramley (1879); in Leeds, where there was little soccer until the 1890s, every church had its own rugby club, Leeds St John (1870) actually confining its membership to the church class. Headingley, after a faltering start, was revived in the mid-1880s by Headingley Hill Chapel's Sunday class.[6]

Nor was this a northern peculiarity. Northampton's sobriquet 'the Saints' dates from the original name of Northampton St James (1873); in the West Country, Newlyn owed its existence to a literary and debating society steered by a local vicar. In the Scottish Borders the Rev Dr James Barclay introduced the game 'to retard the drinking habits of the Canonbie colliers', while examples from Wales might include the Merthyr combinations Penydarren Church Juniors and Dowlais St Illtyd's, and Llanelli's St Peter's Stars and St Paul's United. Places of employment, too, generated their own teams. Camborne (1878) owed its playing strength to the tin workers of the Dolcoath mine, the largest in Cornwall, with some assistance from the ex-public school trainees of the Camborne School of Mines. Pontypridd Chainworks Crusaders and Llanelli's Wern Foundry and Copper Mills Rangers are Welsh examples of works teams. As for neighbourhood or street sides, 'Tinopolis's' Prospect Place Rovers and Gilbert Place Rangers could be matched from across the Bristol Channel by Bridgwater's Barclay Street Hornets, Albert Street Dreadnoughts and Bristol Road Rovers.[7]

Finding a permanent field to play on, however, could be a problem even to more formally organised clubs. Coventry lived a nomadic existence from its foundation in 1873 until it acquired the Coundon Road ground, its sixth, in 1916, while a metropolitan side like Wasps, ever-prey to voracious land developers, were forced to move five times in 12 seasons during the 1890s. By contrast Redruth, formed in 1895 on the initiative of some old Marlburians and Cliftonians in concert with the usual assortment of local petty bourgeoisie, managed to secure support, and a ground, from the Redruth Brewery Company. Patronage from this source was reminiscent of the traditional involvement of the drink trade in public amusements, while prominent local landowners and industrialists were similarly pleased to extend their patronage, from motives as diverse as family tradition, civic pride, personal gratification, and even something as uncomplicated as a love of the game.

A common solution to the problem of finding somewhere to play was to put the facilities of an existing cricket club to wider use. Like Derby County, Preston North End and other soccer teams, many rugby clubs had their beginnings in the desire of cricketers to extend their summer association into the winter. Bradford (1868), Wigan (1876) and Oldham (1876) in the north, Moseley and Coventry (both 1873) in the midlands, and Rosslyn Park (1879) in the south, as well as Swansea (1874) and Cardiff (1876), playing on the park behind the Cardiff Arms in Wales, and Gala (1876) in Scotland, all began as cricket clubs. In Belfast, the North of Ireland CC was persuaded by some of its ex-Cheltenham and Marlborough members to play 'football according to the Rugby rules' between cricket seasons, and NIFC came into existence in 1868.[8]

II

From Hell, Hull and Halifax, good Lord deliver us.
  Old proverb

The Rugby rules underwent a series of modifications throughout the 1870s. Partly from increasing player frustration at a static game of five-minute mauls (ironically, the initial effect of the abolition of hacking was to prolong mass scrummaging), partly through spectator demand for greater entertainment, modes of playing and scoring evolved which made for a more open game. By the late 1870s forwards were expected to heel the ball back and it was to give backs more of the ball and more room to run with it that in 1877 the number of players on each side was reduced to 15 and the forwards whittled down from 10 to 8 by the 1890s. A faster game called for more combination among both backs and forwards and provided for the display of individual skill. With the introduction of a points system of scoring in 1886, standardised throughout the four home countries in 1894, the try began its long march from being merely a preliminary to the initially more valuable kick at goal to being its equivalent, and eventually superior to the conversion. Deciding the outcome of games by points not only simplified the task of keeping score; it also separated winners from losers.

It was the high priority accorded to winning that gave northern, and soon Welsh, rugby its special flavour. As clubs proliferated in the industrial north, to become foci of communal identity and collective achievement, the establishing of the Yorkshire Challenge Cup in 1877 set an example which by 1882 the other northern counties had followed, except Lancashire whose more socially exclusive clubs were averse to this kind of competition. Teams returning with local, district or county trophies were greeted with torchlit processions and boisterous celebrations reminiscent of the unrestrained Wakes of earlier generations – industrialisation had done little to undermine much older habits of carnival and celebration.

Keenly contested cup games also raised the standard of football played, the perfecting of techniques and the elaboration of moves. Strong running centre three-quarters like Bradford's Rawson Robertshaw cultivated the art of carving openings for their wings, and powerfully-built athletic artisan forwards mastered the science of smart footwork, of wheeling the scrum and heeling the ball or dribbling it through in a controlled foot-rush, a speciality of the great Bradford and then Newport sides of the 1880s and 1890s. Although there were no northerners in the English XXs of the early 1870s, there were eleven of them in the England XV that beat Wales in 1892.[9]

Increasingly, seriousness of purpose allied to working-class strength and stamina saw northern sides inflicting consistent defeats on their southern opponents. Once the Rugby Union's county championship was established in 1888, Yorkshire won it for seven of the first eight seasons. By 1890 the county's affiliated 150 clubs constituted almost half the membership of the RFU. The social complexion of northern rugby was different from its southern counterpart dominated by ex-public schoolboys from the professions, occupationally far removed from industry and unsympathetic to it. The northern game was controlled by self-made men in manufacturing and commerce, who came into frequent contact with their employees and shared their enthusiasm for the Saturday afternoon's activities.

Northern rugby, in addition, was a mass spectator sport. In 1891 23,000 watched Yorkshire play Lancashire at Huddersfield; between 1888 and 1893 the Yorkshire Cup Final attracted on average audiences of over 15,000; in 1893 even a third-round cup-tie drew 27,600 to Headingley, more than had watched the FA Cup Final the previous year. Large crowds brought increased gate money, which might be spent on improving facilities to accommodate yet more spectators, or on making it worthwhile for clubs to induce players to forego a day's work in order to play.

Such tendencies were viewed with deep misgivings among the southern-based RFU, whose committee shared the distrust of their class for big crowds, especially working-class crowds, at a time of growing industrial unrest. Cup competitiveness exerted little appeal in the south. When in 1894 the idea was mooted for Middlesex, only seven entries were received. In the north it was too deeply entrenched to be resisted, but a further actively canvassed proposal to form a northern 'alliance' or league of first-class clubs was rejected, on the grounds that this would enhance the priority accorded to commercial considerations and further erode cherished amateur values. Had not the founding of the Football League in 1888 both legitimised and encouraged professionalism? At the RFU's annual meeting in September 1893 a Yorkshire proposal 'that players be allowed compensation for *bona fide* loss of time' was defeated. In August 1895 22 clubs seceded from the RFU to form the Northern Union. By 1898 they numbered 98.[10]

The consequences of 'the Great Schism' were profound. The RFU's intransigence preserved its middle-class ethos intact, but at some cost. It crippled itself numerically and financially. By 1903 the 481 member clubs of 1892 had fallen to 244 and not until the 1920s, a decade of triumphalist amateurism, was the 1893 figure re-attained. As for Yorkshire, having won the County Championship five times consecutively between 1892 and 1896 England's largest county did not win it again until 1926; Lancashire, the 1891 champions, not until 1935. And England? Their prospects were dashed

for nearly 20 years. The English XV did not win the international championship from 1892 to 1910.[11] The power in the land in these years was Wales.

III

> But Cyfartha is like a fisherman's net. The fly [-half] has been too clever. He
> should have passed to his wing long ago, but he is greedy and wants the try
> himself, and on he goes, tries to sell a dummy, and how the crowd is laughing,
> for to sell a dummy to Cyfartha is to sell poison to a Borgia.
>   Richard Llewellyn, *How Green Was My Valley* (1939), ch. 24

It was from England that rugby arrived in Wales, where a centuries-long
tradition of festive, unregulated football began to give way from the mid-
nineteenth century to the new sports emanating from the recently-formed
colleges and revived grammar schools of Lampeter, Llandovery, Cow-
bridge, Brecon and Monmouth. Old Rugbeians, it is true, were responsible
for getting the game established in Llanelli (1875) but the origins of other
clubs lay closer: Llandoverians figure prominently in the early history of
Neath (1871) and Monmouthians in Newport's (1874).[12]

The spread of the game in Wales depended on two other factors. One
was the support of that predictable cluster of upwardly mobile young professional men – solicitors, surveyors, small businessmen and building con-
tractors – who, though constituting still only 3 per cent of the population
of Wales as late as 1911, would retain a firm grasp on the running of its
rugby. Even in Wales it never became the people's game in the sense of
their achieving control over it. In this respect the Welsh experience was
no different from that of England.

In a second respect it was crucially different, for the arrival of rugby
coincided with the climax of the penetration of South Wales by industrial
capitalism. The existing population was quite unable to generate the labour
power necessary to meet the growing demand for Welsh steam-raising coal,
and the consequent high wage-levels attracted enormous migration into
the coalfield, the metal-working centres and the ports. By 1911, when the
population of Wales had increased by nearly a million since 1871, one
in every three occupied males was a miner, 256,000 of them, concentrated
in the southern industrial belt. Nothing has more influenced the outlook
and character of Welsh society, making it significantly different from that
of the large urban areas of England like Merseyside or Birmingham, than
this dependence on the primary production of coal. The observer who
drily remarked in 1923 that 'they know all about mining in Wales and
they apply their knowledge of it to Rugby Football' was nearer the truth
than he knew.[13]

Rugby's arrival in Wales in the 1870s predated that of soccer by 20 years. It met significant needs. It provided dramatic excitement and aesthetic satisfaction. In its appeal to a sense of shared ritual it fulfilled a valuable bonding function; it flourished both as a relief from and an analogue to the work experience, complementing as much as compensating for the sinking of the individual in the collective. At the same time, the aspiring commercial middle class who via the Welsh Rugby Union (1881) sought to control its breakneck growth were able to annex the responsible upper end of the working class as a wedge against the dissolute lumpenproletariat. The game was valued too as a focus for local and communal identity, a prized commodity in the ribbon-developed valleys which lacked appropriate civic foci. But we should never lose sight of the central appeal for an industrial population of a physically vigorous spectator sport: its theatricality, its opportunity for self-expression as well as for entertainment, its affirmation of life after work, of a sense of wholeness denied elsewhere.

What it did not do was instil in the crowd sporting habits or a devotion to clean living, any more than it civilised them or quelled their industrial militancy. It was less an agent of change than of continuity. The public house, for instance, always the favourite milieu of the sporting and sociable, effortlessly adapted itself to new conditions by providing changing rooms, committee facilities, even an early results service. Until they acquired their own premises well into the next century, Pontypridd rugby club was based at the White Hart, Rhymney at the Tredegar Arms, Penygraig at the Butcher's and Gowerton at the Commercial. One Merthyr hostelry even ran its own side, the Cyfarthfa Old Ship Rovers.

Proliferating cup competitions, in South Wales as in the north of England, honed local rivalries to a keen edge. The cup-tie between Bridgend and Neath in 1880 was the occasion for 'semi-savagery' and 'wanton biting'; the Llanelli team at Neath in 1883 'were left to the tender mercies of an infuriated mob and had almost to fight their way to the hotel ... they were hustled and pushed, hooted and pelted with clods, mud and even stones'. Between 1895 and 1900 Neath, Aberavon, Abertillery, Llanelli and Cardiff were among the leading clubs whose grounds were suspended because of rioting spectators. The game was as violent as the society that sustained it. Ferndale's game with Mountain Ash in 1897 was reckoned to be 'a blood bath'. During their traditional Boxing Day derby with neighbouring Dowlais that season, 'most of the Merthyr players were maimed'. Little wonder that the first of a local paper's 'Hints for rugby players' at this time was 'Hint 1: Make your will.'[14]

From an early date Welsh rugby was watched by larger numbers of spectators than anywhere outside the North of England. In 1893–4 when 12,000 watched the Scotland v. England international at Raeburn Place, 20,000 saw Cardiff's club matches with Newport and Swansea. The lustrous Swansea side of the early 1900s regularly drew crowds of 20,000 home and away. Welsh clubs also tended to add several thousand to away gates. In 1903 Bristol's steady 5,000 was increased to 8,000 for the visit of Swansea; 15,000 descended on the Devonport Albion ground to watch them in 1904. Receipts were correspondingly larger for Welsh games too. In 1890–1 Coventry's takings were £113 when Cardiff's were £1,233; by 1893–4 Cardiff's gate-money totalled £2,478, while Rosslyn Park's was £2 5s. 3d. In Wales they charged less and still did better. In 1905 12,000 spectators at Mardyke, Cork, paid £900 to watch Ireland play England, while 40,000 paid £2,000 to see the Irish at Swansea.[15]

Visits from crack northern sides like Dewsbury, Wakefield Trinity and Batley were being reciprocated by Welsh clubs from the mid-1880s, but the distance involved militated against frequent fixtures. Much nearer was English rugby's second heartland, a swathe reaching from the south midlands around the Severn Estuary into Somerset and Devon. The rugby links that were early on forged between the West Country and Welsh clubs anxious to prove themselves against good but also accessible opponents were reinforced by the thousands of immigrants from the metal and coal-mining areas of Somerset and the Forest of Dean, and by the incoming agricultural workers of the western counties attracted by the favourable wages of the Welsh coalfield. Some of the most renowned Welsh players of the period 1890–1914 were West Countrymen by birth. The Hancock brewing family from Wiveliscombe in Somerset, having identified the existence of a large thirst on the other side of the Bristol Channel, in 1883 moved to Cardiff to slake it. In 1884 Frank Hancock played a key role in the Cardiff rugby club's historic decision to field four threequarters and reduce the number of forwards to eight. By 1890 the other countries had also embraced the revolutionary 'Welsh system', a concept as enterprising and innovative as the brash, new, self-confident society that invented it. One of the greatest exponents of the four threequarter system, Cardiff's Gwyn Nicholls, captain of the famous Welsh side of 1905, was born in Gloucestershire.

Chronological priority can play as significant a role as geographical accident in determining cultural preference. Association football, based in northeast Wales near the soccer-playing conurbations of Merseyside and Manchester, began making inroads into South Wales only in the late 1890s. Billy Meredith as yet meant little to South Wales crowds. The name they conjured with was that of Newport's handsome, charismatic Arthur Gould, even to Yorkshire's Frank Marshall in 1893 'the central figure in the football world ... the greatest centre threequarter that has ever played'. In 1897 Gould, who had by then won more caps, scored more points and kicked more goals than any other player in the game, by his brilliance provoked a crisis as potentially destructive as that of 1893 over broken time. The International Rugby Board, founded by representatives of the four home countries in 1884 but at this stage virtually a puppet of the RFU, sought to expel Wales from the rugby community in 1897 for sanctioning a testimonial organised by Gould's countless admirers. The WRU stood its ground and the RFU was soon persuaded by its own clubs, who resented being deprived of their lucrative Welsh fixtures, to urge the restoration of Wales to the international fold in 1898.

For their part, the middle-class controllers of the game in Wales were equally firmly resolved to resist outright professionalism. They were however prepared to condone a certain amount of blindside remuneration in order to maintain amateur rugby's social function in Wales as a focus for a perceived community of interest. If rugby in Wales went professional it would be consigned to being a proletarian game enjoying no more than a regional status. The long-established northern manufacturers who lost no sleep about defying what the *Wigan Observer* in 1895 called 'the thraldom of southern gentry' had a different outlook from the administrators of the Welsh game anxious to assert their national identity within a British framework and to be accepted as equals beyond Wales. To them the creation of the Northern Union provided an avenue for those who wished to play professionally to do so. The activities of 'poachers' seeking to lure players north were less welcome. In 1899 a scout from Wigan was thrown into the sea at Penarth. 'Llanelli in football', wailed a 'Scarlet' supporter in 1897, 'has been to the Northern Union what Rhayader is to Birmingham in the matter of water supply.'[16] But its northern safety valve enabled rugby in Wales to remain firmly under amateur control.

It became indissolubly wedded to ideas of Welsh nationality in the wake of the events of a Saturday afternoon in December 1905, during Edwardian Wales's high noon of optimism and prosperity. The epic nature of that day's encounter is only partially explained in terms of the virtual invincibility of the two sides contending for what a contemporary New Zealand journalist called 'the world's championship in rugby'. Wales, riding the crest of a Golden Era which saw them win six Triple Crowns between 1900 and 1911, had just won their third Triple Crown in five years, while the All Blacks had swept through England, Scotland and Ireland destroying all opposition at club, county and national level, amassing over 800 points to a mere 27. Nor does its centrality pivot solely on Bob Deans' disputed try (conjured up after the match by Harmsworth's sensationalist *Daily Mail*)

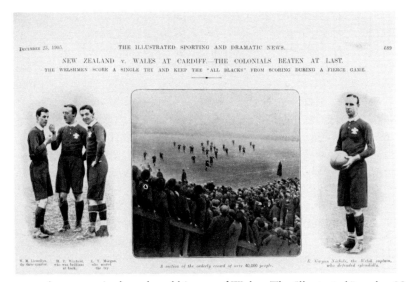

DECEMBER 23, 1905.   THE ILLUSTRATED SPORTING AND DRAMATIC NEWS.   689

NEW ZEALAND v. WALES AT CARDIFF.—THE COLONIALS BEATEN AT LAST.
THE WELSHMEN SCORE A SINGLE TRY AND KEEP THE "ALL BLACKS" FROM SCORING DURING A FIERCE GAME.

10.1 A moment in the cultural history of Wales. The *Illustrated London News*
records the only defeat of the 1905 All Blacks

which, if allowed, would have deprived Wales of a 3–0 victory. It was
not even that this was a victory for the kind of rugby played: the hard,
unrelenting forward power in intelligent combination with brilliant back
play of two smooth-running machines lubricated by well-practised tactical
ploys and ruses. What the victory really indicated was a collective national
achievement, and if there is any connection between sport and ideas of
national character, then 1905 stands out as not merely a landmark in the
history of Welsh rugby, or of rugby generally, but as a shaper of a wider
set of images about the whole culture and identity of a nation.[17] That
December afternoon was a moment in the cultural history of Wales.

IV

I believe that Rugby football . . . is the best instrument which we possess for
the development of manly character.
    H. H. Almond, 'Rugby football in Scottish schools' in Rev F. Marshall (ed.), *Football:
    The Rugby Union Game* (1892), p. 56

The only country able to rival Wales's triumphant advance in the first
decade of the twentieth century was Scotland, as difficult to beat at Inverleith
(Murrayfield was not opened till 1925) as Wales were everywhere else. While
the Scots always had exceptionally able individual players like K. M.

McLeod and 'Darkie' Bedell-Sivright, they subordinated the cult of the star performer to the thrill of the skilfully-controlled forward foot-rush. Nothing was more calculated to inspire the Scots than the cry 'Feet, Scotland', though this was countered by the shout of 'Brains, Wales' at Swansea in 1900.[18]

It was the Scots, too, who were the hardiest defenders of pristine amateurism, from the Gould dispute onwards taking particular exception to the presentation of mementoes. In 1907 they refused Pontypridd permission to make a presentation to their Scottish international D. M. McGregor. When in 1912 Stade Bordelais, the French champions, advertised in a Scottish newspaper offering a good business situation to a suitable outside-half, the SRU moved quickly to get the French authorities to impose life suspensions on the president, coach and committee of the offending club.[19]

Scottish rugby conservatism was personified by J. Aikman Smith, who served on the SRU in various capacities from 1887 to his death in 1931. Aikman Smith was a former pupil of Edinburgh's Royal High School, and Scottish rugby owed its inception, and for many years its character, to the Scottish Academies whose powerful rivalries extended into senior football. The Scottish Rugby Union, founded in 1873, was established and dominated by a closely-knit group of private schools in Edinburgh like the Academy, Merchiston, Loretto and Royal High where, under the aegis of reforming headmasters like H. H. Almond of Loretto, the Rugby School game was introduced in the 1850s by teachers who had studied at English schools and universities. Almond's pronouncements tended to begin with the ominous 'All boys...' All boys in the school had to play rugby unless exempted by the school medical officer; all boys were to be accurately weighed and measured twice a term, for 'nothing makes a boy believe in a good physical system so soon as the increase of his measurements'.[20]

Yet it is not to brawn and bone nor to a Calvinist-induced dour streak that we need look to account for the conservatism of Scottish rugby, but to the simple fact that here was a regime where men at 30 were still playing the same opponents as when they were 15 and in school. This was bound to breed a certain resistance to change. Although the Edinburgh game spread to Glasgow where the West of Scotland CC, former pupils of east coast schools and Glasgow Academy, began to play rugby from 1865, social exclusiveness was again rigidly safeguarded by charging high entry fees, restricting membership to products of particular schools and by careful choice of fixtures. West of Scotland and Glasgow Academicals, for instance, generally ignored requests for fixtures from new clubs, or, if such games were inadvertently arranged, turned out their second teams. Glasgow rugby remained insular, non-competitive and little publicised, 'a minority activity which confirmed and sustained a well-established, shared fellowship among a particular social grouping'.[21]

A quite different kind of atmosphere prevailed in the Borders where the game, radiating out from schools like Galashiels Academy and Kelso High, began to make serious inroads in the 1880s. While Edinburgh's sides were for former pupils in business there, in Langholm (1871), Hawick (1872), Gala (1875) and Melrose (1877) the game was played by weavers, masons and artisans who for studs barred their working boots with strips of leather from the driving belts in the local tweed mills. The small-town self-awareness of the Borders, with their historic rivalries and less marked class divisions – 'it is not too much to say', reported an Edinburgh journalist in 1911, 'that all classes in Melrose from the city fathers and ministers of churches down to the humblest follower have an interest in the doings of the club' – made for communal involvement, fiercely partisan crowds, and rough play. By 1890 crowds of 4,000 and upwards, drawn from a population too scattered to support professional football, congregated noisily for the visits of smart-aleck city sides who were often the recipients of excessive vigour which the SRU punished with swift disciplinary measures.[22]

The former pupils of the Scottish Union were by the beginning of the century barely able to conceal their distrust of the working man's involvement in the game. In 1903 the prominent Scottish referee Crawford Findlay expressed surprise that Wales selected miners, steelworkers and policemen for their international teams when such players should really have joined the Northern Union. It was an attitude the Borders had come to live with. Increasing dissatisfaction at the SRU's high-handedness and constant neglect of local players almost precipitated the secession of the Border clubs in the 1890s. Scotland had been playing international rugby for 20 years before Adam Dalgleish of Gala became the first Border cap, and it was another 10 before a Border player, T. M. Scott of Hawick, actually captained the national side. The establishment of the Border League in 1903, reluctantly sanctioned by the SRU, widened the cultural gap between Border and city rugby but it was intimately connected with Scotland's ability to mount a serious challenge to Welsh pre-war dominance: with the emergence of the Border international player, Scottish rugby had found its equivalent of 'the Rhondda forward'.

Another rugby stronghold characterised by the same mix of social inclusiveness and anti-urbanism was the southwest of England, where in the early years of the century thousands of excursionists travelled to see Weston, Tavistock, Bath and Bridgwater compete for the Somerset Cup, and where fighting among players and spectators was a common occurrence. Further west, Plymouth Albion, already watched by crowds of 6,000 in the 1890s, could draw 19,000 on a Wednesday afternoon in 1905 for the visit of Oxford University. Clearly the extensively-covered All Blacks tour injected English rugby with new blood, and aggravated old problems. Coventry's 1906 Boxing Day match with Moseley degenerated into unlicensed mayhem between players and spectators. As the west midlands became a soccer stronghold, rugby in the east midlands built up an enduring popular base. At Leicester 16,000 watched the All Blacks and 14,000 the 1906 Springboks. Second only to Leicester for enthusiasm were Northampton's 'Saints', by the century's turn enjoying gates of 14,000 for games with their great rivals the 'Tigers', and away support, especially to London, of up to 3,000 followers.[23]

The evident spectator-orientated nature of West Country and midland rugby did not escape the vigilant eye of the player-orientated RFU. Leicester came near to being suspended for broken-time irregularities in 1908, and Coventry *were* in 1909, when a scrutiny of their account books revealed that illegal payments had been disguised as the cost of lemons and towels. Coventry were promptly suspended and watched helplessly as they lost their ground and several players to a professional organisation that joined the Northern Union. Factors at work here were the arrival of NU players from Salford and elsewhere to work in the motor industry, and welling interest in the success of Coventry City AFC which had driven the rugby organisation to adopt protective measures of its own. The rapid incursion of Southern League football into South Wales and the West Country was similarly not unconnected to the attempt to establish professional rugby there between 1908 and 1912.[24] There was an audience for football played seriously and skilfully whatever the shape of the ball. It was amateur rugby's middle-class ideologues, and die-hards on each side, who sought to erect sectarian barriers between the various codes.

A more virulent sectarianism coloured the history of Irish rugby from the beginning. Rugby took root there as a colonial reflection of the structure and social context of the game in England. It arrived via old boys of Rugby and Cheltenham at Trinity College Dublin, notoriously the bastion of Anglo-Saxon Protestant culture, and the early members of the Irish RFU established at TCD in 1874 were mostly schools and colleges. At the end of the nineteenth century the wily Irish critic Jacques McCarthy distinguished between the three kinds of football played in Ireland as follows: 'In Rugby you play the ball, in Association you kick the man if you cannot kick the ball, and in Gaelic you kick the ball if you cannot kick the man.' In the south of Ireland rugby would always suffer from the popularity of Gaelic football, whose practitioners, according to McCarthy, 'are a free and fierce community based in Drumcondra, co. Dublin, conveniently situated between Glasnevin graveyard and the Mater Misericordia Hospital'. The Gaelic Athletic Association's foreign games ban introduced in 1886 inhibited the growth of rugby, especially in rural Ireland; 'the pseudo-Saxon game' made more headway in the towns, though only in Limerick did it acquire anything like a working-class following.[25]

A north–south division manifested itself in the organisation of Irish rugby from the outset. The North of Ireland RU founded in 1875 took almost five years to join the Dublin-based union in 1879. The game began in the north in the Protestant and Royal Schools like the Royal Belfast Academy, Portora, Londonderry Academical Institution and Magee College; and from there to the towns. Collegians (1890) were the former pupils of Belfast Methodist College, and Instonians (1919) those of the Royal Belfast Academical Institution, but rugby in that city remained socially exclusive and after the founding of the Irish FA there in 1880 soccer became Ulster's dominant game.

In some of the moderate-sized towns of the north rugby reached beyond its professional base to embrace a wider audience. Dungannon, all but one of whose side in 1873 were graduates of TCD, was well known in the 1900s for its large and partisan crowd, among the most vociferous a number of elderly ladies in shawls. Rugby could on rare occasions even transcend the religious divide, witness the triumphant homecoming in 1908 of the City of Derry team bearing the Irish Provincial Towns Cup and accompanied by a Protestant *and* Catholic flute band. For the most part the game in the north, with its segregated school system and an embattled Catholic community unable to afford the same ambiguity in its sporting affiliations as the professional classes in the Republic, was and remains almost exclusively a middle-class, Anglophile, Protestant activity.[26]

The history of rugby in Northern Ireland, therefore, like most aspects of life there, can scarcely be understood without reference to its political context. Thus, while rugby on the mainland came to a halt just as the 1914–15 season was about to begin, in Ulster the Home Rule crisis had already brought sporting activity to a standstill nine months earlier. In December 1913, NIFC decided 'that in view of the political crisis all matches for the second half of the season should be cancelled so that members who are identified with the Ulster Volunteer Force and the Unionist Clubs might have more leisure to devote themselves to the work of drilling and otherwise preparing for eventualities'. All fixtures were cancelled from 14 January 1914 and 'North's' Ormeau ground given over to the UVF.[27]

By August 1914 even wider issues were at stake, though not to the Irish: Kevin Barry of UCD Rugby Club and Frederick Browning, President of the IRFU, were both killed during the Easter Rebellion. In Britain the national unions sent out circulars urging all their members to join up. The WRU insured itself against defeat home and away: 'If only every man in every First XV in Wales were to enlist, what a magnificent body there would be at the service of our country and even then there would still be plenty of players left to enable the game to be played as usual.'[28]

Clubs up and down the country surrendered their grounds for recruiting, drilling and other military purposes, and there was no shortage of volunteers. Seven junior clubs in the Llanelli district provided more than 400 men, the Keswick XV presented themselves at their Drill Hall as one body, Leicester's formidable secretary-manager Tom Crumbie personally recruited 4,500, and the WRU's secretary, Walter Rees, was given the title of Captain for his domestic wartime efforts. Rugby was seen by its own as setting a patriotic example that 'others' – meaning the soccer fraternity – might have done better to emulate.[29]

'If the first 100,000 British soldiers in the war had not been sportsmen', asserted a speaker at Bath FC's Golden Jubilee dinner (an event postponed from 1915 to 1919) 'they would not have known how to take defeat and eventually turn back the Germans.' The classic equation between war and sport, familiarly expressed in Newbolt's 'Vitai Lampada' of 1898, with its juxtaposition of the bumping pitch and the jammed Gatling, reached its apotheosis in the hideous carnage of the Western Front. The English fondness for football was seen as an element in their superiority over the Germans. Two years into the war an Old Malvernian took issue in his school magazine with a master who had suggested the school give up rugby: 'Rugger must stay. What a confession of weakness to give it up now.' His letter was dated: The Somme, 14 November 1916.[30] A well-attested expression of the sporting spirit was to kick a football towards the enemy lines and follow it. The annual Mobbs Memorial Match between the East Midlands and the Barbarians was inaugurated in 1921 to commemorate Edgar Mobbs of Northampton and England who used to lead his men into attack by punting a rugby ball into No Man's Land and following it up. This 'preposterous act of bravado', in Paul Fussell's words, terminated his life at Passchendaele at 34 years of age.[31]

Rugby football even had its own Rupert Brooke (himself an old Rugbeian) in Ronald Poulton (-Palmer), educated at Rugby and Balliol and holder of 17 caps for England. He scored five tries in his first Varsity match in 1909 and four on his last international appearance in 1914, the year he inherited the Huntley and Palmer biscuit fortune, provided he added the name Palmer to Poulton. This done he joined the 4th Royal Berkshires and was hit by a sniper's bullet in Belgium at 25 years of age in 1915. The flagrant good looks of 'the wondrous Poulton, the fleet and flaxen' seemed an inseparable element of his sporting achievement and he was sonorously lamented in similar terms to Brooke as a Newboltian hero, a 'golden-haired Apollo' who 'stood as a symbol of the heart of England ... of the golden young men who died faithfully and fearlessly in a war where much that was of value beyond price in an imperfect world perished too'.[32] He was one of 27 English internationals killed, as well as 30 Scottish, 13 Welsh and 9 Irish, excluding those who died of their war injuries later. Bristol, who like many other clubs built a Memorial Ground after the war in tribute 'to those who played the Great Game during season 1914–18', lost 300 players and members; Headingley lost a quarter of its membership. Of the 60 players who turned out in the four teams fielded by London Scottish on the last Saturday of the 1913–14 season, 45 were killed.[33]

V

A man who kicks another intentionally is a blackguard and a coward. Recently a well-known International ... said that a gentleman kicks another with his instep instead of with the toe of the boot. Personally I think no gentleman ever kicks another.

 I. M. B. Stuart, *The Theory of Modern Rugby Football* (1930), pp. 3–4

The sanctimonious tendency to portray rugby's amateurs, who in 1914 had flocked unselfishly to the colours, as more patriotic than soccer's paid professionals, who in 1915 had to be reminded of their duty, was a factor in the pronounced post-war swing towards rugby among 'good' schools and those that aspired to be thought of as such. For a diversity of reasons – disdain for the 'pools and Woodbine' image of professional soccer, desire to revive the public-school ethos, the anxieties aroused by post-war militancy and the perceived 'character-building' quality of the Union game – soccer-playing schools moved over in droves to rugby and to the higher social cachet it brought with it. The drift anticipated from 1910 by Radley, Rossall, Emmanuel and Pocklington soon became a stampede among minor public and socially-ambitious grammar schools: a sample would include Beaumont College (1917), Felstead (1919), Worksop, Wrekin and King's Worcester (1921), Manchester GS (1922), Framlingham and Ipswich (1924), Colchester RGS (1926), Magdalen CS and Wycliffe (1928). This shift took place to a rising accompaniment of literary affectation celebrating 'the rugby spirit'. Public-school fiction, like English rugby whose virtues it extolled, revived in popularity, especially the late Victorian stories of Talbot Baines Reed, who had regaled *Boy's Own Paper* readers with tales of the Cock House of Fellsgarth: ' "Well played indeed, Corder!",' cried his captain to the scholarship boy who has just scored the winning try and put the snobs to shame. 'Oh what music is the sound. What would he dare not now!'[34]

Nor was there any lack of practical advice as to how rugger should be played by these post-war Corinthians. Among the precepts listed by a widely-read 1922 compendium of rugby hints were 'Never dispute the referee's decision', and 'Keep your mouth shut: all good athletes breathe through their nostrils.' *A Manual of Rugby Football for Public Schools* that appeared in 1925 addressed itself to graver issues: 'Nothing looks worse than for a player to have his stockings about his ankles, and it certainly takes yards off his pace. No player who is too slack to go to the trouble of finding a pair of garters is worth his place in any team.'[35]

During the 1920s English rugby enjoyed a period of prolonged success, as if it were actually thriving on its middle-class tennis-and-golf image of suburban sporting gentility. This decade saw the number of clubs in membership of the RFU increase at the fastest rate in its history, with 231 new clubs becoming affiliated to it as opposed to 45 in the years 1901–9. These years too saw the proportion of public-school educated players in the English side at its highest: 572, compared with 422 for 1902–11 and 262 for 1962–71.[36] England won the Triple Crown four times in the 1920s and another twice in the 1930s. Self-confidence expressed itself in a number of tactical innovations centred particularly on the back-row of the scrum from where W. W. Wakefield led the side in robust fashion. Enormous crowds filled Twickenham on international days. While a modest 18,000 had been present for England's opening game there in 1910, 49,000 watched the Calcutta Cup match of 1924, and 73,000 the England v. New Zealand game in 1936. During the inter-war period big matches at Twickenham were social occasions for 'the grand assembly of the Forsyte commonwealth, the parade of the self-possessive class'.[37]

The distinctive feature of the Twickenham crowd, in rugby terms, was its ignorance. It attracted, as it still does and in far greater numbers than other major grounds, thousands of people apparently willing to shout themselves hoarse at what they would not cross the road to see at their local recreation ground. In A. G. Macdonell's satirical *England, Their England* (1933) – it is noticeable how in the inter-war period rugby began to acquire something of the literary status already gained by cricket – Donald attends the 1930 Varsity Match along with 65,000 others 'of whom about 30,000 appeared to be young men, 30,000 young women, and 5,000 parsons'. In the train afterwards there were two schools of opinion, one believing that Cambridge had won 19–6, the other that Oxford had, by either 15–0 or 24–0. Only the evening paper settled the matter: the game had been a 3–3 draw.[38]

As a success symbol Twickenham was rivalled only by Murrayfield,

10.2 The middle-class gambol at Twickenham during the 1932 Middlesex 'Sevens'

opened in 1925 with a capacity of 80,000. Scotland won three Triple Crowns and won or shared five championships between the wars, while the official mind of Scottish rugby remained as fearful of change as ever. Since 1927 Wales and England had worn numbered jerseys, but the SRU would have none of it. When George V mildly inquired at Twickenham in 1928 why the Scots did not similarly identify their players, Aikman Smith told him it was a rugby match and not a cattle market. This was also the attitude of senior players like J. D. Bannerman, who brought pressure to bear on socially inferior Border players to resist numbering, which came about only after the death of Aikman Smith in 1931 and Bannerman's own retirement the following year. International occasions at Murrayfield, as at Twickenham, were great middle-class affairs, the Princes Street pre-match parade being, in Allan Massie's words, 'an affirmation of confidence in the rightness in the way the world was ordered'.[39]

That confidence was less in evidence in the Border textile towns, where contracting markets, declining production and rising unemployment made for a harsher environment. The return to the gold standard and changing fashions – a flapper needed a quarter of the cloth required by an Edwardian woman – drove many producers out of work and those employed in textiles in Scotland fell nearly 25,000 between 1924 and 1935. In these years textile-

10.3 Scottish rugby supporters arrive in London in 1936 for the international. They are not from the Gorbals.

dependent Langholm's rugby fortunes took a sharp downturn, whereas Kelso, to whom farming and agriculture mattered more, enjoyed a much happier period. By contrast, economic malaise affected a community club like Melrose to the extent that in April 1935 it decided that 'damage to dentures during a game would not be paid for in future' and a dentist's estimate was even required for repairs to natural teeth.[40] The late 1930s, when textile manufacture recovered and knitwear production began to cater for an increasing leisure market, brought a revival of Border rugby, though Scotland's 1938 Triple Crown, like those of 1933 and 1925 before it, was won by a side manned almost entirely by former pupils and Anglo-Scots.

Scottish rugby was dealt no more than a glancing blow by the Depression because unemployment, which stood at 25 per cent of the insured Scottish workforce in 1932, was concentrated in the soccer areas of heavy industry in west and central Scotland. The corresponding figure for Wales that year was 40 per cent, and was far higher in the ravaged valleys of Welsh rugby's heartland.[41] During the inter-war years the population of Wales actually fell in absolute numbers for the first time since 1801. The 265,000 miners employed in South Wales in 1920 fell to 138,000 by 1933. With over half the population – 56 per cent in 1930 – engaged in mining and the metallurgical industries, the fall in the wages bill from 65 million pounds to 14 million eddied out into the furthest reaches of the community. By the early 1930s, when unemployment in the southeast of England was around 11 per cent and the 'self-possessive class' paraded at Twickenham, it stood at 43 per cent in the Rhondda, 59 per cent in Merthyr, 76 per cent in Pontypridd and 85 per cent in Abertillery. Nearly half a million people moved out of Wales in these years, the entire national increase of a quarter of a century and another 93,000 as well. Moreover, 50 per cent of those leaving Glamorgan between 1921 and 1937 were in the 15 to 29 age group, a loss which had miserable repercussions for its sport.

South Wales's whole social fabric took a fearful beating as the collective achievements of the pre-war period – chapels, trade unions, workmen's institutes, choirs and rugby clubs – crumbled. The WRU's takings halved during the 1920s as international crowds fell away and clubs defaulted. The Union was besieged by requests for help from clubs desperately trying to keep afloat. Cross Keys, Ebbw Vale, Pontypool, Blaenavon and Pontypridd sought financial assistance during 1926–7 in the aftermath of the crippling coal stoppage of 1926. As soup kitchens opened, rugby clubs closed. Rhymney rugby club closed down completely between 1924 and 1933. Cwmbran had no option when the local colliery laid off 1,300 men within a twelve month in 1926–7. By 1928 the work of two and a half thousand men at Senghenydd had been terminated; in 1929, when nearly every member of the team was unemployed, the club disbanded. So, that year, did Tredegar and Treherbert. Steel-making in Ebbw Vale ceased in 1929 too, putting 10,000 out of work. Despite a reduced admission charge and a catchment area of 40,000, gate receipts at Ebbw Vale Park seldom reached one pound, and in 1932 the club was forced into the indignity of seeking public assistance.

Not surprisingly the tensions of these years spilled on to the field. Since joining the constabulary was one alternative to immigration or long-term unemployment, there were more policemen than miners in Welsh sides of the inter-war years. In 1926 six of the Welsh eight forwards were policemen; Cardiff had on average ten policemen in its First XV every year from 1923 to 1939. As sports personalities these gentle giants were held in some affection; in parts of the coalfield there was less admiration for the institution they represented as strikers and strike-breakers settled their scores in the course of murderously violent matches. In a game in the Swansea Valley one constable, recognised as having swung his truncheon too freely during the 1925 anthracite strike, was crippled for life. In the Afan Valley, in one of the single-industry communities north of Port Talbot where a state of virtual guerrilla warfare prevailed, a referee went on to the field with a revolver strapped to his waist.[42]

Its infrastructure grievously impaired, the Welsh XV's performance in these years was disastrous. They won only 9 games out of 32 between 1923 and 1930 as the other countries began achieving their first victories in Wales since the 1890s. A demoralised Wales lost consistently away from home, even in Paris in 1928; it was 23 years before they won at all at Twickenham. Lack of success was cause and effect of selectorial myopia and administrative inadequacy. Tactical bankruptcy on the field reflected financial insolvency off it.

The marked contrast between the Welsh inter-war experience and that of the rugby-playing areas beyond it is underlined by Wales's human repayment of its pre-1900 debt to the West Country. The ten years from 1926 were, by its own reckoning, 'glorious' ones for Torquay RFC who had three international and countless other Welshmen playing for them. Weston RFC enjoyed similarly unprecedented success, not unconnected to the town council's policy of placing adverts in Welsh newspapers offering work opportunities to the unemployed – 'more particularly centre threequarters and forwards' – so that by the 1930s, when there were up to twelve exiles in the side, they were known as 'Weston Welsh'.[43]

It was not only the West Country that benefited from the Welsh diaspora. The population of Coventry expanded from 128,000 in 1921 to 220,000 in 1939, making it the fastest growing city in Britain. In 1934 its unemployment rate was 5.1 per cent. By 1937 it was estimated that 21.5 per cent of all immigrants to Coventry were Welsh, as thousands of predominantly young males flooded into the west midlands to infuse local politics, trade unionism and an indigenous but ailing rugby tradition with new life.[44] The Welsh in exile brought about a quickening of interest in other quarters, too. In the early thirties Sale increased their gates substantially by urging people to 'come and see the two Welsh centres' Wooller and Davey.[45] In 1935 this pair were the architects of Wales's 13–12 defeat of the Third All Blacks, a victory overshadowed outside Wales by Prince A. Obolensky's two remarkable cinema–newsreeled tries in England's 13–0 win over the tourists the following month. In Wales itself there was no doubting the significance of the narrower victory. Seen as symbolic of a wider process of social and economic recovery, what was gratifying was not merely the manner in which fourteen men had hung on to win, or the open 'schoolboy' rugby they played, but the composition of the team itself, a satisfying blend of college-educated backs and tinplate workers, colliers and policemen in

10.4 This young Welsh supporter looks alone in the Strand, but off-camera are 15,000 of his fellow countrymen, in London for the 1937 match with England

the pack. 'Wales is proud of this victory', declared the conservative *Western Mail*. 'Welsh peers and labourers – with all the intervening stratas [*sic*] of society – were united in acclaiming and cheering the Welsh team. It was... a victory for Wales that probably is impossible in any other sphere.'[46]

VI

A first-class Rugby player is a public figure, a public entertainer, a public servant, and a part of the national life of the country.
    Rowe Harding, *Rugby Reminiscences and Opinions* (1929), p. 141

The return of peace and the lack of alternative outlets for the release of savings brought a sport-starved nation flocking back to the football grounds of Britain. The international rugby tourney was resumed in 1947, to be promptly dominated by Ireland whose slight rugby base had been unscathed by the war. It is tempting to link the consecutive Irish Triple Crowns of the late forties to Ireland's political, economic and cultural transformation in that decade but rugby remained rooted among the urban,

Anglophile, professional sector, reflecting and maintaining class and status identity in the Republic as much as in the North.[47]

The rekindled interest in rugby across the Irish Sea was still no match for the enthusiasm on the British mainland where club matches, in Wales anyway, were watched by crowds equal only to those on international days in Belfast and Dublin and comparable to the high attendances at league soccer games in England and Scotland, whose own rugby clubs could not approach anywhere near the 20–30,000 crowds that consistently turned up to watch the first-class Welsh sides. Even Leicester had a total match attendance of only 21,000 in 1949–50. Bedford, it is true, could show a precisely aggregated figure of 47,449 for that year, but both were exceeded by the 48,500 that watched one match alone, between Cardiff and Newport, in February 1951. This world record for an ordinary club match was not so exceptional at the time; in 1952 40,000 watched Cardiff at Swansea, and by 1955–6 Newport v. Cardiff derbies were still drawing 30,000 to Rodney Parade and 35,000 to the Arms Park.[48] Twickenham attained a record attendance of 75,000 for the Welsh game of 1950, and Murrayfield's 1951 Scotland v. Wales figure of 80,000 remained a record until 104,000 saw the same fixture in 1975, the readiness of 25,000 or more Welshmen, and women, to travel to away games inflating the size of the crowd on both occasions.

Welsh supporters had begun travelling in large numbers in the 1930s. Post-1945 they had greater incentives and improved means to do so as confidence returned to both their society and its rugby. Full employment, substantial capital investment, government-sponsored advance factories and low-interest loans helped diversify Welsh industry. In 1950 Wales won their first Triple Crown since 1911 and did so again in 1952, thanks to a combination of extremely fit ex-servicemen, teacher-training college products and manual workers, for as late as 1950 coal-mining still accounted for one in four industrial jobs in Wales.

Elsewhere in Britain, changes in occupational structure and rising expectations were more pronounced as average real weekly earnings began a rise which saw them almost double between 1950 and 1980. Rugby could not be immune to these changes and by the early sixties their effect was being registered. Attendances at club matches entered on a secular decline as televised Saturday afternoon sport and changing leisure patterns took their toll. A survey of the leading English clubs in the late fifties showed Gloucester to be the best supported with 5,000 a match, Leicester, Bristol and the Harlequins averaging 4,000, and Bath and Coventry barely two thousand. Their best attendances were generally for Welsh sides who brought their own supporters and pulled in Welsh exiles. Although support in Wales held up, the kind of 35,000 crowd that watched Cardiff play Llanelli in 1958 was increasingly the exception as the live televising of international matches brought rugby to its widest-ever audience while sapping its grassroots. When the Calcutta Cup match was shown live in March 1957, Bath's usual crowd of a few thousand for the visit of the United Services was reduced to a paltry 261.[49]

Measures were required to reconcile televised internationals with the demands of regular club fixtures, and to lift the game out of the defensively-minded, low-scoring rut into which it was sinking. One notorious international in 1963 was punctuated by 111 line-outs, while the resurgence of soccer after England's 1966 World Cup triumph finally spurred rugby's administrators into a long-overdue legislative overhaul. The most far-reaching among a flurry of amendments geared to improving the game – many of them borrowed from increasingly televised Rugby League – was the introduction in 1968 of the 'dispensation law' which, by prohibiting direct kicking to touch outside the defending 25-yard line, reduced the number of line-outs, kept the ball in play for longer and encouraged running with the ball. The increased value of the try to four points in 1971 was also in keeping with the liberalising tendencies of the period, though its benefits were soon smothered in a blanket of legislative adjustments that made the goal-kicker the most valued member of his side, as he had been a hundred years earlier. Even Harold Wilson's 1960s catchphrase 'the white heat of the technological revolution' rubbed off on rugby, particularly in Wales which in 1967 became the first country to adopt a national coaching and squad system. These innovations, complemented by a gleaming technical vocabulary which soon became the stock-in-trade of every self-respecting pundit, coincided with the emergence – again in Wales and emanating from changes within the national culture[50] – of a handful of astonishingly gifted performers who brought to the game a new and enterprising awareness of its potentialities. Based on the London Welsh club where mobile young graduate teachers and medical students like John Dawes, Gerald Davies, J. P. R. Williams and Mervyn Davies exploited in a freely chosen, stimulating environment the implications of the new laws, and enhanced by the further inputs of such remarkable players as Gareth Edwards, Barry John, Michael Gibson and David Duckham, British rugby acquired some of the panache of the Dutch total footballers of that era. In the early 1970s, it briefly flared as the most attractive and successful in the world.

Scotland's hidebound past effectively prevented it from making more than spasmodic contributions to British rugby until the 1980s. An enduring legacy of the Aikman Smith era was the instinctive response of the SRU to say 'no' to any new proposal and then think about it. The traditionalism of Scottish rugby, in the hallowed form of the elsewhere long-outmoded 3–2–3 scrum formation, survived well into the 1950s as diehards died very hard in defence of a game by then half a century out of date. A demoralising catalogue of 17 consecutive international defeats between 1951 and 1955 impelled the SRU to set up training courses, though not for club coaches – they would have to wait until 1969 – but, characteristically, for schoolmasters charged with 'the production of better citizens'. By the end of the 1960s it was clear that FP rugby was in terminal decline as the products of Edinburgh Academy, Heriot's and George Watson's preferred to play in the more competitive atmosphere of Border rugby. From the early 1970s Melrose and Hawick replaced the Academies as the principal feeders of the Scottish team. The players' new demand for squad sessions on the Welsh model was partially met by the appointment in 1972 not of a national coach but an 'adviser', a designation evocative of US military personnel in the Third World. In 1973 Scotland then stunned everyone by instituting a national league which did nothing to strengthen the tenuous hold of rugby on Glasgow (in fact it further weakened it as the city's players gravitated to outlying clubs like Kilmarnock and Ayr) but which did forge new links between central and Highland Scotland and the Borders.[51]

The winds of change began gusting through the corridors of English rugby too in the late 1960s. It was not only a new generation of Welsh players that emerged from a society shaped but no longer dominated by a traditional industrial culture. Fran Cotton was born into a mining community near Wigan in 1948. His father had left school to join his six brothers and their father in the local pit. His nonconformist upbringing was suffused with collective memories of the 1920s when the local weekly wage was two pounds and professional rugby players brought home six pounds after a win. Education was the way out, via the eleven-plus to a rugby-playing grammar-school and Loughborough. It was the game played at school that determined the shape of the ball played by other young lads from working-class backgrounds like Steve Smith in Macclesfield, Ian McLaughlan in Ayr and Willie John McBride in rural Antrim.[52]

With the perks that came in the wake of increased media attention in the 1970s, the attractions of the professional game receded for leading players like these. By the end of the decade rugby players were no longer the teachers and sales representatives of the 1950s or even the 1960s; they were increasingly the financial advisers, building society managers and business executives of a commercial world in which rugby personalities were now marketable assets. As the audience for live televised internationals rose to a consistent 8 million, the benefits of advertising did not go unappreciated by the commercial sector, the national rugby unions, or the players themselves.

The appearance from the mid-1970s of advertising hoardings at national and club grounds indicated that commercialisation was encroaching significantly on amateur rugby. Tobacco companies and soft drinks firms pumped money into cup competitions in England and Wales, and by the 1980s international matches were attracting sponsorship worth several hundred thousands of pounds. Some sponsors seemed well suited to their events: it was Dulux Paints who sponsored the 23–3 whitewash of Wales by New Zealand in 1980, while a £1.6 million deal with Courage brewers to establish a club championship in England in 1987 prompted the RFU, mindful of their undistinguished international record over the previous 20 years, to remark that they needed all the Courage they could get.[53] In these circumstances, and where every international match could generate half a million pounds, top players, keenly aware of the vast sums available in other sports, began feeling that the professional standard of performance increasingly expected of them was worth more than generous expenses. The development of sponsorship has accelerated the drive to overt professionalism.

VII

There is practically nothing new to be written about Rugby Football.
P. C. Adams, captain of Old Edwardians in the 1880s, *A Lecture on Rugby Football* (Birmingham, 1926), p. 4

In the last 20 years Rugby Union has transformed both itself and its audience. But not beyond all recognition. It is still, in Scotland, a rallying point for the respectable. It is still, in Wales a barometer of the national condition, whose sorry state for much of the 1980s was reflected in debilitating self-doubt and recurrent defeat. Irish rugby continues, miraculously, to avoid Partition. Politics may never be far from the surface – when the Ulster troubles spilled over into the south in 1972, both Scotland and Wales refused to play in Dublin[54] – but consistency, too, underlies the reassuringly unpredictable fortunes of Irish rugby: in 1979 34 of Ireland's 45 senior clubs were still town-based, and doctors and civil servants still dominated the national side.[55]

Stands English rugby where it did? The clubhouse is less of an aggressively heterosexual male preserve than it once was, even if the ban on ladies entering one in the northeast was lifted only in 1971.[56] Changing patterns in family life, the greater emancipation of women and the attractions of the late-night disco have combined to erode the ritualist subculture of the 'Zulu Warrior' and his drunken acolytes.[57] Even Twickenham's image as a bastion of male chauvinism was severely dented in 1987 when the Women's

Definitely 'The Man's Game' whether

10.5 watching, as tickets for the ball are sold to Rugby League spectators at Leigh in 1949

10.6 or playing, like this South of England Public Schools xv of the same period

10.7 Rugby's version of kissing the Blarney Stone. Irish tomfoolery before the game against England at Lansdowne Road, Dublin, in 1951

RFU final was played there.[58] Beyond, rugby in the shires and on the leafier fringes of urban-industrial England remains little changed from the appearance it presented in 1960, when a study of Banbury showed its 19,000 inhabitants to be part of a society consciously divided by class, where stratification was 'a fact of life', and where rugby was identified with the wealthy professionals in the town and the wealthy agricultural element outside it – with squash, tennis, Freemasonry, Conservatism and the Church of England.[59] This England's spiritual home remains Twickenham, the temple of the lumpenbourgeoisie, where it struck one observer sitting in the stand at an international in the 1980s that the men and women sitting around him seemed never to have been to a game before.[60] This England took grave offence at the invasion of the Twickenham pitch by Bath supporters before the end of the 1987 John Player Cup Final. Had rowdyism returned in the late twentieth century to plague a game initially promoted to eradicate it from the public schools of the early nineteenth? It seemed only to confirm that life imitates television, and that the dividing line between supporters' loyalty and spectator participation always was a fine one.

In any case, pitch invasions were hardly unprecedented, even at Twickenham. They had regularly beset the Springboks' tour of the British Isles in 1969–70, when matches were played in a siege atmosphere and rugby grounds took on the appearance of armed camps. During the controversial 25-match tour one game was abandoned, the venues of two others switched and the 50,000 anti-apartheid demonstrators who turned out required more than 20,000 police to contain them. A confrontation between protesters and 'vigilantes' at Swansea produced some of the worst mob violence seen in Britain since the thirties, while the 10,000 who marched on Lansdowne Road constituted the largest public assembly in Dublin for 50 years.[61]

That Rugby Union should now occupy a central position in the increasingly politicised areas of world sport, a role which rather exaggerates its actual global extent, stems from its imperial past. The great colonising urge of the nineteenth century that saw rugby follow the flag had been supervised by an imperial officer class hardened if not created by keenly contested house matches. The Corinthian attributes of courage, self-control and the exercise of authority and of discipline were learnt on the playing fields of England and Scotland, the training grounds of a colonial command force. 'Public schoolboys of limited academic ability whose compensatory delight was muscle', in J. A. Mangan's words,[62] became governors, commissioners and administrators throughout the Empire, sometimes with unanticipated consequences. Among the more exotic relics of the British colonial legacy in Africa is a Scottish international cap which is one of the most valued items in the ceremonial regalia worn during the installation of the Divine King of the Sudanese Shilluk tribe.[63]

Rugby spread and consolidated its position in the white dominions much as it did at home. The first game to be played in New Zealand under Rugby rules took place at Nelson in 1870, organised by the Sherborne-educated son of the Speaker of the House of Representatives; within ten years there were 78 clubs in the country and in 1892 the various provincial unions came together to set up the NZRFU. It was a game for the elite, not a universal sport like football, and therefore the recreation of a superior social group and the expression of a certain form of civilisation. It demanded the exercise of moral values, and its scope for physical hardness, endurance and shared effort made it an ideal game for pioneers. In South Africa, whose Rugby Football Board was set up in 1889, it came to play both an integrative *and* exclusive role, uniting both white communities but deriving its strength from the ferocious collective discipline of the Boers, whose religious and political distinctiveness it reinforced. Democratic but not common, rugby in white South Africa came to articulate the convictions and aspirations of the Voortrekker past.[64]

The British army, which had introduced early variants of rugby to the Cape in the 1860s, took it to even further outposts of empire. The Welsh Regiment played it in the Khyber Pass in 1893 as well as pioneering it among the Chinese in the 1920s.[65] There has been a more substantial return on the rugby investment in Japan, where the game was introduced by a Cambridge graduate returning to Keio University in 1889. Japan's first rugby fixture took place the following year between Keio and the Yokohama Club, composed of British residents. Evangelical motives took rugby-playing missionaries from New Zealand to Fiji, Tonga and elsewhere in the South Pacific (the Fijian RU was founded in 1913), but it was commercial considerations that impelled British businessmen and railway engineers to Argentina, where the game was played in Buenos Aires in the 1880s and the River Plate RU established before the end of the century.

The British also imported rugby to France where Rosslyn Park were the first side to tour in 1893, playing against the British colony in Paris. The Captain of Racing Club de Paris between 1900 and 1903, and later the French Rugby Federation's first secretary, was a Scot, C. F. Rutherford, who arrived in Paris in 1895 from Epsom College. The spectators at his first game in the Vincennes public park consisted of a few workmen looking at 'un tas d'imbéciles, galopant sur le gazon après un ballon'.[66] Representatives of the wine and coal trades played key roles further south so that by the end of the century there were sides at Nantes, Bordeaux, Lyons and Toulouse. While soccer spread in the ports and industrial towns of northern France, it was in the south-west that rugby particularly flourished as clubs like Bayonne and Béziers came to enjoy a popular following similar to that in South Wales and parts of northern England. Middle-class in inspiration, the small-town sides of Languedoc, Gascony, and the Basque region provided a new focus for traditional sociability and, as in Wales, cultural distinctiveness.[67] The hiring of semi-professional Welsh players as coaches to clubs like Bayonne and Perpignan raised standards of play sufficiently for France, who began playing all four home countries from 1910, to beat Scotland 16–15 in Paris the following year. What finally convinced the *Daily Telegraph*'s correspondent that French sport had come of age was the ten-month long siege of Verdun in 1916 which showed that the French could after all 'stick it out' and therefore succeed at rugby.[68]

Unquestionably they could, better than any of the home countries if France's second place in the inaugural Rugby World Cup held in 1987 was any indication. And the Empire, too, struck back when the first winners of the tournament's William Webb Ellis trophy proved to be New Zealand, demonstrably the finest of more than 100 nations at the end of the twentieth century playing a game popularly if erroneously attributed to a day-boy at Rugby School who 'was . . . generally regarded as inclined to take unfair advantages at football'.

NOTES

For their help in preparing this chapter I would like to thank Timothy Auty, Linda James, John Jenkins and Tony Mason.

1   W. J. Baker, 'William Webb Ellis and the origins of Rugby Football: the life and death of a Victorian myth', *Albion*, 13, pp. 117–30.

2   E. Dunning and K. Sheard, *Barbarians, Gentlemen and Players* (Oxford, 1979), pp. 60–2, 83–6.

3   J. A. Mangan, *Athleticism in the Victorian and Edwardian Public School* (Cambridge, 1981), pp. 136, 206.

4   L. Balaam (ed.), *Manchester Football Club 1860–1985* (Manchester, 1985), pp. 4–5, 19, 28.

5   T. Delaney, *The Roots of Rugby League* (Keighley, 1984), pp. 3–5; A. Service, *Saints in Their Glory* (St Helens, 1985), pp. 1–3.

6   Rev F. Marshall (ed.), *Football: The Rugby Union Game* (1892), pp. 430, 439; T. W. J. Auty, *Headingley FC 1878–1978* (Headingley, 1978), pp. 17–18. See also David Russell, ' "Sporadic and curious": the emergence of rugby and soccer zones in Yorkshire and Lancashire, *c.* 1860–1914', *The International Journal of the History of Sport*, 5, 2, September 1988, pp. 185–205.

7   *Victoria County History: Northamptonshire*, vol. 2 (1906), p. 395; W. Bell, *Langholm RFC 1871–1971* (Langholm, 1971), unpaginated; R. Gethin, *Merthyr Rugby 1876–1976* (Merthyr, 1976), p. 7; M. Rhys (ed.), *Bois y Llan: Llangennech RFC 1885–1985* (Llanelli, 1986), p. 26; W. J. Robbins (ed.), *Rugby in the Duchy* (Camborne, 1934), p. 24; D. Smith and G. Williams, *Fields of Praise* (Cardiff, 1980), pp. 11–12; *Bridgwater and Albion RFC 1875–1975* (Bridgwater, 1975), p. 17.

8   C. C. Hoyer Millar, *Fifty Years of Rosslyn Park* (1929), p. 13; S. Barton (ed.), *The Gala Story 1875–1975* (Galashiels, 1975), p. 15; *North of Ireland Cricket and Football Club 1859–1959* (Belfast, 1959), pp. 9, 13.

9   J. Griffiths, *The Book of English International Rugby 1871–1982* (1982), pp. 11–14, 58.

10 Dunning and Sheard, *Barbarians*, pp. 198–200; Delaney, *Roots*, pp. 14–15, 52–82. In 1922 the Northern Union became the Rugby League.

11 U. A. Titley and R. McWhirter, *The Centenary History of the Rugby Football Union* (Twickenham, 1970), pp. 111–24.

12 Smith and Williams, *Fields of Praise*, pp. 22–7.

13 L. J. Williams, 'The economic structure of Wales since 1850' in G. Williams (ed.), *Crisis of Economy and Ideology: Essays on Welsh Society 1840–1980* (Bangor, 1983), pp. 35–47; Col. P. C. Trevor, *Rugby Union Football* (1923), p. 188.

14   *Bridgend Chronicle*, 2 December 1880; *Llanelly and County Guardian*, 6 December 1883; *Welsh Rugby Union Minute Books*; R. Gethin, *Merthyr Rugby*, p. 8; *Merthyr Express*, 19 September 1903.

15   Griffiths, *English International Rugby*, pp. 67, 100; *South Wales Daily Post*, 5 January 1903; B. E. Matthews, *The Swansea Story* (Swansea, 1968), pp. 25–7; J. R. Barker-Davies (ed.), *One Hundred Years of Coventry Blue 1874–1974* (Coventry, 1974), p. 30; D. E. Davies, *Cardiff Rugby Club 1876–1975* (Cardiff, 1975), pp. 35, 39; Hoyer Millar, *Rosslyn Park*, p. 63; *South Wales Daily News*, 13 March 1905.

16   *South Wales Daily News*, 23 January 1899; G. Hughes, *The Scarlets* (Llanelli, 1986), p. 57, quoting the *Llanelly Mercury*.

17   Smith and Williams, *Fields of Praise*, pp. 145–71. Cf. J. Clarke and C. Critcher, '1966 and all that: England's World Cup victory' in A. Tomlinson and G. Whannel (eds.), *Off the Ball* (1986), pp. 112–26. The rioters who selectively ransacked Tonypandy High Street in 1910 left untouched the chemist's shop of Willie Llewellyn, who had won the last of his twenty international caps against New Zealand in 1905; D. Smith, 'Tonypandy 1910: definitions of community', *Past and Present*, 87, p. 168.

18   *South Wales Daily News*, 29 January 1900.

19   A. M. C. Thorburn, *The Scottish Rugby Union Official History* (Edinburgh, 1985), pp. 25–7, 35.

20   H. H. Almond, 'Rugby Football in Scottish schools' in Marshall (ed.), *Football: The Rugby Union Game*, pp. 51–66.

21   P. Bilsborough, 'The development of sport in Glasgow 1850–1914', Unpublished MLitt thesis, University of Stirling, 1983, pp. 110–13, 209, 254–6, 290.

22   A. Massie, *A Portrait of Scottish Rugby* (Edinburgh, 1984), pp. 111–25; J. Gilbert, *Melrose Rugby Football Club 1877–1977* (Hawick, 1977), pp. 1–2.

23   *Weston-Super-Mare RFC 1875–1975* (Weston, 1975), pp. 26–8; *Plymouth Albion RFC 1876–1976* (Plymouth, 1976), p. 10; Barker-Davies, *Coventry*, p. 30; D. Hands, *Leicester FC 1880–1980* (Leicester, 1981), p. 26; *V.C.H. Northamptonshire*, p. 395; G. Williams, 'Midland manoeuvres: a history of Northern Unionism in Coventry', *Code 13*, 2 December 1986, pp. 9–14.

24   Barker-Davies, *Coventry*, pp. 57–8; Hands, *Leicester*, pp. 19–22; Delaney, *Roots*, pp. 113–15; G. Williams, 'How amateur was my valley: professional sport and national identity in Wales 1890–1914', *British Journal of Sports History*, 2, December 1985, pp. 248–69, esp. pp. 258–65.

25   J. J. McCarthy in Marshall, *Football*, p. 222; E. Van Esbeck, *One Hundred Years of Irish Rugby* (Dublin, 1974), pp. 14–41; M. O'Hehir, *The GAA: 100 Years* (Dublin, 1984), pp. 16–17.

26   *City of Derry RFC 1881–1981* (Londonderry, 1981), pp. 31–2; J. Sugden and A. Bairner, 'Northern Ireland: sport in a divided society' in L. Allison (ed.), *The Politics of Sport* (Manchester, 1986), pp. 100–7.

27   NICFC *1859–1959*, (see 8 above), p. 17.

28   Van Esbeck, *Irish Rugby*, pp. 91–2; *Welsh Rugby Union Minute Books*, 27 August 1914.

29   W. R. Taylor (ed.), *Keswick RUFC 1879–1979* (Keswick, 1979), p. 15; Hughes, *Scarlets*, p. 90; Hands, *Leicester*, p. 33.

30 *Bath FC 1865–1965* (Bath, 1965), p. 27; R. Blumenau, *A History of Malvern 1865–1965* (1965), p. 89.

31 P. Fussell, *The Great War and Modern Memory* (1975), pp. 25–7, 276; Titley and McWhirter, *Centenary History of RFU*, Biographical Section, *s.v.* Mobbs, E. R.

32 E. B. Poulton, *The Life of Ronald Poulton* (1919); A. A. Thompson, *Rugger My Pleasure* (1955), pp. 34–7, 85; H. Marshall (ed.), *Rugger Stories* (1932), p. 161.

33 *Bristol FC Jubilee Book 1888–1938* (Bristol, 1938), p. 23; Auty, *Headingley*, pp. 33–5; W. J. A. Davies, *Rugby Football* (1923), p. 159.

34 F. A. M. Webster, *Our Great Public Schools* (1937); O. L. Owen, *The Growth of a Sporting Venture* (Ipswich, 1952), pp. 39–47; K. Robbins, *The Eclipse of a Great Power* (1983), pp. 158, 254–5; Marshall, *Rugger Stories* (1932); K. Pelmear, *Rugby Football: An Anthology* (1958), pp. 127–34; J. Stevenson, *British Society 1914–45* (Harmondsworth, 1984), p. 387.

35 E. H. D. Sewell (ed.), *Rugby Football Up-to-Date* (1922), p. 13; R. M. Rayner, *A Manual of Rugby Football for Public Schools* (1925), p. 138.

36 Dunning and Sheard, *Barbarians*, pp. 235–8. The first rugby match to be broadcast live on BBC radio was the England v. Wales game at Twickenham, 1927. Capt. Teddy Wakelam, the commentator, mapped out a plan of squares with his producer, Lance Sieveking, who also supplied a blind man to sit outside the commentary box 'in order that I might imagine that I was describing the game to him'. Wakelam was subsequently informed by a listener in Lancashire 'that I was a complete fraud, that I had been reading from a previously prepared script, and that he would like to hear from me *immediately* what had happened'. H. B. T. Wakelam, *The Game Goes On* (1936), pp. 165–74.

37 Ivor Brown in Marshall, *Rugger Stories*, pp. 160–1.

38 A. G. Macdonell, *England, Their England* (1933), chap. 11.

39 Thorburn, *Scottish Rugby Union*, pp. 27–8; Massie, *Portrait*, pp. 36–7. See also Eric Linklater's novel, *Magnus Merriman* (1934), ch. 12.

40 C. Harvie, *No Gods and Precious Few Heroes: Scotland 1914–80* (1981), pp. 42–7; Bell, *Langholm*; A Hastie, *Kelso RFC 1876–1976* (Kelso, 1976), p. 41; Gilbert, *Melrose*, p. 40.

41 For what follows, see G. Williams, 'From Grand Slam to Great Slump: economy, society and Rugby Football in Wales during the Depression', *Welsh History Review*, 9, June 1983, pp. 338–57, and references there cited. In addition, P. T. Atkinson, *Centenary History of Rhymney RFC 1882–1982* (Rhymney, 1982), pp. 41–5; W. G. Boulton, *Senghenydd: The Village and its Rugby Club* (Risca, 1982), pp. 27–34.

42 Davies, *Cardiff RFC*, pp. 197–8; H. Francis, 'The anthracite strike and the disturbances of 1925', *Llafur*, 1, May 1973, p. 19; T. Lewis, *The Mules: A History of Kenfig Hill RFC* (Pyle, 1973), p. 24.

43 *Weston RFC*, pp. 44–50.

44 B. Lancaster and T. Mason (eds.), *Life and Labour in a Twentieth-century City: The Experience of Coventry* (Coventry, 1987), pp. 24, 67, 265. Several other midland clubs, like Rugby, Moseley and Wolverhampton, had 'excellent seasons' in the inter-war years. G. Holmes, *Midland Rugby Football* (Leicester, 1949), pp. 75–100.

45 M. Barak (ed.), *A Century of Rugby at Sale* (Sale, 1961), p. 49.

46 *Western Mail*, 23 December 1935.

47 T. Browne, *Ireland: A Social and Cultural History 1922–79* (Glasgow, 1981), pp. 171–211; Sugden and Bairner, 'Northern Ireland', p. 103.

48 Dunning and Sheard, *Barbarians*, p. 250; Davies, *Cardiff RFC*, pp. 117–20; J. Davis, *One Hundred Years of Newport Rugby* (Risca, 1974), pp. 136–7; Matthews, *Swansea Story*, p. 54.

49 W. J. Morgan and G. Nicholson, *Report on Rugby* (1959), pp. 148–53.

50 Smith and Williams, *Fields of Praise*, pp. 373–6, 414–19; J. Davies, 'Wales in the Nineteen Sixties', *Llafur*, 4, 1987, pp. 78–88.

51 Thorburn, *Scottish Rugby Union*, pp. 45–56; Massie, *Portrait*, pp. 53–4.

52 F. Cotton, *Fran: An Autobiography* (1981), pp. 23–4, 45; S. Smith, *The Scrum Half of My Life* (1984), pp. 15–20; I. McLaughlan, *Mighty Mouse* (1980), pp. 12–13; W. J. McBride, *Willie John* (Dublin, 1976), pp. 13–18. See also D. Hare, *Dusty* (1985), p. 47; P. Wheeler, *Rugby From the Front* (1983), pp. 33–4.

53 *The Independent*, 10 February 1987. The Welsh XV that played New Zealand in 1980 was on average 2 st. 3 lbs. heavier, and two and a half inches taller per man than the 1905 side.

54 In 1954 a crisis that arose when southern players refused to acknowledge the British anthem at Belfast's Ravenhill ground so long as the Republican anthem and tricolour were illegal in the North was 'resolved' only by transferring all subsequent internationals to Lansdowne Road, Dublin. S. Diffley, *The Men in Green: The Story of Irish Rugby* (1973), pp. 48–50. Although Scotland and Wales declined to play in Dublin in 1972, England did so in 1973, and lost. At the after-match dinner, the English captain John Pullin remarked, 'We may not be much good but at least we turn up.' J. Reason and C. James, *The World of Rugby*, (1979), p. 219.

55 N. Carroll, *Sport in Ireland* (Dublin, 1979), p. 37.

56 J. Taylor (ed.), *Middlesbrough RUFC 1872–1972* (Middlesbrough, 1972), p. 23.

57 K. G. Sheard and E. Dunning, 'The Rugby Football Club as a type of 'male preserve': some sociological notes', *International Review of Sport Sociology*, 8, 1973, pp. 5–21. The 'Zulu Warrior', the authors remind us (p. 7) is 'the traditional signal for a ritualistic strip by a member of the group ... usually enacted after the match, either in the club-house bar or, if the team has been playing away, on the coach which is carrying the players home'.

58 A protest from a leading figure on the RFU that 'Ladies don't play rugby' was met with the rejoinder, 'Women do'. *The Independent*, 13 April 1987. The Women's RFU, comprising nearly 50 clubs in a two-divisional league structure, staged an inaugural international between Wales and England at Pontypool in April 1987.

59 R. Frankenberg, *Communities in Britain* (Harmondsworth, 1966), pp. 172–3.

60 G. Davies and J. Morgan, *Sidesteps: A Rugby Diary 1984–5* (1985), p. 85.

61 R. E. Lapchick, *The Politics of Race and International Sport: The Case of South Africa* (Westport, Conn. 1975), pp. 156–68; P. Hain, *Don't Play with Apartheid* (1971), esp. pp. 133, 144, 148; Smith and Williams, *Fields of Praise*, pp. 403–5.

62 Mangan, *Athleticism*, p. 139

63 I. M. Lewis, *Social Anthropology in Perspective* (Harmondsworth, 1971), p. 63.

64 R. Archer and A. Bouillon, *The South African Game: Sport and Racism* (1982), pp. 56–78.

65 J. Maclaren, *The History of Army Rugby* (Aldershot, 1986), pp. 12–23.

66 Sewell, *Rugby Football Up-to-Date*, pp. 216–27.

67 R. J. Holt, *Sport and Society in Modern France* (1981), pp. 68–76; H. Garcia, *Le Rugby* (Paris, 1962), pp. 15–16.

68 Col. P. C. Trevor, *Rugby Union Football*, p. 9.

AFTERWORD

TONY MASON

THINKING ABOUT SPORT

'Strange', mused the Director, as they turned away, 'to think that even in Our Ford's day most games were played without more apparatus than a ball or two and a few sticks and perhaps a bit of netting. Imagine the folly of allowing people to play elaborate games which do nothing whatever to increase consumption. It's madness. Nowadays the Controllers won't approve of any new game unless it can be shown that it requires at least as much apparatus as the most complicated of existing games . . .'

Aldous Huxley, *Brave New World* (1956 Penguin edn), p. 35

Thinking about sport in society has for some time been an expanding area of interest for an expanding number of historians and sociologists. The purpose of this section is to draw the attention of readers to important examples of this growing body of work. There is not the space to present a detailed critique of theories of sport but interested readers can delve more deeply at their leisure and inclination.

One way of thinking about sport's place in society involves setting up a model identifying the main features of sport in the traditional or pre-industrial world and placing it alongside one of modern or industrial society. Sport in the former is characterised by its periodic, unorganised and essentially local nature. There is no generally accepted way of playing nor any widely agreed set of rules. No controlling organisations exist. Sport is not a separate activity pursued for its own sake but closely bound up with the hierarchy, ritual and symbols of the wider social life. Sport in particular, in what was largely an agrarian society, was governed by the religious and seasonal rhythms of that society. It usually took place on the festivals associated with those rhythms.

Sport in modern society, on the other hand, is almost everything which sport in earlier times was not. It is highly organised, structured and regulated. A regular programme of fixtures exists at every level of activity, local, regional, national, even international. Sport at the highest level is specialised, bureaucratised and increasingly commercialised. The goal of the athlete, who for a period of his life does nothing else but prepare for and compete in his or her chosen sport, is victory. Sport has taken on an important role in education, the promotion of health and the making of profits. Sporting performance has contributed to the status of individuals, towns, institutions and countries. What had happened to sport in the change from agrarian to industrial society reflected those societal changes. A backward-looking, traditional, customary way of life had been replaced by a new order based on reason, individual striving and achievement. The transition from traditional to modern sport, so the argument goes, was one of the cultural expressions of a new scientific view of the world.

The main criticism of this kind of approach is that the model can easily obscure the reality. It is important to recognise those moments in particular at which the characteristics of sport in those societies do not fit the abstract models. Tradition and history will often be important in the practice and organisation of individual sports. Such models do not always enable scholars to focus on the conflicts between sport and society.

Perhaps the most impressive analysis of sport, which offers the kind of model-based explanation outlined above, is Allen Guttmann's in his book *From Ritual to Record* (1978).[1] Although much of the raw material is drawn from the author's commanding knowledge of sport in post-Civil War America his aim is to establish the similarities between the nature and role of sport in all modern societies. Guttmann emphasises seven common features of sport in the modern world. Sport is secularised, democratic, specialised, rationalised, bureaucratised, quantified and record orientated. The skilful way in which he presents the evidence to support his characterisation cannot be reproduced in any detail here. But an example of his argument can be seen by looking at his discussion of the egalitarian nature of modern sports.

Sports are democratic in two senses. In the first place conditions of competition for all those involved are the same. Second, and more important, if a comparison is made with the sports of earlier times, then it is clear that modern sports offer much more open access. In ancient and many pre-industrial societies ascription rather than achievement governed participation. Guttmann is aware that, in the nineteenth century for example, attempts were made in several countries to limit involvement in sport to gentlemen. He is also aware that there were class and regional hostilities and that discrimination in sport was practised against blacks and women and that such prejudices have persisted right through the twentieth century. But his conclusion is that opportunities were opened up which had not been available in earlier times in more traditional societies and that more of the less well off, more of the ethnic minorities and more women can and do now take part in sport. Guttmann explains the emergence of modern sport in terms of the slow development of an empirical, experimental, more rational and scientific way of looking at the world.

One of the most important competing theories with which Guttmann is arguing is Marxist in origin. This is a materialist view which begins from the proposition that the dominant class produced by the processes of capitalist production extends its influence to every part of social life including sport. Modern sport helps to keep the workers in a subordinate place by making them fitter for work, socialising them in schools and communities into behaviour patterns which benefit the dominant class, and distracting and compensating them with exciting spectacle. Their minds are thus diverted away from politics and the threat which they would otherwise pose to the ruling group. Capitalist sport celebrates capitalist values such as competition, discipline, hard work and achievement. The growing commercialisation of sport provides further support for this analysis: a sports goods and recreation industry has developed to exploit athletes, workers and consumers.

Eric Hobsbawm and John Hargreaves have tried to refine this basic Marxist position further.[2] Hobsbawm, in a stimulating essay entitled 'Mass-producing traditions: Europe, 1870–1914', noted the role of the British middle class in exporting modern sport to Europe. He argues that 'the middle classes in the broadest sense found subjective group identification unusually difficult'. They were neither small enough, like the aristocracy, 'nor sufficiently united by a common destiny and purpose', like the workers.[3] On the one hand, middle-class sports, like golf and tennis and the elevation of the ideology of amateurism enabled the middle class to segregate themselves from their inferiors. Such segregation buttressed identity. On the other hand the expansion of sport as an international phenomenon provided for both bourgeoisie and workers a medium for national identification. Sport was one of the 'invented traditions' of the 50 years before the outbreak of the First World War. The intention on the part of some individuals and organisations to use it in order to manipulate behaviour was clearly present. But it is unlikely that the manipulation would have been successful if it did not meet 'a felt. . . need among particular bodies of people'.[4]

It cannot be certain, however, that an institution such as sport will be adopted by the target group exactly in the way hoped for by the promoters. Middle-class ideals of sportsmanship, for example, were often ignored or rejected by the workers and partisanship embraced in their place. This more complicated relationship is one of the major points made by John Hargreaves in a study which provides the most systematic and detailed attempt to explain the role of sport in Britain from a Marxist point of view. Hargreaves makes use of Antonio Gramsci's idea of hegemony to emphasise that in modern democracies a process of negotiation takes place between dominant and subordinate groups in sport, as in other areas of social life. But he nonetheless concludes that sport in Britain has contributed to the maintenance of bourgeois hegemony. According to Hargreaves, sport helped produce the fragmentation of the working class by setting enthusiasts against non-enthusiasts, promoting local chauvinism, and, because it has been so much a male-dominated sub-culture, men against women. He too, like Hobsbawm, stresses the role of sport in confirming national identity.

Marxists such as Hargreaves and Hobsbawm have not rejected modern sport but have tried to understand its role in society. Since the later 1960s a group of western European sociologists, of which the best known are probably Jean-Marie Brohm, Bero Rigauer and Gerhard Vinnai, have developed a more austere critique which has judged modern sport by the standards of spontaneous play and found it wanting. Labelled 'neo-Marxists', these critics have identified a division of labour in sport which matches that in the wider economy. Pierre Laguillaumie, quoted by Guttmann, sums up this view neatly. 'The champion is fabricated in the image of the worker and the track in the image of the factory. Athletic activity has become a form of production and takes on all the characteristics of industrial production.'[5] Small numbers of well-paid but exploited athletes perform for the rest. These critics agree that playing or watching sport is a stabilising factor for the capitalist status quo. Watching in particular provides an emotional safety valve for the release of aggressive feelings which might otherwise be turned on the real class oppressors. Sport is no different from work. Especially at the top level the drive for efficiency and maximum production mirrors the central feature of the work experience. Sport is therefore an alienated institution in an alienated society in which both it and work have lost their true meaning. Furthermore the same is true of sport in eastern Europe where the exploiter is the state rather than capitalism.

There can be no doubt that some of these strictures have a good deal of force. Western sport is very commercialised. Sport on both sides of what used to be called the Iron Curtain is exploited for militaristic and especially nationalistic ends. It has also been true that the better off have been able to occupy powerful positions in the hierarchies which have done so much to shape modern sport, simply because they had more money and time. Playing and watching sport does vary with social class. In all kinds of modern societies more middle-class than working-class people take part in both. But class cannot explain everything. The young watch and play more than the old; Protestants more than Catholics, men more than women. It is also doubtful whether the dominant groups in society have ever maintained a monolithic view of what sport ought to be. Sport has occasionally played a part in the opposition to capitalist processes. Like all leisure activities it does contain features which may point the contrast with work. Guttmann has argued that far from sport being an alienated institution in an alienated society there may be less alienation in sport than elsewhere. The achievements of the athlete belong to no one else. They are intelligible to all and win recognition for him or her outside the world of specialist practitioners. Records may come and go but the image and personality of the performer remains in memory and history. The desire for pleasure and enjoyment, sociability and excitement is never completely extinguished.

This quest for excitement, in fact, has also been analysed particularly in the work of Norbert Elias.[6] In comparatively advanced societies, there is limited scope for showing strong feelings. High excitement is looked upon with disapproval and among crowds in public is seen as potentially disruptive. But the act of controlling such feelings, which are clearly present in many individuals, is itself a stress-inducing phenomenon. So much so that most societies have developed counter-measures against it. One group of these has been leisure activities in general and sport in particular. Leisure pursuits allow people to express themselves more freely in 'imaginary settings' created by the activities themselves. These settings are designed to promote the same quality of excitement which 'real-life' situations would produce but without the real dangers and risks associated with it. For Elias, the football match provides a singularly appropriate example.

Thus spectators of a football match may savour the mimetic excitement of the battle swaying to and fro on the playing field, knowing that no harm will come to the players or to themselves. As in real life they may be torn between hopes of success and fear of defeat; and in that case too strong feelings aroused in an imaginary setting and their open manifestation in the company of many others may be all the more enjoyable and perhaps liberating because in society at large people are more isolated and have few opportunities for collective manifestations of strong feelings.[7]

Sport then, in Elias's own elegant phrase, provides 'emotional refreshment' for those interested in it. In advanced societies it has been one manifestation of the 'civilising process' which since the seventeenth century in Britain has led to a society governed by stricter codes of conduct outlawing the more crass forms of self-indulgence and producing the more emotionally controlled societies of the late twentieth century. Such an explanation may not seem to fit the facts of the behaviour of a minority of the crowd at contemporary football matches but Elias argues that it does. He is able to do this by using the notion of the 'de-civilising spurt'. It may be that conditions in the wider society do not provide all its members with controls which are strong enough to contain their excitement. Individual controls against violence become loosened and part of the population may actually find violence enjoyable. Coupled with this is the 'outsider syndrome' by which groups of youths from the lower end of the working class find themselves held in low esteem by society and treated, in other words, like outsiders. Football provides the opportunity for these young men to gather in a crowd and 'without quite knowing what (they) are doing, but enjoying the excitement, one gets one's own back on the establishment'.[8]

It is not clear whether all sports provide what Elias calls the 'battle-excitement' without real casualties, with indeed, the minimum amount of injury to players and spectators. Football seems to fit the theory more snugly than track and field athletics, cricket or tennis, fishing or golf. There is also the question of how far leisure pursuits other than sport produce the kind of excitement which Elias sees as one of their major functions.

It is obvious that the study of sport is attractive because sport tells us something about ourselves. The last decade has seen an expansion of serious writing on a subject which can no longer claim to be neglected. It is important, however, that sport should be kept in perspective; many people, perhaps the majority, are largely untouched by it: and as an effective means of social control sport must be less important than economics or politics.

WHITHER SPORT?

The essays in this book point to the cultural, social, economic and political importance of sport in twentieth-century Britain. It seems unlikely that this importance will be much diminished in the foreseeable future. But prediction is difficult. For one thing it is not clear how long Thatcherite policies of curbing public spending and privatising public services will continue. As long as they do they are likely to damage opportunities to participate in sport in three main ways. Most young people are introduced to sport at school and school playing fields are liable to be sold off with the excuse that temporary falling rolls have made them surplus to requirements. In addition the government's well-publicised national curriculum for state schools, has only allotted 5 per cent of the teaching time to sport and physical education. The sports lobby have suggested that such a proportion is inadequate and an Inner London Education Authority Working Party recommended that it should be doubled.[9] Second, local government has traditionally provided many of the facilities for sport from football pitches and bowling greens to tennis courts and swimming pools. Between 1972 and 1987 the number of local authority sports centres grew from 20 to

1,500. The government is now suggesting that the management of municipal sports and leisure facilities be put out to tender.[10] Activities traditionally not aimed at making profits but with the social goals of improving the fitness and adding to the enjoyment of life have now to be subordinated to the values of the accountant. An increase in the cost of using such facilities seems likely to be at the expense of the participation of the less well off. Finally the growth of commercial sponsorship for sport has clearly suggested to government that it no longer needs to pay out so much from its own coffers in grants. The Sports Council is the main channel through which government funds flow to individual sports organisations. It will be interesting to see what role the Council will have in ten years' time.[11]

Tension is likely to remain between those groups in and out of the schools who favour the expansion of regular but non-competitive physical exercise for all, based on dance, gymnastics and swimming, and those who would like to see a high level of effort continued to be put into the more traditional team games, with their elevation of the best players and their often highly competitive ethos. It seems clear that in the state comprehensive school, a lack of resources and the commitment to providing as wide a sporting choice for the individual boy or girl as possible may lead, for example, to the decline of cricket and rugby in schools. Coupled with the fall in numbers in the 13–24 age group 1982–93, the group mainly attracted by the traditional team games, this would at least suggest that a reduction in the number of potential participants is inevitable. Declining standards may also result. At the same time if the slow expansion of private education continues then the traditional sports of athletics, cricket, football, rowing and rugby are likely to play a much bigger part in middle- and upper-middle-class education than in the education of the majority of the population. One thing that all this suggests is that the sporting participation patterns which several studies have now made familiar are likely to persist. The most active players will continue to be found in the professional and managerial groups, the least active among semi- and unskilled manual workers. There will continue to be few sports where those with the highest incomes are not the most active. Car ownership will remain crucial for many sports. The young will take part more than the old and in spite of a growth in the number of women participating, especially indoors, men will continue to play more than women. As the Sports Council themselves accept, sport for all remains a long way off. It is likely to remain easier to encourage intensification of commitment and greater frequency of participation than to bring in new players.[12]

It also seems safe to predict that sport will remain an essentially voluntary activity in Britain. With about 150,000 sports clubs containing 6.5 million members and serviced by 500,000 officers who give up their spare time for the privilege, sport in Britain is firmly wedded to the voluntary sector and the club form of organisation. Clubs are exclusive. They do not see their role as encouraging mass participation.

The essays in this book clearly chart the process by which the ties between sport and business have become closer as the twentieth century has progressed. They also show that top level sport itself has increasingly taken on the trappings of business, particularly in the last two decades. In the years 1980–6 direct business sponsorship of British sport grew from about £50 million to £160 million per year. Such growth has produced powerful organisations which bring sponsor and sport together and take large sums for matching the one with the other. The International Marketing Group was a pioneer in this field but now there are major competitors. Together with the sports goods manufacturing and retailing sectors these companies provide a powerful vested interest whose influence on the organisation and development of individual sports is likely to be considerable. Sport plays an expanding role in corporate entertainment and promotion. Both company clients and employees may be entertained at top sporting events via packages organised by companies such as Sportsworld PLC. These are particularly popular in the summer at such venues as Ascot, Henley, Lord's and Wimbledon. Volvo explained why they found golf outings so beneficial for staff and customers. It is a world-wide expanding game in which the handicap system enables the good player to take part off the same tee as the less proficient. Work and play provides a happy mix and helps to break down the barriers between sales people and customers. Such largesse encourages the staff and, most important, golf was already played by many of Volvo's customers.[13] In general horse-racing, rowing, cricket, tennis and golf attract most business entertainment packages but rugby internationals and a few top football occasions are also on the corporate sporting calendar. The fact that much sought-after tickets for top events are bought at black market prices depriving the regular fans of the possibility of watching will be one area of controversy which seems unlikely to go away. Short of a disastrous world-wide recession it seems that business will continue to pump money into sport although, as most sports are discovering, two sponsors are better than one and several better than two.

Much of the sponsorship money recently thrown at sport has been dependent on television presence. Without regular coverage sports find sponsors hard to get and harder to keep. Until now BBC and ITV have had the market to themselves. Suddenly technological change is threatening to alter the nature of television transmission. Cable TV can be expected to encourage local firms to sponsor local events, players and teams. Satellite TV will bring into the home top-level sport from all over the world perhaps directly competing in terms of time of performance with the live British variety. Stuart Hall has warned that our national coverage may be lost in a kaleidoscopic chaos of local transmissions on the one hand and global transmissions on the other.[14] Most people cannot yet take cable and it is not clear that there will be a rush to buy the equipment necessary to tune in to Sky. But it would be foolish of British sport not to be preparing for the day – and night – when this multiplicity of channels does become available.

ITV sees cable and satellite as major competitors for their advertising revenue. Declining audiences have forced them to look at their programme schedules including sport. The result has been the removal from ITV screens of bowls, darts, gymnastics and wrestling. Channel 4 has abandoned snooker. These sports, say ITV, are watched by too high a proportion of the over-55s in the lower income groups. Their aim must be a younger more affluent audience who will spend money on the advertisers' products. ITV look to a future which will see them concentrate on fewer sports with live coverage and top events.[15] This explains their determined attempt to buy exclusive rights to top English league football. This leaves the BBC as the sole outlet for the excluded sports and raises the question of how long the Corporation can continue to transmit two-thirds of all sports programmes as it also comes under government, satellite and ratings pressure. Whatever the new *modus vivendi* between sport and television over the next decade, it will not be arrived at without damage being inflicted on the less popular sports. It is a commonplace that television has enhanced the popularity of some sports such as show-jumping, snooker, darts and bowls but what it has given it can also take away and may be about to do so.

Of course TV will continue to select and underline the importance of the leading sportsmen and sportswomen. By its tedious but relentless interviews and pre- and post-match discussions it will make them into celebrities. Financial rewards for the top players seem to add a fourth dimension to the Olympic motto: 'faster, further and higher' are joined by 'bigger and bigger and bigger'. The temptation for the talented is very great and the result is early specialisation, intense training, fierce dedication and competition and a high wastage rate. The full-time athlete now makes use of sports science and sports medicine in order to give him or her a winning edge. And if they don't, perhaps drugs will. A recent study of drug use and abuse in sport concluded that it was 'a chilling thought that we are getting to a point where international sport is concerned only with biologically prepared and pharmacologically manipulated individuals performing to bolster the prestige of particular Governments or ideologies'.[16] It is simple enough to predict that the use of drugs and some of the applications of scientific research will remain one of the most controversial areas of the sporting life. Science has helped make sport a business.

All this suggests that the sport which the professionals play is far removed from that in which the great majority participate and is becoming more reified with every decade. Sport is much more closely aligned with business and consumerism than it was even two or three decades ago. Ten years ago, in an article in the *Times Literary Supplement*, Russell Davies offered the opinion that in spite of all its faults, sport gave pleasure and the opportunity for us to express admiration. 'In sport we generally have to look less hard for the admirable than in any other sphere of public life.'[17] Stan Hey in a recent *Observer* encomium agreed. Sport retains the capacity to 'transcend mere performance and spectacle and to promote virtue'.[18] The question for the immediate future is will it continue to be allowed to do so and are there sufficient people willing to stand up in order to see that it does?

NOTES

1 Allen Guttmann, *From Ritual to Record: The Nature of Modern Sports* (Columbia University Press, 1978). What follows owes much to Guttman and also to Richard Gruneau, 'Modernization or hegemony: two views on sport and social development' in J. Harvey and H. Cantelon, *Not Just a Game: Essays in Canadian Sports Sociology* (Ottawa University Press, 1988).
2 Eric Hobsbawm, 'Mass-producing traditions: Europe, 1870–1914' in Eric Hobsbawm and Terence Ranger (eds.), *The Invention of Tradition* (Cambridge, 1983). John Hargreaves, *Sport, Power and Culture* (Oxford, 1986). Other interesting theoretical treatments of sport can be found in Fred Inglis, *The Name of the Game. Sport and Society* (1977), Jennifer Hargreaves (ed.) *Sport, Culture and Ideology* (1982) and Brian Stoddart, *Saturday Afternoon Fever. Sport in the Australian Culture* (New South Wales, 1986).
3 Hobsbawm 'Mass-producing traditions', pp. 301–2.
4 Ibid., p. 307.
5 Jean-Marie Brohm, *Sport: A Prison of Measured Time*, translated by Ian Fraser (1978). Bero Rigauer, *Sport and Work*, translated by Allen Guttmann (New York, 1981). Gerhard Vinnai, *Football Mania. The Players and the Fans: The Mass Psychology of Football* (1973). Guttmann *Ritual*, p. 66.
6 What follows is mainly based on Norbert Elias and Eric Dunning, *Quest For Excitement. Sport and Leisure in the Civilising Process* (1986). See also Norbert Elias, *The Civilising Process* (1978).
7 Norbert Elias and Eric Dunning *Quest*, p. 43.
8 Ibid., p. 57.

9   *The Guardian*, 12 July 1988.

10 *The Guardian*, 1 July 1988.

11 For the Sports Council's own views of the more immediate future see *Sport in the Community. Into the 90's. A Strategy for Sport 1988–1993* (Sports Council, 1988), 92pp.

12 *Sport in the Community ... Which Ways Forward?* (Sports Council, 1987), p. 16.

13 *Marketing*, 4 February 1988. For Sportsworld Group PLC see *The Corporate Hospitality Book* (Business Entertainment Services, 1988).

14 *The Guardian*, 21 July 1988.

15 *The Guardian*, 2 July 1988. For a good account of the development of television's involvement with sport see Garry Whannel, 'The unholy alliance: notes on television and the remaking of British sport 1965–85', *Leisure Studies*, 5 (1986), pp. 129–45.

16 Tom Donohoe and Neil Johnson, *Foul Play. Drug Abuse in Sports* (Oxford, 1986), p. 126.

17 *Times Literary Supplement*, 10 March 1978.

18 *The Observer*, 27 March 1988.

INDEX

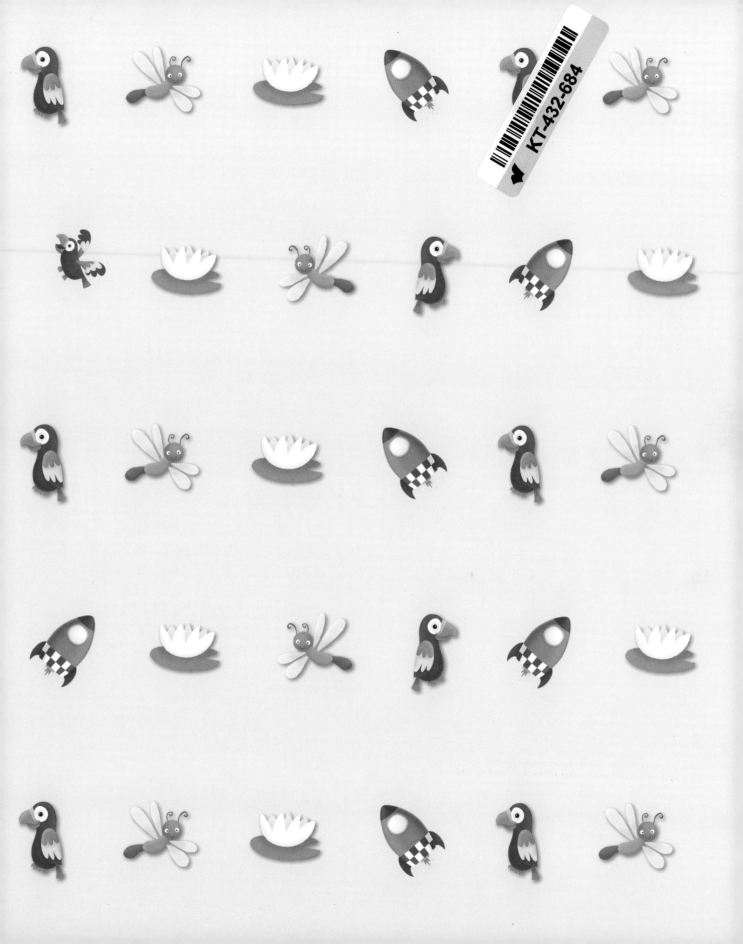

501
Things to Find

igloobooks

Charlie and Freddie are best friends and they love to have adventures together.

Charlie

Freddie

See if you can spot them in each picture in this book. Once you've found them, there will be other things to find as well! Let's have a practice. Can you find Charlie and Freddie in the picture opposite?

2 sharks

4 stingray

6 octopus

Well done! Now you've found Charlie and Freddie, see if you can spot these things, too!

Aquarium

Dino Discoveries!

Charlie and Freddie are having fun
playing with the dinosaurs.
Can you spot where they are?

Can you spot these things, too?

1 T-rex

3 pterodactyls

6 volcanoes

7 dinosaur nests

8 footprints

10 fossils

Theme Park Fun

Charlie and Freddie can't wait to go on all the rides at the theme park! Can you spot where they are in this picture?

MONSTER MANSION

HOOK A PRIZE

Can you spot these items, too?

2 candy stands

3 teddy bears

5 ice creams

Crazy Coaster

PICK-A-PRIZE

6 blue balloons

9 popcorn

10 candy floss

Knights & Dragons

Charlie and Freddie are having an adventure at a cool castle! Can you spot them among the knights and dragons?

Can you spot these things, too?

3 blue dragons

4 ladders

6 gargoyles

7 red shields

9 flags

10 flaming torches

Treasure Hunt

Charlie and Freddie are searching for buried treasure with pirates! Can you spot where they are in this picture?

Can you find these items, too?

2 treasure maps   **3 treasure chests**   **5 compasses**

8 telescopes

9 pirate hats

10 seagulls

Jolly Jungle

Charlie and Freddie are being jungle explorers!
Can you spot where they are hiding?

Can you spot these things, too?

1 rhino

3 leopards

4 toucans

6 venus fly traps

7 monkeys

10 lizards

Haunted House

Charlie and Freddie have found an old haunted house. Can you spot where they are?

Can you find all of these other items, too?

2 clocks

4 skeletons

5 ghosts

6 rats

8 spider's webs

10 bats

Space Adventure

Charlie and Freddie are playing with their alien friends in outer space! Can you spot them in this picture?

Can you spot these things, too?

2 galaxy swirls

4 spotty planets

5 spaceships

6 rockets

8 orange aliens

10 shooting stars

Cool Car Racing

Charlie and Freddie are having lots of fun at the go-cart circuit. Can you spot them?

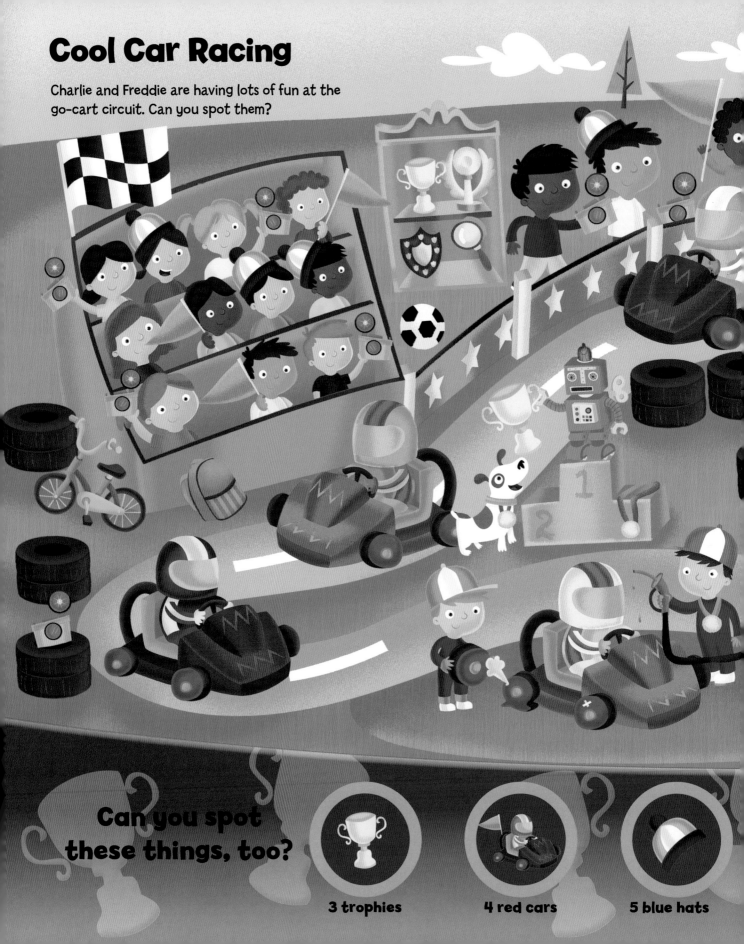

Can you spot these things, too?

3 trophies

4 red cars

5 blue hats

7 medals   **8 orange flags**   **10 cameras**

Futuristic Fun

There are all sorts of cool and exciting things in the future. Can you spot where Charlie and Freddie are?

Can you spot
these things, too?

1 satellite dish

3 space scooters

4 flying cars

7 space helmets

8 robotic birds

10 watches

Monster Party

Charlie and Freddie are at a monster party. Can you spot them? Do you recognise any of the other partygoers?

Can you find all of these items at the party?

2 monster stereos

5 one-eyed monsters

6 glasses of monster pop

8 party hats

10 music notes

20 monster cupcakes

Well done!

You spotted everything! Did you find Charlie and Freddie, too? Were you looking closely? Can you find these ten things in each picture?

1 red cap

1 puppy

1 bicycle

1 kite

1 football

1 robot

1 skateboard

1 backpack

1 magnifying glass

1 truck

Bonus!

Hidden somewhere within this book is this big, toothy fish! Can you spot which picture he is in?

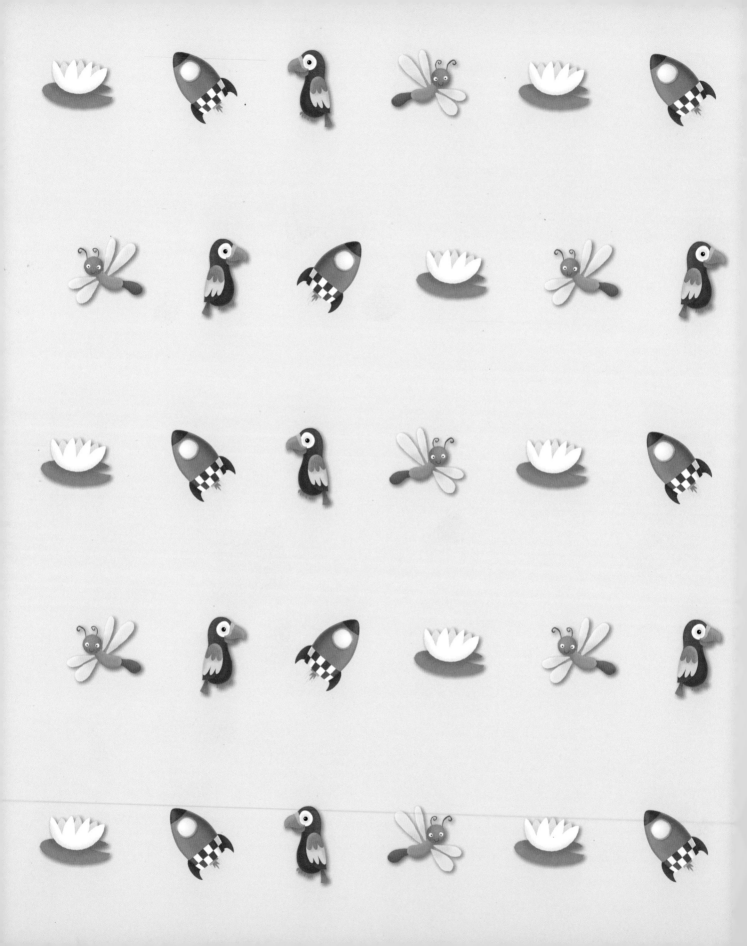